Mathematics for Economics and Business

Mathematics for Economics and Business

An Interactive Introduction

Second edition

JEAN SOPER

Blackwell
Publishing

BLACKWELL PUBLISHING
350 Main Street, Malden, MA 02148-5020, USA
9600 Garsington Road, Oxford OX4 2DQ, UK
550 Swanston Street, Carlton, Victoria 3053, Australia

Screenshots reprinted by permission of Microsoft Corporation.

First edition published 1999
Second edition published 2004 by Blackwell Publishing Ltd

8   2011

Library of Congress Cataloging-in-Publication Data

Soper, Jean.
Mathematics for economics and business : an interactive introduction /
Jean Soper.– 2nd ed.
p. cm.
Includes index.
1. Economics, Mathematical. 2. Business mathematics. I. Title.
HB135.S573 2004
519.5–dc22
2003014252

ISBN 978-1-4051-1126-3 (alk. paper) – ISBN 978-1-4051-1127-0 (pbk. : alk. paper)

A catalogue record for this title is available from the British Library.

Set in 10/12½ Galliard
by Graphicraft Ltd, Hong Kong
Printed and bound in Singapore
by C.O.S. Printers Pte Ltd

The publisher's policy is to use permanent paper from mills that operate a sustainable forestry policy, and
which has been manufactured from pulp processed using acid-free and elementary chlorine-free practices.
Furthermore, the publisher ensures that the text paper and cover board used have met acceptable
environmental accreditation standards.

For further information on
Blackwell Publishing, visit our website:
www.blackwellpublishing.com

Contents

Preface

If you have chosen to study economics you have probably discovered that economic analysis sometimes involves a mathematical approach. Whether you are enthusiastic or wary about using mathematics, you are likely to find that competence in some basic mathematical techniques is an essential prerequisite for success on your course. This book aims to help you learn the methods you need and apply them to economic problems. It may be that much of the mathematics presented here is already familiar to you, or alternatively you may be feeling a bit worried because your economics course includes some mathematics but you haven't studied it for some time. This book and the resources on the accompanying CD are structured so as to be flexible in their use. The book has separate sections for mathematical methods and economics applications and the materials on the CD-ROM are accessed from a menu system so you can choose to use them in the way that is appropriate for you. You can begin by learning the mathematics in a particular chapter or can proceed immediately to the economics examples.

Mathematics is presented in this book with intuitive rather than rigorous explanations. Many of the applications are numerical examples where you can look at the results graphically and thus see how the rules of mathematics work. By following the worked examples and tackling the practice problems you will discover how to use each of the techniques and try them for yourself. Trying the problems is important, because you learn mathematics by doing it. As you practice you become competent and your understanding of the methods improves.

The book can be used on its own, but packaged with it is a CD-ROM containing the MathEcon courseware and other e-learning resources. The interactive MathEcon screens help you to understand more about many of the topics, both in mathematics and in economics. Other resources on the CD-ROM include interactive quizzes that run in a Web browser and plenty of additional practice problems for each chapter in the form of Acrobat documents that you can print out. There are also Excel files to accompany the Excel sections of the book and PowerPoint slides that outline the methods, for use by both lecturers and students. The section that follows gives more information about the features of the book and the electronic resources.

The lecture course from which this book has evolved is attended by students from a wide range of mathematics backgrounds. Some have previously studied both mathematics and economics, but the course brings the two disciplines together in a way that is new to them. For other students, both mathematics and economics are new subjects. Although the course is harder for them, many find in the end that they can do quite well. Practise is the key to success, and to scoring high marks in assessments.

New Material in the Second Edition

The major changes in the second edition are the inclusion of two additional chapters on linear programming and matrix algebra and the addition of sections on the use of Excel to three of the existing chapters. These changes and other more minor ones have been made in response to users' requests. Linear programming problems are solved graphically and by using Excel Solver. The matrix algebra chapter seeks to prepare students to understand the methods used in econometrics.

The use of Excel is in no way seen as a substitute for hand calculations which develop students' understanding of the methods. Instead, Excel is seen as an easy way of producing stylish graphs of functions, of solving more complex problems and of investigating the impact of changes. The Excel facilities described in the book include the use of Chart Wizard, the Paste Function button, constructing your own formulae including array formulae and matrix formulae and the use of Solver for solving equations and for linear programming problems.

There are also additional materials on the CD-ROM. The e-learning resources now include interactive quizzes, many additional practice problems, PowerPoint slides, a new edition of MathEcon and the Excel files.

Acknowledgements

Producing this book together with the MathEcon courseware and other e-learning resources has only been possible with the tremendous help and support I have received from many other people. I would especially like to thank all members of the WinEcon Executive Committee for allowing the WinEcon screens they created to be used in MathEcon. In particular I would like to thank the Project Directors: Phil Hobbs for endorsing MathEcon at the inception stage, Simon Price for all his programming work and David Demery for keeping things running smoothly. Lesley Price has been a continuing source of help and advice in the assembly of the e-learning materials and has produced the CD supplied with this book.

In addition, I would like to thank many of those who have been colleagues and students at Leicester for their ideas and suggestions. The Excel sections owe a great deal to Martin Lee, who co-authored much of what I have previously written about using spreadsheets in teaching. Emma Angell helped produce many of the additional problems and quizzes included on the CD-ROM. For ideas about appropriate course material I am indebted to Michael Gibson and Ian Bradley who taught the course before me. As first year course coordinator, Paul Herrington provided much encouragement. Ziggy MacDonald designed the MathEcon screens that were produced at Leicester, and helped to deal with computing problems. My students over the years have used the material the book contains, and the questions they have raised have shaped the way in which it is presented.

I am very grateful also to Seth Ditchik and his editorial and production teams at Blackwell Publishing, most especially to Elizabeth Wald whose tact and quiet perseverance have ensured that all difficulties were successfully resolved. The suggestions made by several anonymous reviewers have been very helpful and many of their ideas have been incorporated in this second edition. The responsibility for any errors rests with me.

Finally, I would like to thank my family, Philip, Andrew, David and Christopher, for their continuing encouragement and support. This book is dedicated to them.

Features of the Book

- Mathematics sections
- Economics application sections
- Excel calculation sections
- Definitions
- Remember boxes
- Worked examples
- Practice problems
- Analytical results
- e-Learning resources
    MathEcon
    Excel files
    PowerPoint slides
    Quiz questions
    Further practice problems

The features of this book and the accompanying e-learning resources are designed to let you choose your own approach to learning how to apply mathematics in economic analysis. You can, of course, work through the chapters in order but you can also use the book more selectively. You can begin with the mathematics sections, or if you are already familiar with the techniques they describe you can proceed directly to the sections containing economics examples. An outline of relevant economic analysis is included in these sections and more is provided in the MathEcon software on the CD-ROM. Different economics topics are analysed in separate sections so that you can use this book in parallel with your main economics module, selecting what is relevant at a particular time. The contents list will help you choose what sections you want to study. Cross-references are provided in the margins to help you find where different aspects of mathematical relationships and economic models are discussed in other chapters. Some of the chapters conclude with a section that describes how to use Excel to do the calculations and to plot graphs of functions. The Excel files described in these sections are included on the CD-ROM.

Just reading through the book and looking at the computer files, however, will not make you competent at using the mathematical techniques. To help you learn these the definitions and remember boxes give you key points to memorize, for example:

> internal rate of return: the discount rate at which the net present value of a project is 0.

> The marginal product of labour is found by differentiating the production function with respect to labour, i.e.
>
> $$MPL = dQ/dL$$
>
> **Remember...**

Worked examples such as the one shown here illustrate the methods and let you see each step in the analysis:

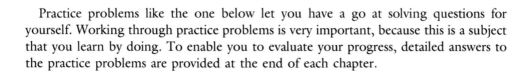

1

Given the total utility function $U = 5x^{0.8}$ find the marginal utility, MU.

Since $U = 5x^{0.8}$ we obtain marginal utility by finding dU/dx.

$$MU = dU/dx = 4x^{-0.2} = 4/x^{0.2}$$

Notice that as x increases, the divisor in the expression for marginal utility, $x^{0.2}$, also increases. The value of marginal utility therefore decreases as x increases, showing that the curve has diminishing marginal utility.

Practice problems like the one below let you have a go at solving questions for yourself. Working through practice problems is very important, because this is a subject that you learn by doing. To enable you to evaluate your progress, detailed answers to the practice problems are provided at the end of each chapter.

1.1 An economy has the consumption function $C = 125 + 0.8Y_d$. All income is subject to income tax at a rate of 0.25, investment is 240 and government spending is 375.

Find the equilibrium income and the government's surplus or deficit.

You may be set other problems as part of your course and want to know the correct approach to use. Looking up either economics or mathematics terms in the index may help you identify the appropriate method. Since this is an introductory text, most of the economic analysis is developed using numerical examples. For some key points, analytical results are also presented in general terms using an algebraic approach.

Show that when TR is a maximum, MR is zero.

If total revenue, TR, is a function of output, Q, we write

$$TR = f(Q)$$

$$d(TR)/dQ = 0 \text{ for maximum total revenue, and so}$$

$$MR = 0 \text{ (substituting } d(TR)/dQ = MR)$$

$$MR = 0 \text{ when total revenue is maximized.}$$

The book is complete in itself, but further e-learning resources are provided on the CD-ROM and there are references to them at various points in the text. For a different perspective on various topics in mathematics and economic analysis you can use the interactive MathEcon courseware. There is more information about this below. The PowerPoint slides include definitions and points from the Remember boxes. Lecturers may find these useful as teaching material. Students can view them as a slide show on screen, or print them as handouts to form a summary of key points that may be useful for revision. If Microsoft PowerPoint is not installed on your computer you can view the slides using the PowerPoint viewer included on the CD-ROM. The Excel files contain the calculations and graphs described in the sections of the book that relate to using Excel. They are produced using Excel 2000 and are readable also in Excel 97.

For students who would like to practise more questions, the CD includes quizzes for you to use on your computer and lots more further practice problems for each chapter in the form of Acrobat documents that you can print.

About MathEcon

MathEcon comprises selected screens on topics in mathematics and in economics from the award-winning WinEcon computer package, which is now Web-enabled (see www.winecon.com for further details). The WinEcon software, published and marketed by the WinEcon Consortium (see below), was developed over a period of three years by a consortium of eight UK universities under the UK higher education funding council's Teaching and Learning Technology Programme. It is designed to offer a student-centred approach to learning economics and associated quantitative techniques.

The MathEcon chapters correspond to those in this book, and each section has an appropriate introduction. If you are using the software separately, the Introduction screens provide a guide to each section. (A list of the MathEcon screens is given in a following section, together with the relevant WinEcon screen numbers, for those students using the WinEcon courseware, and the corresponding book section numbers.)

The courseware offers an interactive and dynamic explanation of many topics, both in mathematics and in economics. Practice problems screens have an easy-to-use answer input mechanism where you get immediate feedback on whether your answer is correct. A calculator is available to help with calculations, and a Help mechanism is provided. Once you have installed MathEcon following the instructions below, the Using MathEcon tab shows you what the different screen buttons do.

MathEcon and Your Computer System

For individual use, MathEcon is only available as a CD-ROM for use on a Windows PC. If you do not have access to a suitable PC, you may be able to access the screens over a network if your university or college has a WinEcon site licence which includes MathEcon. MathEcon would appear on the WinEcon Start up screen as a course entitled Mathematics for Economics and Business. If the networked version of WinEcon you are using does not show this course, ask your course administrator to contact the WinEcon Consortium about an appropriate upgrade (see www.winecon.com for further details).

To contact the WinEcon Consortium write to:

> WinEcon Consortium
> PO Box 4
> Minehead
> TA24 8ZY

or email: enquiries@winecon.com

SYSTEM REQUIREMENTS

The minimum requirements to run MathEcon are:

- PC using a 486 or higher processor, Pentium recommended
- CD-ROM drive
- 8MB RAM (32MB recommended)
- SVGA or higher resolution display
- Hard disk with 50MB free space
- Microsoft Windows 95 / 98 / ME / NT / 2000 or XP

INSTALLING MATHECON

Select Run from the Start menu. Type d:\setup (assuming that your CD is drive D) and click OK. Follow the on-screen instructions to install the program to your hard disk. Once installed select MathEcon from the Programs item in the Start menu. Leave the CD in the drive while you are using MathEcon.

About Using Excel

Excel 2000 was chosen for the spreadsheet examples since it is currently the most popular spreadsheet program and is used in a wide variety of educational and business environments. Chapters 1, 2, 4, 11 and 12 of the book each conclude with a section on using Excel. The spreadsheets they describe, which are listed in the next section, are all available on the CD-ROM for you to explore. The files can also be read in Excel 97.

If you have not previously used a spreadsheet, some key ideas are:

- You lay out your data and calculations with one item in each cell.
- You select a cell where a calculation is to appear, then enter a formula in it to carry out the computation.
- You enter a formula for a calculation in such a way that it can be copied to compute other values.
- The completed spreadsheet can be used for what-if analysis, since changing a value automatically recalculates all values calculated from it.

There is guidance about how to enter relevant formulae in the chapter sections in the book and you can also get information from the Help feature in Excel. Remember that formulae always start with an equals sign and must not contain any spaces. If you encounter a problem in trying to set up your own spreadsheet, load the appropriate file from the CD-ROM, click on the cell showing the value you want to calculate and look in the Formula Bar to see the formula that is being used.

List of Mathecon Screens

MathEcon includes material relating to chapters 1 to 10 of the book. This list shows how the topics are grouped in sections, and also lists the section of WinEcon that contains the topic. From the MathEcon Startup screen, select the Tutorials tab, then choose a chapter and section. The topic titles are then displayed and you can go directly to any of them. Screens indented in this list are supplementary screens. To access them, go to the topic of which they form a part and move to them using the Next Page button.

List of Excel Worksheets

For each of the book chapters listed below there is an accompanying Excel file on the CD. This list shows the names of the files, the worksheets that they contain and the pages of the book where the material is described.

chapter one

Functions in Economics

In this chapter you learn to
- Appreciate why economists use mathematics
- Plot points on graphs and handle negative values
- Express relationships using linear and power functions, substitute values and sketch the functions
- Use the basic rules of algebra and carry out accurate calculations
- Work with fractions
- Handle powers and indices
- Interpret functions of several variables
- Apply the approach to economic variables
- Understand the relationship between total and average revenue
- Obtain and plot various cost functions
- Write an expression for profit
- Depict production functions using isoquants and find the average product of labour
- Use Excel to plot functions and perform calculations

SECTION 1.1: Introduction

We can express economic analysis more precisely when we use mathematics. The approach may not always be appropriate, because economics deals with people and sometimes we may prefer to give a verbal description of their behaviour. The application of mathematics, however, has allowed economic theory to advance and provides the basis for computer models of the economy that have been developed. As you progress in economics you will find mathematics is used in various ways in textbooks and in journal articles.

In introductory economics you study the relationship between various cost curves such as average variable cost, total cost and marginal cost. Mathematics makes relationships explicit and tells us that if one of the cost curves has a particular shape, each of the others has another specific shape. The positions at which the average and marginal curves cross one another can also be exactly determined. In measuring elasticity of demand there can be ambiguity, but mathematics gives us a precise measure in the form of point elasticity, and this resolves the difficulty. Economic models include those representing supply and demand in a market, and models of the economy used in macroeconomics. Each model is expressed as a system of equations. We can investigate how it works and solve the equations to find equilibrium values for the system.

Mathematics is used for modelling financial processes, and it enables us to show how optimization subject to constraints can be achieved. In ways such as these it is useful to businesses. It is therefore a career-relevant subject and a good grade is useful for impressing potential employers. In this chapter you learn how to handle the kinds of functional relationships needed for economic and financial modelling.

The MathEcon chapter 1 screens in the section titled Introductory Mathematics suggest ways of using the screens, give you a dynamic demonstration of plotting points on a graph and highlight important algebraic results. The questions and quizzes challenge your understanding of particular concepts, so be sure to try them. Useful reference material is provided by the Summary of the Basics screen, which lets you access the main rules or methods for each of the previous screens.

The last section of this chapter gives you ideas for using Microsoft Excel to plot graphs and carry out calculations. A computer spreadsheet such as Excel can help you present many kinds of quantitative information. Since it relieves the tedium of computations it makes it possible for you to investigate more aspects of a topic, thus deepening your understanding. The ability to use Excel is a transferable skill and to help you develop it there are example worksheets included on the CD.

To see examples of how mathematics is useful in both microeconomics and macroeconomics, work through the MathEcon section 2 screen titled Economic Problems – Basic Mathematics. Another screen you may like to try is Objectives and Actions: Looking Ahead. This lets you make choices to try to achieve a particular objective. The algebra underlying the model is revealed by the Advanced button.

SECTION 1.2: Coordinates and Graphs

A horizontal and a vertical line form the axes of a graph. Each is marked with a measurement scale. The intervals shown on each scale are chosen for convenience and are not necessarily the same on both axes. The horizontal axis is called, in general, the x axis and the vertical axis the y axis. In a particular example we may give other names to the axes to indicate what is being measured on them. Where the axes intersect, x and y both take the value 0. This is called the origin and is denoted 0. As we move to the right along the horizontal axis the values of x get larger (and y remains at 0). When we move up the vertical axis y increases (and x stays at 0).

> x axis: the horizontal line along which values of x are measured. Values along the axis increase from left to right.
>
> y axis: the vertical line up which values of y are measured. Values on the axis increase from bottom to top.
>
> origin: the point at which the axes intersect, where x and y are both 0.

The pair of values $x = 7$, $y = 2$ can be represented by a point plotted 7 units to the right of the origin and 2 units up from it. This is shown as point A in figure 1.1. A point can be described by its coordinates, which in general are written (x,y). That is, the horizontal, or x distance from the origin is always given first, followed by the vertical, or y distance. The coordinates of point A are $(7,2)$.

To see how we plot points, use the MathEcon screen Coordinates and Graphs. For an example of graph plotting in economics, see The Demand Curve of an Individual screen.

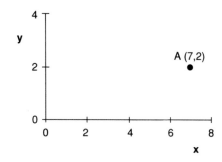

Figure 1.1   Point A has coordinates (7,2)

> coordinates: a pair of numbers (x,y) that represent the position of a point. The first number is the horizontal distance of the point from the origin, the second number is the vertical distance.

PLOTTING NEGATIVE VALUES

A graph like that shown in figure 1.1 lets us plot only positive values of x and y. It is said to comprise the positive quadrant. As economists we sometimes have to deal with negative values. For example, as the quantity sold increases marginal revenue may become negative, and investment may be negative if stocks are run down. To depict negative values we use a graph such as that shown in figure 1.2 where the x and y axes extend in both directions from the origin, dividing the area into four quadrants. As we move leftwards along the x axis the values of x get smaller. To the left of the origin x is negative and as we move further left still it becomes more negative and smaller. So, for example, −6 is a smaller number than −2 and occurs to the left of it on the x axis. On the y axis negative numbers occur below the origin.

---

positive quadrant: the area above the x axis and to the right of the y axis where both x and y take positive values.

1

Plot the points A = (3,0) B = (−5,4) C = (2,−4) D = (−2,−3)

The points are located as shown in figure 1.2.
A (3,0) is 3 units to the right of the origin and on the x axis.
B (−5,4) is 5 units to the left of the origin and 4 units up.
C (2,−4) is 2 to the right of the origin and 4 below the x axis.
D (−2,−3) is 2 to the left of the origin and 3 down from the x axis.

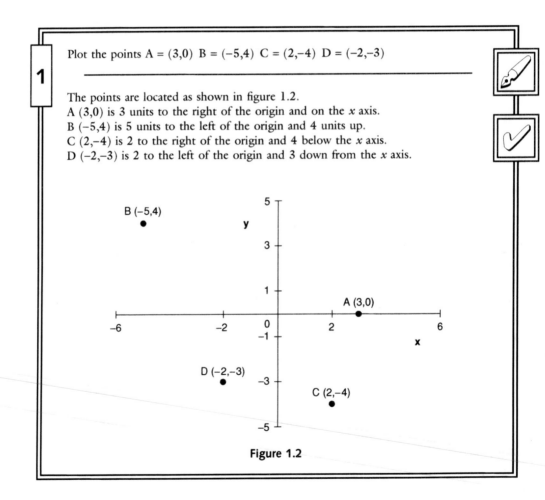

Figure 1.2

1.1 Plot the points A = (6,2) B = (0,5) C = (−7,3) D = (−4,−2) E = (3,−6)

SECTION 1.3: Variables and Functions

A variable takes on different values, perhaps at different times, for different people or in different places. So that we can analyse the relationship between variables, we identify each of them by a letter or symbol. If there are just two variables the values they take can easily be plotted as points on a graph and the variable names x and y are often used, corresponding to the horizontal and vertical axes respectively. We shall use these as our basic variable names, but other letters can also be used and in economics examples we shall choose names as appropriate.

> variable: a quantity represented by a symbol that can take different possible values.
> constant: a quantity whose value is fixed, even if we do not know its numerical amount.

A constant remains fixed while we study a relationship. It could be the proportion of income that is saved, or the level of utility that is achieved on a particular indifference curve. Sometimes we may know the numerical value of a constant, but if we do not or if we want to obtain general results we may use a letter or symbol to represent the constant. Letters commonly used to represent constants are: a, b, c, k.

If one variable, y, changes in a systematic way as another variable, x, changes we say y is a function of x. The mathematical notation for this is

$$y = f(x)$$

where the letter f is used to denote a function. The brackets used in specifying this functional relationship do not indicate multiplication. The variable inside them is the one whose values we need to know to determine the values of the other variable, y, on the left-hand side. Letters other than f can be used to denote a function. If we have more than one functional relationship we can indicate they are different by using different letters, such as g or h. For instance, we may write

$$y = g(x)$$

which we again read as 'y is a function of x'.

An example of a function in economics is that total cost is a function of output. We may choose Q to represent output and write TC as a single variable name standing for total cost. The function can then be expressed as $TC = f(Q)$. We are using Q in place of variable x and TC in place of y.

> function: a systematic relationship between pairs of values of the variables, written $y = f(x)$.

SUBSTITUTION OF X VALUES

A function gives us a general rule for obtaining values of y from values of x. An example is

$$y = 4x + 5$$

The expression $4x$ means $4 \times x$. It is conventional to omit the multiplication sign. To evaluate the function for a particular value of x, multiply that x value by 4 and then add 5 to find the corresponding value of y. If $x = 6$

$$y = (4 \times 6) + 5 = 29$$

These x and y values give us the point $(6,29)$ on the graph of the function. Now let us find the y value when $x = 0$. Substituting for x we obtain $y = (4 \times 0) + 5 = 5$, since multiplying by 0 gives 0.

See section 1.4 on multiplying by 0.

Substituting different values of x gives different points on the graph. Since the function tells us how to obtain y from any x value, y is said to be dependent on x, and x is known as the independent variable. Notice that on a graph the independent variable is plotted on the horizontal axis, and the dependent variable on the vertical axis.

- If y is a function of x, $y = f(x)$.
- A function is a rule telling us how to obtain y values from x values.
- x is known as the independent variable, y as the dependent variable.
- The independent variable is plotted on the horizontal axis, the dependent variable on the vertical axis.

Remember...

LINEAR FUNCTIONS

If the relationship between x and y takes the form

$$y = 6x$$

when we substitute various x values to obtain the corresponding y values we find that all the pairs of x and y values are points lying on a straight line. Listed below are some x values with the corresponding y values:

x	0	5	10
y	0	30	60

The points $(0,0)$, $(5,30)$ and $(10,60)$ all lie on a straight line as shown in figure 1.3. Notice that the line passes through the origin. Each y value is 6 times the x value, and we say that y is proportional to x.

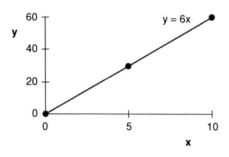

Figure 1.3 A linear function, $y = 6x$

proportional relationship: each y value is the same amount times the corresponding x value, so all points lie on a straight line through the origin.
linear function: a relationship in which all the pairs of values form points on a straight line.

In general, a function of the form $y = bx$ represents a straight line passing through the origin. Since y is always b times x, the relationship between the variables is said to be a proportional one.

shift: a vertical movement upwards or downwards of a line or curve.

Adding a constant to a function shifts the function vertically upwards by the amount of the constant. The function

$$y = 6x + 20$$

has y values that are 20 more than those of the previous function at every value of x. Using the same x values as before we obtain the points: (0,20), (5,50), (10,80). As figure 1.4 shows, the function $y = 6x + 20$ forms a straight line with the same slope as the previous line, but cutting the y axis at 20. This is called the intercept.

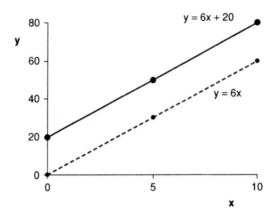

Figure 1.4   Adding a constant shifts the linear function up

intercept: the value at which a function cuts the y axis.

We study linear functions further in section 2.6 Linear Equations.

It is useful to recognize linear functions. If a function has just a term in x and, perhaps, a constant it is linear. A linear function has the general form $y = a + bx$. You can plot the graph of a linear function by finding just two points. Connecting these points with a straight line gives you the graph, and you can extend it beyond the points if you wish.

A function with just a term in x and (perhaps) a constant is a linear function. It has the general form

$$y = a + bx$$

Remember...

POWER FUNCTIONS

> power: an index indicating the number of times that the item to which it is applied is multiplied by itself.

Many of the functions economists use to model relationships are power functions in which the variable x appears raised to a power. Simple examples are

$$y = x^2 \qquad\qquad\qquad (a)$$

$$z = 7x^2 \qquad\qquad\qquad (b)$$

In function (a), the number superscripted to the right of x is called a power. When something is raised to a power we have to multiply that item by itself the number of times shown by the power. In this case, then, $x^2 = x \times x$, and the rule given by function (a) is that we must multiply x by itself to find the value of y. Similarly, function (b) can be written $z = 7 \times x \times x$. To evaluate it for a particular value of x we find x^2 (often called x squared) and then multiply it by 7 to obtain z. If $x = 5$ we have

$$y = 5^2 = 5 \times 5 = 25 \qquad\qquad\qquad (a)$$

$$z = 7 \times 5^2 = 7 \times 25 = 175 \qquad\qquad\qquad (b)$$

Functions often have more than one term and one of them may be a constant, for example

$$y = 140 + 7x^2 - 2x^3$$

In this function the highest power of x that appears is 3. The superscripted symbol x^3 is called x cubed and a power function in which x^3 is the highest power of x is called a cubic function. A function such as

$$y = 25x^2 + 74$$

has x^2 as the highest power of x and is called a quadratic function.

> quadratic function: a function in which the highest power of x is 2. There may also be a term in x and a constant, but no other terms.
> cubic function: a function in which the highest power of x is 3. There may also be terms in x^2, x and a constant, but no other terms.

SKETCHING FUNCTIONS

To help us visualize the nature of the relationship between two variables it is often useful to sketch a graph of the function. This does not have to be a precise graph. We just want to see its general shape. The method is to choose some x values, substitute them in the function to find the corresponding y values, and then plot the graph. Note that in economics it is often only positive values of x that are meaningful. Usually you need to plot a number of points to see the shape of the function, but for a linear function two points are sufficient. The steps in the process are listed below.

> In chapter 6 we will study a method for identifying maximum and minimum values.

To sketch a function   **Remember...**

- Decide what to plot on the x axis and on the y axis.
- List some possible and meaningful x values, choosing easy ones such as 0, 1, 10.
- Find the y values corresponding to each, and list them alongside.
- Look for points where an axis is crossed ($x = 0$ or $y = 0$).
- Look for maximum and minimum values at which the graph turns downwards or upwards.
- If you are not sure of the correct shape, try one or two more x values.
- Connect the points with a smooth curve.

> For information on multiplying negative numbers see section 1.4 Basic Rules of Algebra.

The functions that we use to represent economic relationships are usually single valued functions. When we substitute a value of x in the function we normally obtain a unique value of y that corresponds to it. You should be aware, however, that multivalued functions exist. These have more than one y value corresponding to one x value. For the function $y^2 = x$ there are two y values corresponding to every x value. If x equals 9, say, y is a number which when multiplied by itself gives 9. This implies either $y = 3$ or $y = -3$, since $3 \times 3 = 9$ and $(-3) \times (-3) = 9$.

> Now use the MathEcon screen Variables and Functions to consolidate your understanding. Answer the question it poses, then continue and click the question button to check that you understand the terms constant, variable and function.

USING EXCEL

You can use a computer spreadsheet such as Excel to calculate the values of functions and plot their graphs. You enter the formula for the function once and then copy it, so that calculating a large number of values of the function becomes easy. You can inspect those values for maximum and minimum values, and can plot them on a graph. The file Function.xls contains examples for you to use, including a worksheet called Power function that will plot graphs for you. Further information about this is provided in section 1.13.

2

Sketch and briefly describe the following functions for positive values of x

$$y = 2x^3 - 50x \qquad \text{(a)}$$

$$y = 14 \qquad \text{(b)}$$

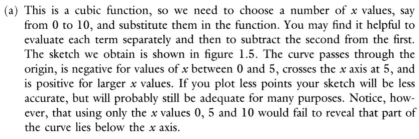

(a) This is a cubic function, so we need to choose a number of x values, say from 0 to 10, and substitute them in the function. You may find it helpful to evaluate each term separately and then to subtract the second from the first. The sketch we obtain is shown in figure 1.5. The curve passes through the origin, is negative for values of x between 0 and 5, crosses the x axis at 5, and is positive for larger x values. If you plot less points your sketch will be less accurate, but will probably still be adequate for many purposes. Notice, however, that using only the x values 0, 5 and 10 would fail to reveal that part of the curve lies below the x axis.

x	0	1	2	3	4	5	6	7	8	9	10
$2x^3$	0	2	16	54	128	250	432	686	1024	1458	2000
$50x$	0	50	100	150	200	250	300	350	400	450	500
$y = 2x^3 - 50x$											
$y =$	0	−48	−84	−96	−72	0	132	336	624	1008	1500

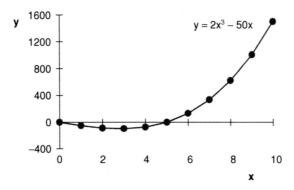

Figure 1.5

(b) The function $y = 14$ says y is a constant. Whatever the value of x, y has the value 14. The graph in figure 1.6 shows a horizontal straight line.

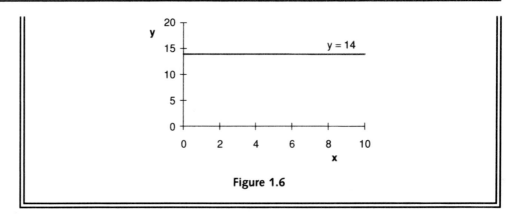

Figure 1.6

1.2 Sketch graphs of the functions for values of x between 0 and 10

(a) $y = 0.5x$ (b) $y = 0.5x + 6$ (c) $y = x^2$ (d) $y = 3x^2$

Which of them are linear? Which is a proportional relationship? What is the effect of adding a constant term?

1.3 Draw the line $y = x$ using equal scales on the horizontal and vertical axes. What angle does the line make with the horizontal axis?

SECTION 1.4: Basic Rules of Algebra

In evaluating algebraic or arithmetic statements certain rules have to be observed about the order in which various operations take place. This means you need to look carefully at an expression before you evaluate it and decide what to calculate first. It is no more difficult to calculate the right answer than the wrong one – you just have to take care in applying the rules about precedence. In an economics example the correct answer should correspond to what would be the diagrammatic solution to the problem, whereas a wrong answer can be completely meaningless – negative price and quantity, for example.

As an illustration, let us find the value of y from the following equation when $x = 3$:

$$y = 10 + 6x^2$$

- We first substitute the value 3 for x and square it, giving 9
- then multiply this by 6, obtaining 54
- and finally add this result to the value 10 giving the answer $y = 64$.

Notice that since $x^2 = x \times x$ it is different from $2x$ (except when $x = 2$). As to the order of the calculation, we have to pick out the term involving exponentiation (raising to a power) and do this first, followed by multiplication and after that addition. Brackets can be used to alter, or clarify, the order in which operations are to take place. Our previous statement is changed if brackets are inserted as shown and x remains 3:

$$y = (10 + 6)x^2$$

A number or symbol immediately before or after brackets implies that everything inside the brackets is to be multiplied by this item. Hence the brackets indicate that what they enclose is to be evaluated first and the result multiplied by the value outside. The above expression could be written

$$y = (10 + 6) \times x^2$$

Evaluating this, we do the bit in brackets first and so add $10 + 6$, giving 16. As before, x^2 is 9 but this is now multiplied by 16 giving a value for the expression of 144. Notice that in writing algebraic statements the multiplication sign is often omitted, or sometimes replaced by a dot.

The reciprocal of x is $1/x$. Instead of dividing by a value we can multiply by the reciprocal of that value. For example, $(y + 11) \div x = (y + 11) \times 1/x$.

---

exponentiation: raising to a power.
reciprocal of a value: is 1 divided by that value.

An expression in brackets immediately preceded or followed by a value implies that the whole expression in the brackets is to be multiplied by that value.

Remember...

The order of algebraic operations is

Remember...

1. If there are brackets, do what is inside the brackets first
2. Exponentiation
3. Multiplication and division
4. Addition and subtraction

You may like to remember the acronym BEDMAS, meaning brackets, exponentiation, division, multiplication, addition, subtraction.

In working with economic models you should use brackets if you substitute an expression for a variable. This helps ensure you keep the calculation correct. In the worked example below notice how the brackets help us get the correct negative sign on the Y term in the answer.

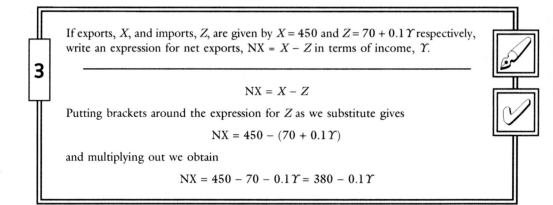

3

If exports, X, and imports, Z, are given by $X = 450$ and $Z = 70 + 0.1Y$ respectively, write an expression for net exports, NX $= X - Z$ in terms of income, Y.

$$NX = X - Z$$

Putting brackets around the expression for Z as we substitute gives

$$NX = 450 - (70 + 0.1Y)$$

and multiplying out we obtain

$$NX = 450 - 70 - 0.1Y = 380 - 0.1Y$$

CALCULATORS AND COMPUTERS

Most modern calculators use algebraic logic, but remember you do have to put in the multiplication signs. Try entering each of the calculations in the above subsection in your calculator in the order in which it is written and check for the correct answer.

Computer spreadsheet programs also allow you to enter arithmetic statements in a format similar to that in which they are written. The computer does need to recognize that you are giving it a value to evaluate. In Microsoft Excel this is done by starting the expression with an equals sign. Signs to indicate multiplication and exponentiation are also needed, and for these the * and ^ are used. Further information and examples on using Excel for calculations are provided in section 1.13.

ORDER WITHIN AN EXPRESSION

Except when the rules about precedence indicate otherwise, we usually evaluate algebraic expressions working from left to right. Sometimes, however, you can make a calculation easier by choosing which part of it you do first. If you do this you must be sure your order of operations is legitimate.

Addition or multiplication of numbers can occur in any order. Take as an example $19 + 27 + 1$. This is the same as $19 + 1 + 27$, which is quicker to add in your head and gives 47.

A multiplicative example is $5 \times 17 \times 2 = 5 \times 2 \times 17$. It is easier first to multiply 5 by 2 than by 17, and so the answer of 170 is easy to work out in your head with the second arrangement.

Brackets may sometimes be used in sums or products to group terms, perhaps because of their economic significance, but the value of the result is not affected. For example

$$(19 + 1) + 27 = 19 + (1 + 27) = 47$$

and

$$(5 \times 2) \times 17 = 5 \times (2 \times 17) = 170$$

In subtraction and division the order of the terms is important. The value following a minus sign is subtracted from the value that precedes it. When a division is specified the first number is to be divided by the second. Interchanging the terms of a subtraction or division would alter the value of the expression and so is not permissible. For example

$$8 - 6 = 2, \text{ while } 6 - 8 = -2$$

and

$$8 \div 4 = 2, \text{ while } 4 \div 8 = 1/2$$

> The MathEcon screen Basic Rules of Algebra describes these properties further. Try the quiz for some practise in evaluating a complex expression.

NEGATIVE NUMBERS

We can regard the x axis as a number scale. The values get bigger as we move to the right and smaller as we move to the left. Addition moves you to the right along the scale and subtraction moves you to the left, if the value being added or subtracted is positive. As you evaluate a complex expression you may have to add or subtract a negative number. The negative sign reverses the direction in which you move. Removing brackets around negative numbers, a plus and a minus sign together become a minus, while two minus signs together become a plus. Hence

$$7 + (-3) = 7 - 3 = 4 \tag{a}$$

Adding a negative number is the same as subtracting a positive number and you move to the left on the number scale. However,

$$7 - (-3) = 7 + 3 = 10 \tag{b}$$

Subtracting a negative number is the same as an addition and you move to the right on the number scale.

When you evaluate an expression that begins with a negative number you start at a position on the x axis to the left of the origin. If you add a positive number you move to the right, while a subtraction moves you to the left. Remember you can reorder the terms in an addition if you wish. Examples are

$$-5 + 6 = 6 - 5 = 1 \tag{c}$$

$$-5 - 6 = -(5 + 6) = -11 \tag{d}$$

Factors and brackets are
explained further in the next
but two subsection.

Both terms in (d) have a negative sign so we may rewrite the expression using brackets as shown. Notice that the result is more negative than the number we started with.

In multiplications involving one or more negative numbers we bring the signs to the front of the terms we are multiplying. Again one plus and one minus sign together become a minus, while two minus signs become a plus. Division is similar to multiplication and the same rules about signs apply. For example

$$2 \times (-5) = -10 \tag{e}$$

$$(-2) \times (-5) = -(-10) = 10 \tag{f}$$

$$10 \div (-2) = -10 \div 2 = -5 \tag{g}$$

$$(-10) \div (-2) = -(-10 \div 2) = 5 \tag{h}$$

Take care in applying these rules to squared terms. Notice that -5^2 is -25 because exponentiation is done first and the negative of the result is taken, whereas $(-5)^2$ is 25 because the brackets instruct us to multiply -5 by itself, so there are two negative signs which yield a positive value.

When two signs come together   **Remember...**

$$- + \text{ (or } + -) \text{ gives } -$$

$$- - \text{ gives } +$$

CALCULATORS AND NEGATIVE SIGNS

If you enter two arithmetic signs consecutively into a calculator, for example, × followed by −, it often assumes the second is a correction for the first. Some calculators have a (−) sign for entering a minus sign that precedes a number. If yours does not, then for correct calculator evaluation of expressions (a), (b) and (e) to (h) you should enter the brackets as shown. If an expression starts with a minus sign as does (c), you may find that if you begin by entering −5 into your calculator the minus sign is not shown. You may, however, get the correct result. To get the calculator to show you it has a negative sign at the start of a calculation you can put the term in brackets. Alternatively, if you have a +/− key you can enter a positive number and press the +/− key to change the sign. Try out your calculator on expressions (a) to (h) so you are sure of how to enter expressions that include negative signs.

MULTIPLICATION AND DIVISION INVOLVING 1 AND 0

When we multiply or divide by 1 the expression is unchanged, whereas if we multiply or divide by −1 the sign of the expression changes. Hence

$$39 \times 1 = 39, \ 23 \times (-1) = -23, \ 92/1 = 92, \ 17/(-1) = -17$$

In algebraic expressions, if we have $2 \times x$ we write $2x$, but if we have $1 \times x$ we simply write x. It is important to know that the 1 is implied, although it is not stated. Also, because multiplication by 1 does not change anything, any expression can be considered as being multiplied by 1. This concept has an important parallel in matrix algebra.

4 Remove the brackets from the expression $y = -(6x^3 - 15x^2 + x - 1)$

Each term inside the brackets is multiplied by -1, so we have

$$y = -6x^3 + 15x^2 - x + 1$$

When we multiply by 0, the answer is 0. For example, consider different multiples of 8

$$3 \times 8 = 24 = 8 + 8 + 8$$

$$2 \times 8 = 16 = 8 + 8$$

$$1 \times 8 = 8 \text{ (there is just one 8 with nothing to add to it)}$$

$$0 \times 8 = 0 \text{ (there are no 8's, and therefore nothing)}$$

Division divides a value into parts, but if there is nothing to begin with the result of division is nothing, for example

$$0 \div 4 = 0$$

Division of 0 gives the answer 0.

Division by 0, however, gives a quite different result, namely one that is infinitely large if it is positive, or infinitely small if it is negative. Check to see what your calculator gives for $14 \div 0$. You should find it does not give you a numerical answer. We sometimes want to exclude the possibility of division by 0 and so, for example, we may define a function for a specified set of values, excluding any that would imply division by 0. To see that division by 0 gives a very large number which may have a negative sign (making it infinitely small), consider dividing 5 by successively smaller numbers:

$$5 \div 1 = 5$$

$$5 \div \frac{1}{2} = 10$$

$$5 \div \frac{1}{10} = 50$$

$$5 \div \frac{1}{100} = 500$$

$$5 \div \frac{1}{1000} = 5000$$

As the number we are dividing by gets closer and closer to 0 in the list above, the result gets larger and larger. It seems that division by 0 gives an infinitely large positive number. But if each of the divisors above were negative, they would still be getting closer and closer to 0, but would be approaching it from the left of zero on the number scale. Each answer would be the negative of the one shown and so division by 0 can give a result of infinitely large magnitude but with a negative sign, so that the value is infinitely small.

The only general statement we can make about the result of dividing 0 by 0, $0 \div 0$, is to say it is undefined. In a particular case it may be possible to study what happens as both the numerator and the denominator get very small.

$1 \times x = x, (-1) \times x = -x$ **Remember...**

- Any value multiplied by 0 is 0.
- 0 divided by any value except 0 is 0.
- Division by 0 gives an infinitely large number which may be positive or negative.
- Be wary of division by 0.

An example of where you may encounter division by zero in studying economics is shown on the MathEcon screen Deriving the Short-Run Average Fixed Cost (AFC) and Average Variable Cost (AVC) Curves. Total fixed cost (FC) is a constant and average fixed cost is found by dividing it by the level of output, Q. The values of Q that we consider are positive values starting from 0. If $Q = 0$, then AFC = FC/Q is infinite. Labour employed, L, determines the values of output, Q, and variable cost, VC. When $L = 0$, both Q and VC are zero. The formula AVC = VC/Q therefore gives $0 \div 0$. This result is meaningless. What we can do instead is use a small fractional value for L. If $L = 0.001$, $Q = 0.35$, VC = 20 and AVC = 20/0.35 = 57.14. If you want to check this, the production function from which the values of Q are calculated is shown on the screen Short-Run Production Functions: A Numerical Example.

FACTORS AND MULTIPLYING OUT BRACKETS

To help us evaluate an expression we may want to take out a common factor from each of several terms, or on other occasions we may wish to perform the opposite operation of multiplying out the brackets. With a bit of practise you will find you can recognize a pattern in the best way to approach a particular type of problem. For example, suppose

$$y = 6x - 3x^2$$

Remembering that this is a shorthand way of writing

$$y = (6 \times x) - (3 \times x \times x)$$

we see that each of the terms on the right-hand side can be exactly divided by $3 \times x$, because $(6 \times x)/(3 \times x) = 2$ and $(-3 \times x \times x)/(3 \times x) = -x$. The amount that we can divide by, $3 \times x$, is called a common factor. We can rewrite the original expression using brackets that contain the terms after they have been divided by the common factor, and with the common factor outside, multiplying the whole. This is called factorizing the expression and gives

$$y = 3 \times x \times (2 - x)$$

It is usual to write this without the multiplication signs as

$$y = 3x(2 - x)$$

> factorizing: writing an expression as a product that when multiplied out gives the original expression.

Alternatively, it may be useful to multiply out brackets and so remove them. If one expression is written immediately next to an expression in brackets, the implication is that these are multiplied together. To multiply out, we multiply each term in the brackets by the expression outside the brackets. Consider, for example

$$3x(2 - x)$$

To multiply out the brackets we multiply 2 by $3x$, then multiply $-x$ by $3x$ giving

$$3x(2 - x) = 6x - 3x^2$$

When two brackets are multiplied together, to remove them we multiply each term in the second bracket by each term in the first bracket. It is then usual to simplify the result by collecting terms where possible. For example

$$(a - b)(-c + d) = -ac + ad + bc - bd$$

Remember to use the rules about signs discussed in the Negative Numbers subsection.

Another example of multiplying out brackets is

$$(x - 7)(4 - 3x) = 4x - 3x^2 - 28 + 21x$$
$$= -3x^2 + 25x - 28$$

Here the simplification involves adding the two terms in x. Notice that since factorization is the reverse process to multiplying out brackets, had you been given the right-hand side of the expression you could have factorized it to obtain the left-hand side, but the

You can see another example on the MathEcon screen Basic Rules of Algebra under the heading Combined Multiplication and Addition.

factors might not have been immediately obvious. Factorizing a quadratic expression involves some intelligent guesswork. You have to look for two expressions that multiply together to give you the one you started with. You should also be aware that not every quadratic expression factorizes to a product of expressions that contain integer values. The following standard results of multiplying out brackets are helpful:

$$(a + b)^2 = a^2 + 2ab + b^2$$

$$(a - b)^2 = a^2 - 2ab + b^2$$

$$(a + b)(a - b) = a^2 - b^2$$

You are asked to show these results in practice problem 1.7 below.

An expression in brackets written immediately next to another expression implies that the expressions are multiplied together.

Remember...

Multiplying out brackets

One pair: multiply each of the terms in brackets by the term outside.

Two pairs: multiply each term in the second bracket by each term in the first bracket.

Factorizing: look for a common factor, or for expressions that multiply together to give the original expression.

ACCURACY

When your calculations give non-integer results it is often appropriate to round your answer. To give an answer correct to two decimal places you round it up if the value in the third decimal place is 5 or over. If such an answer is to be used in a further calculation, however, to maintain as much accuracy as possible you should retain the value in your calculator and continue the calculation. This is especially important when answers to different parts of a calculation are to be multiplied together, since any inaccuracies would be compounded. In evaluating

$$\left(100 \times \frac{5}{9}\right)\left(36 \times \frac{2}{7}\right)$$

you can input this into a calculator in one step as $(^{500}\!/_9) \times (^{72}\!/_7)$ and round up to get an answer of 571.43. But notice that if you do the calculation in steps, rounding up after each one (i.e. $^{500}\!/_9 = 55.56$; $^{72}\!/_7 = 10.29$; then 55.56×10.29), you get the inaccurate result of 571.71 because each of the intermediate results has been rounded up.

1.4 Evaluate each expression without using a calculator and then check your answer using a calculator

(a) $35 - 2x^2$ when $x = 4$ and when $x = 5$

(b) $(25 - 23)x^2$ when $x = 4$ and when $x = -4$

(c) $\dfrac{10}{5} - 4$ 　　　　　　　　(d) $\dfrac{10}{5 - 4}$

(e) $\dfrac{10}{4} - 5$ 　　　　　　　　(f) $2 + (3 \times 5)$

(g) $-6 \times (3 - 7)$ 　　　　　　　(h) $32 - 2 \div 10$

(i) $-12 - 8 \times 3$ 　　　　　　　(j) $-15 - (-9)$

(k) $\sqrt{25}$

1.5 If a consumer spends two-thirds of any increase in income and her income increases by \$100, what is the increase in her spending?

1.6 Factorize

(a) $-10x - 45x^2$ 　　　　　　(b) $143x - 52$

(c) $5x^2 + 5x - 20xy$

1.7 (a) Multiply (or divide) out the brackets and simplify as far as possible

(i) $8x(10 - 7x)$ 　　　　　　(ii) $(2x + 5)(9 - 3x)$

(iii) $(11 - x)(12 - 4x)$ 　　　　(iv) $24 + 0.8(x - 675)$

(v) $\dfrac{1600 - 12x}{0.8}$

(b) Simplify

(i) $232x - 2x^2 - 100 - 150x + 0.36x^2$

(ii) $\dfrac{100 + 150x - 36x^2}{x}$

(iii) $x - 0.8x$ 　　　　　　(iv) $4(x - 0.75x)$

(c) Subtract $150 + 70x - x^2 + 0.5x^3$ from $270x - 3x^2$ and simplify your answer

(d) Evaluate $30 + 18x - 0.6x^2$ when $x = 15$

(e) By writing the square of a term in brackets as the product of terms, show the following results:

(i) $(a + b)^2 = a^2 + 2ab + b^2$ (ii) $(a - b)^2 = a^2 - 2ab + b^2$

(iii) $(a + b)(a - b) = a^2 - b^2$

1.8 (a) Check the following

(i) $(x - 7)$ and $(x + 5)$ are factors of $x^2 - 2x - 35$

(ii) $(3x + 1)$ and $(x + 8)$ are factors of $3x^2 + 25x + 8$

(iii) $(2x + 9)$ and $(x - 1)$ are factors of $2x^2 + 7x - 9$

(b) Factorize

(i) $x^2 + 10x + 21$ (ii) $3x^2 + 14x - 5$

(iii) $2x^2 + 8x - 10$ (iv) $3x^2 + 26x + 55$

SECTION 1.5: Fractions and Sharing

Sometimes the functions economists use involve fractions. For example, $\frac{1}{4}$ of people's income may be taken by the government in income tax, and $\frac{5}{7}$ of disposable income may be spent on consumption. Sometimes an optimal situation is identified when one ratio equals another, as shown by the following example. When the ratio of the prices of two goods equals the ratio of their marginal utilities, spending is optimally allocated between the two goods.

See MathEcon screen Optimal Consumption Choice.

---

fraction: a part of a whole.
ratio: one quantity divided by another quantity.

In numerical calculations you may choose if you prefer to write fractions as decimals, for example, $\frac{1}{4} = 0.25$. But for demonstrating various algebraic results you need to know the basic rules of working with fractions. These rules are listed below.

A fraction is a part of a whole. For example, if a household spends $\frac{1}{5}$ of its total weekly expenditure on housing, the share of housing in the household's total weekly

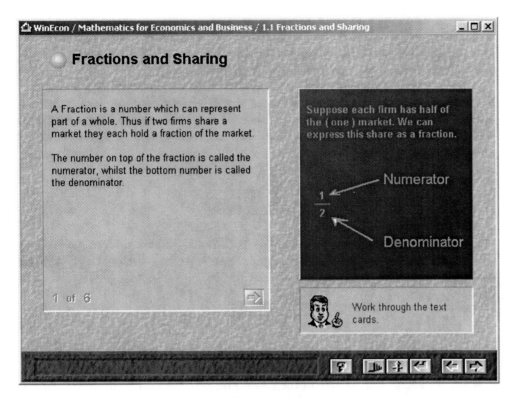

Figure 1.7

expenditure is ⅕. We can find the amount spent by multiplying the share, which is a fraction, by the total amount. If the household's total weekly expenditure is $250, the amount it spends on housing is one fifth of that amount.

Amount spent on housing = share of housing × total weekly expenditure

$$= \frac{1}{5} \times 250 = \$50$$

numerator: the value on the top of a fraction.
denominator: the value on the bottom of a fraction.

The top line of a fraction is called the numerator and the bottom line is called the denominator. The denominator shows how many parts the total amount is considered as being divided into, and the numerator shows the number of those parts that belong to the item we are considering. In the housing expenditure example, total weekly expenditure is considered as being divided into five parts (5 is the denominator) and one of these parts is spent on housing (1 is the numerator).

A fraction can also be written as a ratio of algebraic symbols. For example, if h = amount spent on housing and x = total weekly expenditure, the share of housing = h/x. The rules for working with fractions are first demonstrated numerically, but you then need to practise the same rules with fractions written in algebraic symbols using the examples that follow.

CANCELLING

When working with fractions we can divide both the numerator and the denominator by the same amount and the fraction is unchanged. If we have the fraction $^{30}/_{40}$ we can simplify it by dividing both top and bottom by 10.

$$\frac{30}{40} = \frac{(30 \div 10)}{(40 \div 10)} = \frac{3}{4}$$

10 is said to be a factor of both the numerator and the denominator, and can be cancelled.

When cancelling, if the whole of the numerator (or denominator) is cancelled out it becomes 1. For example, with

$$\frac{14 \times 6}{56 \times 9}$$

dividing by 14 on the top and bottom gives

$$\frac{(14 \div 14) \times 6}{(56 \div 14) \times 9} = \frac{1 \times 6}{4 \times 9} = \frac{6}{36}$$

Dividing the numerator and denominator by 6 simplifies the fraction further

$$\frac{6 \div 6}{36 \div 6} = \frac{1}{6}$$

When a fraction includes algebraic symbols, if the same symbol occurs as a multiplier in both the numerator and the denominator of a fraction, these symbols can be cancelled. For example

$$\frac{20y^2}{5y} = \frac{4(y \times y)}{y} = 4y$$

since the y in the denominator cancels with one of the y's in the numerator.

COMMON DENOMINATOR

Economists often want to compare two fractions to see if they are equal or, if not, which is bigger. They also want to add and subtract fractions. For all of these operations we need to express our fractions as having the same, or common, denominator. For example, to find which is the bigger of $\frac{3}{7}$ and $\frac{9}{20}$ we multiply both numerator and denominator of each fraction by the denominator of the other. This is the reverse operation to cancelling and leaves the value of the fraction unchanged.

$$\frac{3}{7} = \frac{20 \times 3}{20 \times 7} = \frac{60}{140}, \text{ while } \frac{9}{20} = \frac{7 \times 9}{7 \times 20} = \frac{63}{140}$$

Now that both fractions have the same denominator, 140, we can see immediately that the second is bigger because it has a numerator of 63 which is bigger than that of 60 which the first fraction has. Using the symbol > to indicate that the first expression is greater than the second, we write $^{63}/_{140} > {}^{60}/_{140}$, and so $\frac{9}{20} > \frac{3}{7}$. This is an example of an inequality expression, where the inequality sign indicates which of the two values it is separating is the greater.

> \> sign: the greater than sign indicates that the value on its left is greater than the value on its right.
> \< sign: the less than sign indicates that the value on its left is less than the value on its right.

Common denominators are also needed in working with algebraic expressions and we find them in the same way. For example, to put the fractions $3y/5x$ and $7x/y$ on a common denominator we multiply each fraction by the denominator of the other. This gives

$$\frac{3y}{5x} = \frac{3y \times y}{5x \times y} = \frac{3y^2}{5xy} \text{ and}$$

$$\frac{7x}{y} = \frac{7x \times 5x}{y \times 5x} = \frac{35x^2}{5xy}$$

Notice that unless we know the numerical values of x and y we cannot immediately say which of these two fractions is bigger.

ADDITION AND SUBTRACTION OF FRACTIONS

If fractions have the same denominator we can immediately add them or subtract them. We simply add or subtract the numerators and place the result on the common denominator. For example

$$\frac{3}{7} + \frac{1}{7} = \frac{3+1}{7} = \frac{4}{7} \text{ and}$$

$$\frac{9}{11} - \frac{2}{11} = \frac{9-2}{11} = \frac{7}{11}$$

If the denominators are not the same we must find a common denominator for the fractions before adding or subtracting them. For example, to find $^1/_4 + {}^2/_3$ we multiply both numerator and denominator of the first fraction by 3, and of the second fraction by 4. Both fractions then have denominators of 12 and we can add them.

$$\frac{1}{4} + \frac{2}{3} = \frac{3}{12} + \frac{8}{12} = \frac{3+8}{12} = \frac{11}{12}$$

To perform the subtraction $^{24}/_{35} - {}^3/_{10}$ we could use 350 as a common denominator using our basic rule of using the denominator of each fraction to multiply both numerator and denominator of the other. But if we notice that the first denominator is 7×5 and the second is 2×5 we see that the multiplier of 5 is already common to both denominators and we need only multiply by the other term in each denominator. Thus we use 2 as the multiplier for the first fraction and 7 for the second giving us 70 as the denominator. This is said to be the lowest common denominator.

$$\frac{24}{35} - \frac{3}{10} = \frac{48}{70} - \frac{21}{70} = \frac{48-21}{70} = \frac{27}{70}$$

---

lowest common denominator: the lowest value that is exactly divisible by all the denominators to which it refers.

An algebraic example is

$$\frac{2}{x+2} + \frac{5}{x+1}$$

Notice that although 2 appears both in the numerator and denominator of the first fraction it does not multiply the whole of the denominator and hence cannot be cancelled. Choosing the product of both denominators as the common denominator we have

$$\frac{2(x+1) + 5(x+2)}{(x+2)(x+1)}$$

and multiplying out the numerator gives

$$\frac{(2x+2+5x+10)}{(x+2)(x+1)}$$

Collecting terms in the numerator we have

$$\frac{7x+12}{(x+2)(x+1)}$$

MULTIPLICATION AND DIVISION OF FRACTIONS

To multiply two fractions we multiply the numerators and the denominators. For example

$$\frac{1}{2} \times \frac{3}{5} = \frac{1 \times 3}{2 \times 5} = \frac{3}{10}$$

To divide one fraction by another we turn the divisor upside down and multiply by it. You can check that this works by seeing that the reverse operation of multiplication gets you back to the value you started with. For example

$$\frac{5}{7} \div \frac{3}{4} = \frac{5}{7} \times \frac{4}{3}$$

$$= \frac{5 \times 4}{7 \times 3} = \frac{20}{21}$$

Check by multiplying the answer by the value you divided by and cancelling:

$$\frac{20}{21} \times \frac{3}{4} = \frac{20 \times 1}{7 \times 4}$$

$$= \frac{5 \times 1}{7 \times 1} = \frac{5}{7}$$

Algebraic fractions can be multiplied and divided in just the same way. You may then be able to cancel terms, but always check carefully that whole terms are equal before you cancel them. For example

$$\frac{x + 4}{x} \times \frac{x^2}{2} = \frac{(x + 4) \times x^2}{x \times 2} = \frac{(x + 4)x}{2}$$

cancelling the x in the denominator with one of the x's in the numerator x^2. Note that although there is a 4 in the numerator it is added to x and therefore it is not possible to cancel the 2 in the denominator with it.

Use the MathEcon screen Fractions and Sharing for more examples using the rules of fractions. An economic application is choosing what fraction of your income you want to spend on consumption. The screen Objectives and Actions: Looking Ahead lets you take part in a simulation where you choose what fraction or multiple of your income you consume in different time periods.

- Amount of an item = fractional share of item × total **Remember...** amount.
- A fraction is: numerator/denominator.
- Cancelling is dividing both numerator and denominator by the same amount.
- To add or subtract fractions first write them with a common denominator and then add or subtract the numerators.
- Fractions are multiplied by multiplying together the numerators and also the denominators.
- To divide by a fraction turn it upside down and multiply by it.

Evaluate the following without using a calculator

(a) $\dfrac{9}{11} + \dfrac{1}{2}$ (b) $\dfrac{5}{12} \times \dfrac{4}{7}$ (c) $\dfrac{1}{3} \div 4$ (d) $\dfrac{7}{10} - \dfrac{5}{16}$ (e) $\dfrac{8}{15} \div \dfrac{12}{25}$

(f) In a population of 28 million people aged between 20 and 60, $\frac{3}{4}$ are working or looking for work. How many people in the age group are economically active?

5

(a)
$$\frac{9}{11} + \frac{1}{2} = \frac{18 + 11}{22} = \frac{29}{22} \text{ or } 1\tfrac{7}{22}$$

(b) Cancelling the 4's, since $12 = 4 \times 3$
$$\frac{5}{12} \times \frac{4}{7} = \frac{5}{3} \times \frac{1}{7} = \frac{5}{21}$$

(c) Dividing by 4 is the same as multiplying by $\frac{1}{4}$
$$\frac{1}{3} \div 4 = \frac{1}{3} \times \frac{1}{4} = \frac{1}{12}$$

(d) You could use 160 as the denominator, but the lowest common denominator is 80
$$\frac{7}{10} - \frac{5}{16} = \frac{56 - 25}{80} = \frac{31}{80}$$

(e) We turn the fraction we are dividing by upside down and multiply by it
$$\frac{8}{15} \div \frac{12}{25} = \frac{8}{15} \times \frac{25}{12}$$

Cancelling 4's and 5's gives
$$\frac{2}{3} \times \frac{5}{3} = \frac{10}{9} \text{ or } 1\tfrac{1}{9}$$

(f) The economically active population in the age group is those who are working or looking for work. The number economically active $= \frac{3}{4} \times 28 = 21$ million people.

Simplify

(a) $\dfrac{3}{x^2} \times \dfrac{x}{9}$ (b) $\dfrac{5x}{2(x+1)} + \dfrac{3x}{4(x-1)}$

6

(a) Here we can cancel 3's and also x's since $x^2 = x \times x$:
$$\frac{3}{x^2} \times \frac{x}{9} = \frac{1}{x} \times \frac{1}{3} = \frac{1}{3x}$$

(b) Putting both terms on $4(x+1)(x-1)$ as the lowest common denominator gives $[10x(x-1) + 3x(x+1)]/[4(x+1)(x-1)]$. Multiplying out the brackets in the numerator we find
$$\frac{10x^2 - 10x + 3x^2 + 3x}{4(x+1)(x-1)} = \frac{13x^2 - 7x}{4(x+1)(x-1)}$$

1.9 Evaluate the following without using a calculator

(a) $\dfrac{3}{4} - \dfrac{1}{2}$

(b) $12 \times \dfrac{1}{3}$

(c) $\dfrac{1}{6} \times \dfrac{5}{7}$

(d) $\dfrac{3}{10} + \dfrac{7}{15}$

(e) $\dfrac{8}{9} \div 2$

(f) $\dfrac{24}{35} \times \dfrac{7}{8} \div \dfrac{3}{5}$

(g) $\dfrac{11}{12} - \dfrac{7}{18}$

1.10 If your marginal utility in consuming good X is 5 and your marginal utility in consuming good Y is 9 when you are buying X and Y at prices of 30 and 45 respectively, is the ratio of your marginal utilities equal to the ratio of the prices?

1.11 Simplify

(a) $\dfrac{x^2}{4} \times \dfrac{3}{x}$

(b) $\dfrac{15M}{P^2} \times P \div \dfrac{15M}{P}$

(c) $\dfrac{5x^2 - 3x}{x(1 + 3x)}$

(d) $\dfrac{8x}{12x^2 - 16x}$

(e) $\dfrac{7}{x + 2} + \dfrac{5x}{2x - 1}$

SECTION 1.6: Powers and Indices

A power or index applied to a value shows the number of times the value is to be multiplied by itself. For example

$$x^3 = x \cdot x \cdot x$$

and

$$x^5 = x \cdot x \cdot x \cdot x \cdot x$$

index or power: a superscript showing the number of times the value to which it is applied is to be multiplied by itself.

Notice that $x^1 = x$.

When we multiply together expressions comprising the same value raised to a power, we add the indices and raise the value to that new power. An example will show you that this rule works. Multiplying x^3 by x^5 gives three x's and then five x's all multiplied together. So we have eight x's multiplied together, which by definition is x^8.

$$x^3 . x^5 = (x . x . x)(x . x . x . x . x) = x^8$$

The rule gives the same result:

$$x^3 . x^5 = x^{3+5} = x^8$$

To divide two expressions where each is the same variable raised to some power, we subtract the powers to find the power of the variable in the answer. Again you can see by an example that the rule works. Dividing x^5 by x^3 we have five x's divided by three x's. Each of the bottom x's cancels with a top x, leaving two x's in the numerator, so the result is x^2.

$$\frac{x^5}{x^3} = \frac{x . x . x . x . x}{x . x . x} = x . x = x^2$$

Using the rule we obtain the same answer:

$$\frac{x^5}{x^3} = x^{5-3} = x^2$$

In such divisions, if the larger of the two values is the divisor, cancelling gives us a numerator of 1 and the denominator comprises the value raised to an appropriate power. Using the rule about subtracting the powers when we divide we obtain a negative index for our variable, so there are two alternative ways of writing the result. For example

$$\frac{x^3}{x^5} = \frac{x . x . x}{x . x . x . x . x} = \frac{1}{x . x} = \frac{1}{x^2}$$

and

$$\frac{x^3}{x^5} = x^{3-5} = x^{-2}$$

> In chapter 5 we will find that it is important for us to be able to switch between these two alternative formats.

We can now deduce the value of x^0. Using the rule that when we divide we subtract the indices, we see that we get x^0 whenever x to a particular power is divided by x to the same power. Looking at it another way, we see that the numerator and denominator are the same and cancelling them gives us the value 1. Hence $x^0 = 1$. For example

$$\frac{x^4}{x^4} = x^{4-4} = x^0$$

and

$$\frac{x^4}{x^4} = \frac{x . x . x . x}{x . x . x . x} = 1$$

We can also give an interpretation to fractional powers. Consider what happens when we multiply an expression with a fractional power by itself as many times as the denominator of the fraction. For example, multiply together two of $x^{1/2}$

$$(x^{1/2})(x^{1/2}) = x^{1/2+1/2} = x^1 = x$$

But the number that when multiplied by itself gives x is the square root of x, $\sqrt{x}$. This implies that

$$x^{1/2} = \sqrt{x}$$

Similarly, $x^{1/3}$ is the cube root of x since

$$(x^{1/3})(x^{1/3})(x^{1/3}) = x^{1/3+1/3+1/3} = x^1 = x$$

and in general $x^{1/n}$ is the nth root of x.

Any expression can be raised to a power. We use brackets to enclose the expression and write the power outside the brackets. The power shows us how many times the expression is multiplied by itself. If we write this out in full we can then multiply out. Consider for example $(5x)^3$. Writing this as a product of the terms and then multiplying out gives

$$(5x)^3 = (5x)(5x)(5x) = 5^3x^3 = 125x^3$$

It follows that when a product is raised to a power, each term in the product is raised to the power. The general result is written

$$(ax)^n = a^nx^n$$

Now consider an expression with an index which is then all raised to a power, for example $(x^3)^3$. We can rewrite this and multiply out, collecting the terms. We obtain

$$(x^3)^3 = (x^3)(x^3)(x^3) = x^9$$

Notice that

$$x^9 = x^{3\times3}$$

When an expression to a power is raised to a power we combine the powers by multiplying them. In general

$$(x^m)^n = x^{mn}$$

To multiply, add the indices; to divide, subtract the indices.

Remember...

$$x^{-n} = \frac{1}{x^n}$$

$$x^0 = 1$$

$$x^{1/2} = \sqrt{x}$$

$$(ax)^n = a^nx^n$$

$$(x^m)^n = x^{mn}$$

For more practise with powers and indices use the MathEcon screen Powers and Indices. Be sure to try the three types of applications questions and the quiz.

When expressions that contain powers are multiplied or divided by one another we use the above rules to simplify them. Notice that the rules allow us to combine indices for the same symbol that appears more than once in an expression. We cannot combine indices for different variables, so for example there is no way of simplifying x^3/y^2.

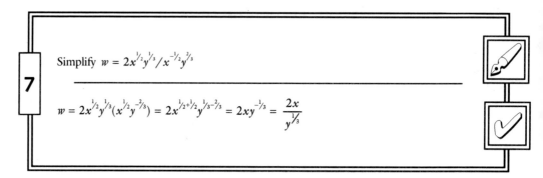

7

Simplify $w = 2x^{1/2}y^{1/3}/x^{-1/2}y^{2/3}$

$$w = 2x^{1/2}y^{1/3}(x^{1/2}y^{-2/3}) = 2x^{1/2+1/2}y^{1/3-2/3} = 2xy^{-1/3} = \frac{2x}{y^{1/3}}$$

POWERS AND YOUR CALCULATOR

Most scientific calculators have a button marked x^y which is used to raise a number to a power. Enter the number, press the x^y button, enter the power to which the number is to be raised and press = to obtain your answer. If the power is negative, precede it by (−) or enter the positive value and press the +/− button followed by the = key. Alternatively, you can put negative or fractional powers in brackets. Try using your calculator to evaluate some expressions involving negative and fractional powers to check that you understand them. For example

$$64^{1/2} = 64^{0.5} = 8 \quad \text{and} \quad 10^{-2} = \frac{1}{10^2} = 0.01$$

SCIENTIFIC NOTATION

If the result of a calculation is very large or very small, calculators and computers usually display it using scientific notation. This takes the form of a number followed by an exponent, telling you that the number is to be multiplied by 10 to that power. For example, if you enter 3000^3 in your calculator using the x^y button you may get the answer 2.7^{10}. This is to be interpreted as 2.7×10^{10}. What this means is that the decimal point in the number shown is to be moved to the right the number of places given in the exponent, so that the value is 27,000,000,000. Another example is $1 \div 970$, where your calculator may give the answer $1.030927835^{-0.3}$. To find the value we move the decimal point three places to the left, which gives 0.001030927835. The reason for the use of scientific notation is that it allows the calculator to show more significant figures in the answer than would otherwise be possible.

exponent: a superscripted number representing a power.

1.12 Simplify

   (a) $x^7 . x^8$ (b) $x^{1/3} . x^{1/4}$

   (c) $\dfrac{x^9}{x^4}$ (d) $x^9 . x^{-4}$

   (e) $\dfrac{x^{3/4}}{x^{1/4}}$ (f) $(x^4)^2$

   (g) $(2x)^4$ (h) $\dfrac{15x^7}{3x^2 . 5x^5}$

   (i) $\dfrac{12x^{1/4}y^{-1/2}}{x^{-3/4}y^{1/2}}$ (j) $\dfrac{x^{a-1}}{x^a}$

1.13 Show that

$$\left(\frac{1}{1+r}\right)^t = (1+r)^{-t}$$

1.14 Evaluate

   (a) 5^2 (b) 2^5

   (c) 9^{-2} (d) 8^0

   (e) $64^{1/2}$ (f) $27^{1/3}$

   (g) $(3^2)^4$ (h) $82 - 3^4$

   (i) $82 + (-3)^4$ (j) $\left(\dfrac{x}{5}\right)^2$ when $x = 35$

   (k) $(x^2 + 40)^{1/2}$ when $x = 9$

SECTION 1.7: Functions of More Than One Variable

In the relationships studied by economists the dependent variable is often thought to depend on a number of other variables. For example, the utility a person obtains may depend on the quantities of several goods that he or she consumes. Another example is that the output a firm produces may depend on the amounts it uses of each of a number of inputs.

> multivariate function: the dependent variable, y, is a function of more than one independent variable.

For the case where the dependent variable, which we shall continue to call y, depends on two variables x and z we express the function

$$y = f(x, z)$$

which we read as y is a function of x and z. In this function there are two independent variables x and z. If we have possible values for x and z we may substitute them to obtain the corresponding value of y. Since there are two independent variables, we may fix one of them, say x, at a particular value and change the other variable, z. This lets us investigate how y changes as z changes. The approach corresponds to comparative statics analysis in economics where economists investigate the effect of changing one variable while other things remain unchanged. We can, of course, also investigate the effects on y of changing x while z is held constant.

- If $y = f(x, z)$ y is a function of the two variables x and z. **Remember...**
- We substitute values for x and z to find the value of the function.
- If we hold one variable constant and investigate the effect on y of changing the other, this is a form of comparative statics analysis.

We shall see an example of substituting values for two independent variables in section 1.12 where we investigate the quantities of output produced by a firm with a specific production function and employing two different factors of production, labour and capital. A more general approach to describing the effects of changing one of the independent variables but not the other will be discussed in chapter 8.

To depict the relationship between three variables graphically using an axis for each requires a three-dimensional graph, but there are also ways of presenting the information as a two-dimensional graph. Economists usually use one of the two-dimensional options as we see in the example in section 1.12.

SECTION 1.8: Economic Variables and Functions

We now investigate and plot various economic functions. The analysis in sections 1.9 to 1.12 corresponds to analysis presented in any elementary microeconomics textbook. This book, however, emphasizes mathematical relationships and shows the shapes of curves that correspond to particular functions. We shall find the rules of algebra helpful in calculating the values to plot, and also in using definitions of the relationships between variables to link one function to another.

Notice that we usually replace the general variable names x and y with names chosen to suit our variables and we label the axes of our diagrams to correspond. Suitable scales for the axes depend on the particular model, but for some economic variables – such as price, quantity, cost and labour employed – only positive values are meaningful. Other variables, such as profit, can take negative values.

It is a general principle of economic modelling to choose a functional form that is as simple as possible while representing the appropriate form of relationship. You will therefore find that linear relationships are used in various contexts and that where a curve is needed to depict the relationship a quadratic or cubic function may be used. The analysis presented in sections 1.9 to 1.11 is concerned with two variable relationships. A multivariate relationship is examined in section 1.12, focusing on particular aspects that can be represented on two-dimensional graphs.

> You can see examples of functional relationships in the MathEcon screens titled Factors Affecting Demand, where you investigate the demand for peaches, and Short-Run Production Functions: A Numerical Example, where you plot a curve representing the short-run production function. The screen Economic Problems – Basic Mathematics has four different economic problems for you to practise.

SECTION 1.9: Total and Average Revenue

When a firm sells a quantity, Q, of goods each at price P, its total revenue, TR, is the price that is paid multiplied by the quantity sold and so

$$TR = P . Q$$

Average revenue, AR, is the revenue received by the firm per unit of output sold. This is its total revenue divided by the quantity sold. Hence,

$$AR = TR \div Q = P$$

substituting the above expression for TR.

The average revenue curve shows the average revenue or price at which different quantities are sold. It therefore shows the prices that people will pay to obtain various quantities of output and so it is also known as the demand curve.

$$TR = P . Q$$

$$AR = \frac{TR}{Q}$$

Remember...

A market demand curve is assumed to be downward sloping. Different prices are associated with different quantities being sold and more is sold at lower prices. There will also be an associated downward sloping marginal revenue, MR, curve but we postpone consideration of its exact relationship with TR and AR until chapter 5.

If average revenue is given by

$$P = 72 - 3Q$$

sketch this function and also, on a separate graph, the total revenue function.

8

___

The average revenue function has P on the vertical axis and Q on the horizontal axis. The general form of a linear function is $y = a + bx$. Comparing our average revenue function we see that it takes this linear form with $y = P$, $a = 72$, $b = -3$ and $x = Q$. We therefore need find only two points on our function to sketch the line, and can then extend it as required. For simplicity we choose $Q = 0$ and $Q = 10$. The corresponding P values are listed, the two points are plotted and the line is then extended to the horizontal axis as shown in figure 1.8.

Chosen values of Q: Q 0   10
Substituting in $P = 72 - 3Q$: P 72   42

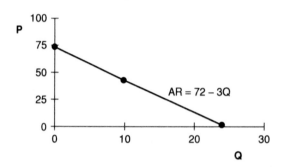

Figure 1.8

We next find an expression for TR.

$$TR = P \cdot Q = (72 - 3Q)Q = 72Q - 3Q^2$$

As before, the horizontal axis is called Q. Revenue values are again being plotted on the vertical axis, but they are now values of TR, which in general is much larger than AR and so a different scale is appropriate. The function is a quadratic one, so we must find a number of points. Choosing some values of Q, say the even numbers between 0 and 16 and also 24, we calculate the value of $72Q$ and of $3Q^2$ and subtract the second from the first to find TR as shown in the table. The graph in figure 1.9 shows a curve which at first rises relatively steeply, then flattens out and reaches a maximum at $Q = 12$, after which it falls. Notice that the curve is symmetric. Its shape to the right of its maximum value is the mirror image of that to the left. The values of TR at 14 and 16 are the same as those at 10 and 8. Notice that a downward sloping linear demand curve implies a total revenue curve which has an inverted U shape.

Q	0	2	4	6	8	10	12	14	16	24
72Q	0	144	288	432	576	720	864	1008	1152	1728
$3Q^2$	0	12	48	108	192	300	432	588	768	1728
TR	0	132	240	324	384	420	432	420	384	0

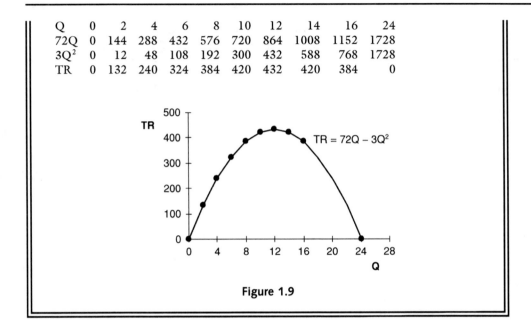

Figure 1.9

symmetric: the shape of one half of the curve is the mirror image of the other half.

Some firms may sell all their output at the same price. This is a feature of firms operating under the market structure known as perfect competition. These firms face a horizontal demand curve and have a total revenue function which is an upward sloping straight line passing through the origin.

There is a description of how to use Excel to plot the above demand and total revenue functions in section 1.13, and the worksheets used are included in the Function.xls file on the CD.

1.15 A firm in perfect competition sells its output at a price of 12. Plot its total revenue function, $TR = 12Q$.

1.16 Sketch the market average revenue function given by

$$AR = 25 - 5Q$$

SECTION 1.10: Total and Average Cost

A firm's total cost of production, TC, depends on its output, Q. The TC function may include a constant term, which represents fixed costs, FC. The part of total cost that varies with Q is called variable cost, VC. We have, then, that TC = FC + VC. Average cost per unit of output is found by dividing by Q. We can find average total cost, denoted AC, which is given by AC = TC ÷ Q, together with average variable cost AVC = VC ÷ Q and average fixed cost AFC = FC ÷ Q. The relationship between marginal cost, MC, and the other cost curves is defined in chapter 5 of this book.

Various cost curve relationships are defined on the MathEcon screen Short-Run Cost Definition.

FC is the constant term in TC.

VC = TC − FC

AC = TC/Q

AVC = VC/Q

AFC = FC/Q

Remember...

9

For a firm with total cost given by

$$TC = 120 + 45Q - Q^2 + 0.4Q^3$$

identify its AC, FC, VC, AVC and AFC functions. List some values of TC, AC and AFC, correct to the nearest integer. Sketch the total cost function and, on a separate graph, the AC and AFC functions.

$$TC = 120 + 45Q - Q^2 + 0.4Q^3$$

$$AC = TC/Q = 120/Q + 45 - Q + 0.4Q^2$$

$$FC = 120 \text{ (the constant term in TC)}$$

$$VC = TC - FC = 45Q - Q^2 + 0.4Q^3$$

$$AVC = VC/Q = 45 - Q + 0.4Q^2$$

$$AFC = FC/Q = 120/Q$$

Some possible values for Q and for each of the terms in the total cost function are shown in the table. The corresponding TC, AC and AFC values are calculated and are plotted in figures 1.10 and 1.11. Notice that when $Q = 0$ the first terms in AC and in AFC involve dividing by zero. To avoid the problem of an infinite result, the smallest value of Q for which AC and AFC are calculated is 0.3.

Q	0	0.3	1	3	5	8	10	12	15
$45Q$	0	13.5	45	135	225	360	450	540	675
Q^2	0	0.09	1	9	25	64	100	144	225
$0.4Q^3$	0	0.0108	0.4	10.8	50	204.8	400	691.2	1350

Correct to the nearest integer

TC	120	133	164	257	370	621	870	1207	1920
AC		445	164	86	74	78	87	101	128
AFC		400	120	40	24	15	12	10	8

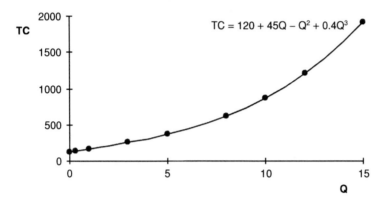

$$TC = 120 + 45Q - Q^2 + 0.4Q^3$$

Figure 1.10

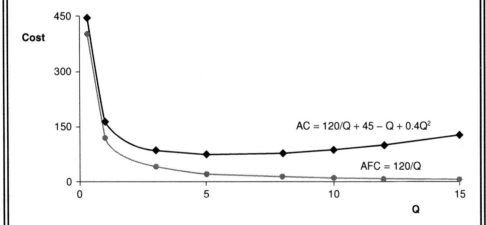

$$AC = 120/Q + 45 - Q + 0.4Q^2$$

$$AFC = 120/Q$$

Figure 1.11 Average Total Cost and Average Fixed Cost

In figure 1.11 notice that the average total cost curve at first falls as output rises, but later the curve rises again. By contrast, average fixed cost is always declining as output increases.

10

Electricity users pay a $15 standing charge each quarter plus $0.10 for each unit of electricity used. Draw a graph showing the total cost per quarter, y, for various possible amounts of electricity used, x. Write an expression for y in terms of x. Write also an expression for the average cost per unit used. How would you describe average cost if only a very small number of units of electricity are used?

If x units of electricity are used the cost for these units is $0.1x$. To this amount we must add the standing charge of $15, so the total cost in dollars is $0.1x + 15$. Some possible values of x and the corresponding y values are shown in the table and the relationship is plotted in figure 1.12. The function can be written as

$$y = 0.1x + 15$$

$$AC = y/x = 0.1 + 15/x$$

If only a very small number of units are used the average cost is very high, because the standing charge of $15 is shared over only the very small number of units.

x	0	1	10	100	500
y	15	15.1	16	25	65

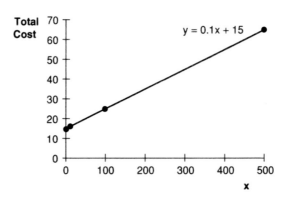

Figure 1.12

1.17 Sketch the average cost curve

$$AC = 9 - Q + 0.5Q^2$$

1.18 A photocopier costs $180 per month to rent, plus $0.05 for each copy produced. Draw a graph showing the total monthly cost, y, for the number of copies made, x (x from 0 to 10,000). Write an expression for total cost in terms of x.

1.19 Sketch the total cost function

$$TC = 300 + 40Q - 10Q^2 + Q^3$$

and write expressions for AC, FC, VC and AVC.

SECTION 1.11: Profit

Profit is the excess of a firm's total revenue, TR, over its total cost, TC, and so we calculate it by subtracting TC from TR. Using the symbol π as the variable name for profit, we write

$$\pi = TR - TC$$

Note that π is used here simply as a convenient variable name. There is no connection with the constant π used, for example, in measuring the area of a circle. Maximization of profits is usually assumed to be the objective of a firm. In chapter 6 we find how to identify the output at which this is achieved.

You can see examples of profit functions in MathEcon. The screen titled Profit Maximization is for a firm with a horizontal demand curve, while the Profit Maximization by a Monopolist screen shows a firm with a downward sloping demand curve.

Profit = π = TR − TC

Remember...

11

A firm has the total cost function

$$TC = 120 + 45Q - Q^2 + 0.4Q^3$$

and faces a demand curve given by

$$P = 240 - 20Q$$

What is its profit function?

$$TR = P \cdot Q = 240Q - 20Q^2$$
$$\pi = TR - TC$$

Since TC comprises several terms we enclose it in brackets as we substitute

$$= 240Q - 20Q^2 - (120 + 45Q - Q^2 + 0.4Q^3)$$

Taking the minus sign through the brackets and applying it to each term in turn gives

$$= 240Q - 20Q^2 - 120 - 45Q + Q^2 - 0.4Q^3$$

and collecting like terms we find

$$\pi = -120 + 195Q - 19Q^2 - 0.4Q^3$$

1.20   If the firm in practice problem 1.19 faces the demand curve

$$P = 100 - 0.5Q$$

find an expression for the firm's profit function and sketch the curve.

SECTION 1.12: Production Functions, Isoquants and the Average Product of Labour

The long-run production function shows that a firm's output, Q, depends on the amounts of factors it employs (always assuming that whatever factors are employed are used efficiently). If a production process involves the use of labour, L, and capital, K, we write $Q = f(L, K)$. This is an example of a multivariate function. The dependent variable, Q, is a function of two independent variables, L and K.

One way of representing this relationship on a two-dimensional graph is to use the vertical axis for the dependent variable, Q, and to choose one of the independent variables to plot on the horizontal axis. This implies we temporarily fix the other independent variable at some particular value. If we choose to fix the value of K and plot L on the horizontal axis we are in fact plotting a short-run production function corresponding to the selected value of K. If K changes we obtain a new curve. The long-run production function may be represented by a series of short-run curves each corresponding to a particular level of K, as shown later in figure 1.13.

An alternative graphical approach shown in figure 1.14 is to use one axis for each of the independent variables, L and K. We then find various combinations of these inputs which give the same values of Q and connect them with a curve. This curve, all points on which have equal output, is called an isoquant. Other isoquants can be found in a similar way so that an isoquant map is obtained.

The average product of labour is used as a measure of labour productivity. Defined as APL = $Q \div L$, it is plotted on the vertical axis against L on the horizontal axis, as shown in figure 1.15.

You can see an example of plotting production functions on the MathEcon screen 1.3 Short-Run Production Functions: A Numerical Example. If you would like to try the method in Excel, the worksheet used to calculate the values used in figure 1.13 is available from the Production Function tab in the Function.xls file for you to explore.

A production function shows the quantity of output obtained from specific quantities of inputs, assuming they are used efficiently.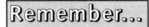

- In the short run the quantity of capital is fixed.
- In the long run both labour and capital are variable.
- Plot Q on the vertical axis against L on the horizontal axis for a short-run production function.
- Plot K against L and connect points that generate equal output for an isoquant map.
- Average Product of Labour (APL) = $Q \div L$

An isoquant connects points at which the same quantity of output is produced using different combinations of inputs.

12

A firm has the production function $Q = 25(L \cdot K)^2 - 0.4(L \cdot K)^3$. If $K = 1$, find the values of Q for $L = 2, 3, 4, 6, 12, 14$ and 16. Sketch this short-run production function putting L and Q on the axes of your graph. Next suppose the value of K is increased to 2. On the same graph sketch the new short-run production function for the same values of L. Add one further production function to your sketch, corresponding to $K = 3$, using the same L values again.

Now sketch another representation of this production function as an isoquant map. Plot L and K on the axes and look for combinations of L and K amongst the values you have calculated which give the same value of Q. Such points lie on the same isoquant.

For the short-run production function with $K = 3$, find and plot the average product of labour function.

The table lists values of L and K and shows the values of Q obtained by substituting each pair of values into the production function $Q = 25(L \cdot K)^2 - 0.4(L \cdot K)^3$. The Q values listed in the row for which $K = 1$ are plotted to give the first short-run production function shown in figure 1.13, and the other production functions are obtained by plotting each of the other rows.

Three shaded cells in the table each contain the Q value 814 (rounded up to the nearest integer) and the other three shaded cells each contain a nearest integer value of 2909. Plotting the pairs of L and K values for which $Q = 814$ and joining them up gives the first isoquant mapped in figure 1.14, and the second isoquant is obtained from the pairs of L and K for which $Q = 2909$.

$K \diagdown L$	2	3	4	6	12	14	16
1	96.8	214.2	374.4	813.6	2908.8	3802.4	4761.6
2	374.4	813.6	1395.2	2908.8	8870.4	10,819.2	12,492.8
3	813.6	1733.4	2908.8	5767.2	13,737.6	14,464.8	13,363.2

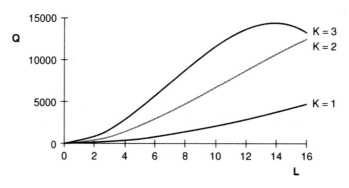

Figure 1.13   Production function for different values of K

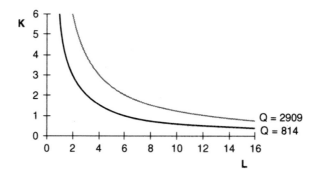

Figure 1.14   Isoquant map

For $K = 3$ we have $Q = 25(3L)^2 - 0.4(3L)^3 = 225L^2 - 10.8L^3$.

$$\text{APL} = Q/L = 225L - 10.8L^2$$

This is plotted in figure 1.15.

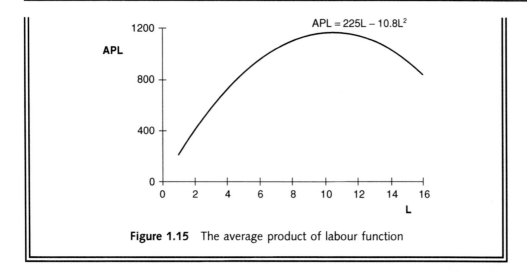

Figure 1.15 The average product of labour function

1.21 A firm has the production function $Q = L^{\frac{1}{2}} \cdot K^{\frac{1}{5}}$. Sketch its short-run production function if $K = 1$, using values for L of 1, 4, 16, 64, 144. If instead $K = 32$, what is the value of Q when $L = 4$? What point on the production function for $K = 1$ gives the same output? Using another graph, sketch the isoquant that passes through these two points. Also find and plot the average product of labour when $K = 1$.

SECTION 1.13: Functions in Excel

You can use Excel to plot graphs and do calculations for you. While getting Excel to plot functions for you is not a substitute for being able to plot them by hand, it is a quick way of producing smart looking graphs, and it does enable you to easily compare the shapes of curves that correspond to different functions. This section sets out some suggestions about how to do this. Often there is more than one way of doing something in Excel. The methods described here may therefore not be the only way of obtaining a particular result, but it is hoped they may provide useful guidelines from which you may develop your own approach. The worksheets described below are included in the file entitled Function.xls on the CD. You may find it helpful to load them for reference as you are creating your own worksheets. For help on a particular topic, use the Help provided in Excel and search for the topic you require.

The worksheet called Power function included in Function.xls and accessed by the tab near the bottom of the screen is designed to let you explore how the shape of a function changes if you change the coefficients of its variables. It is displayed in figure

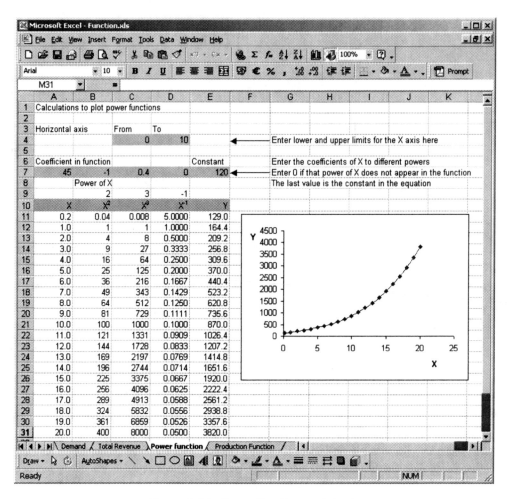

Figure 1.16   Power function worksheet

1.16, set up to show the graph of the Total Cost function plotted earlier in figure 1.10. It is ready for you to use to plot any power function that includes terms in X, X^2, X^3, X^{-1} and a constant.

You enter the appropriate coefficient for each term in the highlighted boxes at the top of each column. If there is a particular term, say X^{-1}, that does not appear in the function you wish to plot, you simply enter a 0 value for its coefficient. Try changing some of the coefficients to see how the graph changes.

You may also like to change the range on the horizontal axis for which values are displayed. You can enter the approximate range of values you want to plot on the horizontal axis in highlighted cells near the top of the screen. A formula then calculates values to plot on the horizontal axis, choosing 20 integer values in or slightly beyond the range you select. If you choose a scale that involves plotting a value for $Q = 0$, the formula chooses to use 0.2 instead to avoid the possible problem of dividing by 0. You can use this worksheet to display the graph for any continuous power function involving powers from −1 to 3. A graph that includes a term in X^{-1} has a discontinuity at $x = 0$. Because of this you should only plot such a graph either for a positive or a negative range of x values.

PLOTTING FUNCTIONS IN EXCEL

To plot a function in Excel you need two columns of values, the left-hand one containing the values to plot on the horizontal axis and the right-hand one comprising the values of the function to be plotted on the vertical axis. You can then use the Chart Wizard to plot the graph. You choose values for the left-hand column in just the same way as you would mark out a scale on the axis if you were drawing the graph by hand, but you can get Excel to fill in the values for you. To obtain the right-hand column of values you enter a formula that calculates the first value of the function and copy it down the column. We shall plot a linear function, the demand curve $AR = 72 - 3Q$ shown in figure 1.8 and available from the demand tab of Function.xls.

THE FILL HANDLE

You could plot a linear function using just two points, but it can be useful to find the values at different points on the line and so we use a more general approach. For the horizontal axis you need to choose a set of values that are not too far apart and in an appropriate range. Just type in the first two or three of them (0, 2, 4 in figure 1.17)

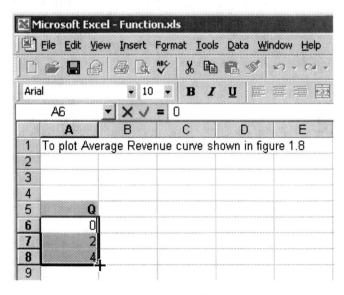

Figure 1.17 The Fill Handle

and then fill in as many values as you want using the Fill Handle. To do this, first select the values you have entered with your mouse and release the mouse button. Next, move your mouse gently at the bottom right-hand corner of the selected cells until you see the thin black cross as shown in figure 1.17. This is the Fill Handle. Click on it and drag down the column to fill in more values of the sequence. In figure 1.18 the values have been filled in steps of 2 to 24, forming a column of values of Q.

EXCEL FORMULAE

For each of the values of Q we need to calculate the corresponding value of AR = $72 - 3Q$, and to do this we need to enter a formula. Although you can type numbers into Excel formulae you make much better use of Excel's capabilities if you enter values into cells where they are displayed and use cell references in the formulae you enter. A cell reference, such as A6, tells Excel to use in its calculation the value that it finds in the cell identified by the column letter and row number. One advantage of this approach is that you can easily do 'what if' analysis. Changing the value in a cell automatically recalculates all the values calculated from it and so lets you see immediately the effect of the change. Appropriate use of cell references also means that a

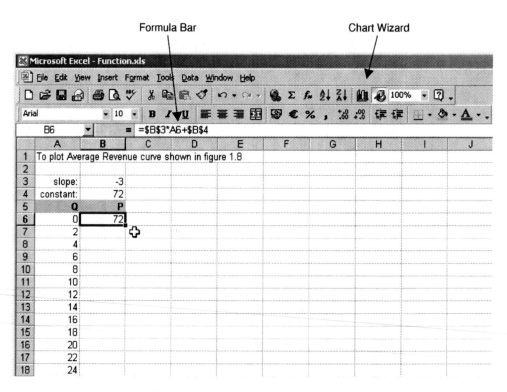

Figure 1.18 The formula entered in B6 displays in the Formula Bar

formula that you enter in one cell can be copied to other cells to complete, say, a column of calculations.

Enter the constant and slope of the line in appropriate cells (B3 and B4 in figure 1.18). Now select the cell where the first value is to be calculated, B6 in figure 1.18. We need a formula to pick up the slope value of −3 from B3, multiply it by the appropriate value of Q, which is the value to the left of the cell where we are entering the formula, and add to this the constant of 72 from B4. So that it will copy, the formula we use is =$B$3*A6+$B$4 which contains both absolute and relative cell addresses. An absolute cell address is indicated by dollar signs in front of the column letter and row number, in this case $B$3. Such an address will not change as the formula is copied, so the calculation will always use the value in the specified cell. A cell address without dollar signs, for example A6, is called a relative address. This means that the calculation will use the value in the cell that is in a particular position with reference to the current cell, here, one cell to its left. This form of address is used to pick up the value of Q so that when we copy the formula down the column a different value of Q is used in each row. Figure 1.18 shows the worksheet once the formula has been entered. Notice that when you select the cell the formula displays in the Formula Bar near the top of the screen.

Formulae in Excel:

Remember...

- Are entered in the cell where you want the result to be displayed
- Start with an equals sign
- Must not contain spaces

Operators:

- Are ( ) brackets, + add, − subtract, * multiply, / divide, ^ raise to the power of
- Relative cell addresses (e.g. A6) change as the formula is copied
- Absolute cell addresses (e.g. $B$3) remain fixed as the formula is copied

---

As you type a formula you can put a cell address into it by clicking on the appropriate cell. This puts the relative version of the address in the formula. To make it absolute, after clicking on the cell you should press function key F4 so that, for example, B3 changes to $B$3. Function key F4 works as a toggle key. If you press it two or three times you get addresses that are part absolute and part relative (two different versions) and if you press it a fourth time you return to a relative address.

To complete the column of values of P you copy the formula in B6 down the column. You can use the usual Edit, Copy, Edit, Paste or you can again make use of the Fill Handle and drag the formula down the column. The two columns of values of Q and P can be seen in figure 1.19.

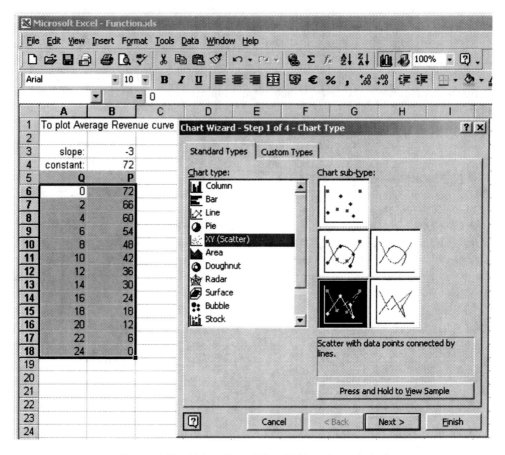

Figure 1.19 Using Chart Wizard XY scatter selected

USING CHART WIZARD

To plot a graph in Excel, you start by selecting the two columns of values that are to be plotted. The left-hand one goes on the horizontal axis and the right-hand one on the vertical axis. Click the Chart Wizard button. You must select the XY (Scatter) type of chart to plot values on the X axis as shown in figure 1.19. All the other types of chart available in Excel simply plot labels on the horizontal axis. Of the subtypes of chart offered, you can choose to connect the points with lines since you are plotting a line (if you were plotting a curve you would want to connect the points with curves) and you may choose to have the data points plotted as well if you wish. Clicking Next gives you a preview of your graph and confirms that Excel has correctly interpreted that the data form two columns (rather than rows). Clicking Next again brings you to the chart options. You can enter a title and axis titles. You can also de-select Major gridlines, and Show legend, since we are only plotting one data series. You can then click Finish and the chart is placed in your worksheet. If you don't want the plot area shaded, right click the mouse over it and choose 'Format Plot Area'. Under 'Patterns Border' select 'None', then to the right under 'Area' select 'None' and click OK. This removes the shading. To alter the direction in which the vertical axis title is plotted, right click over it and choose 'Format Axis Title'. Choose the Alignment tab, move the text orientation pointer until it is horizontal and click OK. You can move the axis titles by clicking on them and dragging. Also, if you click on a blank area of the chart to select the whole chart you can position it in the worksheet as you wish. Once the chart is finished, you can move your mouse cursor over it to display the coordinates of each point, as shown in figure 1.20.

Now that you have a graph of a linear demand curve, it is easy to see how it changes if either the slope or the constant of the line changes. Try typing different values in cells B3 and B4 and watch the effects. Of course, if you type a positive value for the slope you will get an upward sloping line, which may represent supply rather than demand, so you would have to change the title of the graph!

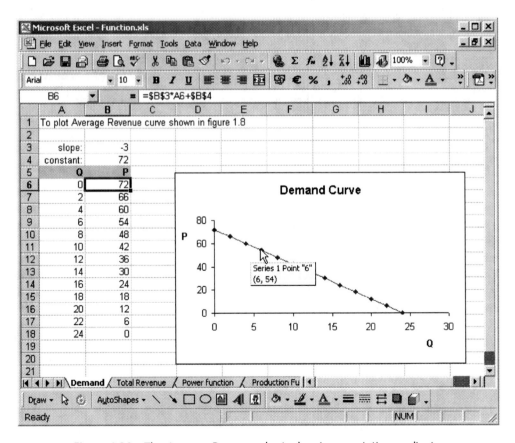

Figure 1.20 The Average Revenue chart, showing a point's coordinates

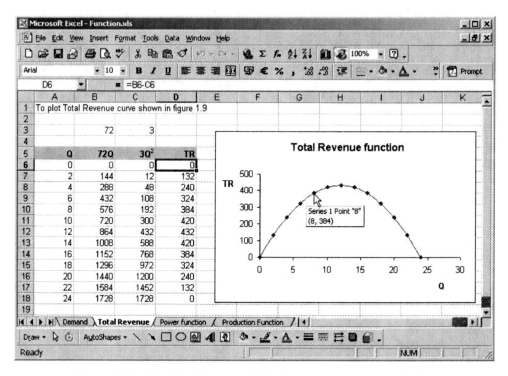

Figure 1.21 The Total Revenue chart, showing a point's coordinates

You may now like to try plotting other economics functions for yourself. There are two more examples for you in the Function.xls workbook so you can see how different formulae are used. Access the different worksheets using the tabs near the bottom of the screen. The total revenue function $TR = 72Q - 3Q^2$ is shown in figure 1.21. Total revenue has been found in stages, calculating each of its terms separately and finding the value of TR in column D. This lets you see exactly what you are calculating and may help you to avoid mistakes. The graph plots the values in column D against those in column A. To select the data in these columns, select those in column A then press and hold Control while selecting the values in column D. Once both columns are selected, release the Control button and you are ready to click the Chart Wizard button as before.

Chapter 1: Answers to Practice Problems

1.1

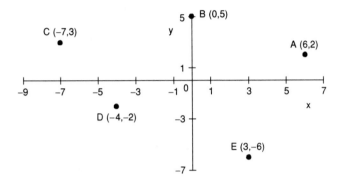

Figure 1.22

1.2   (a) Linear function, proportional relationship between x and y. Whatever value
x takes, y is half of it. Choose two or more values of x, e.g. $x = 0$, $y = 0$;
$x = 10$, $y = 5$.

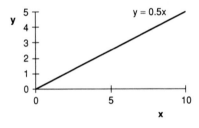

Figure 1.23

(b) Linear, non-proportional relationship. Plotting on the same scale as figure
1.23, the lines are parallel but this one is shifted up by the amount of the
constant and cuts the y axis at 6.

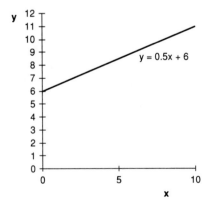

Figure 1.24

(c) Quadratic function. Choose several values of x, say

x	0	1	2	3	4	5	6	7	8	9	10
y	0	1	4	9	16	25	36	49	64	81	100

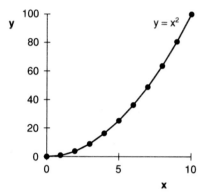

Figure 1.25

(d) This quadratic function also passes through the origin.

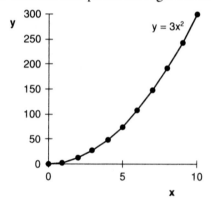

Figure 1.26

1.3   45° angle

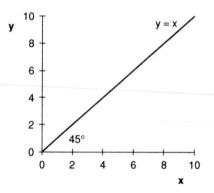

Figure 1.27

1.4   (a) 3, −15   (b) 32, 32

       (c) −2   (d) 10

       (e) −2.5   (f) 17

       (g) 24   (h) 31.8

       (i) −36   (j) −6

       (k) +5 or −5 (does your calculator tell you this?)

1.5 $66.67

1.6   (a) −5x(2 + 9x)   (b) 13(11x − 4)

       (c) 5x(x + 1 − 4y)

1.7   (a) (i) $80x − 56x^2$

             (ii) $−6x^2 + 3x + 45$

             (iii) $132 − 56x + 4x^2$

             (iv) $24 + 0.8x − 540 = 0.8x − 516$

             (v) $2000 − 15x$

       (b) (i) $82x − 1.64x^2 − 100$

             (ii) $100/x + 150 − 36x$

             (iii) $0.2x$

             (iv) x

       (c) $−150 + 200x − 2x^2 − 0.5x^3$

       (d) $30 + 18(15) − 0.6(15^2) = 165$

       (e) (i) $(a + b)(a + b) = a^2 + 2ab + b^2$

             (ii) $(a − b)(a − b) = a^2 − 2ab + b^2$

             (iii) $(a + b)(a − b) = a^2 − ab + ab − b^2 = a^2 − b^2$

1.8   (a) (i)   Yes, product gives $x^2 + 5x − 7x − 35$

             (ii) Yes, product gives $3x^2 + 24x + x + 8$

             (iii) Yes, product gives $2x^2 − 2x + 9x − 9$

       (b) (i) $(x + 3)(x + 7)$

             (ii) $(x + 5)(3x − 1)$

             (iii) $(x − 1)(2x + 10) = 2(x − 1)(x + 5)$

             (iv) $(3x + 11)(x + 5)$

1.9   (a) $\frac{1}{4}$ (b) 4 (c) $\frac{5}{42}$ (d) $\frac{23}{30}$ (e) $\frac{4}{9}$ (f) 1 (g) $\frac{19}{36}$

1.10   Ratio of marginal utilities = $MU_x/MU_y = \frac{5}{9}$, ratio of prices = $P_x/P_y = \frac{30}{45} = \frac{6}{9}$, so the ratios are not equal. (Economic theory shows this indicates you could reallocate your spending on the two goods to increase your total utility.)

1.11   (a) $3x/4$

       (b) $15M \times P \times P/(P^2 \times 15M) = 1$

       (c) $x(5x - 3)/x(1 + 3x) = (5x - 3)/(1 + 3x)$

       (d) $4x \times 2/4x(3x - 4) = 2/(3x - 4)$

       (e) $[7(2x - 1) + 5x(x + 2)]/(x + 2)(2x - 1) = (14x - 7 + 5x^2 + 10x)/(x + 2)(2x - 1)$

           $= (5x^2 + 24x - 7)/(x + 2)(2x - 1)$

1.12   (a) x^{15} (b) $x^{7/12}$

       (c) x^5 (d) x^5

       (e) $x^{1/2} = \sqrt{x}$ (f) x^8

       (g) $16x^4$ (h) 1

       (i) $12x^{1/4}y^{-1/2}(x^{3/4}y^{-1/2}) = 12xy^{-1} = 12x/y$

       (j) $x^{a-1} \cdot x^{-a} = x^{-1} = 1/x$

1.13 $1^t/(1 + r)^t = 1/(1 + r)^t = (1 + r)^{-t}$

1.14   (a) 25   (b) 32

       (c) $1/81 = 0.012$ (d) 1

       (e) 8 or -8 (f) 3

       (g) 6561   (h) 1

       (i) 163   (j) 49

       (k) $(81 + 40)^{1/2} = 11$ or -11

1.15   Price constant, TR a line through the origin. At $Q = 10$, TR = 120.

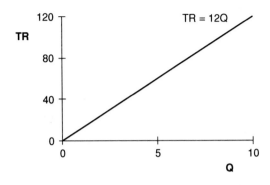

Figure 1.28

1.16 The term in Q is negative, so as Q increases AR decreases.

Q	0	5	6
AR	25	0	−5

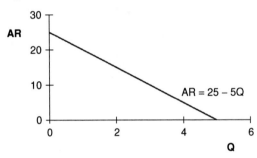

Figure 1.29

1.17

Q	0	1	2	3	4	5	6	7	8	9	10	11	12
AC	9	8.5	9	10.5	13	16.5	21	26.5	33	40.5	49	58.5	69

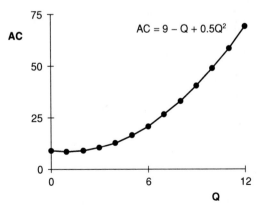

Figure 1.30

1.18 $y = 180 + 0.05x$

x	0	1000	5000	10,000
y	180	230	430	680

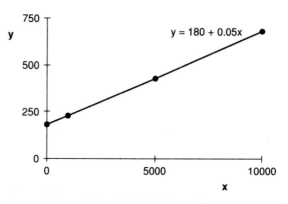

Figure 1.31

1.19

Q	0	1	2	3	4	5	6	7	8	9	10	11	12	13
TC	300	331	348	357	364	375	396	433	492	579	700	861	1068	1327

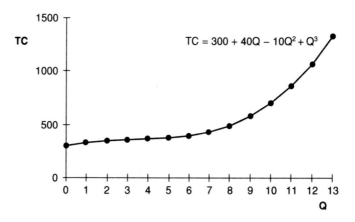

Figure 1.32

$AC = 300/Q + 40 - 10Q + Q^2$

$FC = 300$

$VC = 40Q - 10Q^2 + Q^3$

$AVC = 40 - 10Q + Q^2$

1.20 TR $= P \cdot Q = 100Q - 0.5Q^2$

Profit $=$ TR $-$ TC $= 100Q - 0.5Q^2 - (300 + 40Q - 10Q^2 + Q^3)$

$\qquad = -300 + 60Q + 9.5Q^2 - Q^3$

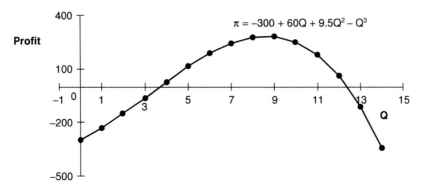

Figure 1.33

1.21 Given $K = 1$ we have

L	1	4	16	64	144
Q	1	2	4	8	12

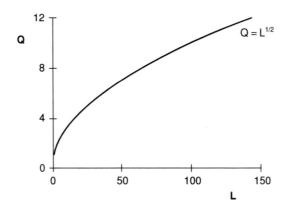

Figure 1.34

If $K = 32$ and $L = 4$, $Q = 4$. This point and the point $K = 1$, $L = 16$ form the basis for the isoquant shown in figure 1.35.

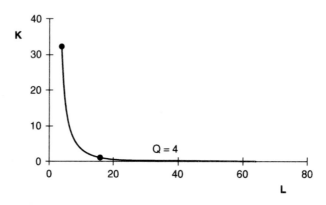

Figure 1.35   Isoquant

when $K = 1$, APL is as shown in figure 1.36.

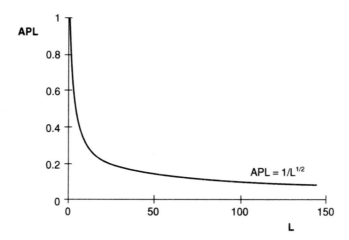

Figure 1.36   Average product of labour

chapter two

Equations in Economics

In this chapter you learn to
- Understand how equations are used in economics
- Rewrite and solve equations
- Substitute expressions
- Solve simple linear demand and supply equations to find market equilibrium
- Carry out Cost–Volume–Profit analysis
- Identify the slope and intercept of a line
- Plot the budget constraint to obtain the budget line
- Appreciate there is a constant rate of substitution as you move along a line
- Solve quadratic equations
- Find the profit maximizing output and also the supply function for a perfectly competitive firm
- Solve simultaneous equations
- Discover equilibrium values for related markets
- Model growth using exponential functions
- Use logarithms for transformations and to solve certain types of equations
- Plot and solve equations in Excel

SECTION 2.1: Introduction

An equation is a statement that two expressions are equal to one another. What is on the left of the equals sign has the same value as what is on the right. In economic modelling we express relationships as equations and then use them to obtain analytical results. Solving the equations gives us values for which the equations are true. If, then,

To improve your skill in handling and solving equations, use the screens in the first section of MathEcon chapter 2. There are lots of examples that use equations in the following two sections.

we can express the condition for market equilibrium as an equation in terms of price, P, solving the equation for P tells us the price at which the market is in equilibrium.

This chapter explains the different techniques needed to solve various kinds of equations. Applications in economic analysis follow each method.

> equation: two expressions separated by an equals sign such that what is on the left of the equals sign has the same value as what is on the right.

This chapter also teaches you the methods needed to solve IS–LM equations, which are discussed in the next chapter, Macroeconomic Models.

Section 2.2: Rewriting and Solving Equations

Solving equations lets us discover where curves intersect. Economists are often interested in such points because they may provide information about equilibrium situations. A graphical solution can be obtained by sketching the curves and reading off the x and y values at the point (or points) where they cross, but the results can only have limited accuracy. Since the x and y values are the same on both curves at such points, we can also obtain an exact solution using algebra. At an intersection of the functional relationships $y = f(x)$ and $y = h(x)$, the two y values are equal and therefore $f(x) = h(x)$. Equating the two functions of x and solving for x gives the x value (or values) at which the curves cross. Substitution of this x value into one of the functions gives the corresponding y value.

The process of rewriting an equation to solve it is called transposition. The general aim is firstly to get all terms containing the variable of interest to the left-hand side of the equation, and then to get just this variable on its own on the left-hand side. This gives the solution of the equation: the variable on the left-hand side is equal to the expression on the right-hand side of the equation.

> transposition: rearranging an equation so that it can be solved, always keeping what is on the left of the equals sign equal to what is on the right.

As you change an equation you decide which terms you would like to move to the other side, but you cannot just put them there! You must keep the two sides of the equation equal to one another. A method for ensuring this is to carry out the same algebraic operation on both sides of the equation. You may add the same term to both sides of an equation, or you may subtract the same quantity from both sides. What you add or subtract is chosen so that on one side of the equation the combined value of this amount and an existing term is 0. For example, to solve for x the equation

$$140 + 6x = -30x + 284$$

you add $30x$ to both sides so that on the right-hand side $-30x + 30x$ becomes 0. We now have the new equation

$$140 + 36x = 284$$

Next subtract 140 from both sides and you get

$$36x = 144$$

To solve for x we divide both sides by 36. This gives

$$x = 4$$

As this last step illustrates, multiplying or dividing both sides of an equation by the same quantity can be a useful operation. You can also square or take the square root of both sides of an equation if you wish. Equations involving a squared term are called quadratic equations and we see how to solve these in section 2.9.

When several terms are involved, use brackets to ensure that you carry out the operation on the whole of each side. If one side of the equation is a fraction, multiply both sides by the denominator so you get rid of the fraction. Division by zero would not give a useful result (see section 1.4) so you should not attempt it. As regards solving the equations in this book, it is not meaningful to try to take the square root of a negative number. If you find yourself apparently needing to do this, the kind of solution you are looking for may not exist.

Another tip is to think about whether your answer makes sense – if it doesn't, check your working. Just a wrong sign can make your answer meaningless. To guard against such a slip, rearrange equations one step at a time. In examinations, mistakes cost marks but you are unlikely to be given extra marks for completing the transposition process in one line.

The MathEcon screen titled Transposition demonstrates rewriting and solving an equation, and has an example for you to try.

When rewriting equations

Remember...

- add to or subtract from both sides
- multiply or divide through the whole of each side (but don't divide by 0)
- square or take the square root of each side
- use as many stages as you wish
- take care to get all the signs correct.

Plot the equations $y = -5 + 2x$ and $y = 30 - 3x$. At what values of x and y do they cross? Find also the algebraic solution by setting the two expressions in x equal to one another.

1

We are asked to plot two linear functions, so plotting two points on each then connecting them will suffice. The table shows x values of 0 and 10 and the corresponding y values for each line. These points are used to plot the lines shown in figure 2.1. Notice that the lines cross at $x = 7$, $y = 9$.

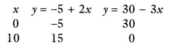

x	$y = -5 + 2x$	$y = 30 - 3x$
0	-5	30
10	15	0

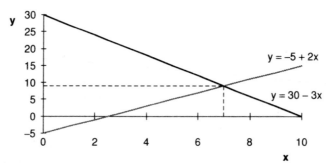

Figure 2.1 Lines intersect at (7,9)

For an algebraic solution, the two y values are equal so we equate the right-hand sides of the expressions and solve for x

$$-5 + 2x = 30 - 3x$$

We want terms in x on the left-hand side but not on the right, so add $3x$ to both sides since $-3x + 3x = 0$. We then have

$$-5 + 2x + 3x = 30$$

or

$$-5 + 5x = 30$$

To remove the constant term from the left-hand side we now add 5 to each side, giving

$$5x = 35$$

and so, dividing by 5, we have

$$x = 7$$

We then find the value for y by substituting $x = 7$ in either of the equations. Using $y = 30 - 3x$ gives

$$y = 30 - 21 = 9$$

which confirms the graphical result. The solution is $x = 7$, $y = 9$.

Solve for x

$$4x - 16 = \frac{8x^2}{2x + 3}$$

This expression looks rather complicated, and the term in x^2 suggests you may have to solve a quadratic equation. But do not give up! If you are asked to attempt a certain question at a particular stage of your course it is likely that the question can in fact be solved with the knowledge you already have. Begin by multiplying both sides by $(2x + 3)$ to remove the fraction and you get

$$(4x - 16)(2x + 3) = 8x^2$$

Multiply out the brackets, which gives

$$8x^2 - 20x - 48 = 8x^2$$

Subtract $8x^2$ from both sides and the term in x^2 disappears, leaving

$$-20x - 48 = 0$$

Now add 48 to each side and we have

$$-20x = 48$$

Divide both sides by -20, remembering that when you divide a positive number by a negative one the result is negative. This gives the solution

$$x = -2.4$$

SOLUTION IN TERMS OF OTHER VARIABLES

Not all of the equations you deal with will have numerical solutions. Sometimes when you solve an equation for x you obtain an expression containing other variables. Use the same rules to transpose the equation. Remember that in the solution x will not occur on the right-hand side and will be on its own on the left-hand side.

If you are given a relationship in the form $y = f(x)$, rewriting the equation in the form $x = g(y)$ is called finding the inverse function. To be able to find the inverse there must be just one x value corresponding to each y value. For non-linear functions there can be difficulties in finding an inverse, but we may be able to do so for a restricted set of values. For example, the function $y = x^2$ has two x values (one positive and one negative) corresponding to every y value, but if we consider the restricted function $y = x^2$, $x > 0$ this function has the inverse $x = \sqrt{y}$. For the linear functions often used in economic models inverse functions can always be found. One reason for finding the inverse function is if the variable represented by y is conventionally plotted in economics on the horizontal axis. Demand and supply equations provide examples of this.

See section 2.4.

inverse function: expresses x as a function of y instead of y as a function of x.

3

Solve for x in terms of z

$$x = 60 + 0.8x + 7z$$

At first glance you seem to already have a solution for x, but notice that x occurs also on the right-hand side of the equation. We must collect terms in x on the left-hand side, so we subtract $0.8x$ from both sides and obtain

$$x - 0.8x = 60 + 7z$$

Since both left-hand side terms contain x we may write

$$(1 - 0.8)x = 60 + 7z$$

which gives

$$0.2x = 60 + 7z$$

To get x with a coefficient of 1 we divide both sides by $0.2 = \frac{1}{5}$, which is the same thing as multiplying both sides by 5. This gives

$$x = 300 + 35z$$

4

Given $y = \sqrt{x} + 5$, obtain an expression for x in terms of y.

Begin by interchanging the sides so that the side with x is on the left of the equation. We then have

$$\sqrt{x} + 5 = y$$

Next subtract 5 from both sides, giving

$$\sqrt{x} = y - 5$$

To find x we must square both sides. This means that the whole of the right-hand side is multiplied by itself, so use brackets. We obtain

$$x = (y - 5)^2$$

Squaring out the bracket we may also write

$$x = y^2 - 10y + 25$$

2.1 Plot the equations $y = 12 + 5x$ and $y = 22 + 4x$. At what point on the graph do they cross? Find also an algebraic solution for the intersection of the two lines.

2.2 Solve for x

(a) $7 - 3x = \dfrac{x}{5}$

(b) $x = 0.8x + 20$

(c) $x = \dfrac{4}{9x}$

(d) $150 - 0.72x = 232 - 4x$

(e) $x = 450 + 0.67x + 250 - 75 - 0.17x$

2.3 Solve for x in terms of y

(a) $6x + y = 12$

(b) $y = 24 - 8x$

Section 2.3: Substitution

When two expressions are equal to one another, either can be substituted for the other. Substitution is a key technique in mathematics. If a question asks you to find the values of several variables and you have found the value of one of them, substituting that value into other functions is often the way of finding the other values you need. Doing the substitution is something you will probably find quite easy. The problem is that the question will not usually tell you it needs to be done, so you have to learn to recognize situations in which substitution is useful. To help you with this, look out for the different ways in which substitution is used. In this chapter we use it to find the quantity supplied and demanded once we have found the equilibrium price, to show the effect of the imposition of a per unit tax on a good, and to solve simultaneous equations.

substitution: to write one expression in place of another.

When substituting, always be sure to substitute the whole of the new expression and combine it with the other terms in exactly the same way that the expression it replaces was combined with them. It is often helpful to put the expression you are substituting in brackets to ensure this. For example if $y = x^2 + 6u$ and $x = 30 - u$, find an expression for y in terms of u. Substituting $30 - u$ for x we obtain

$$y = (30 - u)^2 + 6u$$

which on multiplying out and collecting terms becomes

$$y = 900 - 54u + u^2$$

2.4   Simplify the expression for y

$$y = \frac{1.5p^{0.5} \cdot p}{q}$$

where $q = p^{1.5}$.

2.5   If $Y = C + 350$ and $C = 40 + 0.8Y$, substitute for C and solve for the value of Y.

SECTION 2.4: Demand and Supply

Demand and supply functions in economics express the quantity demanded or supplied as a function of price, $Q = f(P)$. According to mathematical convention the dependent variable, Q, should be plotted on the vertical axis. Economic analysis, however, uses the horizontal axis as the Q axis and for consistency we follow that approach in this text. So that we can determine the points on the graph in the usual way, before plotting a demand or supply function we first find its inverse function giving P as a function of Q.

See section 2.2.

Remember...

• We plot supply and demand with P on the vertical axis.
• Before plotting a supply or demand function, write it so that P is on the left, Q is on the right.

5

Find the inverse function for the demand equation $Q = 80 - 2P$ and sketch the demand curve.

Adding $2P$ to both sides of the demand equation we get

$$2P + Q = 80$$

Subtracting Q from both sides we obtain

$$2P = 80 - Q$$

Dividing each side by 2 gives the inverse function

$$P = \frac{80 - Q}{2} = 40 - \frac{Q}{2}$$

The demand function is linear, so it suffices to plot two points. Selected values of Q are shown in the table together with corresponding values for P. The graph is then drawn as shown in figure 2.2 and extended so that it touches both axes.

Q	$P = 40 - Q/2$
0	40
20	30

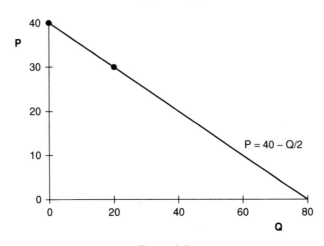

Figure 2.2

2.6

Rewrite these equations expressing P as a function of Q, then plot them on a graph

$$\text{Supply: } Q = 4P$$

$$\text{Demand: } Q = 280 - 10P$$

MARKET EQUILIBRIUM

Market equilibrium occurs when the quantity supplied equals the quantity demanded of a good. The supply and demand curves cross at the equilibrium price and quantity. If you plot both the demand and supply curves you can read off approximate equilibrium values from the graph. Another approach is to solve algebraically for the point where the demand and supply equations are equal. This gives exact values. Suppose we wish to find the equilibrium price and quantity when the quantity demanded, Q_d, is given by

The MathEcon screens titled Factors Affecting Demand and Demand Curve of an Individual let you investigate a demand function, then show you how economists plot a demand curve with Q on the horizontal axis and P on the vertical axis.

$$Q_d = 96 - 4P$$

and the quantity supplied, Q_s, is

$$Q_s = 8P$$

For an algebraic solution we can use the equations in this form. Notice that the use of subscripts helps us distinguish the demand equation from the supply one. The condition under which equilibrium is achieved is that the quantity supplied equals the quantity demanded. We write, therefore

$$Q_s = Q_d \text{ in equilibrium}$$

so

$$8P = 96 - 4P$$

by substituting the right-hand sides. Adding $4P$ to both sides gives

$$12P = 96$$

and dividing by 12 we have

$$P = 8, \text{ the equilibrium price}$$

To find the equilibrium quantity we then substitute P into either the supply or the demand equation. Using the supply equation gives

$$Q_s = 8P = 8 \times 8 = 64, \text{ the equilibrium quantity}$$

As a check we can use the demand equation also

$$Q_d = 96 - 4P = 96 - 4 \times 8 = 96 - 32 = 64$$

You can explore this economic concept in the second section of MathEcon chapter 2, Market Equilibrium.

Since $Q_s = Q_d$ this confirms that we have correctly solved the equations, and we state the solution:

$$\text{Market equilibrium occurs at } Q = 64, P = 8$$

CHANGES IN DEMAND OR SUPPLY

The quantity demanded and the quantity supplied of a good are usually modelled as dependent on a number of factors. All of these except price are assumed to be constant when we draw the demand and supply curves. Changes in factors other than price alter the positions of the curves. For example, suppose we have a multivariate demand function where Q, the demand for good X depends on P, the price of X, together with M, consumer income and P_Z, the price of another good, Z. If the demand function is

$$Q = 80 - 5P + 0.1M + 0.3P_Z$$

when M and P_Z are fixed respectively at 2500 and 60 the demand curve becomes

$$Q_1 = 80 - 5P + 0.1(2500) + 0.3(60) = 348 - 5P$$

where Q is written with a subscript 1 to denote that this is a demand curve for specific values of M and P_Z. If either M or P_Z changes, the demand curve shifts and we change the subscript on Q to 2, to indicate that we now have a different curve. For example, if M falls to 2000 the expression for demand becomes

$$Q_2 = 80 - 5P + 0.1(2000) + 0.3(60) = 298 - 5P$$

We get a new line representing demand, which is parallel to the old one but shifted down from it.

Demand and supply curves can also change their shapes in other ways. For example, suppose a change in tastes causes twice as much to be demanded at any price. If the original demand is given by

$$Q = 55 - 5P$$

denoting the new quantity demanded Q_2 we know that it is twice Q and so we write

$$Q_2 = 2Q = 2(55 - 5P) = 110 - 10P$$

Again the use of subscripts distinguishes two different curves. Notice that with the original demand curve nothing is bought when $P = 11$, and similarly nothing is bought at that price with the new curve. This kind of change in demand causes the demand curve to pivot around its intersection with the P axis.

Shifts in demand and supply curves are discussed in MathEcon screens Shifts in an Individual's Demand Curve and Shifts in the Supply Curve of a Firm.

If you would like to plot graphs of the equations in this section, the file called Equations.xls will help you. The worksheet Supply–Demand can be used for any linear supply and demand curves. It calculates the inverse functions, then plots them on a graph. There is information about how to use this spreadsheet in section 2.15.

6 For the demand and supply functions given, find the inverse functions giving P as a function of Q, sketch the demand and supply curves and mark the equilibrium position.

$$\text{Demand: } Q_d = 110 - 5P$$

$$\text{Supply: } Q_s = 6P$$

If demand increases by 20%, find the new demand function, its inverse and the new equilibrium position on the diagram.

Rewrite the demand equation, adding $(5P - Q_d)$ to both sides. This gives

$$5P = 110 - Q_d$$

Dividing through by 5 we obtain the inverse demand function

$$P = 22 - \frac{Q_d}{5} \qquad \text{(curve D}_1\text{)}$$

For the inverse of the supply equation we interchange the sides, obtaining

$$6P = Q_s$$

and then divide by 6 to get

$$P = \frac{Q_s}{6} \qquad \text{(curve S)}$$

The demand and supply curves D_1 and S are shown in figure 2.3. Equilibrium occurs where they cross, and here the values of P and Q on the demand curve equal those on the supply curve. This is the point $Q = 60$, $P = 10$.

When demand increases, the quantity demanded is 20% greater than before at every price. Hence the new quantity demanded, Q_{d2}, is given by

$$Q_{d2} = 1.2(110 - 5P) = 132 - 6P$$

The inverse function is

$$P = 22 - \frac{Q_{d2}}{6} \qquad \text{(curve D}_2\text{)}$$

This is shown as the new demand curve D_2 in figure 2.3, and the new equilibrium position occurs where this curve crosses the supply curve at the point $Q = 66$, $P = 11$.

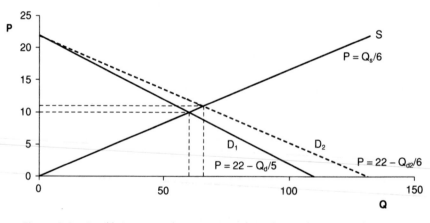

Figure 2.3   Equilibrium P and Q increase when demand increases by 20%

EFFECTS OF A PER UNIT TAX

The information contained in the supply equation about how much producers will supply is based on the prices that they receive. If a per unit tax, t, is imposed, although buyers still pay P for each unit of the good, the suppliers receive only $P - t$. The difference between the price paid and the price received is the per unit tax, t, which is paid to the government. A per unit tax therefore changes the supply equation and causes the supply curve to shift. Whatever the form in which the supply equation is written, we can alter it to incorporate a per unit tax by writing $P - t$ in place of P wherever it occurs. For example, if when there is no tax the supply equation is given by

$$Q_{s1} = -3 + 4P$$

then when a per unit tax of t is imposed the supply equation becomes

$$Q_{s2} = -3 + 4(P - t)$$

where we change the subscript on Q to indicate this is a different equation.

You may be familiar with the diagrammatic analysis which shows a supply curve shifting vertically upwards by t when a unit tax of that size takes effect. We can see this from our equations if we rewrite them expressing P as a function of Q. The original supply equation becomes

$$P = \frac{Q_{s1}}{4} + \frac{3}{4}$$

With $P - t$ for P in the equation and the new subscript on Q, the post-tax supply equation is

$$P - t = \frac{Q_{s2}}{4} + \frac{3}{4}$$

Adding t to both sides this becomes

$$P = \frac{Q_{s2}}{4} + \frac{3}{4} + t$$

A general algebraic result about the size of the price change following the imposition of a per unit tax is shown on the MathEcon screen Economic Problems – Equations.

The post-tax values for P are t more than the original ones, so when we plot the two supply equations with P on the vertical axis the post-tax curve is higher by the amount of the tax. Notice that if the demand curve is downward sloping, equilibrium price does not rise by the full amount of the tax. As price rises, less is demanded and so when a tax is imposed the new equilibrium position occurs at a lower output than the previous equilibrium. The two equilibrium positions can be found by equating each supply equation in turn with the demand equation, as shown in the worked example below.

To obtain the new supply equation when a per unit tax, t, is imposed, substitute $P - t$ for P in the supply equation. **Remember...**

If demand and supply in a market are described by the equations below, solve algebraically to find equilibrium P and Q.

$$\text{Demand: } Q_d = 120 - 8P$$

$$\text{Supply: } Q_s = -6 + 4P$$

If now a per unit tax of 4.5 is imposed, show how the equilibrium solution changes. How is the tax shared between producers and consumers? Sketch a graph showing what changes ensue when the tax is imposed.

7

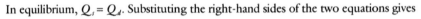

In equilibrium, $Q_s = Q_d$. Substituting the right-hand sides of the two equations gives

$$-6 + 4P = 120 - 8P$$

Adding $8P + 6$ to each side we have

$$12P = 126$$

Dividing by 12 gives

$$P = 10.5$$

Substituting in the supply equation gives

$$Q_s = -6 + 4(10.5) = 36$$

and in equilibrium this equals Q_d. The equilibrium values are $P = 10.5$ and $Q = 36$.

When a tax of 4.5 is imposed the supply curve becomes

$$\text{Supply: } Q_{s2} = -6 + 4(P - 4.5) = -24 + 4P$$

In equilibrium this new quantity supplied equals the quantity demanded, so

$$Q_{s2} = Q_d$$

and substituting right-hand sides we have

$$-24 + 4P = 120 - 8P$$

Adding $8P + 24$ to each side gives

$$12P = 144$$

and so dividing by 12 we find

$$P = 12$$

From the new supply equation we obtain

$$Q_{s2} = -24 + (4 \times 12) = 24$$

The equilibrium values are $P = 12$ and $Q = 24$. Although the tax is 4.5, price has risen by only $12 - 10.5 = 1.5$. One third of the tax has been passed on to consumers as a price increase, but the remainder has been absorbed by the producers. The quantity traded has fallen from 36 to 24.

To plot the curves we write the inverse functions expressing P in terms of Q. We find

Demand, D: $P = 15 - \dfrac{Q_d}{8}$

Original supply, S_1: $P = \dfrac{3}{2} + \dfrac{Q_{s1}}{4}$

Supply after tax, S_2: $P = \dfrac{3}{2} + \dfrac{Q_{s2}}{4} + 4.5 = 6 + \dfrac{Q_{s2}}{4}$

These three linear functions are plotted in figure 2.4. Supply rises vertically by 4.5 when the tax is imposed, as can be seen from the positions at which the two supply curves cut the P axis.

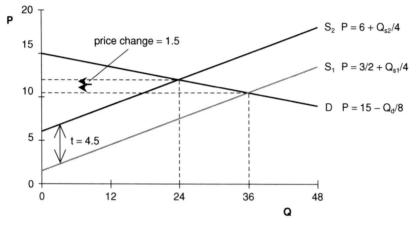

Figure 2.4 Per unit tax raises P and reduces Q

2.7 For the supply function $Q_s = 6 + 12P$ and the demand function $Q_d = 150 - 6P$, write the inverse functions giving P in terms of Q and sketch a graph of them, marking the equilibrium position.

If a difficulty in obtaining components reduces supply so that only half the previous quantity is now supplied at any price, find the new supply function, Q_{s2}. If after this the availability of a substitute product reduces demand so that only half the quantity previously demanded is now demanded at any price, find the new demand function, Q_{d2}. Find the inverse functions, plot the curves and find the new equilibrium positions after each change occurs.

2.8 Market demand is given by $Q_d = 66 - 3P$ and supply is given by $Q_s = 2P - 4$. Find the equilibrium price and quantity. If a per unit sales tax of $t = 5$ is imposed on the good, find the new equilibrium price and quantity.

SECTION 2.5: Cost–Volume–Profit Analysis

Cost–Volume–Profit (CVP) analysis is a method used by accountants to estimate the desired sales level in order to achieve a target level of profit. Two simplifying assumptions are made: namely that price and average variable costs are both fixed.

As in section 1.11 we write that profit is the difference between total revenue and total cost

$$\pi = \text{TR} - \text{TC}$$

We use revenue and cost expressions that were defined in sections 1.9 and 1.10, namely

$$\text{TR} = P \cdot Q$$

$$\text{TC} = \text{FC} + \text{VC}$$

$$\text{AVC} = \frac{\text{VC}}{Q}$$

where P is price, Q is the quantity of output sold, FC is fixed cost, VC is total variable cost, and AVC is average variable cost. Substituting in the profit function for TR and TC gives

$$\pi = P \cdot Q - (\text{FC} + \text{VC}) = P \cdot Q - \text{FC} - \text{VC}$$

Multiplying both sides of the expression for AVC by Q we obtain

$$\text{AVC} \cdot Q = \text{VC}$$

so we may substitute for VC in the profit equation and get

$$\pi = P \cdot Q - \text{FC} - \text{AVC} \cdot Q$$

All the above is generally true, but we now come to the stage where the special assumptions of CVP analysis are used. Instead of a downward sloping demand curve we assume that P is fixed, and whereas AVC might typically be a curve whose values vary with Q, we assume that AVC is fixed also. We have that π is a function of Q but P, FC and AVC are not. This allows us to write the inverse function expressing Q as a function of π. Adding FC to both sides gives

$$\pi + \text{FC} = P \cdot Q - \text{AVC} \cdot Q$$

Interchanging the sides we obtain

$$P \cdot Q - \text{AVC} \cdot Q = \pi + \text{FC}$$

Q is a factor of both terms on the left so we may write

$$Q(P - \text{AVC}) = \pi + \text{FC}$$

The analysis is explained on the MathEcon screens CVP: Graphical Analysis and CVP: Algebraic Analysis (1) and (2). The screen titled Economic Problems – Equations has a Revenue Cost and Profit example which shows a general method for finding the break-even level of output. The special assumptions of CVP analysis are not used.

Dividing through by $(P - \text{AVC})$ gives

$$Q = \frac{\pi + \text{FC}}{P - \text{AVC}}$$

If the firm's accountant can estimate FC, P and AVC, substituting these together with the target level of profit, π, gives the desired sales level.

For a firm with fixed costs of 555, average variable cost of 12 and selling at a price of 17, find an expression for profit in terms of its level of sales, Q. What value should Q be to achieve the profit target of 195? At what sales level does this firm break even? Illustrate your algebraic analysis with a diagram.

$$\pi = \text{TR} - \text{TC} = P \cdot Q - \text{FC} - \text{VC}$$

Writing $\text{VC} = \text{AVC} \cdot Q$ gives

$$\pi = P \cdot Q - \text{FC} - \text{AVC} \cdot Q$$

Substituting costs and price we find

$$\pi = 17Q - 555 - 12Q$$

so

$$\pi = 5Q - 555$$

which is the required expression for profit. Rewriting this to give Q in terms of π we add 555 to both sides so

$$\pi + 555 = 5Q$$

Interchanging the sides gives

$$5Q = \pi + 555$$

and dividing by 5 we have

$$Q = \frac{\pi + 555}{5}$$

Substituting the profit target of 195 gives

$$Q = \frac{195 + 555}{5} = 150$$

A sales level, Q, of 150 is required to achieve the target profit. For the break-even value of Q we substitute instead $\pi = 0$, so

$$Q = \frac{555}{5} = 111$$

$Q = 111$ is the break-even sales level. The conventional diagrammatic analysis is shown in figure 2.5. TR and TC are plotted, and profit is the vertical distance between them.

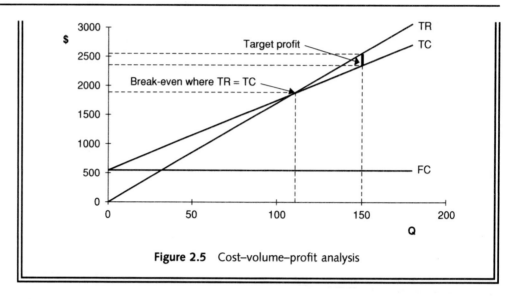

Figure 2.5   Cost–volume–profit analysis

2.9   If a firm has fixed costs of 328, average variable cost of 8 and it sells at a price of 12, what is its desired level of sales, Q, if it has a profit target of 20? Find also its total revenue and total cost for a sales level of Q, and so obtain an expression for profit in terms of Q. Use this to check that the sales level you calculated earlier gives the target profit. At what sales level does this firm break even?

SECTION 2.6: Linear Equations

You can already plot the equation of a line, but we now look further at what it represents. Linear models are much used in economics. They are simple and convenient and often provide a reasonably good description of how variables are related. To interpret linear models we need to be able to identify key features of linear equations. We now discover what the terms 'slope' and 'intercept' of a line mean and we learn to recognize them. We also answer questions such as 'Given a line and a point, how can we tell if the point lies on the line?'

The MathEcon screen shown in figure 2.6 explains how to measure the slope of a line that passes through the points (2,8) and (4,11). The slope of a line is defined to be (distance up) ÷ (distance to right) as you move between two points. The 'distance up' is the second y value minus the first and is denoted Δy. The 'distance to the right' is the second x value minus the first and we denote it Δx.

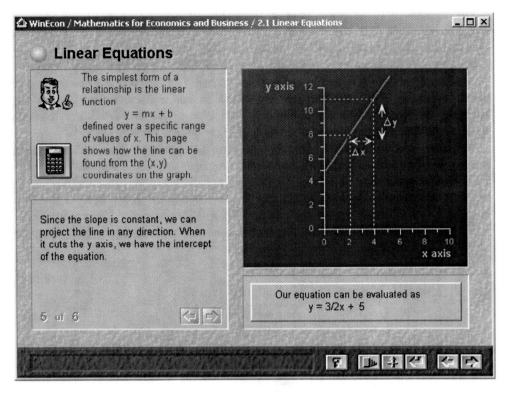

Figure 2.6

The slope of a line can then be defined as

$$\text{slope} = \frac{\Delta y}{\Delta x} = \frac{\text{distance up}}{\text{distance to right}}$$

For the points (2,8) and (4,11) we have $\Delta y = 11 - 8 = 3$ and $\Delta x = 4 - 2 = 2$ and so the slope of the line is $\Delta y/\Delta x = \frac{3}{2}$. Notice that this is the constant that multiplies x, called the coefficient of x, in the equation representing the line, $y = \frac{3}{2}x + 5$.

---

slope of a line: distance up divided by distance moved to the right between any two points on the line.

coefficient: a value that is multiplied by a variable.

intercept: the value at which a function cuts the y axis.

The intercept of a line is the value at which the line cuts the y axis. This is the value y has when x is 0. Our line is given by $y = \frac{3}{2}x + 5$. If we substitute $x = 0$ into this equation we get the value 5, which is the intercept.

We can now interpret the equation of a line which we recognize as having the general form $y = mx + b$ where m and b are constants. The variables in a linear equation simply appear as they are. They are not raised to any powers, or we can say that implicitly the variables have the power of 1 since $x^1 = x$. The coefficient of x, m, is the slope of the line and the constant term, b, is the intercept on the y axis.

The slope and intercept of a line can be zero or negative. A line with zero slope is just a constant and its graph is a horizontal line, as in figure 2.7. As x increases there is no change in the value of y along the line. Lines with zero intercept pass through the origin as illustrated in figure 2.8. If a line slopes downwards to the right as shown in figure 2.9, y goes down rather than up as we move to the right. The change in y is in the negative direction, and therefore such a line has a negative slope. With a negative

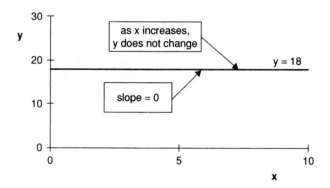

Figure 2.7 A horizontal line has zero slope

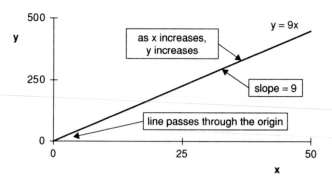

Figure 2.8 Positive slope, intercept at zero

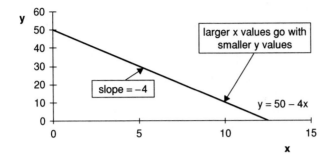

Figure 2.9 Negative slope, positive intercept

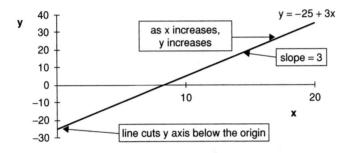

Figure 2.10 Positive slope, negative intercept

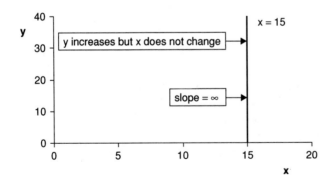

Figure 2.11 A vertical line has infinite slope

slope y gets smaller as x gets bigger. A negative intercept implies that the line cuts the y axis below the origin, as shown in figure 2.10. When a line is vertical, y can take any value but x does not change. However large a value of Δy we consider, Δx is zero and so $\Delta y/\Delta x$ is infinite. A vertical line has infinite slope, as shown in figure 2.11.

> **Remember...**
> - A line can be represented as $y = mx + b$.
> - The constant term gives the y intercept.
> - The slope of a line is the coefficient of x.
> - Slope = $\Delta y / \Delta x$ = (distance up)/(distance to right).
> - Lines with positive slope go up from left to right.
> - Lines with negative slope go down from left to right.
> - Horizontal lines have zero slope.
> - Vertical lines have infinite slope.

You can measure the slope of a line between any pair of points on it, because a line has the same slope throughout its length. If you consider a larger change in x, the change in y values between the two points increases proportionately so that the ratio $\Delta y / \Delta x$ stays the same.

In economic analysis we may want to know whether a particular point (x_1, y_1) complies with a linear relationship we have modelled, $y = mx + b$. To discover this we calculate the y value on the line in our model that corresponds to x_1. We do this by substituting x_1 in the equation of the line. We then compare this y value with y_1. If the values are different, the point does not lie on the line. For points above the line $y_1 > mx + b$ and for points below the line $y_1 < mx + b$.

A linear model can be used to predict the effect on y of a change in x. Since

$$\text{slope} = \frac{\Delta y}{\Delta x}$$

multiplying this through by Δx and interchanging the sides gives

$$\Delta y = \text{slope} \times \Delta x$$

Hence we multiply the change in x by the slope of the line to find the predicted resulting change in y. You can use this to find the intercept of a line from the coordinates of its points, as shown in the worked example below.

For the equation of a line $y = mx + b$ we have said that m and b are constants, and indeed they are for any specific line. They are better described, however, as parameters since we may be interested in what happens when they change, as discussed for supply and demand in section 2.4. If the constant term in the equation changes, the intercept is altered and the line shifts. That is, it moves to a new position parallel to its original one, because it still has the same slope. If the coefficient of x in the equation changes, the slope of the curve is altered. The line pivots about its intersection with the y axis.

The MathEcon screen titled Linear Equations demonstrates how we find the slope and intercept of a line and lets you try it for yourself with some quiz questions.

> parameter: a value that is constant for a specific function but that may be changed to give other functions of the same type.

9

Does the point (7,6) lie on the line connecting points (4,8) and (10,5)?

The line connecting (4,8) and (10,5) has slope = $\Delta y/\Delta x = (5 - 8)/(10 - 4)$ = $-\frac{3}{6} = -\frac{1}{2}$. The intercept is the y value when $x = 0$. From the point (4,8) where $x = 4$ and $y = 8$ we need $\Delta x = -4$ to make $x = 0$. To find the corresponding Δy we rewrite the expression for the slope, giving $\Delta y = -\Delta x/2$ and substitute Δx. This gives $\Delta y = -(-4)/2 = 2$. The intercept is $y + \Delta y = 8 + 2 = 10$, and so the line connecting the points is given by $y = 10 - x/2$.

We find the point on the line with an x value of 7 by substituting this in the equation, giving $y = 10 - \frac{7}{2} = 6.5$. This shows that the point (7,6.5) lies on the line and that therefore the given point (7,6) lies below the line connecting the two points. For the given point, $y < 10 - x/2$. Figure 2.12 illustrates the points and the line.

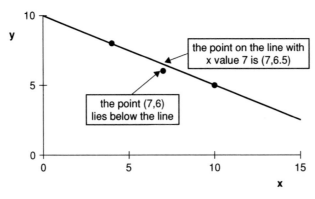

Figure 2.12 Line connecting (4,8) and (10,5)

2.10 Find the slope and intercept of a line passing through each of these pairs of points, and write the equation of the line in each case

(a) (0,12) (10,52)

(b) (0,45) (15,15)

(c) (5,8) (7,10)

2.11 Which of the following points lie on the line $84 - 7x$?

(10,14) (6,40) (5,48)

SECTION 2.7: Budget Lines

The budget constraint is a line showing combinations of two goods X and Y that are just affordable when a consumer spends a given amount of income on them. Quantities of the two goods form the axes of the graph. Since negative quantities cannot be purchased, the budget constraint is plotted only for the positive quadrant where X and Y take positive values. The easiest way of plotting the line is to find the points at which it cuts the horizontal and vertical axes. These correspond to the purchase of only X (Y = 0) and only Y (X = 0) respectively. The equation of a budget line is obtained by assuming that all the consumer's income, M, is spent on these goods, X and Y, which are bought at prices P_x and P_y.

The budget line equation is $x . P_x + y . P_y = M$.   **Remember...**

Points that lie above the budget constraint cannot be afforded because $x . P_x + y . P_y > M$, while for points below the budget line the consumer has unspent income, since $x . P_x + y . P_y < M$. We now see a worked example of how a budget constraint is plotted and how the equation for it is obtained. This is followed by the derivation of a general budget line expression that can be used to show how a budget line alters if prices or the consumer's income change.

10

A backpacker budgets $198 per month for hostels and excursions. Hostels cost $6 per night (sometimes the backpacker sleeps on the bus, or with friends) and excursions cost $18 each. Plot the backpacker's budget line and obtain the budget constraint expression. If the backpacker plans to spend 30 nights in hostels, how many excursions can he or she afford? How many nights of free accommodation are needed for the backpacker to be able to afford one extra excursion?

Let x be the number of excursions, so at $18 each the amount spent on excursions is $18x$. Let y be the number of nights spent in hostels, so $6y$ is spent on them. Total expenditure is the sum of these amounts, and this must equal the budget of $198. We have

$$18x + 6y = 198$$

This is the basic expression for the budget constraint. It shows that total expenditure equals total income. To find where the line intersects the x axis we set $y = 0$ in the expression and solve for x. This gives $18x = 198$ or $x = 11$. The point (11,0) is where the budget line meets the x axis. It shows that if the backpacker spends all of his or her budget on excursions, 11 of them can be bought. We now substitute $x = 0$ in the budget constraint. This gives $6y = 198$ or $y = 33$. The budget line therefore intersects the y axis at the point $(0,33)$, showing that if no excursions are bought, the backpacker can afford hostel accommodation for 33 nights. Plotting these two points and connecting them with a straight line gives the budget line shown in figure 2.13.

To write the budget constraint in the form of the general expression for a line $y = b + mx$, we need to rearrange the expression above. We start by subtracting $18x$ from both sides and get

$$6y = 198 - 18x$$

Dividing through by 6 gives

$$y = 33 - 3x$$

This shows y as a function of x. The line has an intercept on the y axis of 33 and a slope of -3.

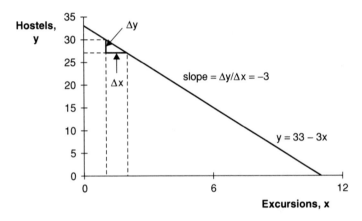

Figure 2.13   Budget line

If $y = 30$ we have $30 = 33 - 3x$ which solves to give $x = 1$. If 30 nights are spent in hostels the backpacker can afford one excursion.

One extra excursion implies $\Delta x = 1$. To find the corresponding change in y, Δy, we multiply Δx by the slope of the line

$$\Delta y = -3\Delta x = -3$$

For an extra excursion the value of y must be reduced by 3, so three nights of free accommodation are needed. You may have answered this part of the question by saying that the price of an excursion is three times that of a night in a hostel, so three hostel nights must be relinquished to obtain one extra excursion. Algebraically we may write $P_x = 3P_y$, which gives $P_x/P_y = 3$. The example illustrates the general result that as y is exchanged for x along the budget line $\Delta y = -(P_x/P_y)\Delta x$.

Find general expressions for the budget line and the points at which it intersects the axes for a consumer with income M who buys two goods, X and Y, at prices P_x and P_y. What is the slope of this budget line? How does the position of the line alter as P_x, P_y and M change?

If the consumer buys x units of good X at price P_x, expenditure on good X is $x \cdot P_x$. Similarly, an expenditure of $y \cdot P_y$ buys y units of good Y. The consumer's total expenditure is $x \cdot P_x + y \cdot P_y$, and the budget line comprises points where total expenditure equals income, M

$$\text{Budget line: } x \cdot P_x + y \cdot P_y = M$$

Where the line meets the x axis only x is bought. To find this point we set $y = 0$ in the expression and solve for x. This gives $x \cdot P_x = M$ or $x = M/P_x$. The budget line meets the x axis at the point $(M/P_x, 0)$. The intersection with the y axis, the intercept of the line, is found by substituting $x = 0$ in the budget constraint. This gives $y \cdot P_y = M$ or $y = M/P_y$. The intercept is at the point $(0, M/P_y)$.

To rewrite the budget constraint giving y as a function of x, subtract $x \cdot P_x$ from both sides so that

$$y \cdot P_y = M - x \cdot P_x$$

Now divide both sides by P_y, which gives

$$y = \frac{M}{P_y} - \frac{x \cdot P_x}{P_y}$$

so rearranging the second term to show the coefficient of x, the budget line is given by

$$y = \frac{M}{P_y} - \left(\frac{P_x}{P_y}\right)x$$

From the discussion of the form of a straight line in section 2.6, we recognize the coefficient of x as the slope of the line. The slope of the budget line is $-P_x/P_y$, the negative of the ratio of the prices of the goods and the intercept is the constant term in the equation, M/P_y. Changing P_x rotates the line about the point where it cuts the y axis. If P_y alters, both the slope and the y intercept change. The line rotates about the point where it cuts the x axis. An increase or decrease in income M alters the intercept but does not change the slope. The line shifts outwards or inwards.

To learn more about the budget line and to discover for yourself the effects of various changes in prices or incomes, use MathEcon screen Changing the Budget Line. The budget line is used in conjunction with indifference curves on the screen Optimal Consumption Choice.

indifference curve: connects points representing different combinations of two goods that generate equal levels of utility for the consumer.

2.12 A consumer has an income of 750 and spends it on two goods, X and Y, whose prices are 37.5 and 2 respectively. Plot the consumer's budget line. The consumer is indifferent between each of the following combinations of x and y: (1,900) (8,225) (27,100). If the consumer's utility function is $U = x^{1/3}y^{1/2}$ find the level of utility achieved at each of these points. Do any of the points lie on the budget line? Add the indifference curve to your graph.

SECTION 2.8: Constant Substitution Along a Line

When we consider different points on a negatively sloping straight line, we see that a larger value of x implies having less y, and we can exchange y for x at a constant rate. This is the case, for example, with budget lines discussed above. It contrasts with situations where economic theory suggests that substitution takes place at a non-constant rate.

For example, consumer indifference curves are usually assumed to have a diminishing marginal rate of substitution and so to have a shape which is curved towards the origin like that in figure 2.14. The curve passes through points A (3,20) and B (5,10), indicating that the consumer is indifferent between them. What can we say about how this person would rank 4 units of X and 15 units of Y? First notice that point C (4,15) lies on the line joining the two points between which the consumer is indifferent. Since indifference curves bend towards the origin, the new point (4,15) must lie on a higher indifference curve, and the consumer prefers that point to the other two.

To study this in more depth, use the screens Discovering Indifference Curves and Assumptions of Indifference Curves in section 3 of MathEcon chapter 2.

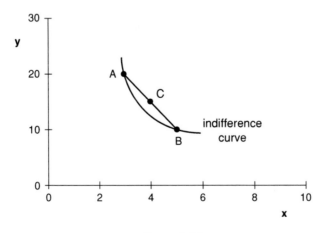

Figure 2.14

> diminishing marginal rate of substitution: as a consumer acquires more of good x in exchange for good y, the rate at which he substitutes x for y diminishes because he becomes less willing to give up y for a small additional amount of x.

> The rate at which y is substituted by x is constant along a downward sloping line, but not along a curve.   **Remember...**

Section 2.9: Quadratic Equations

In economic modelling we work with the simplest function that can adequately represent a relationship, but sometimes a curve rather than a straight line is required. In sections 1.9 and 1.10 we used quadratic functions to represent total revenue and average variable cost. Such functions have the general form

$$y = ax^2 + bx + c$$

where a, b and c are constants. When you sketch a quadratic function you find it has either a hill or a U shape, and that generally two values of x give the same value of y.

A quadratic equation has a term in x^2 but no higher powers of x. To solve for x we first write it in the form $ax^2 + bx + c = 0$. The value(s) of x for which this equation is true can be found graphically by plotting $y = ax^2 + bx + c$ and looking to see where $y = 0$. In figure 2.15 the graph cuts the x axis twice and there are two values of x at which $y = 0$, x_1 and x_2. If it happens that a quadratic function just touches the x axis at its highest or lowest point, there is only one value of x that provides a solution to the equation. If the curve turns before it reaches the x axis, the value of $y = 0$ does not occur for any value of x, and so the equation $ax^2 + bx + c = 0$ does not have a solution. An example of this is a U-shaped average variable cost curve.

The MathEcon screen titled Quadratic Equations lets you discover how the shape of a quadratic function depends on the signs of a and b. The screen also shows you a general algebraic method for solving a quadratic equation. The derivation of the formula used is available from the M button. If you would like to plot and solve quadratic equations in Excel, the Quadratic worksheet in the file called Equations.xls will help you. There is a description of how to use it in section 2.15.

Algebraic methods are more accurate than graphical ones, but the squared term means we need a special technique. Sometimes factorizing the expression helps. Consider for example

$$5x^2 - 20x = 0$$

Since each term is divisible by $5x$ we can factorize the left-hand side and write

$$5x(x - 4) = 0$$

There are now two terms multiplied together, $5x$ and $(x - 4)$. For their product to be 0, one of the terms must be zero. This means either $5x = 0$ or $(x - 4) = 0$.

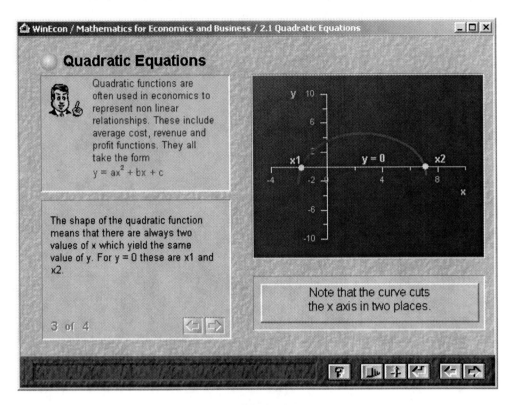

Figure 2.15

If $5x = 0$, dividing by 5 we find that $x = 0$ and this is one possible solution to the equation. If $x - 4 = 0$, adding 4 to both sides we find that $x = 4$, which is the other possible solution.

The graph of the function is plotted in figure 2.16. It cuts the x axis at $x = 0$ and $x = 4$, confirming that these are the two solutions to the equation.

A more general method for solving the quadratic equation $ax^2 + bx + c = 0$ uses a formula, the derivation of which is shown on the MathEcon screen. Whereas factorization is not always possible, the formula approach can always be used, although sometimes it may tell you that no solution exists. This happens if the curve does not cut the x axis.

A quadratic equation takes the form $ax^2 + bx + c = 0$ **Remember...**

- You can solve it graphically
- or sometimes by factorizing it
- or by using the formula

$$x = \frac{-b \pm \sqrt{b^2 - 4ac}}{2a}$$

where a is the coefficient of x^2, b is the coefficient of x and c is the constant term.

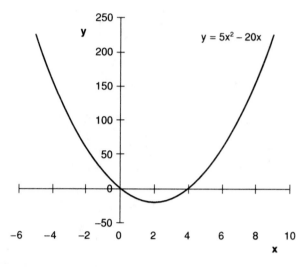

Figure 2.16

The symbol ± means 'plus or minus'. It is a shorthand way of telling us to compute two answers, using the + sign in one calculation and the − sign in the other.

To see how we use the formula let us solve the equation

$$8x^2 - 20x + 3 = 0$$

We identify a = 8, b = −20 and c = 3. Notice that the sign of the coefficient must be included. Begin by calculating the expression within the square root sign, called the discriminant. This gives

$$b^2 - 4ac = (-20)^2 - (4 \times 8 \times 3) = 400 - 96 = 304$$

We take the square root of this value and obtain 17.436. Substituting this result, −b and a into the formula gives

$$x = \frac{20 \pm 17.436}{16}$$

Using the positive sign we get x = 37.436/16 = 2.34, while the negative sign gives x = 2.564/16 = 0.16. The solution of the equation is x = 2.34 or x = 0.16.

Negative values of the discriminant $b^2 - 4ac$ can occur. This will not usually happen in the economics examples in this book, so if you find you have a negative value it is worth checking your calculation. If the negative value is genuine, do not try to take the square root of the expression. You are dealing with a curve which does not cut the x axis, so you cannot solve the equation for values of x at which y = 0.

2.13 Solve the following equations, or state that they cannot be solved

(a) $3x^2 - 18x + 15 = 0$ (b) $4x^2 - 12x + 9 = 0$

(c) $16x^2 - 64 = 0$ (d) $-8x^2 + 6x + 50 = 0$

(e) $7x^2 - 63x = 0$ (f) $5x^2 - 9x + 18 = 0$

(g) $-3x^2 + 10x + 25 = 0$

SECTION 2.10: Intersection of MC with MR or AVC

Quadratic equations arise in economics when we want to discover where a quadratic function, say marginal cost, cuts another quadratic function, say average variable cost, or cuts a linear function, say marginal revenue. We equate the two functional expressions, then subtract the right-hand side from both sides so that the value on the right becomes zero. After collecting terms we solve the quadratic equation using one of the methods explained above.

11 A firm has the marginal cost function $MC = 3Q^2 - 32Q + 96$ and marginal revenue function $MR = 236 - 16Q$. Find the firm's profit maximizing output.

To maximize profits the firm chooses to produce where marginal cost equals marginal revenue, as we shall see in chapter 6. Equating the MC and MR functions we have that

$$3Q^2 - 32Q + 96 = 236 - 16Q$$

Subtracting the right-hand side from both sides gives

$$3Q^2 - 32Q + 96 - (236 - 16Q) = 0$$

Removing the brackets gives

$$3Q^2 - 32Q + 96 - 236 + 16Q = 0$$

and by collecting terms we obtain

$$3Q^2 - 16Q - 140 = 0$$

We now use the formula for solving a quadratic equation, so

$$Q = \frac{-b \pm \sqrt{b^2 - 4ac}}{2a}$$

where $a = 3$, $b = -16$ and $c = -140$. Calculating the expression within the square root sign gives

$$b^2 - 4ac = (-16)^2 - 4 \times 3 \times (-140) = 256 + 1680 = 1936$$

so $\sqrt{(b^2 - 4ac)} = 44$. We then have

$$Q = \frac{16 \pm 44}{2 \times 3} = \frac{60}{6} \text{ or } \frac{-28}{6}$$

so $Q = 10$ or $Q = -4.67$. Only the positive value is economically meaningful, so profit maximization occurs when $Q = 10$.

To ensure that this is a profit maximizing position, strictly we should also check that MC cuts MR from below.

You can see these MC and MR functions plotted in the Quadratic worksheet in the Excel file Equations.xls. The solution to the above quadratic equation is also found. For an explanation of the relevant economics, see the screen Profit Maximization (2) in section 3 of MathEcon chapter 2. Another method of finding the profit maximizing output is presented in chapter 6.

12

A firm in perfect competition has the average variable cost function $\text{AVC} = 0.85Q^2 - 11.9Q + 102$ and the marginal cost function $\text{MC} = 2.55Q^2 - 23.8Q + 102$. What is the firm's minimum supply price?

The individual firm in perfect competition is too small to influence price, P, which is set by the industry. The firm therefore faces a horizontal demand, AR, curve which is also its marginal revenue, MR, curve and so $\text{MR} = \text{AR} = P$. Since a profit maximizing firm chooses to produce where $\text{MC} = \text{MR}$, for the firm in perfect competition this is a point where $\text{MC} = P$. The firm supplies the quantity that corresponds to the existing value of P, as determined by its MC curve. The short-run supply curve of the firm is its marginal cost curve above the point where MC and AVC intersect. This intersection represents the point at which the firm is just covering its average variable cost. At any lower price it will cease production. By equating MC and AVC we find the lowest output the firm would supply and by substitution in MC we find the minimum supply price.

We have $\text{MC} = \text{AVC}$ which gives

$$2.55Q^2 - 23.8Q + 102 = 0.85Q^2 - 11.9Q + 102$$

Subtracting the right-hand side from both sides gives

$$2.55Q^2 - 23.8Q + 102 - (0.85Q^2 - 11.9Q + 102) = 0$$

and so

$$2.55Q^2 - 23.8Q + 102 - 0.85Q^2 + 11.9Q - 102 = 0$$

By collecting terms we have

$$1.7Q^2 - 11.9Q = 0$$

Factorizing we find

$$Q(1.7Q - 11.9) = 0$$

Hence $Q = 0$ or $(1.7Q - 11.9) = 0$. We are looking for a point where MC cuts AVC from below, which does not occur at $Q = 0$. The other value of Q comes from $1.7Q = 11.9$, which gives $Q = 7$ as the output where MC and AVC intersect.

If the horizontal price line cuts MC at this point, a quantity of 7 is supplied and the price is the same as the value of MC. We substitute $Q = 7$ in the marginal cost function to find the required price. This gives

$$MC = 2.55(7)^2 - 23.8(7) + 102 = 60.35$$

and so the minimum supply price is 60.35. The supply curve is $P = 2.55Q^2 - 23.8Q + 102$ for $P \geqslant 60.35$. Figure 2.17 shows the solution diagrammatically.

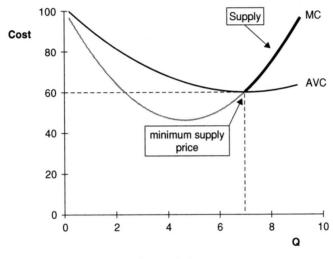

Figure 2.17

The economic analysis is shown in the supplementary screen, Short-Run Supply, accessed by the Next Page button from the screen titled Fixed and Variable Costs in section 3 of MathEcon chapter 2.

2.14 What is the profit maximizing output for a firm with the marginal cost function $MC = 1.6Q^2 - 15Q + 60$ and marginal revenue function $MR = 280 - 20Q$?

2.15 What is the minimum supply price for a perfectly competitive firm which has the average variable cost function $AVC = 1.4Q^2 - 24Q + 250$ and the marginal cost function $MC = 4.2Q^2 - 48Q + 250$?

SECTION 2.11: Simultaneous Equations

When economists model how markets operate, they often use different equations to represent different aspects of the market. For market equilibrium, the values of the variables are such that the equations are true simultaneously. Graphically, these values correspond to where the curves intersect. An example is the demand and supply model (section 2.4). Quantity demanded and quantity supplied are functions of price, P. In equilibrium these quantities are equal. To solve for equilibrium values, we equate the two expressions in P, thus eliminating Q. We obtain an equation which we can solve for P. Once we have a value for P we can substitute it into either equation to find Q. Eliminating variables by substitution is one method of solving simultaneous linear equations.

Another method of eliminating a variable is to subtract (or add) the left-hand sides and the right-hand sides of a pair of equations. Before doing this we need to ensure that one variable has the same coefficient (ignoring the sign) in both equations. If necessary we multiply through each equation by the coefficient in the *other* equation of the variable we wish to eliminate. The equations are subtracted if the variable to be eliminated has the same sign in both equations, and added if the signs are different.

13

Solve the simultaneous equations

$$2x + 4y = 20$$
$$3x + 5y = 28$$

For ease of reference we number the equations

$$2x + 4y = 20 \tag{1}$$
$$3x + 5y = 28 \tag{2}$$

We choose the variable to be eliminated, say x. We need to get x with the same coefficient in both equations. Using x's coefficient in the other equation, we multiply through equation (1) by 3, and equation (2) by 2. This gives

$$6x + 12y = 60 \tag{3}$$
$$6x + 10y = 56 \tag{4}$$

Now that x has a coefficient of 6 in both equations we subtract the corresponding sides of equations (3) and (4). We obtain

$$0 + 2y = 4$$

Since $2y = 4$, $y = 2$ is the solution for y. Now substitute it into either equation, say (1). We get

$$2x + 4(2) = 20$$

or

$$2x + 8 = 20$$

Subtracting 8 from both sides gives

$$2x = 12$$

and so $x = 6$.

As a check, substitute $x = 6$, $y = 2$ in equation (2). The left-hand side is

$$3(6) + 5(2) = 18 + 10 = 28$$

which is the value of the right-hand side, so the values are correct.

The solution of the equations is $x = 6$, $y = 2$.

A similar approach to that above is used to solve a larger set of equations. Usually simultaneous equations can be solved if the number of equations is the same as the number of unknown variables for which we are finding values. However, this condition does not guarantee that a solution exists. For example, if two equations represent parallel lines, as shown in figure 2.18, they do not intersect and so a solution cannot be found. Also, if one

Use the MathEcon screen Simultaneous Equations to discover more about solving these equations. If you would like to use Excel to solve simultaneous equations, section 2.15 explains how to do this with Excel's Solver tool.

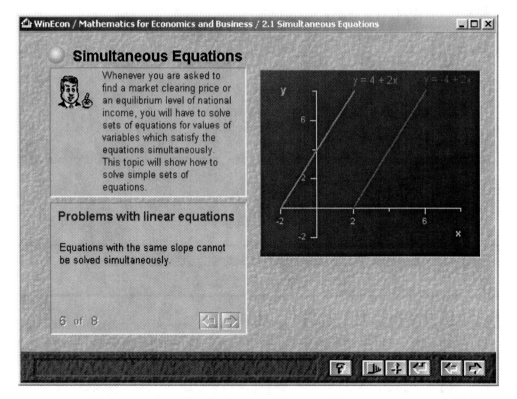

Figure 2.18

equation is a multiple of another equation they are in fact the same equation and do not contain enough information for us to find a unique solution.

Simultaneous equations can usually (but not always) be solved if

Remember...

number of equations = number of unknowns

Solution methods for two simultaneous equations include

- finding where functions cross on a graph
- eliminating a variable by substitution
- eliminating a variable by subtracting (or adding) equations.

Once you know the value of one variable, substitute it in the other equation.

2.16   Solve the equations, or say if no unique solution exists

(a) $4x + 5y = 33$

$7x + y = 19$

(b) $2x + 11y = 72$

$8x + 12y = 96$

(c) $10x - 2y = 26$

$5x + 2y = 40$

(d) $2x + 8y = 46$

$3x + 12y = 69$

SECTION 2.12: Simultaneous Equilibrium in Related Markets

Demand and supply in two related markets forms an example of an economics model using simultaneous equations. Demand in each market depends both on the price of the good itself and on the price of the related good. To solve the model we use the equilibrium condition for each market and equate the quantity supplied to the quantity demanded in that market. This gives two equations in two unknowns, which we then solve.

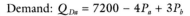

The market for activity holidays is represented by the functions

$$\text{Demand: } Q_{Da} = 7200 - 4P_a + 3P_b$$

$$\text{Supply: } Q_{Sa} = -1200 + 12P_a$$

and the market for beach holidays is represented by the functions

$$\text{Demand: } Q_{Db} = 1800 - 3P_b + \frac{1}{3}P_a$$

$$\text{Supply: } Q_{Sb} = -400 + 3P_b$$

where P_a and P_b are the prices of activity and beach holidays and Q_{Da}, Q_{Sa}, Q_{Db} and Q_{Sb} are the quantities demanded and supplied respectively of each type of holiday. Find the equilibrium prices and quantities of each type of holiday.

For the activity holiday market to be in equilibrium

$$Q_{Sa} = Q_{Da}$$

and substituting, we get

$$-1200 + 12P_a = 7200 - 4P_a + 3P_b$$

or

$$16P_a - 3P_b = 8400 \tag{1}$$

and for the beach holiday market to be in equilibrium

$$Q_{Sb} = Q_{Db}$$

which on substituting gives

$$-400 + 3P_b = 1800 - 3P_b + \frac{P_a}{3}$$

or

$$-\frac{P_a}{3} + 6P_b = 2200 \tag{2}$$

We now have two simultaneous equations to solve for P_a and P_b. Multiply equation (1) by 2, which gives

$$32P_a - 6P_b = 16,800 \tag{3}$$

Adding equations (2) and (3) we find

$$31\frac{2}{3}P_a + 0P_b = 19,000$$

so

$$95P_a = 57,000$$

multiplying both sides by 3 to remove the fraction, and

$$P_a = 600$$

We can now find P_b from equation (2)

$$-\frac{1}{3}(600) + 6P_b = 2200$$

or

$$-200 + 6P_b = 2200$$

Adding 200 to each side we have

$$6P_b = 2400$$

Dividing by 6 gives

$$P_b = 400$$

We can find the quantities of holidays most easily from the supply equations. For activity holidays

$$Q_{Sa} = -1200 + 12P_a$$

which gives

$$Q_{Sa} = -1200 + 12(600) = -1200 + 7200 = 6000$$

Using the beach holidays supply equation

$$Q_{Sb} = -400 + 3P_b$$

which gives

$$Q_{Sb} = -400 + 3(400) = 800$$

The solution is

$$P_a = 600, \; P_b = 400, \; Q_a = 6000, \; Q_b = 800$$

Check by substituting in the demand equations

$$\text{Activity holidays: } Q_{Da} = 7200 - 4P_a + 3P_b$$

The right-hand side gives

$$7200 - 4(600) + 3(400) = 7200 - 2400 + 1200 = 6000 = Q_{Sa}$$

$$\text{Beach holidays: } Q_{Db} = 1800 - 3P_b + \frac{P_a}{3}$$

The right-hand side gives

$$1800 - 3(400) + \frac{600}{3} = 800 = Q_{Sb}$$

Therefore, the solution is correct.

Notice that the form of the demand equations shows activity and beach holidays to be substitutes. As P_a rises Q_{Da} falls and Q_{Db} rises. Less activity holidays and more beach holidays are demanded.

2.17 The market for boots is described by the following equations

$$\text{Demand: } Q_{Db} = 87 - \frac{P_b}{6} + \frac{P_t}{5}$$

$$\text{Supply: } Q_{Sb} = -56 + 2P_b$$

and the market for trainers is modelled by the equations

$$\text{Demand: } Q_{Dt} = 417 - 3P_t + \frac{P_b}{4}$$

$$\text{Supply: } Q_{St} = 110 + 2P_t$$

where P_b is the price of boots, P_t is the price of trainers, Q_{Db}, Q_{Sb}, Q_{Dt} and Q_{St} are the quantities demanded and supplied of boots and trainers respectively. Find the quantities and prices at which both markets are in equilibrium.

SECTION 2.13: Exponential Functions

With an exponential function, the variable occurs in the power. An example is $y = 5^x$. We say that x is the exponent and the number that is raised to the power, 5 in this case, is called the base. For a particular value of x, say 4, to evaluate the y value on a calculator you enter the base, press the button marked x^y, type the exponent and press = to obtain the answer. Try evaluating 5^x when $x = 4$. The answer is $y = 5^4$ = 625.

> exponential function: has the form a^x where the base, a, is a positive constant and is not equal to 1.

In economics the preferred base for exponential functions is a mathematical constant denoted e, which has the value 2.71828. . . . To plot exponential functions using base e you need to calculate $y = e^x$ for various values of x. Don't type in a value for e to your calculator or computer – there are more decimal places after 2.71828. Scientific calculators have a button marked e^x. Press the e^x button, enter x and press = to

Use the MathEcon screen Exponential Functions in section 1 of chapter 2 to discover
more. The screen Economic Problems –
Equations in the following section has an example called Wine Economics where an exponential function is used to model a growth
pattern that rises and then falls over time.

get the answer. On some calculators you enter the x value and then press
the e^x button to obtain the required value. Negative exponential functions
have negative exponents. If the power is $-x$ use the $(-)$ key before entering
x, or the $+/-$ key after entering x. Try out your calculator on the worked
examples.

- The exponential function most used in economics is **Remember...**
  $y = e^x$.
- The independent variable is in the power and the base is
  the mathematical constant e = 2.71828. . . .
- Use your calculator or computer to evaluate e^x.

15

Evaluate e^x for $x = -3, -2, -1, 0, 1, 2, 3$. Sketch the curves for $y = e^x$ and
$y = e^{-x}$.

x	-3	-2	-1	0	1	2	3
e^x	0.049787	0.135335	0.367879	1	2.718282	7.389056	20.08554
e^{-x}	20.08554	7.389056	2.718282	1	0.367879	0.135335	0.049787

The curves for $y = e^x$ and $y = e^{-x}$ are plotted in figures 2.19 and 2.20. The
shape of the curve for $y = e^{-x}$ is the curve for $y = e^x$ reflected about the
y axis.

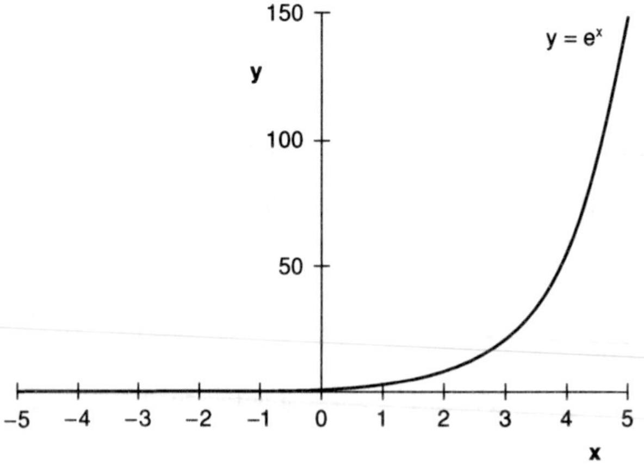

Figure 2.19   Exponential function

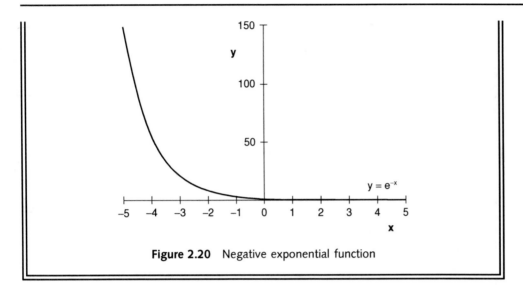

Figure 2.20   Negative exponential function

Exponential functions give us flexibility to model relationships in different ways. One application is to describe a continuous growth process where the value of y depends on the time period. The independent variable, then, is time which we denote t. If y grows at a continuous compound rate R, its value at any time t is given by $y = y_0 e^{Rt}$ where y_0 is the initial value of y and R is a decimal.

> The model is explained in section 4.3.

16

If y grows at a continuous compound rate of 12% per annum from an initial value of 50, find the value of y after 1, 3, 5 and 10 years.

We use the formula $y = y_0 e^{Rt}$ where $R = {}^{12}/_{100} = 0.12$ and $y_0 = 50$. Since R is given as an annual rate of interest, t is the time in years from the starting point. The results are:

t	1	3	5	10
$y_0 e^{Rt}$	56.37	71.67	91.11	166.01

Values of this function are calculated and plotted using Excel in the Exponentials and Logarithms worksheet of Equations.xls.

A model's earnings rise and then fall over her 12 year career, being represented t years from the start ($t = 0$) in units of $'000 by

$$y = 5e^{(1+0.5t-0.05t^2)}$$

What are her earnings in years 0, 5 and 10? Sketch a graph of her earnings over her career.

17

Substituting various values for t in the formula gives the y values listed. The graph of earnings is shown in figure 2.21.

t	0	1	3	5	7	10	12
y	13.59141	21.31557	38.83951	47.43868	38.83951	13.59141	04.093654

Her earnings in years 0, 5 and 10 are $13,591.41, $47,438.68 and $13,591.41 respectively.

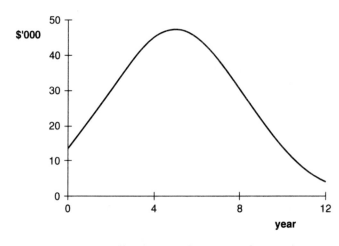

Figure 2.21 Earnings

2.18 If $Y_0 = 1000$ and t is the number of years, evaluate $Y = Y_0 e^{0.05t}$ after 1, 2, 5 and 10 years.

2.19 Evaluate $y = (1 + 1/w)^w$ when $w = 5$, $w = 50$, $w = 500$ and $w = 5000$.

> **2.20** The percentage of households, y, that have watched a programme on a new television channel t years after it starts broadcasting is modelled by
>
> $$y = 100 - 95e^{-0.5t}$$
>
> Find the percentage of households that have watched the new channel after 1 year, 3 years and 10 years.

SECTION 2.14: Logarithmic Functions

It is sometimes useful in economics to measure in variables which are the logarithms of the original units. This lets you immediately compare rates of change or growth. If a variable Y is growing at a constant rate so that its graph has a shape that curves upwards plotting the logarithm of the variable, $\log Y$, gives a straight line function. A graph with a logarithmic scale lets you immediately compare whether growth is constant, increasing or slowing down. You therefore need to be able to find the logarithms of values and you can do this using a calculator or computer.

To see what a logarithm is we express a number in exponential form, as a base raised to a power. For example, we write $1000 = 10^3$. The logarithm of the number is the exponent of the base, so that $\log 1000 = 3$ and the base used is 10.

> logarithm: the power to which you must raise the base to obtain the number whose logarithm it is.

Common logarithms use 10 as a base and are denoted log or $\log_{10}$. Using a calculator to find a logarithm, you press the key marked log or $\log_{10}$, enter the number and press =. On some calculators you enter the number first and then press the log button. Practise using these examples

$\log 1000 = 3$, $\log 1015 = 3.006$, $\log 20 = 1.3010$, $\log 10 = 1$, $\log 5 = 0.6990$

Notice that while the difference of 15 between 1015 and 1000 is the same as that between 20 and 5, the logarithms of the two larger numbers are much closer together than are the logarithms of the smaller numbers. Working with logarithms compresses large numbers more than it compresses smaller ones and can provide a better model for economic data than one using the original variables. Another important feature of logarithms is seen by comparing $\log 20$, $\log 10$ and $\log 5$. The difference of 0.3010 between $\log 20$ and $\log 10$ is the same as that between $\log 10$ and $\log 5$. Comparing the original numbers we see that 20 is twice 10, and 10 is twice 5. Equal differences between logarithms occur for the same proportional changes in the original values.

Another useful base for logarithms, as for exponential functions, is e. Logarithms to base e are called natural logarithms and are denoted either by $\log_e$ or ln. Scientific calculators have an appropriate button for obtaining values. Check the following for yourself

$$\ln 4 = 1.3862, \ln 2 = 0.6931, \ln 1 = 0, \ln 0.5 = -0.6931, \ln(e^{10}) = 10$$

By comparing the first four logarithms you can again see that pairs of numbers which are the same multiple of one another (either twice or four times) have logarithms which are the same difference apart (either 0.6931 or 1.3862). Notice also that the logarithm of 1 is 0. This is true for any base. Positive fractions, such as 0.5, have negative logarithms. You cannot find the logarithm of 0 or of negative numbers.

- Common logarithms, denoted log or $\log_{10}$, are to base 10.
- Natural logarithms, denoted ln or $\log_e$, are to base e and are more useful in analytical work.
- Equal differences between logarithms correspond to equal proportional changes in the original variables.

In MathEcon chapter 2, section 1, use the screen Logarithmic Functions for an explanation of the rules of logarithms, and to see that they are true whichever base is used. To see how useful logarithms are in economics and finance, use the MathEcon screen Trends in Levels and Logarithms, which is at the end of the third section. On the screen Economic Problems – Equations, in section 2, the Growth Ratios example models two countries growing at different growth rates. The one which initially has the larger national income grows at the slower rate and you solve an equation to find when the two countries have the same national income. The equation involves exponential functions but is easy to solve once you take logarithms. If you would like to use Excel to calculate and plot logarithmic functions you can see an example in the Exponentials and Logarithms worksheet of the Equations.xls file.

When you take the natural logarithm of an exponential function such as $\ln(e^{10})$, the result is the exponent. This verifies the definition of a natural logarithm, that if $y = e^x$, $\ln(y) = x$. To take the natural logarithm of an exponential function, you therefore simply write down the power as the answer. Consider also what happens when you evaluate $\ln(e^{10})$ in a calculator. You are finding e^{10} and then taking its natural logarithm to arrive back where you started! Exponentiating is the reverse procedure to taking the natural logarithm of a number. It follows that if you have $\ln(y)$ and want to find y, you exponentiate using the button marked e^x. Try finding $\ln 4$ and then $e^{\ln 4}$. You should get the answer 4. Given the relationship between logarithms and exponential functions, another use of logarithms is in solving equations that contain exponential functions.

Since logarithms are powers, the logarithm of a product is the sum of the logarithms, $\log(xy) = \log(x) + \log(y)$; and the logarithm of a ratio is the difference of the logarithms, $\log(x/y) = \log(x) - \log(y)$. Using the rule about the logarithm of a product we can find the logarithm of a variable raised to a power

$$\log(x^3) = \log(x \,.\, x \,.\, x) = \log(x) + \log(x) + \log(x) = 3\log(x)$$

In general this implies $\log(x^n) = n\log(x)$.

Logarithmic graphs are discussed in section 4.6.

$$\log (xy) = \log (x) + \log (y)$$

$$\log \left(\frac{x}{y}\right) = \log (x) - \log (y)$$

$$\log (x^n) = n \log (x)$$

$$\ln (e^x) = x$$

Remember...

The reverse process to taking the natural logarithm is to exponentiate.

18

A firm has the production function $Q = AL^{0.5}K^{0.4}$. Write an expression for $\ln Q$.

Using the rule $\log (xy) = \log (x) + \log (y)$ we may write

$$\ln Q = \ln A + \ln (L^{0.5}) + \ln (K^{0.4})$$

Applying the rule $\log (x^n) = n \log (x)$ gives

$$\ln Q = \ln A + 0.5 \ln L + 0.4 \ln K$$

This function is linear in the logs of the variables, which has advantages if the model is to be tested with statistical data.

19

A firm's turnover, y, at year t is described by the function $y = 30e^{0.08t}$. What is its turnover in year 0 and in year 2? After how many years will its turnover have doubled since it started trading?

At year 0 when the firm starts up its turnover is $y = 30e^0 = 30$. At year 2 its turnover is $y = 30e^{0.16} = 35.21$. We require t such that $30e^{0.08t} = 60$. Dividing both sides by 30 we obtain

$$e^{0.08t} = 2$$

Take natural logarithms of both sides

$$0.08t = \ln 2 \text{ (since } \ln (e^x) = x)$$

Evaluating $\ln 2$ gives

$$0.08t = 0.6931$$

and so

$$t = 8.66$$

After 8.66 years the firm's turnover will have doubled.

2.21 If $Y_0 = 1000$, t is the number of years and $Y = Y_0 e^{0.05t}$ evaluate $\ln(Y)$ after 1, 2, 5 and 10 years.

2.22 The percentage of households, y, that have watched a programme on a new television channel t years after it starts broadcasting is modelled by

$$y = 100 - 95e^{-0.5t}$$

After how many years will 80% of households have watched the new channel?

2.23 A model's earnings rise and then fall over her 12 year career, being represented t years from the start (in units of \$'000) by

$$y = 5e^{(1+0.5t-0.05t^2)}$$

In which years are her earnings above \$40,000?

2.24 Quantity demanded, Q, depends on price, P, and income, M, and is given by the expression $Q = 1.3P^{-2}M^{0.08}$. Find the logarithmic demand function giving an expression for $\ln Q$. What advantage could there be in using the logarithmic form?

SECTION 2.15: Plotting and Solving Equations in Excel

You can use Excel to plot equations and to look for an intersection of two curves as the solution to these equations. You can also input formulae into Excel to calculate logarithms, exponentials or the solution to a quadratic equation. Excel has an in-built tool, Solver, that we shall use to solve simultaneous equations. The worksheets described are all included in the Equations.xls workbook file on the CD.

The worksheet Supply–Demand is available for you to explore the graphs of different supply and demand functions. The functions that are plotted when you open the file are those in practice problem 2.7. You can examine other linear functions by changing the parameters. For functions in the form $Q = f(P)$ you enter the parameters in the shaded cells shown in figure 2.22. The formulae that are already entered calculate the parameters of the inverse functions and plot the lines for you. If you want to plot just one supply and demand function, enter the same parameters for both supply functions and for both demand functions.

If you wish to use this spreadsheet to plot various different demand and supply functions, you may like to save each of them using File, Save As and a different file name. Of course, the original version of the file will always be available for you on the CD.

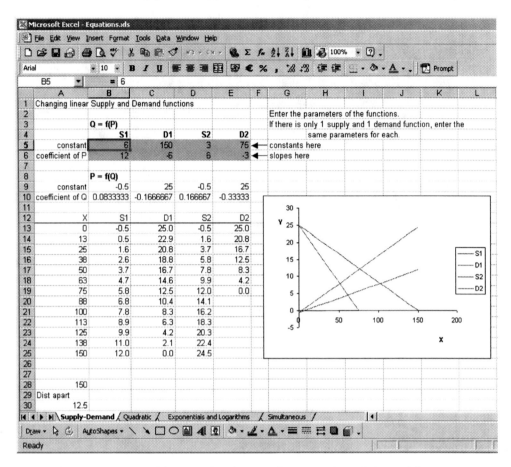

Figure 2.22 Spreadsheet to plot changing linear supply and demand functions

You know that market equilibrium is achieved when the values of price and quantity on the demand curve equal those on the supply curve, and therefore you may be looking at the table of values to see whether you can identify equilibrium points. Unless an equilibrium quantity happens to be one of the values plotted, your scrutiny of the data will not reveal the exact equilibrium values. You can, however, enter your own quantity values and the formulae will all recalculate using them. Hence, if you type 102 to replace 100 in the column of X values, you will see that the prices shown in the S_1 and D_1 columns both become 8, identifying the first equilibrium position as $Q = 102$, $P = 8$.

PLOTTING TWO FUNCTIONS ON THE SAME GRAPH

Let us plot the marginal cost function and marginal revenue function discussed in worked example 11, namely $MC = 3Q^2 - 32Q + 96$ and $MR = 236 - 16Q$. You will

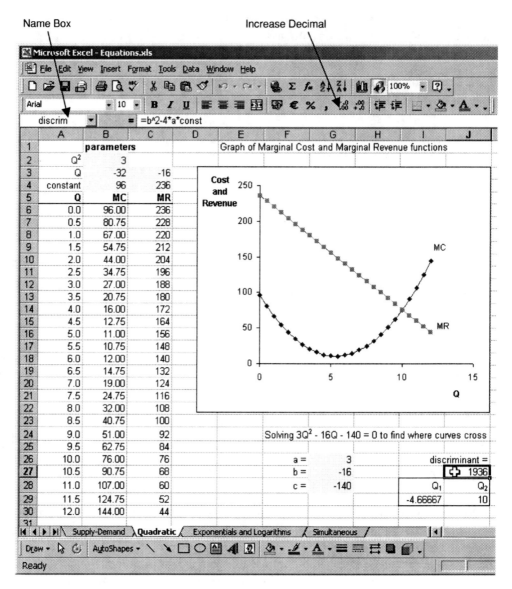

Figure 2.23 Marginal cost and marginal revenue functions
(showing Increase Decimal and Name Box)

have to guess suitable values for the Q axis, but if you wish to change them later you can do so and your calculations will then change to use the new values of Q. Values from 0 to 12 in steps of 0.5 are shown in figure 2.23 and in the Quadratic worksheet. When you fill in the values, some are integers and some have 1 decimal point. Clicking the increase decimal button shows them all with 1 decimal place.

Enter the parameters of each function at the top of the column where its values are to be calculated. Enter formulae and plot the graphs as described in section 1.13. Some formatting is needed to obtain the spreadsheet shown in figure 2.23. Label the curves by selecting the graph, typing MC (or MR) and pressing return. The text appears over the graph in a text box and you can click and drag it to the position you wish. To format an axis on a graph you select it, then right click the mouse and choose Format Axis. Choose the Number tab and reduce the number of decimal places to 0. To subscript or superscript items in Excel you select the individual item, then choose Format Cells and the Number tab where you can check the appropriate box.

SOLVING A QUADRATIC EQUATION

You can enter formulae in Excel to calculate the two possible solutions to a quadratic equation. In the formula

$$x = \frac{-b \pm \sqrt{b^2 - 4ac}}{2a}$$

the term $b^2 - 4ac$ is called the discriminant and it is convenient to calculate it first. To make formulae easier to understand you can name cells and use the names instead of cell references. By default, names are interpreted in Excel as absolute cell references. To name a cell, select it, type its name in the Name Box and press the Enter key. In the Quadratic worksheet cells have been named a, b, const and discrim. It is not possible to use c or r as cell names in Excel, since they stand for 'column' and 'row'. The formula typed to calculate the discriminant is then =b^2-4*a*const and the formulae for the two values of Q are =(-b-discrim^0.5)/(2*a) and =(-b+discrim^0.5)/(2*a).

EXPONENTIAL AND LOGARITHMIC FUNCTIONS

Excel includes many in-built functions that you can type in or access by clicking the Paste Function button. Those for exponentials and logarithms are =EXP() and =LN() where the cell reference for the value to which the function is to be applied goes inside the brackets. Figure 2.24 shows calculations that are available in the Exponentials and Logarithms worksheet for the function discussed in worked example 16. The function is $y = y_0 e^{Rt}$ where $R = 0.12$ and $y_0 = 50$.

Since R is an annual rate we let t equal the value of the year and fill in values from 0 to 10 in steps of 0.5. R and y_0 are parameters of the model, so we enter them in suitable cells ready to use them in our calculations. We first calculate Rt, entering the formula =$B$2*A5 in B5. We then enter the formula =EXP(B5) in the adjacent cell C5, and in D5 we enter the formula =$D$2*C5 to multiply by the value of y_0. These formulae can all be simultaneously copied down their columns and the graph of f(t) is then plotted. Values of the natural logarithm of f(t) are found by entering the formula =LN(D5) in E5 and copying it down. Notice that the graph of the logarithmic function is a straight line.

Paste Function

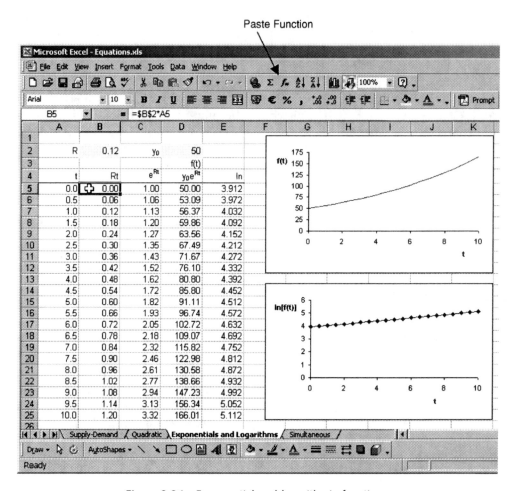

Figure 2.24   Exponential and logarithmic functions

SOLVING EQUATIONS WITH EXCEL SOLVER

Excel includes a Solver tool that is designed to solve a set of equations or inequalities. You can use it to solve two simultaneous equations if you set out the data they contain in a suitable format. Finding the solution is then just a matter of interacting with the Solver dialogue box. Having a computer to find a solution for you is very convenient, but do make sure that you can also solve the equations by hand in case you need to do so. Excel does not actually solve the equations the same way as you do when working by hand. It uses an iterative method, trying out different possible values for the variables to see if they fit the requirements you have specified. We discover how to use Excel by applying it to the equations in worked example 13.

We designate a column for each variable and a row for each equation as shown in figure 2.25 and the worksheet Simultaneous. For each equation, enter the coefficients

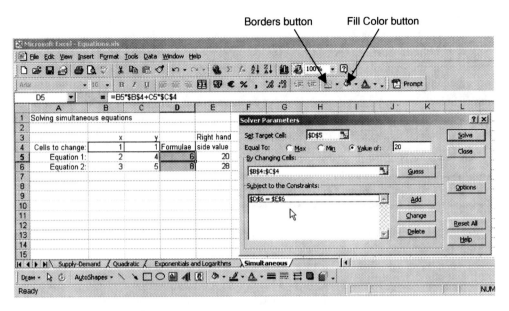

Figure 2.25 Using Solver to solve simultaneous equations
(showing Borders button, Fill Color button)

of the variables in the appropriate cells as shown, and enter the right-hand side values of the equations in column E. Each number requires a separate cell so that it can be used in calculations.

Now choose a cell to contain the value of each variable. In figure 2.25 these are B4 for x and C4 for y. They have been outlined with a box (using the Borders button) to help you identify them. Excel needs a trial value in each of these cells to start its solution process, so the value 1 has been entered in the cells. When the solution is found the trial values are replaced by the solution values of x and y. Solver also needs to know how to calculate the left-hand side of each equation, and to provide this information we must enter formulae using cell addresses. The formula in cell D5 is =B5*$B$4+C5*$C$4 and the forms of addresses chosen make it possible to copy it to cell D6. These cells containing the formulae are shaded using the Fill Color button to help you identify them.

We are now ready to use Solver to obtain the solution. The first time you use Solver you have to make it available by choosing Tools, Add-Ins on the menu, checking the Solver box and clicking OK. You can now choose Tools, Solver to bring up the Solver dialogue box. You set the Solver choices in turn, clicking first in a Solver box and then on the cell or cells in the spreadsheet that it is to use. These cells are outlined or shaded in figure 2.25. Solver is designed to solve more complex problems than ours but we can use it by regarding one of our equations as the target and the other as a constraint. The various steps in the process are set out below.

Click in the Set Target Cell box and then click on the spreadsheet cell containing one of the equation formulae, say D5. Choose Equal to Value of, and type in the right-hand side value which is **20**. Next click in the By Changing Cells box and select the cells containing the trial values of x and y. Click in the Subject to the Constraints box and choose Add. Enter the second equation as a constraint, clicking on the cell containing its formula, D6, for the Cell Reference, choosing the equals sign and selecting the right-hand side value as the Constraint. Clicking OK returns you to the main Solver dialogue box shown in figure 2.25. You can now choose Solve to let Solver find the solution. The values $x = 6$ and $y = 2$ appear in the outlined cells, and the Solver Results box tells you that Solver found a solution.

Chapter 2: Answers to Practice Problems

2.1   Plotting the points in the table and joining them gives the lines shown in figure 2.26.

x	$y = 12 + 5x$	$y = 22 + 4x$
0	12	22
20	112	102

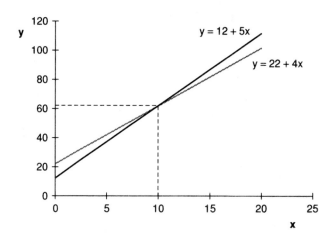

Figure 2.26

Using algebra

$$12 + 5x = 22 + 4x$$

$$12 + x = 22 \ (4x \text{ subtracted from both sides})$$

$$x = 10$$

Substitute this in $y = 12 + 5x$

$$y = 12 + 5(10) = 62$$

2.2 (a) $5(7 - 3x) = x$ (both sides multiplied by 5 to remove the fraction)

$35 - 15x = x$

$x = 35 - 15x$ (sides interchanged)

$16x = 35$ ($15x$ added to both sides)

$x = 2\frac{3}{16}$

(b) $x - 0.8x = 20$

$x(1 - 0.8) = 20$

$0.2x = 20$

$x = 100$ (both sides multiplied by 5)

(c) $9x^2 = 4$ (both sides multiplied by $9x$)

$x^2 = 4/9$

Taking the square root of both sides we must remember that either two positive or two negative values multiply together to give a positive. This implies

$x = \frac{2}{3}$ or $x = -\frac{2}{3}$

(d) $3.28x = 82$ ($4x - 150$ added to both sides)

$x = 25$

(e) $x = 625 + 0.5x$ (terms collected on the right-hand side)

$0.5x = 625$ ($0.5x$ subtracted from both sides)

$x = 1250$ (both sides multiplied by 2)

2.3 (a) $6x = 12 - y$ (y subtracted from both sides)

$x = (12 - y)/6 = 2 - y/6$ (both sides divided by 6)

(b) $8x = 24 - y$ ($8x - y$ added to both sides)

$x = (24 - y)/8 = 3 - y/8$ (both sides divided by 8)

2.4 $y = 1.5p^{0.5} \cdot p/(p^{1.5})$ (substitution for q)

$y = 1.5p^{1.5}/(p^{1.5})$ (terms collected)

$y = 1.5$ (terms in p cancelled)

2.5 $Y = (40 + 0.8Y) + 350$ (substitution for C)

$= 390 + 0.8Y$

$0.2Y = 390$ ($0.8Y$ subtracted from both sides)

$Y = 1950$ (both sides multiplied by 5)

2.6   Supply: $4P = Q$ (sides interchanged)

so $P = Q/4$

Demand: $10P = 280 - Q$ ($10P - Q$ added to both sides)

so $P = 28 - Q/10$

Figure 2.27 is plotted from the values shown in the table

	Supply	Demand
Q	$P = Q/4$	$P = 28 - Q/10$
0	0	28
280	70	0

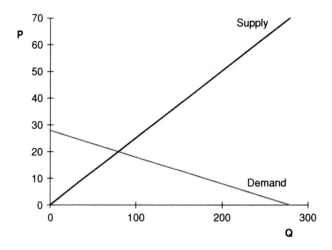

Figure 2.27

2.7   Supply: $P = Q_s/12 - 0.5$ (curve S_1 in figure 2.28)

Demand: $P = 25 - Q_d/6$ (curve D_1)

Equilibrium is at A, where $Q = 102$, $P = 8$.

Reduction in supply: new supply function is $Q_{s2} = 3 + 6P$ or $P = Q_{s2}/6 - 0.5$ (curve S_2)

New equilibrium is where $Q_{s2} = Q_d$. This occurs at B, with $Q = 76.5$, $P = 12.25$.

Reduced demand: new demand function is $Q_{d2} = 75 - 3P$ or $P = 25 - Q_{d2}/3$ (curve D_2)

New equilibrium is where $Q_{s2} = Q_{d2}$. This occurs at C, with $Q = 51$, $P = 8$. Notice that price is now the same as it was originally, and quantity is half what was traded at point A.

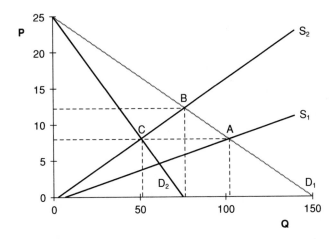

Figure 2.28

2.8   In equilibrium, $Q_s = Q_d$

so $2P - 4 = 66 - 3P$

$5P = 70$ $(3P + 4$ added to both sides)

$P = 14$

Substitution gives

$Q_s = 2(14) - 4 = 24$

After tax supply curve is

$Q_{s2} = 2(P - 5) - 4$ $(P - 5$ written for $P)$

$Q_{s2} = 2P - 14$

The new equilibrium is where $Q_{s2} = Q_d$

$2P - 14 = 66 - 3P$

$5P = 80$ $(3P + 14$ added to both sides)

$P = 16$

Substitution in the new supply curve gives

$Q_{s2} = 2(16) - 14 = 18$

Price rises by 2 when the sales tax of 5 is imposed and quantity traded falls from 24 to 18.

2.9 $Q = (\pi + FC)/(P - AVC)$

$Q = (20 + 328)/(12 - 8)$ (by substituting $\pi = 20$, $FC = 328$, $P = 12$, $AVC = 8$)

$Q = 348/4 = 87$

$TR = P . Q = 12Q$

TC = FC + AVC . Q = 328 + 8Q

π = TR – TC = 12Q – 328 – 8Q

π = 4Q – 328

As a check, substitute Q = 87

π = 348 – 328 = 20

which is the target profit. To find the break-even Q, substitute π = 0 in the expression for Q, keeping the other values as before

Q = (0 + 328)/(12 – 8) = 328/4 = 82

2.10 (a) Slope 4, intercept 12, y = 4x + 12.

   (b) Slope –2, intercept 45, y = 45 – 2x.

   (c) Slope 1. For intercept: Δy = slope.Δx; substitute Δx = –5 to give Δy = (1)(–5) = –5; intercept = y + Δy = 8 – 5 = 3. Therefore, y = x + 3.

2.11 Using x values for the points listed, the points on the line are (10,14) (6,42) (5,49). Of the points listed, the first lies on the line but the others do not.

2.12 Budget line: 37.5x + 2y = 750, or y = 375 – 18.75x. This is plotted with the indifference curve in figure 2.29. Substituting the x and y combinations given into the utility function, we find U = 30 at each point, as shown in the table. Substituting the x values into the equation for the budget line gives the budget line y values listed. The point (8,225) lies on the budget line and is in fact the optimal consumption position for the consumer. For each of the other points, y > 375 – 18.75x. These points give equal utility, but lie above the budget line so they cannot be afforded.

x	y	$x^{1/3}$	$y^{1/2}$	U	Budget line y
1	900	1	30	30	356.25
8	225	2	15	30	225
27	100	3	10	30	–131.25

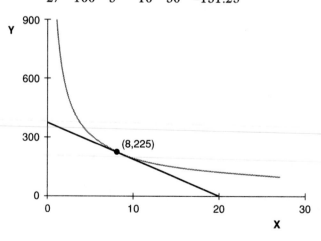

Figure 2.29

2.13 (a) $x = \dfrac{18 \pm \sqrt{(-18)^2 - 4(3)(15)}}{2(3)}$

$x = 1$ or $x = 5$.

(b) $x = \dfrac{12 \pm \sqrt{(-12)^2 - 4(4)(9)}}{2(4)}$

Just one solution, $x = 1.5$, since $(-12)^2 - (4)(4)(9) = 0$.

(c) Since there is no term in x, the formula is unnecessary:

$16x^2 = 64$ gives $x^2 = 4$, so $x = 2$ or $x = -2$.

(d) $x = \dfrac{-6 \pm \sqrt{6^2 - 4(-8)(50)}}{2(-8)} = \dfrac{-6 \pm \sqrt{36 + 1600}}{-16}$

$= \dfrac{34.45}{-16}$ or $\dfrac{-46.447}{-16}$

$x = -2.153$ or $x = 2.903$.

(e) $7x^2 - 63x = 7x(x - 9) = 0$ (factorizing)

$x = 0$ or $x = 9$.

(f) $x = \dfrac{9 \pm \sqrt{(-9)^2 - 4(5)(18)}}{2(5)} = \dfrac{9 \pm \sqrt{81 - 360}}{10}$

No solution, since $81 - 360 = -279$ and we cannot take the square root of a negative number.

(g) $x = \dfrac{-10 \pm \sqrt{10^2 - 4(-3)(25)}}{2(-3)} = \dfrac{-10 \pm \sqrt{100 + 300}}{-6}$

$= \dfrac{10}{-6}$ or $\dfrac{-30}{-6}$

$x = -1.667$ or $x = 5$.

2.14 MC = MR (condition for profit maximization)

$1.6Q^2 - 15Q + 60 = 280 - 20Q$

$1.6Q^2 + 5Q - 220 = 0$

$Q = \dfrac{-5 \pm \sqrt{5^2 - 4(1.6)(-220)}}{2(1.6)} = -13.392$ or 10.267

Only 10.267 is economically meaningful. It is the required output.

2.15 AVC = MC (intersection is at minimum supply price)

$1.4Q^2 - 24Q + 250 = 4.2Q^2 - 48Q + 250$

$-2.8Q^2 + 24Q = 0$

$$Q(-2.8Q + 24) = 0$$

$$Q = 0 \text{ or } Q = 8.5714$$

The value that is economically meaningful is 8.5714. Substitute it in MC.

$$MC = 4.2(8.5714)^2 - 48(8.5714) + 250 = 147.14$$

which is the minimum supply price.

2.16   (a) $y = 19 - 7x$ (by rewriting the second equation)

        $4x + 5(19 - 7x) = 33$ (substituting for y in the first equation)

        $4x + 95 - 35x = 33$ (by multiplying out)

        $-31x = -62$ (by collecting terms and subtracting 95 from both sides)

          $x = 2$

        $y = 19 - 7(2) = 5$ (substituting for x in the second equation)

        Check using the first equation

        $4(2) + 5(5) = 33 = $ right-hand side

        Therefore, the solution $x = 2$, $y = 5$ is correct.

   (b) $8x + 44y = 288$ (by multiplying the first equation by 4)

        $8x + 12y = 96$ (the second equation)

        $0x + 32y = 192$ (by subtraction)

        $32y = 192$

          $y = 6$

        $8x + 12(6) = 96$ (substituting for y in the second equation)

               $8x = 24$ (by subtracting 72 from both sides)

          $x = 3$

        Check using the first equation

        $2(3) + 11(6) = 72 = $ right-hand side

        Therefore, the solution $x = 3$, $y = 6$ is correct.

   (c) Add the two equations

        $15x + 0y = 66$

          $15x = 66$

            $x = 4.4$

$5(4.4) + 2y = 40$ (substituting for x in the second equation)

$2y = 18$ (by subtracting 22 from both sides)

$y = 9$

Check using the first equation

$10(4.4) - 2(9) = 26$ = right-hand side

Therefore, the solution $x = 4.4$, $y = 9$ is correct.

(d) Multiplying the first equation by 3 gives $3(2x + 8y) = 3 \times 46$

or $6x + 24y = 138$

Multiplying the second equation by 2 gives $2(3x + 12y) = 2 \times 69$

or $6x + 24y = 138$

The second equation is the first equation multiplied by 1.5, so in fact the two equations are the same and we cannot find a unique solution.

2.17   For boots market equilibrium

$Q_{Sb} = Q_{Db}$

$-56 + 2P_b = 87 - \frac{1}{6}P_b + \frac{1}{5}P_t$

Adding $56 + \frac{1}{6}P_b - \frac{1}{5}P_t$ to both sides

$2.1667P_b - 0.2P_t = 143$ (1)

For trainers market equilibrium

$Q_{St} = Q_{Dt}$

$110 + 2P_t = 417 - 3P_t + \frac{1}{4}P_b$

Adding $3P_t - \frac{1}{4}P_b - 110$ to both sides

$-0.25P_b + 5P_t = 307$ (2)

$54.1667P_b - 5P_t = 3575$ (multiplying equation (1) by 25)

$53.9167P_b = 3882$ (adding these equations)

$P_b = 72$, $P_t = 65$, $Q_b = 88$, $Q_t = 240$.

2.18   1051.271, 1105.171, 1284.025, 1648.721

2.19   2.48832, 2.691588, 2.715569, 2.71801

Notice that the values are getting closer to 2.71828. . . . As w becomes infinitely large the expression gives the value of e.

2.20 42.38%, 78.80%, 99.36%

2.21 $\ln \Upsilon = \ln \Upsilon_0 + 0.05t = 6.9078 + 0.05t$. Hence values of $\ln (\Upsilon)$ after 1, 2, 5 and 10 years are 6.9578, 7.0078, 7.1578 and 7.4078 respectively. These values lie on a straight line.

2.22 We require

$$100 - 95e^{-0.5t} = 80$$

$$-95e^{-0.5t} = -20$$

$$e^{-0.5t} = 0.2105 \text{ (both sides divided by } -95)$$

$$-0.5t = -1.5581 \text{ (by taking natural logarithms)}$$

$$t = 3.1 \text{ years}$$

2.23 A graph of this data is plotted in figure 2.21. If we can find two years with earnings at \$40,000, between those years she earns above that amount. Solve for t

$$40 = 5e^{(1+0.5t-0.05t^2)}$$

$$8 = e^{(1+0.5t-0.05t^2)}$$

$\ln 8 = 1 + 0.5t - 0.05t^2$ (taking natural logarithms)

$0.05t^2 - 0.5t + 1.0794 = 0$

$$t = 3.2 \text{ and } 6.8$$

In year 3 her earnings have not yet reached \$40,000, and in year 7 they fall below that level. In years 4, 5 and 6 her earnings exceed \$40,000.

2.24 $\ln Q = \ln 1.3 - 2 \ln P + 0.08 \ln M$ (by taking natural logarithms)

$\ln Q = 0.262 - 2 \ln P + 0.08 \ln M$

Using variables transformed to logarithms, the demand function is linear and, therefore, easier to estimate. This model may be the most appropriate one for particular data. There is also an advantage in estimating elasticities, as we see in section 8.8 Logarithmic demand functions.

chapter three
Macroeconomic Models

OBJECTIVES

In this chapter you learn to
- Appreciate the role of macroeconomic modelling
- Understand the notation used throughout this book for macroeconomic models
- Write down a condition for macroeconomic equilibrium, substitute and then solve to find equilibrium income
- Use Keynesian cross models to analyse the goods market
- Apply IS–LM analysis, which includes the money market

SECTION 3.1: Introduction

This chapter shows how a simple economy can be modelled by a set of simultaneous equations. We specify a condition for macroeconomic equilibrium and solve the equations to find equilibrium values for national income, consumption and other macroeconomic variables. There are no new mathematical techniques in this chapter. You apply the rules of algebra and the methods of solving equations that you have already learnt. A study of macroeconomic models often involves finding multipliers. We postpone this until chapters 5 and 8 so that we can find multipliers using the differentiation techniques you learn in those chapters.

You can use the MathEcon screens to study how the equilibrium level of national income is determined. The macroeconomic analysis is presented with diagrams and also as numerical models. Work through both approaches and check that the results correspond. Discover how various functional relationships are typically represented in section 2 of chapter 3, and see how the circular flow of income works. Study the Keynesian cross model which provides a representation of the goods sector of the economy in section 4. Section 5 extends the description of the economy to include the money market. You derive the LM and IS equations, and solve them to obtain values of income, Y, and rate of interest, R, at which equilibrium is achieved simultaneously in both the money market and the goods market. There are no Excel spreadsheets for this chapter, but you can use the methods described in sections 1.13 and 2.15 if you would like to plot the functions for yourself.

SECTION 3.2: Notation and Model Specification

Macroeconomic models throughout this book are specified using the following notation:

$$Y = \text{income}$$

$$Y_d = \text{disposable income}$$

$$AD = \text{aggregate demand}$$

$$C = \text{consumer expenditure}$$

$$I = \text{investment expenditure}$$

$$G = \text{government expenditure}$$

$$X = \text{exports}$$

$$Z = \text{imports}$$

$$T = \text{total net direct taxation}$$

$$t = \text{rate of income tax}$$

$$S = \text{saving}$$

$$W = \text{withdrawals}$$

$$J = \text{injections}$$

$$R = \text{rate of interest}$$

$$MD = \text{total demand for money}$$

$$MS = \text{money supply}$$

This notation is identical with that used in MathEcon, apart from the addition of the term Y_d to identify disposable income. We shall be building simple models to illustrate different aspects of how the economy works. Not all of the above terms will occur in every model.

The term Y represents national income, the income that goes to households in return for their contribution to the production of goods and services in the economy.

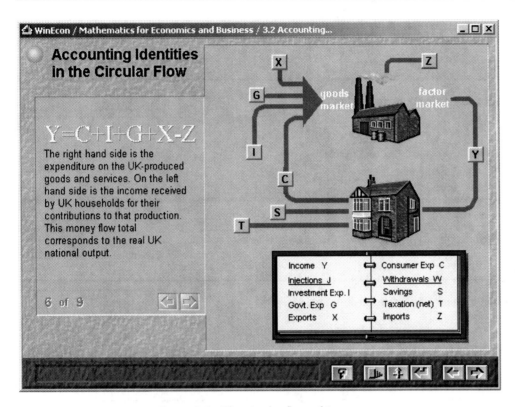

Figure 3.1 The circular flow of income

This money flow corresponds to real national output, and so Y also represents aggregate output. This is explained on the MathEcon screen shown in figure 3.1.

Due to government activity, not all of the national income is available to people to spend. Direct taxation is taken out of the income flow before it reaches households. This is the only form of taxation in our models. The government may also distribute some benefits such as social security payments, which in effect are negative taxes. For simplicity, T incorporates these and is defined as total direct taxation net of any benefit payments. T represents the net flow from the household sector to the government after allowing for social security benefits.

In this book we model T in one of two ways. The first is that T is fixed, as occurs if taxation takes the form of a lump sum tax or poll tax. Alternatively we may specify an income tax at rate t, where we write t as a decimal and assume the same rate of tax applies to all income.

The proportional income tax model is described on the MathEcon screen titled Taxation.

Under a proportional income tax model

$$T = tY$$

Remember...

The income that is then available for people to spend or save as they wish is called disposable income.

Disposable income is defined as   **Remember...**

$$Y_d = Y - T$$

or, with a proportional income tax

$$Y_d = (1 - t)Y$$

Disposable income is either consumed or saved.

Using a linear consumption function we write   **Remember...**

$$C = a + bY_d$$

Substituting $Y_d = Y - T$ shows that consumption is also a function of income, namely

$$C = a + b(Y - T)$$

This is shown on MathEcon screen Consumer Demand and Disposable Income in section 2 of chapter 3.

We can identify b, the coefficient of Y_d in the consumption function, as the marginal propensity to consume out of disposable income. It is the slope of the line and so represents the fraction of a change in disposable income which is used for consumption. We write $b = \Delta C / \Delta Y_d$. If there is no taxation in the economy being modelled, $Y_d = Y$ and the consumption function relates consumption directly to income. We have

$$C = a + bY$$

if there is no taxation.

Since whatever is not consumed is saved, saving is defined   **Remember...**
by

$$S = Y_d - C$$
$$= Y - T - C$$

This is shown in MathEcon on the screen titled Saving. Substituting for C in the expression for saving gives

$$S = Y_d - (a + bY_d)$$

which on taking the sign through the bracket becomes

$$S = Y_d - a - bY_d$$

and so collecting terms we have

$$S = -a + (1 - b)Y_d$$

which is the saving function, expressing saving as a function of disposable income. The coefficient of Y_d, which is $(1 - b)$, gives the slope of the line. This represents $\Delta S/\Delta Y_d$ and so $(1 - b)$ is the marginal propensity to save out of disposable income.

For the consumption function $C = a + bY_d$ **Remember...**

- the marginal propensity to consume out of disposable income is b
- the saving function is $S = -a + (1 - b)Y_d$
- and the marginal propensity to save out of disposable income is $1 - b$.

1

In an economy where the consumption function is $C = 30 + 0.65Y_d$, what is the marginal propensity to consume out of disposable income? If disposable income increases from 1400 to 1500, what is the change in consumption? Check your answer by comparing the two levels of consumption.

The marginal propensity to consume out of disposable income is $0.65 = \Delta C/\Delta Y_d$. Multiplying both sides by ΔY_d, we find that ΔC is given by

$$\Delta C = 0.65 \times \Delta Y_d$$

Since $\Delta Y_d = 1500 - 1400 = 100$, substituting this gives

$$\Delta C = 0.65 \times 100 = 65$$

which is the change in consumption. To check we calculate the two levels of consumption. If $Y_d = 1400$

$$C = 30 + 0.65 \times 1400 = 940$$

and if $Y_d = 1500$

$$C = 30 + 0.65 \times 1500 = 1005$$

The change in consumption is $1005 - 940 = 65$, as before.

The consumption function for a simple economy is given by $C = 310 + 0.7Y_d$.

(a) Write an expression for saving in the economy. Sketch the consumption and saving functions if there is no direct taxation.

(b) Express consumption in terms of Y when direct taxation is levied (i) as a lump sum tax, $T = 300$, or (ii) as a proportional income tax, $t = 0.4$. Add these consumption functions to your diagram showing the consumption function without taxation, and comment.

2

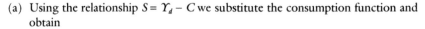

(a) Using the relationship $S = Y_d - C$ we substitute the consumption function and obtain

$$S = Y_d - (310 + 0.7Y_d) = Y_d - 310 - 0.7Y_d$$

Collecting terms gives the saving function

$$S = -310 + 0.3Y_d$$

With no direct taxation $Y_d = Y$ and the consumption and saving functions become

$$C = 310 + 0.7Y$$

$$S = -310 + 0.3Y$$

These are plotted in figures 3.2 and 3.3 respectively.

(b) (i) With direct taxation $Y_d = Y - T$. When $T = 300$ the consumption function becomes

$$C = 310 + 0.7(Y - 300) \text{ or}$$

$$C = 310 + 0.7Y - 210 = 100 + 0.7Y$$

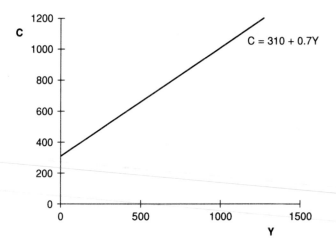

Figure 3.2 Consumption function, no taxation

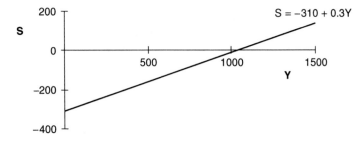

Figure 3.3 Saving function, no taxation

This line is identified as the lump sum tax line on figure 3.4. A lump sum tax shifts the consumption function down parallel to the original consumption function.

(ii) Using the relationship that with a proportional income tax $Y_d = (1 - t)Y$, since $t = 0.4$ we have $Y_d = (1 - 0.4)Y = 0.6Y$. Substituting this in the consumption function gives

$$C = 310 + (0.7 \times 0.6Y) = 310 + 0.42Y$$

The line $C = 310 + 0.42Y$ is identified as the income tax line on figure 3.4. It has the same intercept but a shallower slope than the original consumption function. Raising an income tax makes the consumption function pivot downwards.

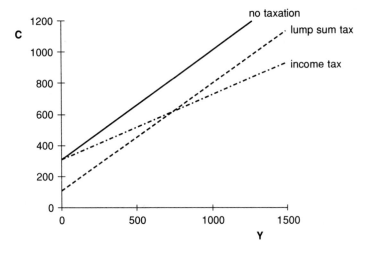

Figure 3.4 Consumption function under different taxation systems

Some variables are exogenous, meaning that their values are determined outside the model being used. Throughout this book, government expenditure, G, and exports, X, are treated as exogenous variables. Some of our models consider taxation, T, and investment, I, to be fixed and therefore exogenous. In other models (for example, with a proportional income tax) these variables are endogenous, meaning that their value is determined within the model. In section 3.5 we see that I may be a function of the rate of interest, R, or income, Y, or both. The term autonomous, meaning independent of income, is used to describe the constant term in an expression for a macroeconomic variable.

---

exogenous variable: its value is determined outside the model.
endogenous variable: its value is determined within the model.
autonomous: independent of the level of income and therefore exogenous.

We represent exogenous variables in our models just using the appropriate letters in the list above.   **Remember...**

Demand for goods and services comes from consumers, forming consumption expenditure, C; from firms undertaking investment expenditure, I; and also from the government, whose expenditure is denoted G. If part of our economy's output is sold overseas we must add exports, X, to aggregate demand, while if part of our domestic expenditure is on goods or services produced overseas these imports, Z, must be subtracted since they do not form part of the national product of our economy.

Aggregate demand for home produced goods and services is therefore given by   **Remember...**

$$AD = C + I + G + X - Z$$

The key feature of aggregate demand is that it is a function of income, Y. We have already seen how consumption and sometimes investment are modelled as functions of income. Imports, Z, are also usually considered to show a positive linear relationship with Y.

Investment, government expenditure and exports are types of expenditure generated outside the circular flow of income of the economy. They constitute injections into the circular flow and, taken together, they are designated J. By contrast, money flows out of the circular flow of income are called withdrawals, W. These occur through saving, taxation and imports.

Injections and withdrawals are defined as follows   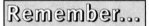 **Remember...**

$$J = I + G + X$$

$$W = S + T + Z$$

The government's surplus is measured as its income from taxation minus its expenditure on goods and services, that is, by $T - G$. If this quantity is negative, the government is running a deficit. To examine the private sector financial balance we compare S and I. When firms spend more on investment than households save, a deficit occurs. Similarly we find the foreign trade balance by computing $X - Z$. If exports X are greater than imports Z there is a foreign trade surplus.

Terms comprising withdrawals and injections are defined together with aggregate demand in section 2 of MathEcon chapter 3 on the screen Accounting Identities in the Circular Flow. The screen Aggregate Demand in the Goods Market has a numerical example. The model shown does not include taxation and considers I, G and X to be autonomous. Since C and Z are functions of income you find that AD is a function of Y and that the coefficient of Y is the marginal propensity to consume minus the marginal propensity to import.

$T - G$ = government budget surplus   **Remember...**
$S - I$ = surplus in the private sector financial balance
$X - Z$ = foreign trade surplus

The Keynesian cross model which we study in section 3.4 does not include the money market. The terms MD (representing the total demand for money) and MS (the supply of money) are used in section 3.5 when we develop the IS–LM model.

3

In an economy with no direct taxation or government expenditure, consumption is given by $C = 30 + 0.84Y$ and imports are given by $Z = 15 + 0.12Y$. If $Y = 500$, $I = 40$ and $X = 85$, find the values of C, S and Z. What is the foreign trade surplus? Show whether $W = J$.

Substituting $Y = 500$ in the consumption function gives

$$C = 30 + (0.84 \times 500) = 30 + 420 = 450$$

Since there is no direct taxation, $S = Y - C$ and substituting we obtain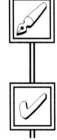

$$S = 500 - 450 = 50$$

Using the import function and substituting for Y we get

$$Z = 15 + (0.12 \times 500) = 15 + 60 = 75$$

$$\text{foreign trade surplus} = X - Z = 85 - 75 = 10$$

In this model with no government activity

$$W = S + Z = 50 + 75 = 125 \text{ and}$$

$$J = I + X = 40 + 85 = 125$$

which shows $W = J$.

3.1 A simple economy with no taxation has the consumption function

$$C = 90 + 0.75Y$$

What is the marginal propensity to consume? Find an expression for the savings function. If $Y = 800$, what is the level of consumption and saving in the economy?

3.2 The consumption function for an economy is modelled as $C = 25 + 0.8Y_d$. The government raises 220 in lump sum direct taxation and spends 240 on goods and services. There is private sector investment of 355.

What is the marginal propensity to consume out of disposable income? What is the government's budget surplus or deficit? If $Y_d = 2000$ find the values of Y, S, W and J.

Suppose the government decides to replace the lump sum tax by a proportional income tax. Assuming Y is unchanged, what tax rate would produce the same amount of tax revenue?

SECTION 3.3: Identifying Equilibrium Income

Macroeconomic equilibrium occurs when total planned spending or aggregate demand in a particular time period, AD, matches the flow of income, Y, generated by the production of output in the economy. The equilibrium condition can therefore be stated as $Y = \text{AD}$.

The key to finding the level of income at which macroeconomic equilibrium occurs is to write the expression for AD and recognize that some of the components of expenditure are themselves functions of income. We solve a set of simultaneous equations about the economy by substituting appropriately, collecting terms that include Υ and thus solving for Υ. Our general model is

$$AD = C + I + G + X - Z$$

and so the macroeconomic equilibrium condition implies

$$\Upsilon = C + I + G + X - Z$$

In any particular case we substitute in the right-hand side of AD as appropriate. After then substituting for AD in the equilibrium condition, we collect terms containing Υ on the left-hand side of the equation and solve for Υ. We shall always solve for macroeconomic equilibrium using the requirement that $\Upsilon = AD$. The method is a general one that is used in sections 3.4 and 3.5 and again in chapters 5 and 8 when we find multipliers.

This is stated as an identity on card 6 of the MathEcon screen Accounting Identities in the Circular Flow.

The method is described on the MathEcon screen Solution Method 1: Aggregate Demand equals Aggregate Output/Income.

Remember...

To find equilibrium income:

- State the equilibrium condition $\Upsilon = AD$.
- Write an expression for aggregate demand: $AD = C + I + G + X - Z$
- and by substituting the components, obtain term(s) containing Υ.
- Substitute for AD in the equilibrium condition.
- Collect terms in Υ on the left-hand side and solve for Υ.

Another macroeconomic equilibrium requirement, ensuring that plans are satisfied, is that withdrawals equal injections, $W = J$. This condition provides an alternative approach to finding equilibrium and we shall use it as a cross-check. The method is to write expressions for W and J and substitute into them as appropriate. Notice that this method requires you to find the value of savings, which may not be explicitly specified.

This alternative approach is explained on the MathEcon screen Solution Method 2: Planned Withdrawals equals Planned Injections. Card 3 points out that although in the model shown all injections are autonomous, this need not be so.

SECTION 3.4: Keynesian Cross Model

We now use the Keynesian cross model to study the interrelationship between expenditure and income. The algebraic approach outlined in section 3.3 is used to determine equilibrium income. The effects of certain changes in planned expenditure are also investigated. We can check that our results correspond to those found by diagrammatic analysis. When aggregate demand, AD, is plotted on the vertical axis against Υ, which measures income and actual output, on the horizontal axis, macroeconomic equilibrium occurs where these are equal. Using equal scales on the axes, possible equilibrium positions

Once you have found equilibrium income you substitute to find values for the other variables, as shown on the MathEcon screen Equilibrium Values for Other Variables.

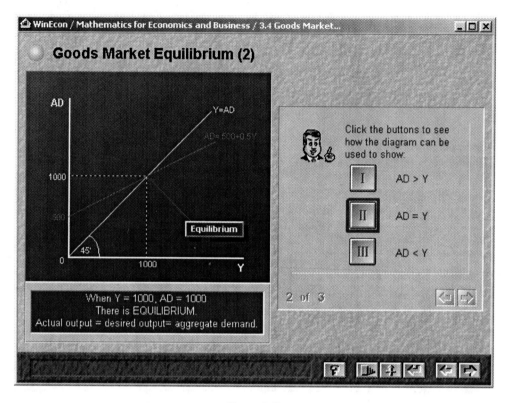

Figure 3.5

fall on a line at 45° to the Y axis. Equilibrium income corresponds to the point at which the AD function cuts the 45° line. The diagrammatic approach is explained on the MathEcon screen shown in figure 3.5.

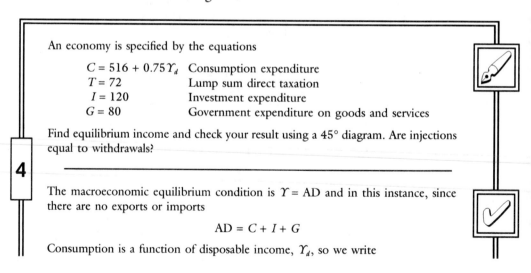

An economy is specified by the equations

$C = 516 + 0.75Y_d$	Consumption expenditure
$T = 72$	Lump sum direct taxation
$I = 120$	Investment expenditure
$G = 80$	Government expenditure on goods and services

Find equilibrium income and check your result using a 45° diagram. Are injections equal to withdrawals?

4

The macroeconomic equilibrium condition is $Y = AD$ and in this instance, since there are no exports or imports

$$AD = C + I + G$$

Consumption is a function of disposable income, Y_d, so we write

$$Y_d = Y - T = Y - 72$$

Substituting this in the consumption function gives an expression in Y

$$C = 516 + 0.75(Y - 72) = 516 + 0.75Y - 54$$

and so

$$C = 462 + 0.75Y$$

As we substitute for C, I and G the expression for aggregate demand becomes

$$AD = 462 + 0.75Y + 120 + 80$$

Collecting terms we obtain

$$AD = 662 + 0.75Y$$

Substituting in the equilibrium condition we find

$$Y = 662 + 0.75Y$$

Subtracting $0.75Y$ from both sides gives

$$(1 - 0.75)Y = 662$$

and so

$$0.25Y = 662$$

and dividing by 0.25 we find $Y = 2648$, which is the equilibrium income.
The diagrammatic approach plots AD against Y as shown in figure 3.6.

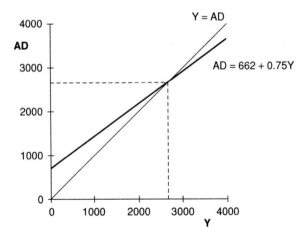

Figure 3.6

By dropping a vertical to the Y axis from the point at which AD cuts the 45° line we can read off the Y value representing equilibrium income. It is 2648, as we found algebraically.

We now separately evaluate injections, J, and withdrawals, W, to see if they are equal. For this closed economy

$$J = I + G = 120 + 80 = 200$$

and

$$W = S + T$$

We find S using the relationship

$$S = Y_d - C$$

We can now evaluate Y_d and C

$$Y_d = Y - T = 2648 - 72 = 2576$$

and

$$C = 516 + 0.75Y_d = 516 + (0.75 \times 2576) = 2448$$

and so

$$S = 2576 - 2448 = 128$$

This gives

$$W = S + T = 128 + 72 = 200$$

Thus $W = J$, as we expect.

The consumption function for a closed economy is given by $C = 64 + 0.8Y_d$. There is a proportional income tax at a rate of $t = 0.25$. The government spends 230 on goods and services and private investment is 50. Find equilibrium income and the government budget surplus. Do these change if the government reduces its expenditure to 190?

5

The macroeconomic equilibrium condition is $Y = AD$. Writing an appropriate expression for AD gives

$$AD = C + I + G$$

With a proportional income tax $T = tY$ and $Y_d = (1 - t)Y$. Substituting $t = 0.25$ we have $T = 0.25Y$ and $Y_d = 0.75Y$. Substituting for Y_d in the consumption function gives

$$C = 64 + (0.8 \times 0.75)Y = 64 + 0.6Y$$

We can now substitute into AD and obtain an expression in Y. This is

$$AD = 64 + 0.6Y + 50 + 230 = 344 + 0.6Y$$

Using the equilibrium condition we obtain

$$Y = 344 + 0.6Y$$

Subtracting $0.6Y$ from both sides gives

$$(1 - 0.6)Y = 344$$

and so

$$0.4\Upsilon = 344$$

Dividing both sides by 0.4 we find $\Upsilon = 860$, which is the equilibrium income.

To find the government's budget surplus we need the value of T. We have $T = 0.25\,\Upsilon = 0.25(860) = 215$

$$\text{Budget surplus} = T - G = 215 - 230 = -15$$

The negative value shows there is a budget deficit of 15.

If the government reduces its expenditure to 190, the aggregate demand function becomes

$$AD = 64 + 0.6\Upsilon + 50 + 190 = 304 + 0.6\Upsilon$$

The equilibrium condition gives $\Upsilon = 304 + 0.6\Upsilon$ from which $0.4\Upsilon = 304$ and so $\Upsilon = 760$ is the new equilibrium income. National income has fallen by 100 as a consequence of government spending being reduced by 40.

The new value of $T = 0.25 \times 760 = 190$. This equals the new value of government expenditure and so the government budget is now balanced. We have

$$T - G = 190 - 190 = 0$$

3.3 A closed economy with no government, no banking system and all investment autonomous has the consumption function $C = 440 + 0.78\Upsilon$.

Write down the equilibrium condition and find the equilibrium level of income if $I = 66$ and if $I = 88$. What is the marginal propensity to consume and by how much does consumption change between these two levels of income?

3.4 A simple open economy with no government has the consumption and import functions

$$C = 140 + 0.72\Upsilon$$

$$Z = 10 + 0.12\Upsilon$$

$$I = 380, \; X = 170$$

Write an expression for AD, showing that it is a function of Υ. Set $\Upsilon = AD$ and solve for equilibrium income. Find the equilibrium values of W and J.

3.5 An economy has the consumption function $C = 125 + 0.8\Upsilon_d$. All income is subject to income tax at a rate of 0.25, investment is 240 and government spending is 375.

Find the equilibrium income and the government's surplus or deficit.

3.6 A simple open economy is modelled by the following equations

$$C = 350 + 0.6Y$$

$$Z = 50 + 0.1Y$$

$$I = 480, \quad X = 310$$

Find the equilibrium level of income. Check that withdrawals equal injections. Does saving equal investment? What can you say about the foreign trade balance?

3.7 An economy has an equilibrium income of 2200. Consumption is described by the expression $C = 170 + 0.75Y_d$. Investment, government spending and taxation are all autonomous. $I = 330$ and the government budget is balanced. Find the values of T and G.

SECTION 3.5: IS–LM Analysis

In this section we extend our model to include the money market where the supply of and demand for money are brought into equilibrium by changes in the interest rate. We use R to denote the rate of interest which is expressed as a decimal, for example, 0.1. An interest rate is often quoted as a percentage, for example, 10% which means $10/100 = 0.1$. In calculations we work with R as a decimal.

We need to specify the demand for money, MD. This depends on Y, R and the price level, P. Larger values of Y and P generate a greater transactions demand for money because people want more money to spend, while a lower rate of interest makes people prefer money to bonds and increases the speculative demand for money. We model real money demand with a linear function such that real money demand increases as Y rises or R falls. The real money supply, MS, is assumed to be determined by the central bank and so to be exogenous. Equilibrium in the money market occurs when the rate of interest is such as to equate the real supply and real demand for money, given the level of income. At different levels of income different rates of interest are required if equilibrium is to occur. The various combinations of real aggregate income, Y, and the rate of interest, R, at which the money market is in equilibrium comprise points on the LM curve. We shall find the equation of the LM curve.

You can see the demand for money function on the screen titled The Money Market and Equilibrium Interest Rate in section 3.5 of MathEcon.

Money market equilibrium occurs when MD = MS. **Remember...**

6

Real Money Demand: $MD = 0.85Y - 1700R$ where Y is real aggregate income and R is the rate of interest expressed as a decimal
Real Money Supply: $MS = 4284$
Find the equation for the LM curve.

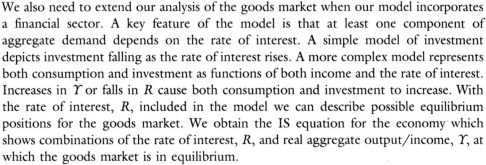

For money market equilibrium $MD = MS$. Substituting for these gives

$$0.85Y - 1700R = 4284$$

Adding $1700R$ to both sides we find

$$0.85Y = 4284 + 1700R$$

Dividing by 0.85 gives an expression for Y from the money market equilibrium condition

$$Y = 5040 + 2000R$$

This is the LM equation.

We also need to extend our analysis of the goods market when our model incorporates a financial sector. A key feature of the model is that at least one component of aggregate demand depends on the rate of interest. A simple model of investment depicts investment falling as the rate of interest rises. A more complex model represents both consumption and investment as functions of both income and the rate of interest. Increases in Y or falls in R cause both consumption and investment to increase. With the rate of interest, R, included in the model we can describe possible equilibrium positions for the goods market. We obtain the IS equation for the economy which shows combinations of the rate of interest, R, and real aggregate output/income, Y, at which the goods market is in equilibrium.

As before we begin by stating the macroeconomic equilibrium condition that $Y = AD$. We then write an expression for AD using the components of expenditure that our model specifies. Since C, I and Z are now all functions of Y and/or R, when we substitute in the equilibrium condition we find that both Y and R appear on the right-hand side of the equation. Rearranging the expression to show Y as a function of R gives us the IS equation.

7

The economy whose money market is described in worked example 6 has no government or external trade. Its goods market is modelled by the equations

Consumption: $C = 108 + 0.82Y$
Investment: $I = 900 - 900R$

Write down the condition for equilibrium in the goods market and obtain an expression for the IS curve.

For equilibrium in the goods market $Y = \text{AD}$ and we have

$$\text{AD} = C + I$$

Substituting for C and I we obtain terms in Y and R on the right-hand side

$$\text{AD} = 108 + 0.82Y + 900 - 900R = 1008 + 0.82Y - 900R$$

Substituting in the equilibrium condition gives

$$Y = 1008 + 0.82Y - 900R$$

Subtracting $0.82Y$ from both sides we find

$$0.18Y = 1008 - 900R$$

Dividing by 0.18 we obtain an expression for Y in terms of R, namely

$$Y = 5600 - 5000R$$

This is the equation of the IS curve.

Once we have obtained the LM and IS equations we can find the values of Y and R that give equilibrium in both the money market and the goods market. The IS and LM equations form a pair of simultaneous equations in two unknowns, Y and R. Setting the expressions for Y equal to one another lets us solve for R, and substituting that value of R back into either the IS or the LM equation lets us find the equilibrium Y. The LM and IS curves can also be plotted on a diagram and the equilibrium values read from the values on the axes at the intersection of the curves. The convention in economics is to plot the diagram with R on the vertical axis. To do this we need to rewrite our equations, expressing R as a function of Y in each case.

Overall macroeconomic equilibrium requires that Y in the **Remember...**
LM equation equals Y in the IS equation.

Find the equilibrium values of Y and R for the economy described in worked examples 6 and 7.

Suppose then that autonomous investment increases by 25.2. What are the effects of this change? Illustrate your results using an IS–LM diagram.

8

Overall macroeconomic equilibrium requires that the values of Y and R satisfy the conditions for equilibrium in both markets. The LM equation and the IS equation constitute a pair of simultaneous equations in two unknowns, Y and R. We have the equations

$$Y_{LM} = 5040 + 2000R \text{ (LM equation)}$$

$$Y_{IS} = 5600 - 5000R \text{ (IS equation)}$$

adding subscripts to the Ys to identify the equation to which each belongs. For equilibrium in both markets

$$Y_{LM} = Y_{IS}$$

and substituting the right-hand sides gives

$$5040 + 2000R = 5600 - 5000R$$

Collecting terms, we have

$$7000R = 560$$

$$R = 0.08$$

Substituting R back into the LM equation gives

$$Y_{LM} = 5040 + (2000 \times 0.08) = 5200$$

and we can confirm this by substituting for R in IS

$$Y_{IS} = 5600 - (5000 \times 0.08) = 5200$$

Equilibrium Y and R are 5200 and 0.08 respectively.

An increase of 25.2 in autonomous investment changes the investment function to

$$I_2 = 925.2 - 900R$$

For goods market equilibrium we now require

$$Y = 1033.2 + 0.82Y - 900R$$

or

$$0.18Y = 1033.2 - 900R$$

The new IS curve is therefore

$$Y_{IS2} = 5740 - 5000R$$

The LM curve is unchanged by the rise in autonomous investment, so overall equilibrium is achieved when

$$Y_{LM} = Y_{IS2}$$

and substituting the expressions gives

$$5040 + 2000R = 5740 - 5000R$$

Collecting terms we have

$$7000R = 700$$

and so we find that at the higher level of investment $R = 0.1$. Substituting into the LM equation gives

$$Y_{LM} = 5040 + (2000 \times 0.1) = 5240$$

The new equilibrium is at $Y = 5240$, $R = 0.1$.

With the increase in autonomous investment, income has increased and the interest rate has risen. The increase in the interest rate chokes off induced investment. To see this we compute the level of investment in the two equilibrium situations. In the first situation

$$I = 900 - 900R \text{ and } R = 0.08, \text{ so } I = 828$$

After autonomous investment has increased by 25.2 we have

$$I_2 = 925.2 - 900R \text{ with } R = 0.1, \text{ so } I_2 = 835.2$$

The overall change in investment is 835.2 − 828 which is a rise of only 7.2. The overall increase is less than the change in autonomous investment, because of the rise in the interest rate.

For diagrammatic analysis we rewrite each curve expressing R as a function of Y. The LM curve $Y_{LM} = 5040 + 2000R$ becomes $R = Y_{LM}/2000 - 2.52$. The original IS curve, IS_1, was $Y_{IS} = 5600 - 5000R$ and is rewritten in the form $R = 1.12 - Y_{IS}/5000$. The new IS curve of $Y_{IS2} = 5740 - 5000R$ becomes $R = 1.148 - Y_{IS2}/5000$ and is denoted IS_2. These three curves are plotted in figure 3.7. We can identify the original and new equilibrium positions, E_1 and E_2 respectively, at the intersections of LM with the IS curves. Equilibrium values of Y and R can be read off from the axes. They correspond to those we found by solving the equations.

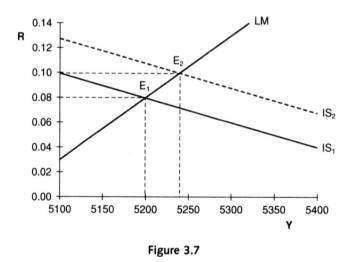

Figure 3.7

There are several associated screens in section 5 of MathEcon chapter 3. These are described in the adjacent text.

The determination of equilibrium in the money market is shown using both graphs and equations on the MathEcon screen The Money Market and Equilibrium Interest Rate. The screen titled The LM Curve and Equation defines the LM curve. You can see an example of finding an LM curve on the screen LM Curve: Equation Derivation.

Turning to the goods market, the screen titled The Consumption Demand Function shows a function where consumption is affected by the rate of interest as well as by income. Investment demand also depends on both the rate of interest and the level of aggregate output, Y, as shown on The Investment Demand Function screen. The screen entitled The IS Equation and Curve: Equation Approach shows how to find the IS curve.

Bringing together the LM and IS curves, the screen IS–LM Equilibrium explains how the values of Y and R are found.

 3.8 The following equations describe an imaginary economy

$C = 45 + 0.75Y_d$	Consumption
$Y_d = Y - T$	Disposable income
$T = 70$	Lump sum tax
$G = 90$	Government expenditure
$I = 350 - 1000R$	Investment, where the rate of interest, R, is a decimal
$MD = 190 - 2000R + 0.4Y$	Money demand
$MS = 450$	Money supply

Find equations for the IS and LM curves. What are the equilibrium values of Y and R?

Is the government budget in deficit or surplus?

Check that injections equal withdrawals. What is the effect of a reduction in the supply of money to $MS = 360$?

In the original equilibrium situation, suppose the lump sum tax is replaced by an income tax. What tax rate, t, is required to yield 70 in tax?

3.9 An economy with no direct taxation is described by the equations

$$C = 260 + 0.6Y - 240R$$

$$I = 314 + 0.2Y - 1200R$$

$$G = 60$$

$$MD = 200 + 0.5Y - 900R$$

$$MS = 1425$$

Find expressions for the IS and LM curves, and the values of Y and R. If G increases by 108, what are the effects?

Chapter 3: Answers to Practice Problems

3.1   Marginal propensity to consume = 0.75. With no direct taxation, consumption is a function of Y

$$S = Y - C = Y - (90 + 0.75Y)$$

$$S = -90 + 0.25Y$$

If $Y = 800$, $C = 690$ and $S = 110$.

3.2   Marginal propensity to consume = 0.8.

$T - G = 220 - 240 = -20$. The government's surplus is -20 (or its deficit is 20).

$Y_d = Y - T$, so $Y = Y_d + T = 2000 + 220$

$Y = 2220$

$C = 25 + (0.8 \times 2000) = 1625$

$S = Y_d - C = 2000 - 1625 = 375$

$W = S + T = 375 + 220 = 595$

$J = I + G = 355 + 240 = 595$

We need to find t such that $tY = T = 220$

$t = T/Y = 220/2220 = 0.099$

The appropriate tax rate is $t = 0.099$ or 9.9%.

3.3 $Y = AD$

If $I = 66$

$AD = C + I = 440 + 0.78Y + 66 = 506 + 0.78Y$, substitute in the equilibrium condition.

$Y = 506 + 0.78Y$, so $(1 - 0.78)Y = 506$, hence $Y = 506/0.22 = 2300$

If $I = 88$

$AD = Y = 528 + 0.78Y$ from which $Y = 528/0.22 = 2400$

Marginal propensity to consume = 0.78

$\Delta Y = 2400 - 2300 = 100$

$\Delta C = 0.78 \times 100 = 78$

Levels of consumption are

$C = 440 + (0.78 \times 2300) = 2234$ and

$C = 440 + (0.78 \times 2400) = 2312$

which again shows $\Delta C = 2312 - 2234 = 78$

3.4 $AD = C + I + X - Z$

$\quad = 140 + 0.72Y + 380 + 170 - 10 - 0.12Y$

$\quad = 680 + 0.6Y$

For equilibrium $Y = 680 + 0.6Y$ and subtracting $0.6Y$ from both sides gives

$0.4Y = 680$

$\quad Y = 1700$

$S = Y - C = Y - 140 - 0.72Y = -140 + 0.28Y = -140 + 0.28(1700) = 336$

$Z = 10 + 0.12Y = 10 + 0.12(1700) = 214$

$W = S + Z = 336 + 214 = 550$

$J = I + X = 380 + 170 = 550$

3.5 $Y_d = Y - tY = Y - 0.25Y = 0.75Y$

$C = 125 + 0.8Y_d = 125 + (0.8 \times 0.75Y) = 125 + 0.6Y$

For equilibrium $Y = C + I + G$

$Y = 125 + 0.6Y + 240 + 375$

$Y - 0.6Y = 740$

$\quad 0.4Y = 740$

$\quad\quad Y = 1850$

$T = 0.25Y = 462.5$

$T - G = 462.5 - 375 = 87.5 =$ government surplus

3.6 For equilibrium, $Y = C + I + X - Z$ so

$Y = 350 + 0.6Y + 480 + 310 - 50 - 0.1Y = 0.5Y + 1090$

$0.5Y = 1090$ (by subtracting $0.5Y$ from both sides)

$\quad Y = 2180$ is equilibrium income

$S = -350 + 0.4Y = 522$, which does not equal I

$Z = 50 + 0.1Y = 268$

$W = S + Z = 790$

$J = I + X = 790$, so withdrawals equal injections

$X > Z$, so foreign trade is in surplus.

3.7 $Y_d = Y - T$

Equilibrium $Y = C + I + G$

Substituting for C, Y_d and I gives

$Y = 170 + 0.75Y - 0.75T + 330 + G$ or

$0.25Y = 500 - 0.75T + G$

But $T = G$ and so

$0.25Y = 500 + 0.25G$

Multiplying by 4 gives equilibrium income

$Y = 2000 + G = 2200$

and so $G = 2200 - 2000 = 200 = T$

3.8   Goods market equilibrium is where $Y = AD = C + I + G$

Substituting for Y_d in the consumption function we have

$C = 45 + 0.75(Y - T)$

Multiplying out the brackets and substituting in the equilibrium condition we obtain

$Y = 45 + 0.75Y - (0.75 \times 70) + 350 - 1000R + 90$

so

$0.25Y = 432.5 - 1000R$

$Y_{IS} = 1730 - 4000R$ is the IS equation.

For money market equilibrium MD = MS

$190 - 2000R + 0.4Y = 450$

$0.4Y = 260 + 2000R$

$Y_{LM} = 650 + 5000R$ is the LM equation.

For equilibrium in both markets we equate the two expressions for Y giving

$Y_{LM} = Y_{IS}$ or

$650 + 5000R = 1730 - 4000R$

from which we find $R = 0.12$ and therefore $Y = 1250$. These are the equilibrium values of R and Y.

Government surplus $= T - G = 70 - 90 = -20$

There is a government budget deficit of 20.

Injections $= J = I + G = 350 - 1000R + 90 = 320$

Withdrawals $= W = S + T$

Find $S = Y_d - (45 + 0.75Y_d) = -45 + 0.25Y_d$

Since $Y_d = Y - T$, $Y_d = 1250 - 70 = 1180$

Substituting in S gives

$S = -45 + (0.25 \times 1180) = 250$

and so

$W = S + T = 250 + 70 = 320$

so withdrawals equal injections.

If $MS_2 = 360$, the equation for the IS curve is unchanged and the new LM equation is given by $MD = MS_2$

$190 - 2000R + 0.4Y = 360$

$0.4Y = 170 + 2000R$

$Y_{LM2} = 425 + 5000R$

The new equilibrium R is obtained from

$Y_{LM2} = Y_{IS}$ implying

$425 + 5000R = 1730 - 4000R$

so that $R = 0.145$ and $Y = 1150$

In this model, the rate of interest rises and equilibrium income falls when the money supply is reduced.

In the original situation $Y_d = Y - T$ where, with an income tax, $T = tY$. The values of Y and t have to be such that T is unchanged at 70, so the analysis of equilibrium in the goods market will start with

$Y = 45 + 0.75Y - (0.75 \times 70) + 350 - 1000R + 90$

and hence the same value of Y, namely 1250, will be generated, so

$t = T/Y = 70/1250 = 0.056$ is the appropriate rate of income tax.

3.9 $AD = C + I + G = 634 + 0.8Y - 1440R = Y$ for goods market equilibrium. This gives

$0.2Y = 634 - 1440R$ or

$Y_{IS} = 3170 - 7200R$ as the IS equation.

For money market equilibrium MD = MS and so

$200 + 0.5Y - 900R = 1425$ or

$0.5Y = 1225 + 900R$ from which we find

$Y_{LM} = 2450 + 1800R$ is the LM equation.

For overall equilibrium, equate the two expressions for Y

$Y_{LM} = Y_{IS}$ giving

$2450 + 1800R = 3170 - 7200R$ or

$9000R = 720$ and so

$R = 0.08$ in equilibrium.

Substituting in LM gives

$Y = 2450 + 144 = 2594$, the equilibrium income.

An increase in G alters aggregate demand to AD $= 742 + 0.8Y - 1440R$, giving

$Y_{IS2} = 3710 - 7200R$ as the new IS curve.

LM is unchanged, so overall equilibrium occurs when

$Y_{LM} = Y_{IS2}$

$2450 + 1800R = 3710 - 7200R$

This gives $R = 0.14$ and substituting gives $Y = 2702$

chapter four

Changes, Rates, Finance and Series

OBJECTIVES

In this chapter you learn to
- Measure interest and growth rates as percentages or decimals
- Calculate percentage changes and percentage points changes
- Calculate the future value of a principal earning simple or compound interest and use different frequencies of compounding
- Find the annual equivalent rate of interest as a standardized measure
- Compute the real rate of interest
- Understand why logarithmic graphs are useful for representing variables that are growing over time, and calculate the average growth rate over a period
- Calculate depreciation using the straight line and reducing balance methods
- Use net present value and internal rate of return for investment appraisal
- Recognize a series and find the sum of a geometric progression
- Carry out loan and annuity calculations involving regular payments
- Find how the price of bills and bonds changes with the rate of interest
- Use Excel to carry out financial calculations

SECTION 4.1: Introduction

Key concepts in this chapter are rates and series. Financial calculations involve interest rates and are often concerned with a sequence of monetary values over a period of time. Growth rate calculations follow a similar pattern and are included here also.

Rates are often quoted as percentages. You may read in the papers that a bank is offering savers a 6% interest rate, or that national income is growing at 2%. For calculations, however, a percentage rate needs to be written as a decimal. The term percentage means divided by 100, so 6% = 6/100 = 0.06. Rates are applied by multiplication. To find how much interest is earned by a sum of money, we multiply it by the rate. If you put $1000 in a deposit account at 6% rate of interest, the interest that is added at the end of the time period is $0.06 \times 1000 = \$60$. We use R to denote a rate expressed as a decimal.

Interest rates and growth rates relate to time periods of a particular length. Often the time period is a year, and this may be implied rather than stated. Take care with this, though, because different time lengths such as one month or one quarter (of a year) are sometimes used. Above we dealt with just one time period, but often we consider processes that continue for several time periods. Throughout this chapter we represent the value at time t as V_t, where the subscript t indicates the time period. At the start of the process t is 0, after one time period it is 1, when two time periods have elapsed t is 2, and so on. For the example above, $t = 0$ at the time when the money is put in the deposit account and $t = 1$ after one time period. We write

$$V_0 = 1000 \text{ (this is the initial value put into the deposit account) and}$$

$$\text{interest} = R \times V_0 = 0.06 \times 1000 = 60$$

This is added to V_0 to find V_1, so

$$V_1 = V_0 + (R \times V_0) = V_0(1 + R)$$

$$= 1000 + 60 = 1000(1.06) = 1060$$

Rates are often quoted as percentages, but they are used as decimals in calculations.

Remember...

The amount with interest added after one time period is

$$V_1 = V_0(1 + R)$$

where R is a decimal.

The screens in MathEcon chapter 4 show calculations relating to some of the finance and growth processes studied in this chapter. These include, in section 2, Nominal and Real Interest Rates and Trends in Levels and Logarithms and in section 3, Net Present Value. Section 4 explains sequences and series, shows you how to find the sum of a geometric progression and gives an example of an annuity calculation.

Other rates used by economists include tax rates and exchange rates. Again, these are applied by multiplication so that the amount paid in sales tax is the tax rate multiplied by the pre-tax price of the item purchased. Exchange rates are quoted for one unit of another currency. If 1 Euro = 1.123 US$, we say that the US$/€ exchange rate is 1.123. Multiplying a number of Euros by this rate gives the equivalent number of US dollars.

Many of the calculations carried out in this chapter can very easily be done in Excel, either by using an in-built formula or by creating a column of values to show the value in each time period separately. There are some examples in the file titled Finance.xls on the CD and some suggestions about methods in section 4.12.

4.1 Express 5.7% as a decimal.

4.2 If a firm has an annual turnover of $2.5 million and sales are growing at 20% per year, what will its turnover be in a year's time?

4.3 A company borrows $86,000 for a year at 14% interest. How much does it have to pay back at the end of the loan period?

4.4 A pack of paving slabs costs $148.60, plus sales tax at 17.5%. What is the total amount you pay for the pack?

4.5 Assuming that the US$/€ exchange rate is 1.123 and ignoring any commission that may be charged

(a) If you have 500 Euros with which you wish to buy US dollars, how many dollars can you buy?

(b) If a book is priced at US$59 and you buy it with your credit card which you pay for in Euros, what price do you pay?

SECTION 4.2: Percentage Changes

Percentage changes are widely used because they make comparisons easy. If the average price level is rising at 3% per year but the price of a season ticket to your favourite sporting event rises by 12.5%, then the season ticket becomes relatively more expensive and you may consider not buying one and using your money in other ways. Let us see how to calculate the percentage change for a season ticket whose price rises from $400 to $450. We find the actual change, divide by the initial value and multiply by 100 to express the result as a percentage.

The formula can be written **Remember...**

$$\text{percentage change} = \frac{V_1 - V_0}{V_0} \times 100$$

In the above example $V_0 = 400$ and $V_1 = 450$, so

$$\text{percentage change} = \frac{450 - 400}{400} \times 100 = 12.5\%$$

1

If the price of a season ticket falls from $450 to $400, what is the percentage change? How does it compare with the percentage change when the price rises from $400 to $450?

We substitute in the formula

$$\text{percentage change} = \frac{V_1 - V_0}{V_0} \times 100$$

$$= \frac{400 - 450}{450} \times 100\% = -11.11\%$$

The change is negative because the price has fallen, but the size of the percentage change is different from that for a change in the opposite direction because the value of V_0 is different.

A percentage change shows how a variable is changing over a period of time. If we calculate the percentage change over a time period for a sum of money on which interest is paid, we are in fact finding the rate of interest paid on that money over the time period.

2

Suppose you borrow $600 and have to pay $700 when you repay the loan 1 year later. What is the annual rate of interest you pay?

Using the formula for a percentage change we have

$$\% \text{ rate} = \frac{V_1 - V_0}{V_0} \times 100 = \frac{700 - 600}{600} \times 100 = 16.67\%$$

Check your result using the formula for the amount with interest added after one time period to see whether $600 at an interest rate of 16.67% grows to $700 after one time period. Use

$$V_1 = V_0(1 + R)$$

Remember, R must be a decimal, so we write $R = 16.67/100 = 0.1667$. Substituting for V_0 and R gives

$$V_1 = 600(1 + 0.1667) = 700$$

This confirms that finding the percentage change for an amount of money loaned or invested gives the percentage rate of interest over the period.

Notice that when we compare two percentages, the difference between them is measured in percentage points (pp). When your season ticket price rises by 12.5% and the average price level rises by 3%, the difference between these is 9.5pp.

PROPORTIONATE CHANGES AND ARC ELASTICITY

A proportionate change is measured by $(V_1 - V_0)/V_0$. It is the same as a percentage change, except that it is not multiplied by 100. If a variable increases and then decreases again by the same amount, the two changes are the same size, but the first is positive and the second is negative. The proportionate changes, however, have different numerical values because the V_0 values are different, just as we saw with percentage changes. This presents a problem with the measurement of elasticity in economics, where the basic formula is

$$\text{elasticity} = \frac{\text{proportionate change in quantity}}{\text{proportionate change in price}}$$

$$= \frac{Q_1 - Q_0}{Q_0} \div \frac{P_1 - P_0}{P_0}$$

This formula gives different elasticities for the same change, depending on the direction in which it takes place. One way of obtaining a unique measure of elasticity is to use averages of the initial and final values of Q and P as the divisors in calculating the proportionate changes. This gives the measurement known as arc elasticity.

> Point elasticity, which also gives a unique measurement, is discussed in section 5.9.

The formula can be written

Remember...

$$\text{arc elasticity} = \frac{Q_1 - Q_0}{(Q_1 + Q_0)/2} \div \frac{P_1 - P_0}{(P_1 + P_0)/2}$$

3

A company raises the cost of an annual car parking permit from \$120 to \$200, and the number of employees who buy one falls from 480 to 460. What is the arc elasticity of demand for parking permits?

$Q_0 = 480$, $Q_1 = 460$, $P_0 = 120$, $P_1 = 200$

$$\text{arc elasticity} = \frac{Q_1 - Q_0}{(Q_1 + Q_0)/2} \div \frac{P_1 - P_0}{(P_1 + P_0)/2}$$

$$= \frac{460 - 480}{(460 + 480)/2} \div \frac{200 - 120}{(200 + 120)/2}$$

$$= -\frac{20}{470} \div \frac{80}{160} = -\frac{4}{47}$$

4.6 A company's share price increases from 156.4 to 187.2. What is the percentage change?

4.7 You put $3600 in a gold star savings account, and when interest is added you have $3794.40 one year later. What rate of interest has been paid, and how does it compare with the 4% offered by a bank deposit account?

4.8 A cinema raises the price of a ticket from $3 to $3.40. Weekly ticket sales fall from 2600 to 2200. What is the arc elasticity of demand for cinema tickets?

SECTION 4.3: Simple and Compound Interest

When a loan extends over several time periods, interest is payable in each period.

SIMPLE INTEREST

With simple interest the same amount of interest is paid in each time period. We saw in section 4.1 that the interest due at the end of the initial time period is $R \times V_0$. Over n time periods, therefore, $n \times R \times V_0$ is payable in simple interest and the value of the outstanding debt is $V_n = V_0 + (n \times R \times V_0) = V_0(1 + n \cdot R)$.

With simple interest at rate R, where R is a decimal   **Remember...**

$$V_n = V_0(1 + n \cdot R)$$

COMPOUND INTEREST, COMPOUNDED ANNUALLY

When money is lent at compound interest over successive time periods, interest is paid not only on the money originally lent but also on the interest that has accrued so far. Most loans and savings accounts calculate interest as compound interest. For example, if you borrow $200 for a 3-year period at 7% compound annual rate of interest the money you owe builds up over the period as follows.

Year	Value outstanding	Interest $(R = 0.07)$
t	V_t $(\$)$	$R \times V_t$
0	$V_0 = 200$	14
1	$V_1 = 214$	14.98
2	$V_2 = 228.98$	16.03
3	$V_3 = 245.01$	

The number of years from the start of the loan is identified by t. V_0 is the amount you borrow, and interest during the initial year is calculated as $R \times V_0 = 0.07 \times 200 = 14$. This interest is added to what you already owe, giving an outstanding debt 1 year after the loan was taken out of V_1, where

$$V_1 = V_0 + (R \times V_0) = V_0(1 + R) = 200 + 14 = 214$$

Thus far the calculation is identical to what we have done previously, but now compound interest is charged on the amount outstanding, so you pay interest on V_1. The interest then is $R \times V_1 = 0.07 \times 214 = 14.98$, and this is added to V_1 to get V_2. We have

$$V_2 = V_1 + (R \times V_1) = V_1(1 + R) = 214 + 14.98 = 228.98$$

Two years after the loan was taken out, V_2 is the amount outstanding. Interest is then payable on V_2 and is $R \times V_2 = 0.07 \times 228.98 = 16.03$, which gives an outstanding debt 3 years from the start of the loan of

$$V_3 = V_2 + (R \times V_2) = V_2(1 + R) = 228.98 + 16.03 = 245.01$$

When you borrow at compound interest the amount of interest payable rises successively each year because you are paying interest both on your original loan and also on the interest already incurred.

The formulae above link the value at each time period with the value in the previous time period. By substituting back we can link the value at any time period with the amount originally borrowed, V_0. For example, we have

$$V_2 = V_1(1 + R)$$

Substituting into this the expression $V_1 = V_0(1 + R)$ gives

$$V_2 = V_0(1 + R)(1 + R) = V_0(1 + R)^2$$

This shows that to find the amount owing after two time periods we multiply the original amount V_0 by $(1 + R)^2$. Similarly for V_3 we have

$$V_3 = V_2(1 + R) = V_0(1 + R)^3$$

For every time period the loan continues the amount outstanding is multiplied by another $(1 + R)$. In general, for a loan that extends over n time periods at compound interest we have

$$V_n = V_0(1 + R)^n$$

The amount originally lent, V_0, is called the principal and the amount to which it grows by the end of the loan period, V_n, is called the future value.

With interest compounded for each time period at rate R, where R is a decimal

Remember...

$$V_n = V_0(1 + R)^n$$

where V_0 is the principal and V_n is the future value.

4

You put $380 in a deposit account that pays 6% interest compounded annually. How much is in your account at the end of 4 years?

Using the formula $V_n = V_0(1 + R)^n$ we have $V_0 = 380$, $R = 6/100 = 0.06$ and $n = 4$. Substituting these values gives

$$V_4 = 380(1 + 0.06)^4$$

Doing the bit in brackets first gives 1.06; we raise this to the power 4 using the calculator button marked x^y, and finally we multiply by 380 to obtain

$$V_4 = 479.74$$

Your savings are worth $479.74 at the end of 4 years.

4.9 A student borrows $1200 for 3 years at an annual rate of compound interest of 4.6%. How much does she owe at the end of the 3-year period?

4.10 A rich uncle has given you $5000 which you plan to save for 5 years. Would you prefer to put it in an account offering 7% simple interest or one offering 6% compound interest?

COMPOUNDING MORE FREQUENTLY

Different time periods can be used for compounding and interest rates can be quoted in different ways. For example, compounding can take place every quarter, every month or every week. The formula we have been using is still appropriate, providing we choose as unit time the frequency with which compounding occurs and we ensure that n and R refer to this time period. If necessary we adjust them appropriately. The worked examples show some of the possibilities that may arise. Notice that the rate of interest may be an annual one even if compounding takes place more often. For a particular annual rate, the greater the frequency of compounding, the larger the future value.

You can see examples of Excel calculations using annual and continuous compounding in the worksheet titled Compound Interest in the file Finance.xls. There are some notes on its construction in section 4.12.

5

$500 is borrowed for 2 years at a monthly compound rate of interest of 2%. How much is outstanding at the end of the period?

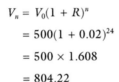

Interest is compounded monthly, so we choose 1 month as our unit of time. The rate of interest quoted relates to this time period. It is 2% per month. We have, then, that $R = 2/100 = 0.02$. The time period at the end of 2 years is denoted by n. But we are now measuring time in months and so $n = 12 \times 2 = 24$ months. Applying the formula

$$V_n = V_0(1 + R)^n$$
$$= 500(1 + 0.02)^{24}$$
$$= 500 \times 1.608$$
$$= 804.22$$

The amount outstanding at the end of 2 years is $804.22. Notice how quickly the debt builds up with monthly compounding although 2% may superficially look quite a low rate of interest.

6

A principal of $250 earns interest at a rate of 6% compounded quarterly over an 18-month period. Find the future value. If instead the interest is compounded weekly, what is the future value?

For the first part of the question we choose a quarter of a year as our unit of time. The interest rate is stated to be 'a rate of 6% compounded quarterly'. The underlying assumption about interest rates, unless something else is very clearly stated, is that they are annual. What we have here is an annual rate of interest of 6%, but the interest is calculated and added on four times a year using $1/4$ of the annual interest rate. The quarterly rate of interest is therefore $6/4$% or 1.5%. Expressing this as a decimal we have $R = 0.015$. The loan period is 18 months, but we are working in units of a quarter of a year or 3 months so the loan is for $18 \div 3 = 6$ quarters of a year. This gives us $n = 6$. We now substitute in the formula to find the future value.

$$V_n = V_0(1 + R)^n$$

$$= 250(1 + 0.015)^6$$

$$= 250 \times 1.093$$

$$= 273.36$$

The future value in 18 months' time is $273.36 with quarterly compounding.

In the second part of the question compounding occurs weekly and so we use 1 week as our unit of time. The interest rate must be allocated over the 52 weeks in the year which gives a weekly interest rate of 6/52%. Writing this as a decimal we find $R = 0.00115$. With 52 weeks in a year, in 1.5 years there are $52 \times 1.5 = 78$ weeks and so $n = 78$. The new future value is

$$V_n = V_0(1 + R)^n$$

$$= 250(1 + 0.00115)^{78}$$

$$= 250 \times 1.094$$

$$= 273.53$$

The future value is $273.53, somewhat larger than before, when the frequency of compounding is increased to weekly.

CONTINUOUS COMPOUNDING

As the previous worked example illustrates, the more frequently compounding takes place over a particular time period, the larger the future value. Theoretically we can increase the frequency of compounding until it is going on all the time. This is called continuous compounding. To calculate the future value when continuous compounding is taking place we use the formula

$$V_n = V_0 e^{Rn}$$

where e is a mathematical constant used in exponential functions.

On your calculator you evaluate e^{Rn} and then multiply by the value for V_0 to find V_n. The values are said to follow a pattern of exponential growth.

Exponential functions are discussed in section 2.13.

With continuous compounding the future value is given by

$$V_n = V_0 e^{Rn}$$

Remember...

7

A principal of $250 earns interest at a rate of 6% compounded continuously over an 18-month period. Find the future value.

With continuous compounding the future value is given by the formula $V_n = V_0 e^{Rn}$. We can choose whatever time units we like for measuring R and n, so long as they are compatible. If we use 1 year as our unit of time, the rate of interest is 6% and $R = 6/100 = 0.06$. With unit time 1 year, 18 months should be written as 1.5 years and so $R.n = 0.06 \times 1.5 = 0.09$. Using the calculator button marked e^x we obtain $e^{Rn} = 1.094$ and multiplying this by 250 gives $V_n = 273.54$.

The future value is $273.54 with continuous compounding, just slightly more in this case than with weekly compounding (see worked example 6).

4.11 Find the future value after 5 years of a principal of $1000 which earns interest at a rate of 3% per quarter, compounded quarterly.

4.12 If a loan of $400 is taken out at a rate of interest of 18% for 2 years, calculate the final outstanding debt if the interest is compounded (a) quarterly (b) monthly (c) continuously.

4.13 A principal of $320 attracts interest at a rate of 7.5% compounded continuously for 4 years. What is the future value?

4.14 You borrow $750 for 3.5 years at an interest rate of 15%. How much difference does it make to the final amount you owe whether the interest is compounded annually or continuously?

SECTION 4.4: Annual Equivalent Rate

Since compound interest can be calculated with different frequencies of compounding using interest rates based on different time periods, it can be difficult to compare alternative loans or savings opportunities.

The Annual Equivalent Rate (AER) is widely recognized as providing a standardized method of interest calculation that gives a basis for immediate comparison of alternatives. The annual equivalent rate measures interest as a compound annual rate and expresses this as a percentage. If interest is actually charged on any other basis the AER shows the compound annual rate that is equivalent, in the sense that the total amount of interest paid during a year would be the same. The AER is calculated by finding the total interest payable in a year and expressing it as a percentage of the principal.

If compounding takes place m times a year, we use $1/m$th of a year as unit time and the future amount at the end of 1 year (or m time periods) is given by the formula for compound interest as

$$V_m = V_0(1 + R)^m$$

$$\text{total interest payable in a year} = V_m - V_0 = V_0(1 + R)^m - V_0$$

$$= V_0[(1 + R)^m - 1]$$

To find the AER we divide by V_0 and multiply by 100 to convert to a percentage. This gives

$$\text{total interest payable as a percentage of } V_0 = 100 \times \frac{V_0[(1 + R)^m - 1]}{V_0}$$

Cancelling the terms V_0 we see that the AER can be found from the formula below.

8

A credit card account charges interest at 2.15% per month. What is the AER?

Use the formula $\text{AER} = 100 \times [(1 + R)^m - 1]$ where $m = 12$ and $R = 0.0215$, the monthly rate of interest expressed as a decimal. This gives

$$\text{AER} = 100 \times [(1 + 0.0215)^{12} - 1]$$

$$= 100 \times (1.2908 - 1)$$

$$= 29.08\%$$

Notice that this is substantially more than 12 times the monthly rate ($12 \times 2.15\%$ = 25.8%).

To find the AER when the quoted interest rate offers continuous compounding we begin with the formula

$$V_1 = V_0 e^R$$

We find the total interest paid as the difference between the amounts at the end and the start of a year. We obtain

$$\text{total interest paid} = V_1 - V_0 = V_0(e^R - 1)$$

To find the AER we express this as a percentage of V_0 and find

$$\text{total interest paid as a percentage of } V_0 = 100 \times \frac{V_0(e^R - 1)}{V_0}$$

Cancelling the terms in V_0 gives the formula we require for the AER.

With continuous compounding

Remember...

$$\text{AER} = 100 \times (e^R - 1)$$

9

Find the AER for a loan charging interest at 16.5%, compounded continuously.

The appropriate formula is

$$\text{AER} = 100 \times (e^R - 1)$$

Writing the rate of interest as a decimal we substitute $R = 0.165$ which gives

$$\text{AER} = 100 \times (1.1794 - 1)$$

$$= 17.94\%$$

4.15

Find the AER for each of these nominal interest rates

(a) 4.2% compound per quarter
(b) 15% with quarterly compounding
(c) 12.5% with monthly compounding
(d) 16.8% compounded continuously
(e) 1.9% compound per month

SECTION 4.5: Nominal and Real Interest Rates

When you compare the interest rates paid by different financial institutions on deposit accounts you are comparing nominal interest rates. These rates show how much money you will have at the end of a particular time period, but they do not tell you what that money will be worth. In a time of inflation the quoted rate of interest may appear to be high. For example, a rate of interest of 25% sounds like a very good return on your money. However, if prices are simultaneously rising at 25% the future value of money invested at 25% will just enable you to buy the same set of goods you could have bought in the original time period. You will not be able to buy any additional goods and therefore the real rate of return on your money is zero.

The nominal percentage rate of interest is the number of $ earned if $100 is lent for 1 year. By contrast the real rate of interest is defined in terms of goods. The real rate is the extra goods or services that can be bought if $100 is lent for 1 year. If prices change between the time when the loan is made and when it is repaid, the real rate does not equal the nominal rate. The real rate of interest is adjusted for inflation and can in fact be negative although the nominal rate of interest is positive.

When inflation is expected, nominal interest rates tend to rise to maintain the value of real interest rates. This has implications for government monetary policy, because if a policy designed to reduce interest rates also generates expectations of increasing inflation these expectations put pressure on interest rates to rise, and therefore the overall effect on nominal interest rates is uncertain.

In MathEcon chapter 4, the topic Nominal and Real Interest Rates in section 2 distinguishes between these rates and gives an explanation of the exact formula for the real rate. Use the two supplementary screens to see comparisons of nominal and real interest rates, including examples of negative real interest rates, as shown in figure 4.1.

Approximately, we may measure the real rate of interest, RR, as the difference between the nominal rate of interest, R, and the inflation rate, p, giving RR = $R - p$. This approximation holds for small percentage changes in R and p and is usually acceptably close to the true value for changes of up to 10%.

The exact formula for calculating the real rate of interest is

$$RR = \frac{1 + R}{1 + p} - 1$$

where R, p and RR are decimals.

Real rate of interest = RR.

Approximately, RR = $R - p$ (valid for rates < 10%)

The exact formula is

$$RR = \frac{1 + R}{1 + p} - 1$$

Remember...

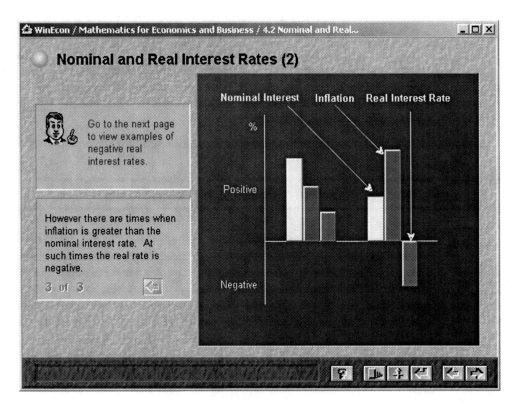

Figure 4.1

---

10 A deposit account offers interest at 25%, but prices are rising at 17%. Use both an approximate and an exact formula to find the real rate of interest.

$R = 0.25$, $p = 0.17$

$$\text{Approximately RR} = R - p = 0.25 - 0.17 = 0.08$$

Using the approximate formula the real rate of interest is 8%.
  The exact formula is

$$\text{RR} = \frac{1 + R}{1 + p} - 1$$

$$\text{RR} = \frac{1 + 0.25}{1 + 0.17} - 1 = 0.0684$$

Using the exact calculation we find the real rate of interest is 6.84%.
  The approximation is not very close, because the changes are larger than those for which the approximate formula is recommended.

4.16 Compare the approximate and exact answers to the following

(a) An investment account offers a nominal interest rate of 10%. If prices are rising at 6.5% per annum, what is the real rate of interest?

(b) If prices are rising at 36% and you borrow money at 48%, what is the real rate of interest you pay?

SECTION 4.6: Growth Rates and Logarithms

Logarithms are explained in section 2.14.

The MathEcon screen Trends in Levels and Logarithms lets you see plots of a variable growing at a constant rate, both for the original units of measurement and after taking logarithms of the variable. If you would like to try this in Excel, the worksheet titled Compound Interest in the file Finance.xls will help you. The notes in section 4.12 explain how you can use two vertical axes, one for V_t and the other for $\log_e(V_t)$ on the same graph.

When compound interest is added to a sum of money over a number of years, or indeed if any variable is growing at a steady growth rate, the graph of the variable plotted at various points in time takes the form of a curve. If, however, we take logarithms of the values of the variables and plot them against time, the graph takes the form of a straight line. Graphs using a logarithmic scale for the variable are useful because they allow us to see immediately the rate at which the variable is growing. They show steady growth as a straight line, a growth rate which is increasing over the time period as a curve bending upwards, and growth at a decreasing rate as a curve that bends downwards.

11

A company's sales are growing at 45% compound per annum. If they are worth $100 million now, what will they be worth in each of the next 4 years? Plot graphs showing the sales figures, and also $\log_e$(sales).

When V_0 grows at a compound growth rate R, its value in any year t is

$$V_t = V_0(1 + R)^t$$

The figure for each year is $(1 + R)$ times that for the previous year. The company's sales figures over the 4-year period are shown in the table. Each is found by multiplying the previous value by $(1 + R) = 1.45$. This gives the sales figures listed. Each value is a 45% increase on the previous value. The next column shows the logarithms to base e of the sales figures. These values increase by a constant amount. Equal distances apart on a logarithmic scale represent equal percentage changes in the original variable. The graph in figure 4.2 plots the actual sales values on the left-hand vertical axis, showing the growth in values of the variable. The logarithms of the sales values are plotted on the right-hand vertical axis and form a straight line.

Year	Sales ($m)	ln Sales
t	V_t	ln V_t
0	100	4.605
1	145	4.977
2	210.25	5.348
3	304.86	5.720
4	442.05	6.091

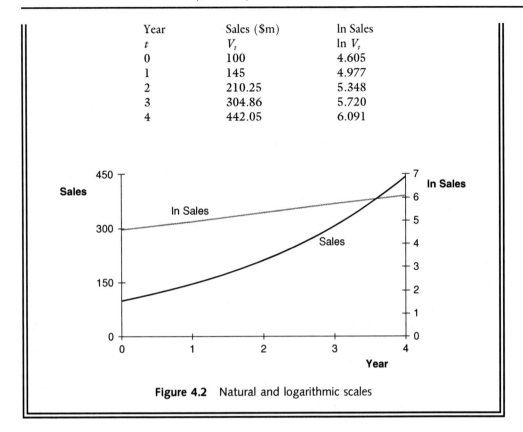

Figure 4.2 Natural and logarithmic scales

We can see why plotting a constant growth variable on a logarithmic scale gives us a straight line graph by applying the rules of logarithms explained in section 2.14. We have

$$V_t = V_0(1 + R)^t$$

Taking logarithms of each side gives

$$\ln(V_t) = \ln(V_0) + t \times \ln(1 + R)$$

Since $\ln(V_0)$ and $\ln(1 + R)$ are just numbers (although we don't know their values), the expression for $\ln(V_t)$ is a linear function of t, giving a straight line graph.

For exponential growth where we have continuous compounding, plotting the logarithm of the variable again yields a straight line graph. The expression for V_t is

$$V_t = V_0 e^{Rt}$$

Taking logarithms we find

$$\ln(V_t) = \ln(V_0) + Rt$$

Since $\ln(V_0)$ and R are constants this is a linear function of t, which again gives us a straight line graph.

FINDING GROWTH RATES AND TIME PERIODS

When a variable grows at compound interest for n time periods and we know its initial and final values, to find the average growth rate we have to substitute into the appropriate formula for V_n and solve to find R. This method is necessary because of the curvilinear growth path when growth is compounded either once per time period or continuously. Another question which arises is how long a sum of money has to be invested at a specified interest rate for it to reach a particular future value. Using the same formula, in this instance we solve to find n. When an equation contains an expression to the power of n, taking logarithms is a useful step in finding its solution.

12

You buy a bond for $800 and sell it 5 years later for $1231.60. What rate of annual compound interest has it earned?

The appropriate formula is

$$V_n = V_0(1 + R)^n$$

We have $V_0 = 800$, $V_n = 1231.60$ and $n = 5$. Substituting these values gives

$$1231.60 = 800(1 + R)^5$$

Dividing each side by 800 we have

$$1.5395 = (1 + R)^5$$

Take the natural logarithm of each side

$$0.4315 = 5\ln(1 + R)$$

Dividing both sides by 5 gives

$$0.0863 = \ln(1 + R)$$

Now exponentiate both sides to remove the logarithm

$$e^{0.0863} = 1.0901 = 1 + R$$

Subtracting 1 from both sides we find

$$R = 0.0901 = 9.01\%$$

13

You consider investing $1500 at 6% compounded continuously. How long would it take for your investment to be worth $2000?

The appropriate formula is

$$V_n = V_0 e^{Rn}$$

We have $V_0 = 1500$, $V_n = 2000$ and $R = 0.06$. Substituting these gives

$$2000 = 1500 e^{0.06n}$$

Dividing both sides by 1500 we find

$$1.333 = e^{0.06n}$$

Taking natural logarithms of both sides we obtain

$$0.2877 = 0.06n$$

Dividing by 0.06 we find

$$n = 4.79$$

It would take 4.79 years for your investment to be worth $2000.

4.17 Demand for thin screen plasma televisions is predicted to grow exponentially at 70% per year. A shop sells 40 this year. How many can it expect to sell in each of the next 4 years? Plot a graph of the values against time. Also plot a graph showing logarithms of sales against time. If sales continue at this rate, when will the shop be selling 2000 thin screen televisions a year?

4.18 You borrow $1000 and 3 years later you are asked to pay back $1845.32. What annual rate of compound interest have you been charged?

SECTION 4.7: Depreciation

In calculating depreciation the value of an asset falls in each consecutive time period. The values follow a path of negative growth, so we calculate the value of an asset in year t, V_t, putting the rate of depreciation, R, into the appropriate interest rate formula with a negative sign. We again use V_0 to represent the initial value of the asset.

STRAIGHT LINE DEPRECIATION

The straight line method of depreciation spreads the loss of value evenly over the lifetime of an asset. It provides an easy way of giving the asset value net of depreciation at any time period using the formula for simple interest with negative R.

Straight line depreciation   **Remember...**

$$V_t = V_0(1 - t \cdot R)$$

REDUCING BALANCE METHOD OF DEPRECIATION

If you have bought, or considered buying, a new car you are probably aware that a car depreciates fastest when it is new, and more slowly as it gets older. The reducing balance method of depreciation models this kind of pattern of asset values. The approach uses the compound interest formula with negative R. The asset value reduces by the same proportion each year but by smaller amounts in later years, because the value is already smaller. This is the usual method of calculating depreciation.

Reducing balance depreciation   **Remember...**

$$V_t = V_0(1 - R)^t$$

14

A firm buys computerized machinery costing \$650,000. If it depreciates at 12% per year, what will it be worth in 5 years' time? Compare the values given by the straight line and reducing balance methods.

We have $V_0 = 650,000$ and $R = 0.12$. Substituting in the straight line formula $V_t = V_0(1 - t \cdot R)$ gives

$$V_5 = 650,000(1 - 5 \times 0.12) = 650,000 \times 0.4 = 260,000 \text{ in 5 years' time}$$

Using the reducing balance method where $V_t = V_0(1 - R)^t$

$$V_5 = 650,000(1 - 0.12)^5 = 650,000 \times 0.528 = 343,026 \text{ in 5 years' time}$$

> **4.19** If assets valued at $3 million depreciate at 7% per annum, what will be their value in 8 years' time? Use both the straight line and reducing balance methods.

SECTION 4.8: Net Present Value

Would you prefer to be given $200 today or $200 in 3 years' time? Most people would choose the money now in preference to the same amount in 3 years' time. One reason for this is that the money could be put into an interest bearing account and would therefore accumulate to a larger sum at the end of the 3-year period. In section 4.3 we saw that $200 at 7% compound annual rate of interest is worth $245.01 3 years later. Looking at this the other way round, we can say that $245.01 available to you in 3 years' time is worth $200 today if the rate of interest is 7%. We call the equivalent value today of some future amount its present value.

> present value: the value of some future amount in the current time period, obtained by discounting.
> discount rate: used in the discount factor formula, it is a rate that represents the cost of capital.
> discount factor: the amount by which a future value is multiplied to obtain its present value.
> net present value: the sum of the present values of the discounted net returns over the lifetime of a project.

In the context of deciding whether an investment project is worthwhile, we begin by estimating the costs and revenues it will generate and finding the net return (revenue minus cost) for each year of the project's life. These are denoted V_t. Recognition that money promised in the future is worth less than if it were available today then leads us to discount future values, reducing them to their present values. We want to find corresponding values V_0 and we can do this by rearranging the compound interest formula. Assuming annual compounding we have

$$V_t = V_0(1 + R)^t$$

Interchanging sides and dividing through by $(1 + R)^t$ gives the expression for V_0

$$V_0 = \frac{V_t}{(1 + R)^t}$$

The process of finding a present value, V_0, is called discounting. The rate of interest, R, used for this is called the discount rate. It represents the cost of capital and is expressed as a decimal in the formula. The net present value, NPV, of a project is found by summing the stream of discounted net returns over the lifetime of the project. The proposed investment is worthwhile if its NPV is greater than zero. This basic rule may have to be modified if you are choosing between alternative projects or there is capital rationing. Although other methods of project appraisal are sometimes used, the NPV approach is generally preferred, because it takes into account the time value of money. You will find it convenient to set out your calculation in a table using a row for each year. It is usual to show the discount factor for each year, $1/(1 + R)^t$. The values V_t are multiplied by the discount factors to obtain the present values V_0.

To find the net present value of a project   Remember...

- for each year, list the net return (revenue − cost)
- choose an appropriate discount rate, R, writing it as a decimal
- find the discount factor for each year $1/(1 + R)^t$
- for each year, multiply the net return, V_t, by the discount factor to find the present value V_0
- sum the present values to obtain the NPV of the project.

Decision rule: undertake the project if its NPV is greater than zero.

15

A firm is considering a project of installing new machinery which costs $500,000. It is expected to yield returns of $200,000 in each of years 1 and 2, and $100,000 in years 3 and 4, after which it will be replaced. Assuming a discount rate of 8% and using the net present value criterion, is the new machinery worth buying?

We list the net return for each year of the project. The cost is incurred at the start of the project and so is shown for year 0 with a negative sign. There are positive returns in each of years 1 to 4.

Year t	Net return ($'000) V_t	Discount factor $1/(1 + R)^t$	Present value ($'000) V_0
0	−500	1.0000	−500
1	200	0.9259	185.19
2	200	0.8573	171.47
3	100	0.7938	79.38
4	100	0.7350	73.50
			NPV = 9.54

The discount factor column shows the appropriate figure to be applied for each year of the project. Notice that when t is 0 in year 0 the discount factor is 1, and that every successive year the discount factor gets smaller. In year 4 it is $1/(1 + 0.08)^4 = 0.7350$. Each net return is multiplied by the discount factor in the same row to find the present value shown in the final column. The sum of the present values gives the NPV for the project. It is 9.54, or in the original units $9540. It satisfies the criterion of being bigger than zero, so we recommend that the new machinery is worthwhile and the project should go ahead.

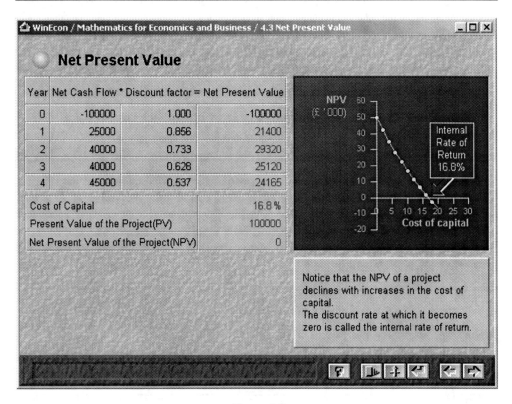

Figure 4.3

This example is calculated in Excel on the Present Value worksheet in the Finance.xls file and there is information about the method in section 4.12. The concept of net present value is explained in section 3 of MathEcon chapter 4 on the screen titled Present Value and Cash Flow. The screen Net Present Value shown in figure 4.3 sets out the calculation of discount factors and NPV step by step. You can see graphically that if the discount rate increases, the NPV of the project falls. Notice that the discount rate at which NPV is zero is called the internal rate of return. The next MathEcon screen allows you, as its title says, to evaluate your own project. You may like to use it to check your hand calculations for the practice problems below. Alternatively you may like to calculate NPV using Excel, as described in section 4.12.

INTERNAL RATE OF RETURN

The internal rate of return, IRR, of a project is the rate of discount at which the NPV is zero. With the MathEcon screen or a computer spreadsheet such as Excel it is easy to enter different values for R, let the computer recalculate the net present value and continue trying values until you find the one at which NPV = 0. The IRR for the project analysed in the worked example above is 8.99%. The IRR decision rule is to undertake the project if the IRR is greater than the discount rate. Since 8.99% exceeds the discount rate of 8%, our conclusion is the same as before: the new machinery is worth buying. For simple problems the IRR method always gives the same decision as the NPV rule. The IRR approach is useful if you are uncertain of the correct discount rate to use, because for any discount rate lower than the IRR the project is worthwhile.

> internal rate of return: the discount rate at which the net present value of a project is 0.

If you do not have a computer available, reworking the NPV calculation for different values of R is somewhat tedious. A suggestion is that if your first value of R gives a positive NPV, choose the next R value substantially bigger so that you get a negative NPV. Plot NPV and R, the cost of capital, on a graph, as in figure 4.3. The relationship is actually curved, but you can approximate with a straight line and so estimate at what value of R NPV will be zero.

> IRR = rate of discount at which NPV = 0
>
> **Remember...**
>
> Decision rule: undertake the project if the IRR is greater than the discount rate.

4.20 A firm is considering a proposed project with an initial cost of $390,000 and projected revenues (in thousands of dollars) of successively 100, 200 and 150 in the next 3 years. Show whether the firm should go ahead with the project if the appropriate discount rate is 5%. Would you recommend a different decision if the discount rate is 10%?

4.21 A proposed investment project costs $870,000 and is expected to generate revenues (in thousands of dollars) in the next 4 years of 230, 410, 390, 170. At a discount rate of 7% is the project worthwhile? What is the internal rate of return of the investment project?

SECTION 4.9: Series

A list of numbers each of which is formed from the previous one in some regular pattern is called a sequence. One type of sequence is where each number is multiplied by a particular amount to form the next number. For example, if each number is multiplied by 3 and if the first number in the list happens to be 5, then the sequence of terms is

$$5, 15, 45, 135, \ldots$$

We can write this sequence as

$$5, 5 \times 3, 5 \times 3^2, 5 \times 3^3, \ldots$$

Notice that because each term is a multiple of the previous term, the numbers quickly become quite large.

---

geometric progression: a sequence of terms each of which is formed by multiplying the previous term by the same amount.

common ratio: the amount by which each term in a geometric progression is multiplied to form the next term in the sequence.

series: a sum of a sequence of terms.

The number used as a multiplier to form each new term of the sequence is called the common ratio and is denoted by c. In the above example, $c = 3$. The first term of the sequence is in general identified as a. The type of sequence where each term is formed by multiplying the previous one by a common ratio is called a geometric progression, or GP. Adding the terms in a sequence gives us a sum of terms which is called a series. We use the notation S_n to denote such a series, where the subscript n indicates the number of terms it contains.

The sum of a GP to n terms is given by the formula

Remember...

$$S_n = \frac{a(1 - c^n)}{1 - c}$$

16

Find the sum of the first six terms of the series 5, 15, 45, 135, . . .

We have $a = 5$, $c = 3$ and $n = 6$. Substitute in the formula

$$Sn = \frac{5(1 - 3^6)}{(1 - 3)} = 1820$$

To convince yourself that the formula works, add up the four terms listed together with the next two terms, which are 405 and 1215. You should again get 1820.

Suppose c is a fraction, say $\frac{1}{2}$. Then if $a = 8$ the sequence of numbers is

$$8, 4, 2, 1, \tfrac{1}{2}, \tfrac{1}{4}, \tfrac{1}{8}, \tfrac{1}{16}, \ldots$$

We see that multiplying by a number less than 1 implies that each number is smaller than the one that precedes it.

In section 4, the MathEcon screen Sequences and Series shows how to find the formula for the sum to n terms of a GP. You can see graphs of S_n for various values of n on cards 4 and 5.

When a sequence has a common ratio of less than 1, if we list a large number of terms the later values in the list get successively closer to 0. The sum of the series does not then go on getting bigger and bigger. Instead, as the series is extended to extra terms, ever smaller amounts are added to the previous total, making the sum of the series approach some particular value. The sum of the GP is said to converge to a finite total.

The formula for the sum of a large number of terms, n, of a GP with $c < 1$ is given by

Remember...

$$S_n = \frac{a}{(1 - c)}$$

17

Find the sum to eight terms of the geometric progression with $a = 8$, $c = 1/2$. Compare this with the value for the sum to a large number of terms, as given by the formula.

The first eight terms of this sequence are listed above and we now form their sum. We obtain

$$S_8 = 8 + 4 + 2 + 1 + \tfrac{1}{2} + \tfrac{1}{4} + \tfrac{1}{8} + \tfrac{1}{16} = 15.94$$

Since $c = 1/2$, which is less than 1 we may use the formula for a large number of terms, which gives

$$S_n = \frac{a}{1 - c} = \frac{8}{1 - 0.5} = \frac{8}{0.5} = 16$$

Notice that even for just eight terms the values for S_8 and S_n are quite close. If we were to add more terms to the series they would all be very small, and so the sum does not get larger than 16 however many terms we add. The GP is said to converge on the value 16.

4.22 Sum to seven terms the GP with $a = 10$, $c = 4$.

4.23 Find the sum to a large number of terms of the series

$$6, 2, \tfrac{2}{3}, \tfrac{2}{9}, \tfrac{2}{27}, \ldots$$

Section 4.10: Savings and Loans with Regular Payments

Savings schemes and loans may combine the application of compound interest to the amount outstanding with regular payments. As an example, suppose someone saving for retirement puts $2500 in a gold savings account and adds $90 to it each month. Until there is $5000 in the account, interest is 4.8%, compounded monthly. Amounts over $5000 earn 6% interest. The value in the gold savings account for three months after the start of the saving scheme is shown in the table. Compound interest is, as usual, calculated on the amount outstanding and is added to that value, but now the regular payment has to be added also to find the value outstanding for the next time period.

Month t	Regular payment ($) W	Value outstanding ($) V_t	Interest ($R = 0.004$ per mth) $R \times V_t$
0		$V_0 = 2500$	10
1	90	$V_1 = 2600$	10.4
2	90	$V_2 = 2700.4$	10.8016
3	90	$V_3 = 2801.2016$	

To find an appropriate general formula, using W for the regular payment we write

$$V_1 = V_0(1 + R) + W$$
$$V_2 = V_1(1 + R) + W$$
$$V_3 = V_2(1 + R) + W$$

Substituting so that the value outstanding at each time period is related to V_0 gives

$$V_2 = V_0(1 + R)^2 + W(1 + R) + W$$

and

$$V_3 = V_0(1 + R)^3 + W(1 + R)^2 + W(1 + R) + W$$

The value after n time periods, V_n, has first term $V_0(1 + R)^n$ and a series corresponding to the regular payments of

$$W(1 + R)^{n-1} + \ldots + W(1 + R)^3 + W(1 + R)^2 + W(1 + R) + W$$

Writing this series in the reverse order lets us see that it is a GP. It is

$$W + W(1 + R) + W(1 + R)^2 + W(1 + R)^3 + \ldots + W(1 + R)^{n-1}$$

To use the formula for a sum of a GP we identify $a = W$ and $c = (1 + R)$. The series has n terms because the power of $(1 + R)$ is 1 for term two, 2 for term three and therefore $n - 1$ for term n. To find the sum we substitute in the formula

$$S_n = \frac{a(1 - c^n)}{1 - c} = \frac{W[1 - (1 + R)^n]}{1 - (1 + R)} = \frac{W[1 - (1 + R)^n]}{-R}$$

Multiplying numerator and denominator by -1 and reordering the terms in square brackets gives

$$S_n = \frac{W[(1 + R)^n - 1]}{R}$$

Adding this to the term in V_0 gives the following formula.

For regular payments

$$V_n = V_0(1 + R)^n + \frac{W[(1 + R)^n - 1]}{R}$$

Remember...

18

For the gold savings account described above, show that the amount outstanding first exceeds $5000 after 24 monthly payments have been made.

Use the formula with $V_0 = 2500$, $W = 90$ and $R = 0.004$ since the annual rate of interest of 0.048 is divided by 12 to obtain the monthly rate.

$$V_n = V_0(1 + R)^n + \frac{W[(1 + R)^n - 1]}{R}$$

$$V_{24} = 2500(1.004)^{24} + \frac{90[(1.004)^{24} - 1]}{0.004} = 5013.71$$

This amount exceeds $5000, but by less than $90. The 24th monthly payment has brought the total in the account to more than $5000 and the higher rate of interest will now be earned.

You can see the sequence of values outstanding over the 24-month period in the Regular Payments worksheet of the Finance.xls file.

SINKING FUND

A sinking fund is a fixed sum of money saved at regular intervals and then withdrawn one period after the last payment into the account. A firm may use a sinking fund to make provision for replacement of equipment. It follows a similar pattern to the gold savings account example above, but all payments are the same amount so $V_0 = W$ and also there is no payment into the account in time period n when the money is withdrawn. Adapting the regular payments formula gives

$$\text{sinking fund } V_n = W(1 + R)^n + \frac{W[(1 + R)^n - 1]}{R} - W$$

$$= \frac{W[(1 + R)^n(R + 1) - 1 - R]}{R}$$

This can be written as shown below.

Sinking fund

Remember...

$$V_n = \frac{W(1 + R)[(1 + R)^n - 1]}{R}$$

19

A firm sets aside $3000 per quarter for the purchase of new computer equipment. At an interest rate of 2% compound per quarter, how much is in the sinking fund at the end of 4 years?

We have $W = 3000$; time period is a quarter so $n = 16$, $R = 0.02$. Substituting in the sinking fund formula gives

$$V_n = \frac{W(1 + R)[(1 + R)^n - 1]}{R}$$

$$= \frac{3000(1.02)[(1.02)^{16} - 1]}{0.02} = \$57,036.21$$

ANNUITIES

If you buy an annuity of a particular value you pay that sum now, V_0, and are then entitled to receive a specified regular amount, A, for an agreed length of time. To enable us to apply the regular payments formula we let n be the number of payments that will be received under the annuity. Since you are receiving the regular payments instead of making them we have $A = -W$. After the last payment there is nothing left in the annuity fund and so $V_n = 0$. Rewriting the regular payments formula to give the value of the annuity, V_0, we have for regular payments

$$V_n = V_0(1 + R)^n + \frac{W[(1 + R)^n - 1]}{R}$$

but $V_n = 0$ and $A = -W$ and so

$$V_0(1 + R)^n = \frac{A[(1 + R)^n - 1]}{R}$$

Dividing through by $(1 + R)^n$ we divide this into each of the terms in the square brackets to obtain the formula shown below.

Annuity value   **Remember...**

$$V_0 = \frac{A[1 - (1 + R)^{-n}]}{R}$$

See the example on the MathEcon screen Economic Problems – Sequences.

This annuity value is calculated using Excel's Present Value function in the Regular Payments worksheet of the Finance.xls file.

The amount by which the annuity payment is multiplied to find the value of the annuity, $[1 - (1 + R)^{-n}]/R$, is called the annuity factor. The formula for the annuity value sums the discounted values of the annuity payments, A, taking into account the time period at which they are payable. A special kind of annuity, called a perpetuity, has no time limit on the length of time for which it is paid. If n is a very large number, $(1 + R)^{-n}$ is effectively 0 and the annuity value formula simplifies to

---

Perpetuity value   **Remember...**

$$V_0 = \frac{A}{R}$$

20

What is the value of an annuity that pays $1000 every 6 months for 15 years? Assume interest is at a compound rate of 4.6% every 6 months.

We have $A = 1000$, $R = 0.046$, $n = 30$ and so the annuity value is

$$V_0 = \frac{A[1 - (1 + R)^{-n}]}{R} = \frac{1000[1 - 1.046^{-30}]}{0.046} = \$16,098.97$$

MORTGAGE REPAYMENTS

When you take out a mortgage to buy a house you borrow an amount now and make regular payments over a time period until you have paid back the money borrowed plus interest. This implies $V_n = 0$. Letting M be the amount you borrow, in terms of the regular payments formula $M = -V_0$. Interest payments are often calculated annually on the money owing at the start of the year, although it may be part of your mortgage agreement that you pay back an amount each month. To use the regular payments formula the time period of the payments must correspond to that on which the interest is charged. Rearranging the formula shows W, the required repayment each period.

Using $V_n = V_0(1 + R)^n + W[(1 + R)^n - 1]/R$ with $V_n = 0$ and $M = -V_0$ we have

$$M(1 + R)^n = \frac{W[(1 + R)^n - 1]}{R}$$

which, dividing through by $(1 + R)^n$, gives

$$M = \frac{W[1 - (1 + R)^{-n}]}{R}$$

Rewriting this to obtain an expression for W gives the formula shown below.

Mortgage repayment

Remember...

$$W = \frac{M.R}{1 - (1 + R)^{-n}}$$

The capital recovery factor is the name given to $R/[1 - (1 + R)^{-n}]$. The factor is multiplied by the amount you borrow to determine the size of the repayments required.

21

What is the annual repayment on a $75,000 mortgage over a 25-year period if the rate of interest is 8%?

We have $M = 75,000$, $n = 25$ and $R = 0.08$ so the mortgage repayment is

$$W = \frac{M.R}{1 - (1 + R)^{-n}}$$

$$= \frac{75,000 \times 0.08}{1 - (1.08)^{-25}}$$

$$= \$7025.91 \text{ per year}$$

4.24 A firm puts $800 per month in a sinking fund at an interest rate of 1% compound per month. What is the value of the fund at the end of 5 years?

4.25 What is the annual repayment on a $59,000 mortgage over 20 years at a compound annual interest rate of 7%? If instead the interest rate is 9%, what is the annual repayment?

SECTION 4.11: Prices of Bills and Bonds and the Rate of Interest

BILLS

Bills, or bills of exchange, are a method of short-term borrowing used by firms and the government. A bill is initially sold below its face value, and the person holding the bill at its maturity date receives the sum stated as the bill's face value. The return to the lender is the margin between what was paid and what is received. This can be expressed as an interest rate.

22

If you pay $97 for a $100 bill which is redeemed at its face value after 3 months, what rate of interest over the quarter do you receive?

$$R = \frac{V_1 - V_0}{V_0} \times 100$$

$$= \frac{100 - 97}{97} \times 100$$

$$= 3.09\%$$

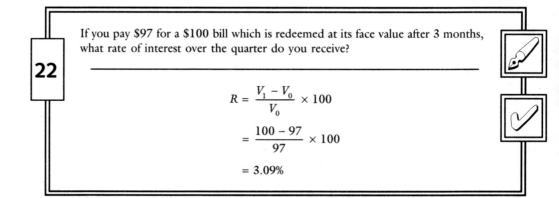

BONDS

Bonds are a longer term form of borrowing. They pay interest each year at the coupon rate stated on the bond, and the face value of the bond is payable on maturity. There are also perpetual bonds with no maturity date. People buy perpetual bonds for the return on them that they will receive. Since the coupon rate on the bond is fixed, the bond price varies at different times to bring its yield into line with the current interest rate, R. As R rises, people will pay less for a bond that offers a particular coupon payment and bond prices therefore fall. There is an inverse relationship between R and bond prices.

Remember...

For a perpetual bond

- coupon payment = coupon value of bond × coupon rate
- bond price = coupon payment ÷ R
- bond price falls as R rises.

23

A \$1000 perpetual bond has a coupon rate of 8%. What price will the bond sell for if the current interest rate is (a) 5% (b) 8% (c) 12%?

The coupon payment is $1000 \times 0.08 = 80$. Therefore, the prices of the bond at the various interest rates are

(a) $\dfrac{80}{0.05} = 1600$

(b) $\dfrac{80}{0.08} = 1000$

(c) $\dfrac{80}{0.12} = 666.67$

A fixed term bond repays the face value of the bond at its redemption date as well as paying the coupon rate of interest. All these payments, together with the times at which they occur, have to be taken into account in calculating the overall return to the purchaser of the bond. The price of a bond at a particular time is given by the net present value of the stream of returns it generates over the remainder of its term, using the current interest rate, R, as the discount rate. We calculate the bond price using the NPV method explained in section 4.8.

Remember...

For a fixed term bond

- bond price = NPV of returns to bond holder
- bond price falls as R rises.

24

A $1000 bond with 3 years to its redemption date has a coupon rate of 8%. What price will the bond sell for if the current interest rate is (a) 5% (b) 8% (c) 12%?

Calculating present values in a table gives

		(a)		(b)		(c)	
Year t	Return	$R = 0.05$ $1/(1 + R)^t$	Present value	$R = 0.08$ $1/(1 + R)^t$	Present value	$R = 0.12$ $1/(1 + R)^t$	Present value
1	80	0.952	76.19	0.926	74.07	0.893	71.43
2	80	0.907	72.56	0.857	68.59	0.797	63.78
3	1080	0.864	932.94	0.794	857.34	0.712	768.72
			1081.70		1000.00		903.93

The bond prices are $1081.70, $1000 and $903.93, the price being lower if the interest rate is higher.

The screens in section 5 of MathEcon chapter 4 give more information.

4.26 A $500 perpetual bond has a coupon rate of 10%. If the current interest rate is (a) 4% (b) 10% (c) 15%, what is the bond's price?

4.27 A $2000 bond with a yield of 12% has 4 years left before its redemption date. What is the bond's price if the current interest rate is (a) 6% (b) 12% (c) 16%?

SECTION 4.12: Financial Calculations with Excel

In Excel, you can do financial calculations either by inputting a single formula to find the value in the final time period, or by creating a column that shows the values for each time period. The advantage of the latter approach is that you can see exactly what is being calculated as you work it out one step at a time. The three worksheets in the Finance.xls file contain examples of both methods.

The spreadsheets are constructed using a similar process to that described in sections 1.13 and 2.15. We enter parameters in appropriate cells and fill in a column of values of time, t. Appropriate formulae are then entered and copied down to obtain values for each time period.

In the Compound Interest worksheet shown in figure 4.4, with annual compounding the interest payment is calculated for each year and then added to the current value

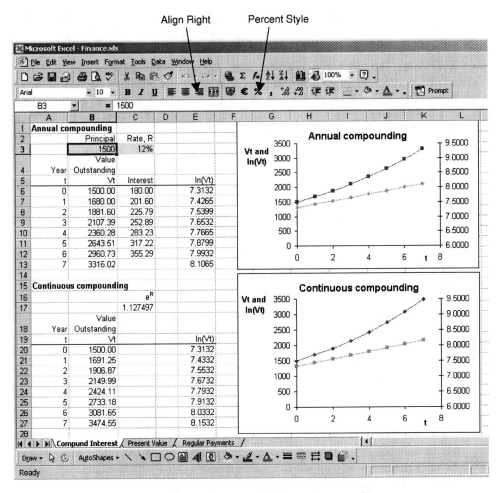

Figure 4.4 Compound interest calculations showing the Percent Style and Align Right buttons

outstanding to obtain the next value outstanding. The formulae used are =B6*Rate to obtain the amount of interest and =B6+C6 to find the new value outstanding. With continuous compounding each year's value is found by multiplying the previous one by e^R. It is useful to find the value of e^R first and this is done in cell C17 using the formula =EXP(Rate). It is then applied from row 21 downwards to obtain the column of values with the formula =B20*$C$17. Columns of logarithms of the V_t values are also found using the =LN() function.

You may be interested in some of the formatting techniques that have been used in this worksheet. The interest rate, R, is actually entered as a decimal in cell C3, but the Percent Style button has been clicked to display it as a percentage. Text normally aligns to the left of the cell, but the Align Right button has been used to display column titles over the values. The title Value Outstanding has been put on two lines by selecting Format Cells from the menu and choosing Alignment, Wrap text. The columns of values have been formatted to show a specific number of decimal places. You can do this by choosing Format, Cells, Number from the menu and choosing the number of decimal places you require, or you can use the Increase Decimal and Decrease Decimal buttons.

The graphs displayed each plot two data series that are measured in very different units and therefore require separate scales. To use two different vertical axes you begin by plotting your chart in the usual way, selecting all the data and choosing an XY scatter chart type. This just gives you the usual axis at the left and one of the data series may be barely visible because its values almost coincide with the x axis. Select that series, right mouse click over it and choose Format Data Series from the pop up menu. Choose the Axis tab and select 'Plot series on secondary axis'. Excel automatically chooses a range of axis values and brings up the secondary axis. You can now adjust the scale on each axis by selecting it in turn and using the Format Axis command. Select the Scale tab and type numbers in the boxes to get the series presented in the way you want.

The Present Value worksheet in figure 4.5 sets out the calculation of present value and internal rate of return for the project in worked example 15. We calculate the first discount factor by entering the formula =1/(1+$C$3)^A7 in cell C7. Notice that an absolute address is used for the discount rate cell and a relative one for the cell containing the year, which forms the power used in the denominator. This formula can then be copied down the column. Notice also that the formula is applicable in year 0

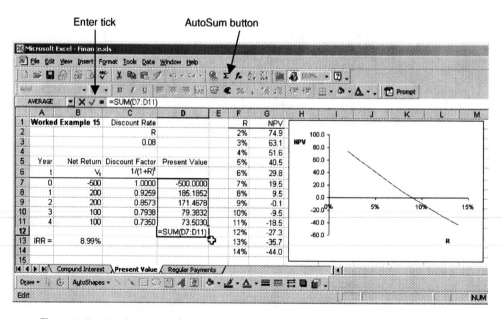

Figure 4.5 Net Present Value calculation, showing AutoSum button and Enter tick

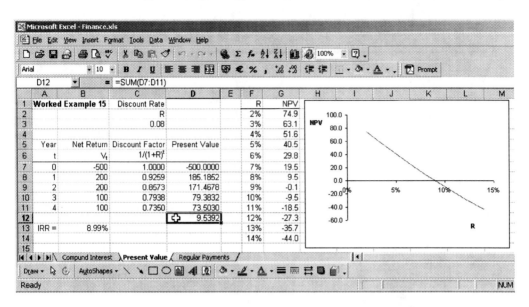

Figure 4.5 (*cont'd*) Shows sum calculated when Enter tick is clicked

(it gives the value 1). The present value of each net return is now obtained by multiplying by the appropriate discount factor. We enter the formula =B7*C7 in cell D7 and copy it down the column. The Net Present Value of the project is then obtained by summing the column of Present Values. If you select the cell at the foot of a column of values and click the AutoSum button, Excel will suggest adding the values above. In this case these are the values we want, so you can click the Enter tick to the left of the formula bar to enter the formula. If the values that Excel suggests are not in fact the values you want to sum, you just change them to those that you want.

Excel has an in-built Net Present Value function that just requires you to specify the discount rate it should use and the net returns it should include. However, the first net return that you specify must relate to year 1, since the function does not include year 0. If you use this function you must add the year 0 net return to it to obtain the net present value of the project. The Net Present Value function is used in column G of the worksheet to find the net present values of the project at different discount rates. The formula =NPV(F2,$B$8:$B$11)+$D$7 is entered in cell G2 and copied down the column. A graph of the NPV values is plotted against the rate of interest R. The point at which the graph cuts the R axis is where NPV = 0, and so the value of r at that point is the Internal Rate of Return of the project. Excel also includes an IRR function which uses the series of net returns, including the one for year 0, to calculate the IRR. This function is used in cell B13 where the formula =IRR(B7:B11) is entered. If you use the Paste Function button to enter this function you will see that it offers you the opportunity to guess the internal rate of return, but in simple problems it is not necessary to do so.

Chapter 4: Answers to Practice Problems

4.1   0.057

4.2 $3 million

4.3 $98,040

4.4 $174.61

4.5   1 Euro = 1.123 US$, so (a) 500 × 1.123 = $561.5 (b) 1 US$ = 1/1.123 €, so the €/US$ exchange rate is 0.890 and the price is €52.54.

4.6   19.69%

4.7   5.4%, 1.4pp higher

4.8   −4/3

4.9 $1373.33

4.10   7% simple interest gives $6750 while 6% compound interest gives $6691.13, so 7% simple interest is preferable.

4.11   Unit time = 1 quarter

$n = 20$, $R = 0.03$

$V_n = \$1806.11$

4.12   (a) 1 quarter is unit time

$R = 0.045$, $n = 8$

$V_n = \$568.84$

(b) 1 month is unit time

$R = 0.015$, $n = 24$

$V_n = \$571.80$

(c) $V_n = V_0 e^{Rn}$

$= 400 \times 1.433$

$= \$573.33$

4.13 $V_n = \$431.95$

4.14   Annual compounding: V_n = \$1223.22

Continuous compounding: V_n = \$1267.84

You owe \$44.62 more if compounding is continuous.

4.15   (a) 17.89%   (b) 15.87%   (c) 13.24%

(d) 18.29%   (e) 25.34%

4.16   (a) Approximately: 0.035 = 3.5%

Exactly: 0.0329 = 3.3%

The approximation is quite close.

(b) Approximately: 0.12 = 12%

Exactly: 0.0882 = 8.82%

The approximation is not good for such large changes.

4.17 $V_t = V_0 e^{Rt}$

Year, t	Sales	ln Sales
0	40	3.69
1	80.55	4.39
2	162.21	5.09
3	326.65	5.79
4	657.79	6.49

Substituting gives

$2000 = 40e^{0.7n}$

$3.912 = 0.7n$

$n = 5.59$

After 5.59 years the shop will be selling the televisions at 2000 per year.

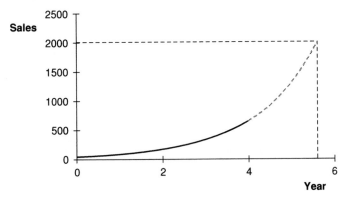

Figure 4.6   Sales of thin screen televisions

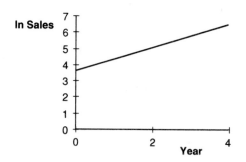

Figure 4.7 In Sales of thin screen televisions

4.18   22.66%

4.19 $1,320,000, $1,678,745

4.20
Year	Discount factor	PV
0	1.0000	−390.00
1	0.9524	95.24
2	0.9070	181.41
3	0.8638	129.58
		16.22

NPV = 16.22 > 0, so the project should go ahead. At 10% discount rate, NPV = −21.1 < 0: recommendation now is not to undertake the project.

4.21   Yes, NPV = 151.11

IRR = 14.63%

4.22   54,610

4.23 $a = 6$, $c = \frac{1}{3}$, $S_n = 9$

4.24 $65,989.09

4.25 $5569.18, $6463.24

4.26 $1250, $500, $333.33

4.27 $2415.81, $2000, $1776.15

chapter five

Differentiation in Economics

In this chapter you learn to
- Understand that differentiation lets us identify marginal relationships in economics
- Measure the rate of change along a line or curve
- Find dy/dx for power functions and practise the basic rules of differentiation
- Apply differentiation notation to economics examples
- Differentiate a total utility function to find marginal utility
- Obtain a marginal revenue function as the derivative of the total revenue function
- Differentiate a short-run production function to find the marginal product of labour
- Understand the relationship between total cost and marginal cost
- Measure point elasticity of demand and supply
- Find the investment multiplier in a simple macroeconomic model

SECTION 5.1: Introduction

Differentiation is a mathematical technique which is useful for studying economic relationships. This chapter shows you how to differentiate functions used in economic modelling. You find that differentiating a total cost or revenue function gives you the corresponding marginal cost or revenue function. The rules used are not difficult. You just learn them and apply them.

Screens in MathEcon chapter 5 Differentiation in Economics link with this chapter. They offer you a detailed step-by-step approach to the methods, but if you already know some of the mathematical rules you can use the summaries and then move directly to section 5.3 Application to Economic Analysis.

SECTION 5.2: Using Differentiation in Economics

Economists often analyse the effects of changes. For example, as a firm increases the quantity of output it sells, the total revenue it receives changes. We would like a way of measuring the rate at which one variable alters in response to changes in another.

Suppose y = total revenue and x = output. If output x is increased by a small amount we denote the change that occurs in x as Δx, and the corresponding change in total revenue y we denote Δy. If total revenue is a straight line, for any Δx the resulting Δy is such that the ratio $\Delta y/\Delta x$ equals the slope of the line. Figure 5.1 shows the line $y = 3x$, where if x increases from 3 to 4, y increases from 9 to 12. We have $\Delta x = 1$, $\Delta y = 3$ and so $\Delta y/\Delta x = 3$. Also, if x changes from 5 to 15, an increase of 10 units, the corresponding increase in y is from 15 to 45, a rise of 30, so the change in y per unit increase in x is $\Delta y/\Delta x = 30/10 = 3$. The rate at which y changes per unit change in x, $\Delta y/\Delta x$, is the same along a straight line regardless of where it is measured. If y is total revenue, $\Delta y/\Delta x$ represents marginal revenue, the rate at which total revenue changes as output increases.

> For more about linear functions see section 2.6.

For a linear function, the rate of change of y with respect to x is measured by the slope of the line which is found from

Remember...

$$\Delta y/\Delta x = \text{(distance up)} \div \text{(distance to the right)}$$

A total revenue function may take the form of a curve. For example, figure 5.2 shows the curve $y = 56x - 4x^2$, where y represents total revenue. At point A the curve is sloping steeply upwards. The curve continues to slope upwards as x increases, but its slope becomes less and less steep so that at B the slope is fairly shallow and then at $x = 7$ the curve reaches a maximum and turns downwards. For values of x that are greater than 7, such as C, the curve has a negative slope. A curve changes at different rates at different points. If y is total revenue, we would like to find the rate at which it changes as output changes, since this represents marginal revenue. When total revenue takes the form of a curve, marginal revenue takes different values at different output levels. We can find a general expression for marginal revenue using the mathematical

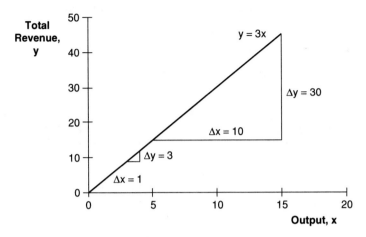

Figure 5.1 Linear function, $\Delta y/\Delta x$ is constant

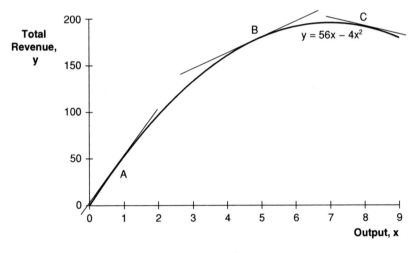

Figure 5.2 Different slopes at different points on a curve

technique of differentiation. The expression we obtain is called the derivative of the function and its value at any point measures the slope of the curve. To find the value of the derivative we note that the slope of the curve at a point is the same as the slope of the tangent to the curve at that point, and we obtain the derivative by finding the slope of that line. The lines drawn on figure 5.2 are tangents to the curve at points A, B and C respectively. Notice that the tangent at point A has a steeper slope than that at B, and that the tangent at C has a negative slope.

Use the MathEcon screen Why Economists use Differentiation in section 1 to see animated examples of measuring the slopes of lines and curves.

> differentiation: finding the derivative of a function.
> tangent: a line that just touches a curve at a point.

SECTION 5.3: The Basic Rules of Differentiation

For measuring the slope of a line we have the notation $\Delta y/\Delta x$ which represents the ratio of measurable changes in y and x. Differentiation is concerned with measuring the slope of a curve at a point. A derivative tells us how y changes if x changes by a very tiny amount and we need a new notation for this. Differentiating $y = f(x)$ gives us the derivative of y with respect to x which is written as dy/dx. The expression dy/dx should be regarded as a single symbol and you should not try to work separately with parts of it. A derivative measures the rate of change of y with respect to x and can only be found for smooth curves. To be differentiable, a function must be continuous in the relevant range. The derivative dy/dx is itself a function of x. If we wish we can evaluate it for any particular x value by substituting that value of x.

> derivative of a function: the rate at which a function is changing with respect to an independent variable, measured at any point on the function by the slope of the tangent to the function at that point.

We continue to use symbols Δy and Δx to denote actual changes in y and x respectively. We can predict the effect on y, Δy, of a small change in x, Δx, by multiplying the change in x by the derivative dy/dx. Note that this method is approximate and is valid only for small changes in x. This is the small increments formula.

> The derivative of y with respect to x is denoted dy/dx.   **Remember...**
> For small changes Δx it is approximately true that
>
> $$\Delta y = \Delta x \cdot dy/dx$$

A derivative dy/dx is an expression that measures the slope of the tangent to the curve at any point on the function $y = f(x)$. To find derivatives in practice we apply the rules listed below. As an illustration of how the rules come about we begin with an example worked from first principles.

Find the derivative dy/dx for the curve $y = 3x^2$, which is shown in figure 5.3.

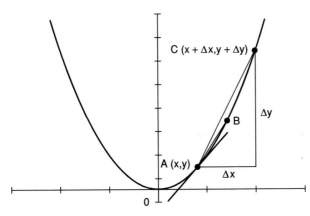

Figure 5.3 Finding dy/dx for the curve $y = 3x^2$

The derivative of the curve at point A is the slope of the tangent shown in figure 5.3. We need to obtain a general expression for the slope of this tangent, relating it to the function we are differentiating. To do this we find an expression for the slope of a line between point A with coordinates (x,y) and point C, another point on the curve with coordinates $(x + \Delta x, y + \Delta y)$. The line AC is drawn in the figure and we see that its slope, which is $\Delta y/\Delta x$, differs somewhat from the slope of the tangent that we seek. We now consider what happens to the slope of AC if we bring point C closer and closer to point A. When point C reaches B, the slope of AC becomes the slope of AB and we see from the lines drawn that its slope is closer to the slope of the tangent at A. Continuing to move point C, as it becomes so close to A that the two points are indistinguishable, the slope of AC is the slope of the tangent at A. When this occurs Δx is extremely tiny and very close to 0. The process of seeing what happens as point C moves to point A is called finding the limit as $\Delta x \to 0$ (we say 'the limit as delta x tends to 0'). We now find an expression for the slope of AC, $\Delta y/\Delta x$, and take the limit as $\Delta x \to 0$ to obtain the derivative dy/dx.

Since points A and C lie on the curve, both sets of coordinates (x,y) and $(x + \Delta x, y + \Delta y)$ satisfy the function $y = 3x^2$. Substituting the coordinates for point C in the function we have

$$y + \Delta y = 3(x + \Delta x)^2$$

Squaring out the brackets we obtain

$$y + \Delta y = 3[x^2 + 2x\Delta x + (\Delta x)^2]$$

Multiplying out and subtracting y from both sides gives

$$\Delta y = 3x^2 + 6x\Delta x + 3(\Delta x)^2 - y$$

Substituting the functional relationship for y we find

$$\Delta y = 3x^2 + 6x\Delta x + 3(\Delta x)^2 - 3x^2$$

so the two terms in x^2 cancel leaving

$$\Delta y = 6x\Delta x + 3(\Delta x)^2$$

The slope of AC is $\Delta y/\Delta x$ and so to find it we divide through both sides of the equation by Δx, which gives

$$\Delta y/\Delta x = 6x + 3\Delta x$$

The derivative dy/dx is the limit of $\Delta y/\Delta x$ as $\Delta x \to 0$. Taking this limit, the term $3\Delta x$ becomes 0 and so

$$dy/dx = 6x$$

From section 2 of MathEcon chapter 5, use the screens The Basic Rules of Differentiation, Worked Examples, A Summary of the Basic Rules of Differentiation and Practice Differentiation to develop your understanding and skills.

The basic rules of differentiation for functions of the form $y = f(x)$ are now stated in turn and worked examples are given. In sections 5.5 to 5.10 we apply these rules to a range of economic problems, so you get lots of practise at differentiation. As we look at relationships between various economics curves, a graphical approach is also used. This helps you understand what a derivative is. We learn and apply the rules of differentiation without proving each of them separately. Standard mathematics books use the above approach to obtain the general rules.

THE CONSTANT RULE

When y is a constant, different values of x all correspond to the same y value. Suppose $y = 8$, as shown in figure 5.4. The graph is a horizontal line, and so its slope is 0. For any change in x, y does not change. There is a zero change in y corresponding to any change in x.

Constants differentiate to zero, i.e.

     if $y = c$ where c is a constant, $dy/dx = 0$

Remember...

2

Find dy/dx for the function shown in figure 5.4, $y = 8$.

For $y = 8$, $dy/dx = 0$, by the constant rule.

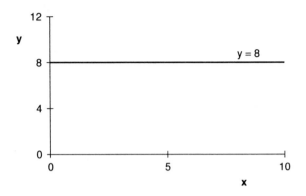

Figure 5.4 A horizontal line has slope = 0

POWER-FUNCTION RULE

A power function has the variable with respect to which we are asked to differentiate raised to a power. Examples of power functions are

$$y = x^4$$

$$y = \frac{20}{x^2}$$

To differentiate a power function you follow the rule: multiply by the power and reduce the power by 1.

Remember...

If $y = ax^n$ where a and n are constants

$$dy/dx = n . ax^{n-1}$$

Multiply by the power, then subtract 1 from the power.

Notice the rule implies that if you differentiate a function of x^3, dy/dx is a function of x^2. While if y is a function of x^2, dy/dx is a function of x. And if you begin with a linear function where y is a function of x, differentiation yields a constant. Another way of handling the constant a in the function $y = ax^n$ is to write it down as you begin differentiating and multiply it by the derivative of x^n. This is possible because of the following rule.

The derivative of a constant times a function is the constant times the derivative of the function, i.e.

Remember...

$$\frac{d(ax^n)}{dx} = a \cdot \frac{d(x^n)}{dx}$$

When differentiating power functions, remember the following from the rules of indices

Remember...

$$x^1 = x$$

$$x^0 = 1$$

$$\frac{1}{x^n} = x^{-n}$$

$$\sqrt{x} = x^{0.5} = x^{1/2}$$

Differentiate each of the power functions listed, finding dy/dx in each case.

(a) $y = x^3$ (b) $y = 3x^2$

(c) $y = -9x^5$ (d) $y = 22x$

(e) $y = 4/x^2$ (f) $y = -18\sqrt{x}$

3

(a) $y = x^3$

To find dy/dx we multiply by the power, which is 3, then subtract 1 from the power, giving

$$dy/dx = 3x^{3-1} = 3x^2$$

(b) $y = 3x^2$

The rule says we should multiply by the power, which is 2, and then subtract 1 from the power. This gives

$$dy/dx = 2 \times 3x^{2-1} = 6x^1 = 6x$$

The power function rule gives the same result as we found from first principles in worked example 1.

(c) $y = -9x^5$

Using our rule we multiply by 5, as it is the power of x, and we then reduce that power by 1. We find

$$dy/dx = 5 \times (-9)x^{5-1} = -45x^4$$

(d) $y = 22x$

In this function x has a power of 1, so multiplying by it leaves the value 22 unchanged. When we reduce the power by 1 we obtain a power of zero, and so must use the rule that $x^0 = 1$.

$$dy/dx = 1 \times 22x^{1-1} = 22x^0 = 22$$

(e) $y = 4/x^2$

In this function x^2 forms the divisor of the constant, 4, and we need to rewrite the expression before differentiating. Since $1/x^2 = x^{-2}$ we write

$$y = 4x^{-2}$$

We then apply our rule, noting that here we are multiplying by a negative number, and that subtracting 1 from a negative power makes the power more negative.

$$dy/dx = -2 \times 4x^{-2-1} = -8x^{-3} = -8/x^3$$

(f) $y = -18\sqrt{x}$

Again this function should be rewritten before we differentiate it. We have that $\sqrt{x} = x^{1/2} = x^{0.5}$ and so we may write

$$y = -18x^{0.5}$$

As we use our rule to differentiate, this time we are multiplying by a fraction and when 1 is subtracted from the power it becomes a negative fraction.

$$dy/dx = 0.5 \times (-18)x^{0.5-1} = -9x^{-0.5} = -9/x^{0.5} = -9/\sqrt{x}$$

Differentiate $y = -5x^2$ and use the small increments formula to predict the change in y if x increases from 3 to 4. Find also the exact change in y by substituting in the function.

4

$$y = -5x^2$$

Differentiating with respect to x we multiply by the power, which is 2, and then subtract 1 from the power so that

$$dy/dx = 2 \times (-5)x^{2-1} = -10x^1 = -10x$$

The small increments formula is

$$\Delta y = \Delta x \cdot dy/dx$$

As x increases from 3 to 4, $\Delta x = 1$ and so we predict $\Delta y = dy/dx = -10 \times 3 = -30$, substituting the initial value of x. The small increments formula suggests y will fall by 30.

Substituting the two x values in turn we find if $x = 3$, $y = -45$ and if $x = 4$, $y = -80$. Actually, y changes by $-80 - (-45) = -35$, a fall of 35.

5.1 Differentiate (i.e. find dy/dx) for each of the following functions

(a) $y = x^4$ (b) $y = 3x^3$

(c) $y = -2x^5$ (d) $y = 95$

(e) $y = 5x$

5.2 Differentiate each function with respect to x

(a) $y = 8x^{-1}$ (b) $y = -6x^{-2}$

(c) $y = 15x^{\frac{1}{3}}$ (d) $y = 10/x$

(e) $y = -3/x^2$ (f) $y = -22\sqrt{x}$

(g) $y = x$

5.3 Differentiate $y = 0.5x^2$ and use the small increments formula to predict the approximate change in y if x changes from 1 to 2. Calculate also the exact change.

SUM-DIFFERENCE RULE

If y is the sum or difference of terms which contain the same variable, x, this rule is used. We differentiate each term separately and then add or subtract them corresponding to the signs in the original function, y.

If $y = f(x) + g(x)$ **Remember...**

$$\frac{dy}{dx} = \frac{d[f(x)]}{dx} + \frac{d[g(x)]}{dx}$$

The derivative of a sum is the sum of the derivatives.

If $y = f(x) - g(x)$

$$\frac{dy}{dx} = \frac{d[f(x)]}{dx} - \frac{d[g(x)]}{dx}$$

The derivative of a difference is the difference of the derivatives.

Differentiate each function with respect to x

(a) $y = 11x + 9x^2$

(b) $y = 8x^2 - 22x + 33$

(c) $y = 7x^3 - 10x^2 + 3x - 4$

(d) $y = 27x + 18 - \dfrac{5}{x^2}$

(e) $y = -\dfrac{4}{x} + \dfrac{18}{\sqrt{x}}$

(f) $y = 2x^7 - 12x^4 + 45x - \dfrac{13}{x}$

(g) $y = c + mx$ (where c and m are constants)

(a) $y = 11x + 9x^2$
To differentiate this sum of terms we differentiate each separately and then add. The derivative of $11x$ is 11 and the derivative of $9x^2$ is $18x$ by the power function rule. So adding the derivatives we get

$$dy/dx = 11 + 18x$$

(b) $y = 8x^2 - 22x + 33$
Taking the terms separately we find $8x^2$ differentiates to $16x$, $22x$ differentiates to 22 and 33 differentiates to 0. Subtracting and adding these results as appropriate gives

$$dy/dx = 16x - 22 + 0 = 16x - 22$$

(c) $y = 7x^3 - 10x^2 + 3x - 4$
Applying the power rule of differentiation to each term in turn we see $7x^3$ differentiates to $21x^2$, $10x^2$ differentiates to $20x$, $3x$ differentiates to 3 and 4 differentiates to 0. Using the sum-difference rule gives

$$dy/dx = 21x^2 - 20x + 3 - 0 = 21x^2 - 20x + 3$$

(d) $y = 27x + 18 - 5/x^2$
Since one of the terms involves division by x^2, we rewrite the function before differentiating and obtain

$$y = 27x + 18 - 5x^{-2}$$

Separately, the derivative of $27x$ is 27, of 18 is 0, and of $5x^{-2}$ is $-10x^{-3}$. Hence

$$dy/dx = 27 + 0 - (-10x^{-3}) = 27 + 10/x^3$$
(since multiplying two minus signs gives a plus)

(e) $y = -4/x + 18/\sqrt{x}$
This function can be rewritten as

$$y = -4x^{-1} + 18x^{-1/2}$$

Taking the terms in turn, $-4x^{-1}$ differentiates to $4x^{-2}$, since two minus signs multiplied together give a plus, $18x^{-1/2}$ differentiates to $-9x^{-3/2}$, since $-1/2$ multiplied by 18 gives -9. Using the sum rule we obtain

$$dy/dx = 4x^{-2} - 9x^{-3/2} = 4/x^2 - 9/x^{3/2}$$

(f) $y = 2x^7 - 12x^4 + 45x - 13/x$
Rewriting the function gives

$$y = 2x^7 - 12x^4 + 45x - 13x^{-1}$$

Differentiating each term separately, $2x^7$ differentiates to $14x^6$, $12x^4$ differentiates to $48x^3$, $45x$ differentiates to 45 and $13x^{-1}$ differentiates to $-13x^{-2}$. Adding or subtracting the terms as appropriate gives

$$dy/dx = 14x^6 - 48x^3 + 45 - (-13x^{-2}) = 14x^6 - 48x^3 + 45 + 13/x^2$$

(g) $y = c + mx$ (where c and m are constants)

Separately differentiating the terms we find c differentiates to 0, because it is a constant, and mx differentiates to $1 \times mx^0 = m$ because m is a constant, $x = x^1$ and $x^0 = 1$. Using the sum-difference rule we add the derivatives, giving

$$dy/dx = 0 + m = m$$

5.4 Find the derivative, dy/dx, for each of the following functions

(a) $y = 20x + 5x^2$ (b) $y = 6x - 3x^2 + 4x^3$

(c) $y = 92 - 7x + 8x^2 - 0.2x^3$ (d) $y = \dfrac{8}{x} + 25 - 12x + 6x^2$

(e) $y = 8\sqrt{x} - 4 + 2x$

LINEAR-FUNCTION RULE

Economists choose to model relationships between variables in as simple a way as possible, which means that straight line functions are often used. Worked example 5 (g) above shows that the power-function rule and the sum-difference rule together allow us to find the derivative of a linear function, $y = c + mx$. Since we frequently want to differentiate linear functions it is useful to set out the result as a separate rule.

If $y = c + mx$ **Remember...**

$$dy/dx = m$$

The derivative of a linear function is the slope of the line.

The result of differentiating a linear function is the same as measuring the slope of a line by $\Delta y/\Delta x$ as we did in section 5.2. Notice that if we differentiate $y = mx$ we find $dy/dx = m$, the same as the derivative of $y = c + mx$. So a line passing through the origin, for which c is 0 and a parallel line with an intercept on the y axis both have the same derivative.

A constant multiplied by the variable with respect to which we are differentiating, such as mx, often forms one term of a more complex function.

> **Remember...**
>
> If $y = mx$
>
> $$dy/dx = m$$
>
> The derivative of a constant times the variable with respect to which we are differentiating is the constant.

6

Differentiate

(a) $y = 16x$ (b) $y = 32 + 16x$

(c) $y = 75 - 11x$

(a) $y = 16x$

Applying the linear-function rule, $16x$ differentiates to 16.

$$dy/dx = 16$$

Notice that $y = 16x$ represents a line passing through the origin with a slope of 16.

(b) $y = 32 + 16x$

By the linear-function rule, the derivative of $32 + 16x$ is 16.

$$dy/dx = 16$$

In this case the function y represents a line which intersects the y axis at 32 and which has a slope of 16.

(c) $y = 75 - 11x$

$$dy/dx = -11$$

Notice that this linear function has a negative slope.

5.5 Find dy/dx for the following linear functions. Check your answers by choosing two values of x and finding $\Delta y/\Delta x$.

(a) $y = 3x + 10$ (b) $y = 64 - 2x$

(c) $y = 28$ (d) $y = 0.5x - 4$

(e) $y = ax + b$ (where a and b are constants)

INVERSE-FUNCTION RULE

If we are given a function of the form $x = f(y)$ we can differentiate with respect to y, obtaining dx/dy, and then take the reciprocal of the result to find dy/dx. As we differentiate with respect to y we use y in place of x in the rules we have learnt. We obtain dy/dx as a function of y. This method allows us to find an expression for dy/dx without having to obtain the inverse of the original function, but it is only applicable when there is just one y value corresponding to each x value so that the inverse function exists. We may need to restrict the y values we consider to achieve this, as shown in part (b) of the following worked example.

To find dy/dx, we may obtain dx/dy and turn it upside down, i.e.

$$dy/dx = \frac{1}{dx/dy}$$

Remember...

Find dy/dx for the functions given

(a) $x = 9y^5$

(b) $x = 81 + 30y + 5y^2$, where $y > 0$

7

(a) $x = 9y^5$

First find dx/dy applying the rule 'multiply by the power then subtract 1 from the power', to the term in y on the right-hand side

$$dx/dy = 45y^4$$

Now take the reciprocal

$$dy/dx = \frac{1}{45y^4}$$

(b) The restriction $y > 0$ ensures there is just one y value corresponding to each x value. If negative y values were allowed, we would find, for example, that $y = -7$ gives $x = 116$ and so does $y = 1$.

$$x = 81 + 30y + 5y^2$$

First find dx/dy

$$dx/dy = 30 + 10y$$

Now take the reciprocal

$$dy/dx = \frac{1}{30 + 10y}$$

5.6 (a) If $x = 64 + 5y$ find dy/dx

(b) If $x = y^2$ and $y > 0$ find dy/dx

SECTION 5.4: Application to Economic Analysis

In economic modelling we usually represent the variables by letters indicating their economic meaning. For example, if utility depends on the amount of x consumed we write $U = f(x)$ or $TU = f(x)$. Before differentiating we can if we wish substitute y for U or for TU and return to the standard form $y = f(x)$. It is useful, however, to learn to work with different variable names. We retain the original notation and differentiate with respect to x, obtaining dU/dx or $d(TU)/dx$, as appropriate.

Different variable names are also used instead of x. Some that commonly occur in economics examples are: P, price; Q, quantity; L, quantity of labour used; I, investment. If appropriate we can differentiate with respect to any of these variables, in effect substituting the appropriate variable name for x in the rules of differentiation we have learnt.

Letters are also used to denote constants. Examples are m and c in the expression $y = mx + c$. Such constants stand for numerical values, but the use of letters rather than numbers allows us to obtain more general results. Letters such as a, b, c are commonly used as constants. Notice that when we differentiate, constants are treated as if they were numbers.

Implicitly we assume that our functions are defined for values that are meaningful in economics. Some variables are restricted to positive values, although the marginal functions we find in this chapter can often take negative values.

Ascertain which letters represent constants.
Identify the variable with respect to which you are differentiating and use it as x in the rules.

Remember...

SECTION 5.5: Utility Functions

For utility analysis we define a function which represents total utility, $U = f(x)$. It shows how much utility an individual obtains from consumption of different amounts of good *x*. As the amount of *x* consumed changes, so the individual's total utility changes. You may already be accustomed to defining marginal utility as the change in total utility when one additional unit of good *x* is consumed. Differentiation provides a more general approach, giving us a statement about marginal utility which is true for all values of *x*. When the total utility function is the kind of smooth curve that economists usually draw its derivative dU/dx is the appropriate way of measuring marginal utility. The derivative shows the rate at which total utility is changing at any point on the curve. The unit-changes approach is an approximation which does give exactly the same values for marginal utility if the utility function is linear.

To find an expression for marginal utility, differentiate the total utility function, i.e.

$$MU = \frac{dU}{dx}$$

Remember...

8

If total utility, $U = 10.5x - 0.75x^2$, find marginal utility, MU. By plotting the total utility and marginal utility functions say how total and marginal utility change as *x* increases. Does the function satisfy the law of diminishing marginal utility?

Marginal utility is found by differentiating the total utility function. Since $U = f(x)$ we find dU/dx using the rules we have learnt for differentiating with respect to *x*. Given

$$U = 10.5x - 0.75x^2$$

$$MU = \frac{dU}{dx} = 10.5 - 1.5x$$

Substituting values of *x* from 0 to 9 into each function gives the values in the table, which are then plotted in figure 5.5.

x	0	1	2	3	4	5	6	7	8	9
Total utility	0	9.75	18	24.75	30	33.75	36	36.75	36	33.75
Marginal utility	10.5	9	7.5	6	4.5	3	1.5	0	−1.5	−3

As *x* increases from 0, total utility rises steeply at first but then more gradually until at $x = 7$ it reaches a maximum and begins to fall. Marginal utility falls steadily from the value of 10.5 when $x = 0$. It reaches 0 at $x = 7$ and is negative at larger values of *x*. The function satisfies the law of diminishing marginal utility because marginal utility falls as *x* increases. Notice that when total utility reaches its maximum value, marginal utility is zero. We study how to identify maximum values and other turning points of functions in chapter 6 Maximum and Minimum Values.

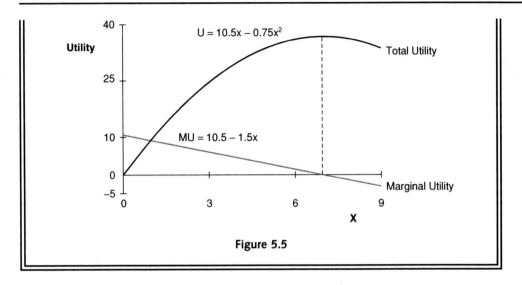

Figure 5.5

9

Given the total utility function $U = 5x^{0.8}$ find the marginal utility, MU.

Since $U = 5x^{0.8}$ we obtain marginal utility by finding dU/dx.

$$MU = \frac{dU}{dx} = 4x^{-0.2} = 4/x^{0.2}$$

Notice that as x increases, the divisor in the expression for marginal utility, $x^{0.2}$, also increases. The value of marginal utility therefore decreases as x increases, showing that the curve has diminishing marginal utility.

Use the screen Example One – Utility Functions in section 3 of MathEcon chapter 5 to see another worked example.

5.7 If total utility $U = 3x - \frac{1}{4}x^2$ find marginal utility, MU. Plot the total utility and marginal utility functions for values of x from 0 to 8. What shapes do the curves take? What can you say about them when $x = 6$?

5.8 A utility function is given by $U = 10x^{1/4}$. Find the corresponding marginal utility function. Is it diminishing? Sketch the two curves using x values of 0, 1, 16 and 81. Why are these convenient values to choose?

> **5.9** Suppose $U = f(x)$ is a function expressing the utility a household obtains from consuming a quantity x of a commodity. How does utility change with x for each of the following functions? (Does it increase, decrease, or what?) How does marginal utility change with x? Do the functions exhibit diminishing marginal utility?
>
> (a) $U = 0.66x$ (b) $U = 0.5x^2$ (c) $U = 6x^{0.5}$

SECTION 5.6: Revenue Functions

In section 1.9 we found that average revenue, AR, equals price, P, and we showed that its relationship with total revenue, TR, is given by $TR = P.Q$. If the demand curve is written in the form $P = f(Q)$ and we substitute it in the expression for TR this gives TR as a function of Q. We can then find marginal revenue, MR, by differentiating $TR = g(Q)$ with respect to Q. The marginal revenue function tells us how total revenue

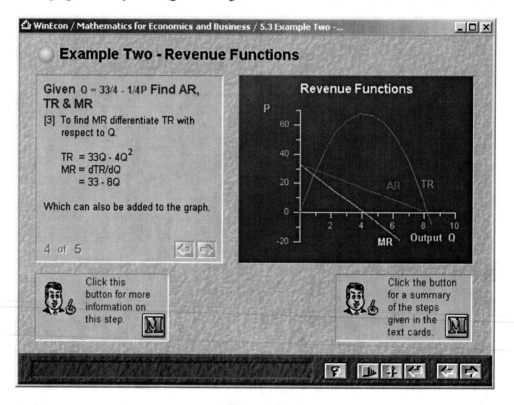

Figure 5.6

is changing as the quantity traded of the item increases. You may be accustomed to defining marginal revenue as the increase in total revenue when quantity sold increases by one unit. Differentiation provides a more general approach, and for linear functions it gives the same values of marginal revenue. We differentiate using the same rules as before, treating Q as if it were x.

To find marginal revenue, MR, differentiate total revenue, **Remember...**
TR, with respect to quantity, Q.

$$MR = \frac{d(TR)}{dQ}$$

Every demand curve has particular total revenue and marginal revenue functions associated with it. The worked examples provide some illustrations.

Use the MathEcon screen Example Two – Revenue Functions to see a total revenue function obtained from a linear demand function and the marginal revenue function which we get by differentiating.

10

Find the AR and MR functions if total revenue is given by TR = $56Q - 4Q^2$. What is the value of MR at $Q = 1, 5, 7, 8$?

AR is defined to be TR/Q, so AR = $(56Q - 4Q^2)/Q = 56 - 4Q$ which is a linear function. To find marginal revenue we differentiate total revenue with respect to Q.

$$MR = d(TR)/dQ = 56 - 8Q$$

This is another linear function. Substituting the various values for Q gives

Q	1	5	7	8
Marginal revenue	48	16	0	−8

If you plot the average and marginal revenue functions against Q on the horizontal axis you see that both are downward sloping straight lines and that MR slopes down twice as steeply as AR.

From the discussion in section 5.2 you may remember that MR is also the slope of the tangent to the total revenue function and the function used in this example is plotted (using x in place of Q) in figure 5.2. Points A, B and C marked on that function correspond to values of Q of 1, 5 and 8. We can now say that the slopes of the tangents at these points are 48, 16 and −8 respectively. Notice that when the total revenue function reaches a maximum at $Q = 7$, MR = 0. We consider the implication of this further in chapter 6.

11

If total revenue is given by $TR = 25Q$ find expressions for AR and MR. In what kind of market might this total revenue function occur?

$TR = 25Q$, and for average revenue we divide both sides by Q which gives $AR = 25$, so AR (or price) is a constant.

Differentiate TR with respect to Q to find $MR = 25$, so MR is a constant, and the same value as AR.

As figure 5.7 shows, the demand curve and marginal revenue curves coincide and are horizontal. Total revenue is an upward sloping line through the origin. Curves with these shapes are characteristic of firms in a perfectly competitive market.

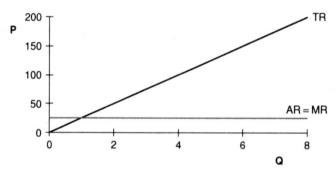

Figure 5.7 Revenue functions for a firm in perfect competition

---

12

Demand is given by $P = 15/Q$. What form do the total revenue and marginal revenue functions take?

Using $TR = P.Q$ we have $TR = 15Q/Q = 15$. This is a constant total revenue function. Whatever output is sold, the total revenue remains at 15. The demand curve is shown in figure 5.8. To obtain MR we differentiate TR. Since TR is a constant

$$MR = d(TR)/dQ = 0$$

As Q, the output traded, increases TR remains constant and so there is no marginal revenue associated with the output change.

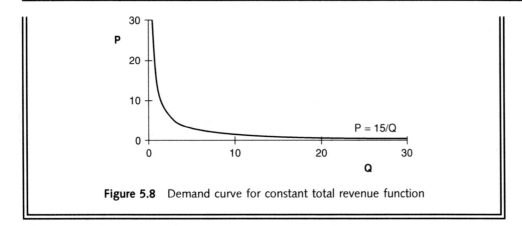

Figure 5.8 Demand curve for constant total revenue function

For linear demand functions we now obtain a general result about the relationship between the demand and marginal revenue functions. To do this we represent the constants in our model by the letters a and b. If it seems more difficult to work with models in this form, remember that the constants are just numbers and in any particular case you could substitute values such as those in worked example 10 above.

For the general form of linear demand function $P = a - bQ$ show that the associated marginal revenue function MR is also linear with the same intercept on the P axis. Show too that MR slopes downwards twice as steeply as AR.

Using the demand function $P = a - bQ$ where a and b are positive constants, we multiply both sides by Q to find TR

$$TR = aQ - bQ^2$$

We now differentiate TR with respect to Q

$$MR = \frac{d(TR)}{dQ} = a - 2bQ$$

Since a and 2b are constants, $MR = a - 2bQ$ is a linear function of Q. Its intercept is a, the same as the demand function's, while its slope of $-2b$ is twice as steep as that of the demand function, which is $-b$. AR and MR are shown in figure 5.9.

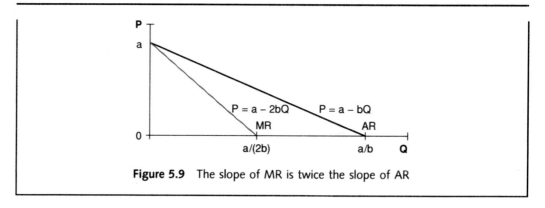

Figure 5.9   The slope of MR is twice the slope of AR

5.10   For the demand curve given by $P = 60 - 0.3Q$, find the total revenue and marginal revenue functions.

5.11   If $TR = 10x - 0.1x^2$, find MR and AR.

5.12   For the demand curve $P = 6/Q$, find expressions for total and marginal revenue.

5.13   Given $TR = 62Q$, find both MR and AR.

5.14   For the demand curve $P = 28 - 3.5Q$, find expressions for total and marginal revenue.

SECTION 5.7: Short-run Production Functions

> Examples of production functions are given in section 1.12, where the average product of labour is defined as Q/L.

A production function shows the quantity of output produced given the input factors used. In the short run, capital is assumed to be fixed and we shall suppose that there is only one factor of production, namely labour, whose use can be varied. Output produced, Q, is therefore a function of the quantity of labour employed, L.

$$Q = f(L)$$

If we differentiate the production function with respect to L, obtaining dQ/dL, we find the rate at which output changes as the quantity of labour employed increases. You may be accustomed to think of marginal product as the additional output obtained when an extra person is employed, but if we draw a smooth shaped production function the derivative dQ/dL is the appropriate measure of the marginal product of labour, MPL. dQ/dL shows how output changes at employment level L when a very small additional amount of labour time is used. The derivative provides a general expression for marginal product into which specific L values can be substituted.

Remember...

The marginal product of labour is found by differentiating the production function with respect to labour, i.e.

$$MPL = \frac{dQ}{dL}$$

13

Given the production function $Q = 22L^{0.5}$, find the marginal product of labour. Does the function exhibit diminishing marginal returns? Sketch graphs of the functions. If four people are employed, what output is produced and what is the marginal product of labour?

The marginal product of labour, MPL, is found by differentiating $Q = 22L^{0.5}$ which gives

$$MPL = \frac{dQ}{dL} = 11L^{-0.5} = \frac{11}{L^{0.5}}$$

As L increases, so does $L^{0.5}$ and as we divide by this larger number $11/L^{0.5}$ decreases. There are diminishing marginal returns to labour.

Figure 5.10 plots the production function and the marginal product of labour. As L increases from 0, output rises, but at a decreasing rate, and MPL falls.

Substituting $L = 4$ into $22L^{0.5}$ to find the output produced gives $Q = 44$ and substituting into $MPL = 11/L^{0.5}$ gives a value for the marginal product of labour of $MPL = 5.5$ when four people are employed.

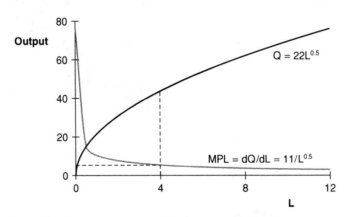

Figure 5.10   Output and marginal product

5.15 Given

$$Q = 350L + 25L^2 - 1.5L^3$$

find the marginal product of labour. What output is produced and what is the marginal product of labour if three people are employed?

(This production function is graphed on the MathEcon screen Short-Run Production Functions: A Numerical Example.)

5.16 For the production function $Q = 8L^{0.75}$ find the marginal product of labour.

SECTION 5.8: Cost Functions

Cost curves in economics can take a variety of shapes. You are probably accustomed to drawing U-shaped average and marginal cost curves but you may also have seen these curves depicted as a horizontal line or as downward sloping curves like those in figure 5.11. Whatever their shapes, certain relationships exist between the various cost

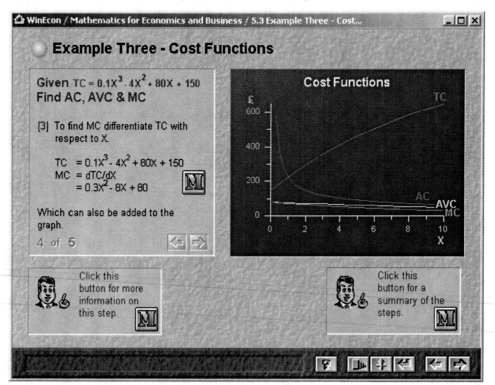

Figure 5.11

curves for a firm. We studied total and average cost in section 1.10 and distinguished between fixed and variable cost. We now define marginal cost, MC, as the derivative of total cost, d(TC)/dQ. This measure is appropriate if total cost is a smooth curve, although you may be accustomed to measure MC as the change in total cost resulting from a unit change in output. d(TC)/dQ shows us the rate at which total cost, TC, is changing and is the slope of the total cost curve. We saw in section 1.10 that TC = VC + FC. As we differentiate TC the constant term representing fixed cost differentiates to zero. This implies d(TC)/dQ = d(VC)/dQ and so you can also find MC by differentiating total variable cost, VC. Fixed cost has no impact on marginal cost, because it does not alter as output changes.

MC does not take negative values, but it may be falling or rising. The corresponding shapes for the TC curve are that it bends downwards or that it bends upwards. Worked example 14 demonstrates this.

Marginal cost is the derivative of TC with respect to Q, the quantity of output, i.e.

Remember...

$$MC = \frac{d(TC)}{dQ}$$

When MC is falling, TC bends downwards. When MC is rising, TC bends upwards. Marginal cost is also the derivative of VC with respect to Q, i.e.

$$MC = \frac{d(VC)}{dQ}$$

14

Find expressions for marginal cost and average total cost for a firm with the total cost function

$$TC = 0.4Q^3 - 4.8Q^2 + 30Q + 2$$

What shapes do the curves take?

MC = d(TC)/dQ and so

$$MC = 1.2Q^2 - 9.6Q + 30$$

$$AC = \frac{TC}{Q} = 0.4Q^2 - 4.8Q + 30 + \frac{2}{Q}$$

Figure 5.12 shows the shapes of the curves. The marginal cost curve never cuts the horizontal axis, so marginal cost is always positive. TC is always rising. While MC is falling, TC is bending downwards. When MC starts to rise, TC begins to bend upwards. MC intersects AC at its minimum point.

(We see how to identify the values of Q corresponding to minimum MC and minimum AC in chapter 6.)

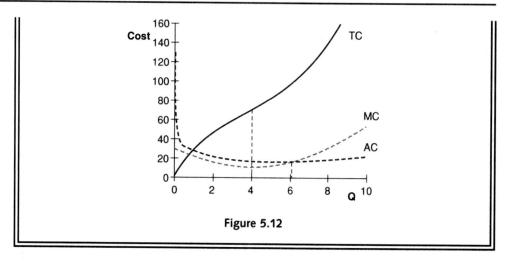

Figure 5.12

The total cost curve for firm A is

$$TC_A = 1650Q - 5Q^2 + 0.6Q^3$$

while the total cost curve for firm B is

$$TC_B = 2500 + 1650Q - 5Q^2 + 0.6Q^3$$

Find the marginal cost curve for each firm and comment.

15

Differentiating each total cost function to find marginal cost gives for firm A

$$MC_A = 1650 - 10Q + 1.8Q^2$$

and for firm B

$$MC_B = 1650 - 10Q + 1.8Q^2$$

The two firms have identical marginal cost functions, because their total variable cost functions are the same, but firm B has fixed costs of 2500 while firm A has none.

 5.17 If $TC = 0.1x^2$, find MC.

 5.18 If $TC = 19 + 0.1x^2$, find MC and compare your answer with that for practice problem 5.17.

5.19 If $TC = 3x^3 - 18x^2 + 40x + 9$, find an expression for marginal cost. Identify fixed cost and total variable cost, and hence find average variable cost. Plot a graph showing total cost, marginal cost and average variable cost and comment on the relationships between them.

5.20 A natural monopoly has an average cost function

$$ATC = \frac{70}{Q} + 125 - 0.125Q \text{ for } 0 < Q < 500$$

Find the total and marginal cost functions, and comment on the shapes of the curves.

SECTION 5.9: Point Elasticity of Demand and of Supply

Elasticity (E) is a numerical measure of the responsiveness of the quantity demanded or supplied to a change in price. It is defined as

$$\text{Elasticity} = \frac{\text{proportionate change in quantity}}{\text{proportionate change in price}}$$

The basic formula for calculating elasticity for a demand or supply function given by $Q = f(P)$ is therefore

$$\text{Elasticity} = \frac{(\Delta Q/Q)}{(\Delta P/P)}$$

In section 4.2 we noticed that this formula gives different elasticities for the same change, depending on the direction in which it takes place, and we defined a measurement known as arc elasticity as one way of overcoming the problem. Since demand and supply functions are usually drawn as smooth curves, a neater and more general approach is to find point elasticities. Remembering the rule that when an expression is divided by a fraction we can turn that fraction upside down and multiply by it, we can rewrite the formula

$$\text{Elasticity} = \frac{(\Delta Q/Q)}{(\Delta P/P)} = \frac{(\Delta Q)}{Q} \times \frac{P}{\Delta P}$$

Rearranging this gives

$$\text{Elasticity} = \frac{\Delta Q}{\Delta P} \times \frac{P}{Q}$$

To calculate point elasticity for the function $Q = f(P)$ we replace $\Delta Q/\Delta P$ by dQ/dP where dQ/dP is the derivative of quantity demanded or supplied with respect to price. This gives the following general expression.

> **Remember...**
>
> Point price elasticity $= \dfrac{dQ}{dP} \times \dfrac{P}{Q}$

To find price elasticity of demand using this formula we work with the equation for the demand curve. We differentiate it to find dQ/dP and then substitute as appropriate. Supply elasticity is found from the supply equation in a similar way. If the demand or supply equation is given to us in the form

$$Q = f(P)$$

differentiating it with respect to P gives dQ/dP, the derivative we require for calculating elasticity. If instead the function is in the form

$$P = g(Q)$$

the easiest way to find dQ/dP is to differentiate with respect to Q, obtaining dP/dQ and then to use the inverse function rule of differentiation to get dQ/dP.

> **Remember...**
>
> By the inverse function rule
>
> $$dQ/dP = \dfrac{1}{dP/dQ}$$

For downward sloping demand curves, dQ/dP is negative. This leads to a negative value for point elasticity, reflecting the fact that as price falls the quantity demanded responds by rising. A demand curve is more elastic when quantity is more responsive to price changes. An elasticity of -5 represents greater elasticity than one of -2. Yet -5 is numerically less than -2. To facilitate interpretation of demand elasticities, it is conventional to ignore the negative sign in discussing them. Larger numbers then represent greater elasticities.

> **Remember...**
>
> Demand elasticities are negative, but we ignore the negative sign in discussion of their size.

As you move along a demand or supply curve, elasticity usually changes but we shall identify particular types of functions with constant elasticity. We begin by working through some examples and then we show that any linear demand curve has elasticity changing from infinite to zero along its length, while any linear supply function is either elastic or inelastic at all points. Knowing the elasticity of a demand curve lets you predict how total revenue will change in response to a price change. This important relationship is considered in chapter 7.

You can see examples of calculating point elasticity by finding the slopes of lines on the screens 5.3 Point Elasticity – Demand (1) to (4) in section 3 of MathEcon chapter 5.

Suppose that demand in a certain market is given by

$$Q = 32 - 4P$$

Calculate the point price elasticity of demand at the following prices

$$8, \quad 6, \quad 4, \quad 2, \quad 0$$

If demand changes so that twice as much is demanded at any price, find elasticity at the same prices and say how it has changed.

Calculate elasticities also for the demand curve $Q = 80 - 12P$ at prices of 6 and 4.

Sketch the three curves and say how their elasticities compare.

We begin by finding dQ/dP for the first demand curve. It is given by

$$dQ/dP = -4$$

Now using the definition of point elasticity we have

$$\text{Price elasticity of demand} = \frac{dQ}{dP} \cdot \frac{P}{Q} = -4 \cdot P/Q$$

This is a general statement giving the price elasticity of demand at any point on the first demand curve. We now evaluate elasticity at the specified prices by first finding the corresponding values of Q from the demand curve and then substituting as appropriate. Remember that multiplying by zero gives zero, while dividing by zero gives infinity.

P		8	6	4	2	0
Q		0	8	16	24	32
Elasticity $= \dfrac{dQ}{dP} \cdot \dfrac{P}{Q} = -4 \cdot P/Q$		$-\infty$	-3	-1	$-\tfrac{1}{3}$	0

Notice that as the price falls the linear demand curve becomes less elastic. The magnitude of elasticity (ignoring the sign) gets less. At $P = 8$ the curve is infinitely elastic, while at $P = 0$ it is wholly inelastic. Unitary elasticity occurs halfway between these prices at $P = 4$. The curve is plotted as D_1 in figure 5.13.

If demand doubles at every price, we have the new demand curve $Q = 64 - 8P$. We now have $dQ/dP = -8$ and calculate values of elasticity as before.

P		8	6	4	2	0
Q		0	16	32	48	64
Elasticity $= \dfrac{dQ}{dP} \cdot \dfrac{P}{Q} = -8 \cdot P/Q$		$-\infty$	-3	-1	$-\tfrac{1}{3}$	0

Notice that elasticity has not changed. We obtain the same values as before at every price. When you plot the demand curve, which is labelled D_2 in figure 5.13, you might think it is more elastic than D_1 because it has a shallower slope. In fact two demand curves which intersect the P axis at the same point have equal elasticities at every price.

We now compare the demand curve $Q = 80 - 12P$. For this curve $dQ/dP = -12$ and calculating elasticities as before at the specified prices we find the results shown

P			6	4
Q			8	32
Elasticity $= \dfrac{dQ}{dP} \cdot \dfrac{P}{Q} = -12 \cdot P/Q$			-9	-1.5

This curve is more elastic than the other curves at the same prices. For example, at a price of 4 the first two demand curves have $E = -1$, but the third demand curve has $E = -1.5$. The reason for this is that the third demand curve has a lower value intercept on the P axis. This curve is shown as D_3 in figure 5.13.

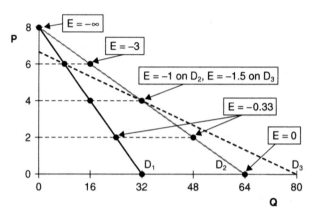

Figure 5.13   At any price, D_1 and D_2 have the same elasticity; D_3 is more elastic

---

17

Calculate point price elasticity of supply for the supply function given by

$$P = 3Q - 10$$

What is the elasticity at $Q = 5$, 10 and 50?

To calculate elasticity we first find $dP/dQ = 3$. We then find dQ/dP

$$dQ/dP = \frac{1}{dP/dQ} = \frac{1}{3}$$

$$\text{Supply elasticity} = \frac{dQ}{dP} \cdot \frac{P}{Q} = \frac{P}{3Q}$$

Substituting $Q = 5$, 10 and 50 in the supply function gives $P = 5$, 20 and 140.
   Point price elasticity of supply $= \frac{1}{3}, \frac{2}{3}$ and $\frac{14}{15}$ respectively. Elasticity of supply is positive because at a higher price suppliers are willing to supply more. As you move along this supply curve, elasticity gets closer to 1, but does not reach it. This supply curve is inelastic at all prices.

Now that we have seen some numerical examples, we obtain some general results about elasticity for particular types of demand and supply curves.

Show that a demand function of the form $Q = k/P$, where k is a constant, has unitary elasticity at all prices.

We write the demand function as $Q = kP^{-1}$. Differentiating it gives

$$\frac{dQ}{dP} = -kP^{-2} = -\frac{k}{P^2}$$

$$\text{Elasticity} = \frac{dQ}{dP} \cdot \frac{P}{Q} = -\frac{k}{P^2} \cdot \frac{P}{Q} = -\frac{k}{P \cdot Q}$$

We now substitute for Q from the demand function. Turning the expression for Q upside down and multiplying by it gives

$$\text{Elasticity} = -\frac{k}{P} \cdot \frac{P}{k} = -1$$

The demand function $Q = k/P$ is a constant elasticity demand function with unitary elasticity at all points on the curve. Since $P \cdot Q = k$, this function is also a constant total revenue function. Figure 5.8 shows such a function with $k = 15$.

The next piece of analysis provides a generalization of the way elasticity varies along a straight line, which we saw in worked example 16.

Show that the linear demand curve $P = a - bQ$ has elasticity varying from $-\infty$ to 0 at different prices, and that when $P = a/2$ elasticity is -1.

The demand curve is shown in figure 5.14 with an intercept of a on the P axis. $dP/dQ = -b$, so $dQ/dP = -1/b$.

$$\text{Elasticity} = \frac{dQ}{dP} \cdot \frac{P}{Q} = -\frac{1}{b} \cdot \frac{P}{Q}$$

We are interested in how elasticity varies with price and so we need to substitute for Q in the formula. To do this we rewrite the demand function expressing Q as a function of P. This gives

$$Q = \frac{a}{b} - \frac{P}{b} = \frac{a - P}{b}$$

Substituting we find

$$\text{Elasticity} = -\frac{1}{b} \cdot \frac{P \times b}{a - P} = -\frac{P}{a - P}$$

The elasticity (E) of a linear demand curve at different prices depends on a, the intercept of the line on the P axis, but not on b, the slope of the line. We saw this in worked example 16, but it is generally true for straight line demand curves.

$$E = -1 \text{ when } \frac{P}{a - P} = 1, \text{ or } P = \frac{a}{2} \text{ (i.e. at a price which is half the intercept)}$$

At the point where the demand curve meets the P axis, $P = a$. Substituting this gives

$$E = -\frac{a}{a - a} = -\frac{a}{0} = -\infty \text{ at the } P \text{ axis}$$

At the Q axis, $P = 0$. This gives

$$E = -\frac{0}{a - 0} = 0$$

Along a linear demand curve elasticity varies from $-\infty$ to 0 as shown in figure 5.14.

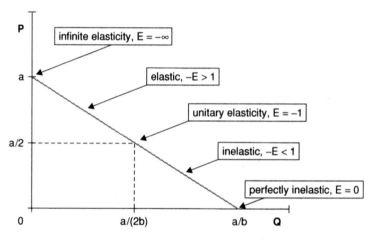

Figure 5.14 Elasticity along the demand curve $P = a - bQ$

For linear demand curves

Remember...

- Elasticity varies from $-\infty$ to 0 as you move down the curve.
- Two demand curves with the same intercept on the P axis have the same elasticity at every price.
- For two demand curves with different intercepts on the P axis, the one with the lower intercept has the greater elasticity at every price.

Our next general result is about linear supply functions.

For a linear supply function $Q = c + mP$ (m > 0), show that whether supply is elastic or inelastic depends on whether c, the intercept of the line on the Q axis, is negative or positive.

Differentiation of the supply function gives $dQ/dP = m$. Therefore

$$E = \frac{dQ}{dP} \cdot \frac{P}{Q} = \frac{mP}{Q} = \frac{mP}{c + mP}$$

substituting for Q from the supply function.

If c is positive, $c + mP > mP$ and so elasticity is a fraction that is less than 1. Supply is inelastic at all points on a linear supply function that has a positive intercept on the Q axis. An example is shown in figure 5.15 where c = 33.4.

If c is 0, $c + mP = mP$ and the value of elasticity is 1. A linear supply function which passes through the origin has unitary elasticity at all points.

If c is negative, the line cuts the horizontal axis to the left of the origin and has a positive intercept on the P axis. Although c is negative, $c + mP$, which equals Q, must be positive. Since c is negative, $c + mP < mP$. Dividing mP by something smaller than itself gives a result that is greater than 1. A linear supply function is elastic at all points if it has a positive intercept on the P axis.

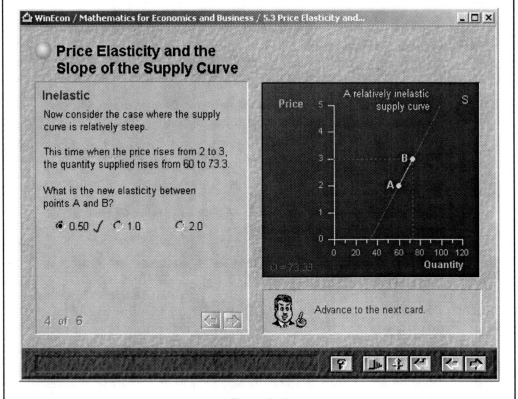

Figure 5.15

See the examples on the MathEcon screen 5.3 Price Elasticity and the Slope of the Supply Curve.

5.21 Find an expression for the point price elasticity of demand for the curve $Q = 240 - 28P$, and evaluate it at $P = 8$ and 6.

5.22 Sketch the two straight line demand functions given and find values for elasticity at prices of 12, 8, 6, 2 and 0

(a) $Q = 144 - 12P$ (b) $Q = 48 - 4P$

Before starting your calculations, did you think one curve was more elastic than the other? Looking at your calculations, how do they compare? At what point on each curve is $E = -1$? How do these curves compare with the demand curve in practice problem 5.21?

5.23 For the function $P = 5 + 0.5Q$, find the point price elasticity of supply at $Q = 10$ and at $Q = 30$.

5.24 Calculate point price elasticity of supply for each of the functions, and evaluate it when $P = 10$.

(a) $Q = 5P + 6$ (b) $Q = 7P^2$

5.25 The following are all examples of constant price elasticity demand functions. Calculate elasticity in each case.

(a) $Q = \dfrac{18}{P}$ (b) $Q = \dfrac{5}{P^3}$

(c) $Q = 9P^{-0.3}$ (d) $Q = AP^{-n}$

What general statement can you make about the value of elasticity for constant elasticity demand functions?

5.26 Calculate elasticity for the following supply functions and show it is independent of price in each case.

(a) $Q = P^2$ (b) $Q = 3P$

(c) $Q = P^3$ (d) $Q = aP^3$

(e) $Q = P^{1.4}$ (f) $Q = AP^n$

What feature of these functions makes elasticity independent of price? What determines its numeric value?

SECTION 5.10: Investment Multiplier

In a simple macroeconomic model of the economy the marginal propensities to consume and save are found as the derivatives of the consumption and saving functions respectively. We can also find the investment multiplier by seeing how income changes in response to a change in investment. We use the method set out in section 3.3 for finding macroeconomic equilibrium.

To find the investment multiplier, use the following steps 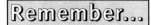 **Remember...**

1. Write down the equilibrium condition for the economy

$$Y = AD$$

Income = Aggregate Demand

2. Write an expression for AD

$$AD = C + I + G + X - Z$$

Substitute into this, but do not substitute a numerical value for the autonomous expenditure I. This gives

$$AD = f(Y, I)$$

and so using the equilibrium condition we obtain an equation where Y occurs on both sides.

3. Collect terms in Y on the left-hand side and solve for Y.
4. Now differentiate. If Y = income and I = investment, dY/dI is the investment multiplier.

A closed economy with no government and all investment autonomous has the consumption function

$$C = a + bY$$

Find the marginal propensities to consume (MPC) and save (MPS). Write down the equilibrium condition and show that the investment multiplier is $1/(1 - MPC)$.

The marginal propensity to consume is the derivative of the consumption function with respect to income, so

$$MPC = \frac{dC}{dY} = b$$

With no taxation the saving function S is given by

$$S = Y - C$$

and substituting for C we find

$$S = -a + (1 - b)Y$$

The marginal propensity to save is the derivative of the saving function with respect to income, so

$$MPS = \frac{dS}{dY} = 1 - b$$

To find the multiplier we write the equilibrium condition

$$Y = AD$$

Since the only expenditures are consumption and investment we have

$$AD = C + I$$

and substituting the consumption function gives

$$AD = a + bY + I$$

Using the equilibrium condition we obtain

$$Y = a + bY + I$$

Subtracting bY from both sides gives

$$Y - bY = a + I$$

Since Y is a factor of the terms on the left-hand side we write

$$(1 - b)Y = a + I$$

Dividing through by $(1 - b)$ we find

$$Y = \frac{a}{1 - b} + \frac{I}{1 - b}$$

The investment multiplier can now be found by differentiating with respect to I

$$\frac{dY}{dI} = \frac{1}{1 - b}$$

We found MPC = b and MPS = 1 − b. Hence in this simple economy the investment multiplier = 1/MPS = 1/(1 − MPC).

5.27 In a simple economy investment, I is autonomously determined and the consumption function is

$$C = 820 + 0.8Y$$

Write down the equilibrium condition if there is no government and no external trade. Find the investment multiplier. Use it to predict the change in Y if I increases by 20.

Chapter 5: Answers to Practice Problems

5.1   (a) $4x^3$ (b) $9x^2$

       (c) $-10x^4$ (d) 0

       (e) 5

5.2   (a) $-8x^{-2} = -8/x^2$ (b) $12x^{-3} = 12/x^3$

       (c) $5x^{1/3-1} = 5x^{-2/3} = 5/x^{2/3}$ (d) $-10x^{-2} = -10/x^2$

       (e) $6x^{-3} = 6/x^3$ (f) $-11x^{-1/2} = -11/\sqrt{x}$

       (g) 1

5.3 $dy/dx = x$, so for $\Delta x = 1$ we predict $\Delta y = x = 1$, the initial value of x. At $x = 1$, $y = 0.5$ and at $x = 2$, $y = 2$ so the exact change is $2 - 0.5 = 1.5$.

5.4   (a) $20 + 10x$ (b) $6 - 6x + 12x^2$

       (c) $-7 + 16x - 0.6x^2$ (d) $-8/x^2 - 12 + 12x$

       (e) $4/\sqrt{x} + 2$

5.5   (a) 3 (b) -2

       (c) 0 (d) 0.5

       (e) a

5.6   (a) $dx/dy = 5$, so $dy/dx = 1/5$

       (b) $dx/dy = 2y$, so $dy/dx = 1/(2y)$. The restriction is needed to ensure only one y value corresponds to each x value.

5.7 $3 - x/2$
       The curves are shown in figure 5.16. Total utility rises steeply at first, then less steeply reaching a maximum at $x = 6$ after which it declines. Marginal utility is a downward sloping straight line.

5.8 $MU = 2.5/x^{3/4}$
       Yes, as x increases MU decreases. Values are 0^4, 1^4, 2^4, 3^4, so they have exact fourth roots of 0, 1, 2 and 3 respectively. Figure 5.17 shows the curves.

5.9   As x increases, utility increases for all the functions. It increases most rapidly for function (b), least rapidly for function (c). For the separate functions we have:
       (a) $MU = 0.66$, a constant. No, constant marginal utility.
       (b) $MU = x$, increasing linear function. No, increasing marginal utility.

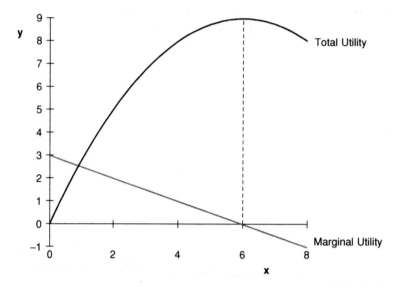

Figure 5.16   Maximum utility at $x = 6$ when MU = 0

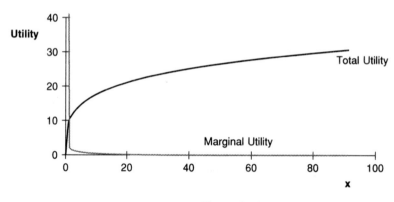

Figure 5.17

(c)   MU $= 3x^{-0.5} = 3/x^{0.5}$. Since the term in x is in the divisor, MU gets smaller as x increases. Yes, diminishing marginal utility.

5.10   TR $= 60Q - 0.3Q^2$, so MR $= 60 - 0.6Q$

5.11   MR $= 10 - 0.2x$; AR $= 10 - 0.1x$

5.12   TR $= P . Q = 6$; MR $= 0$ (constant total revenue function)

5.13   MR $= 62 =$ AR (applicable to a firm in perfect competition)

5.14 $TR = 28Q - 3.5Q^2$, so $MR = 28 - 7Q$

5.15 $MPL = 350 + 50L - 4.5L^2$; 1234.5, 459.5

5.16 $MPL = 6L^{-0.25} = 6/L^{0.25}$

5.17 $MC = 0.2x$

5.18 $MC = 0.2x$, the same upward sloping straight line as problem 5.17, which shows fixed cost does not affect marginal cost.

5.19 $MC = 9x^2 - 36x + 40$; $FC = 9$ and $TVC = 3x^3 - 18x^2 + 40x$, so $AVC = 3x^2 - 18x + 40$. The curves are shown in figure 5.18. When MC reaches a minimum, TC changes from curving downwards to curving upwards. MC crosses AVC at its minimum point.

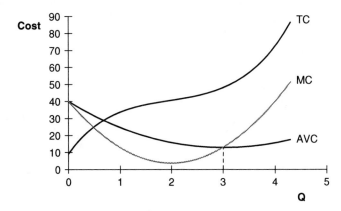

Figure 5.18 Cost functions

5.20

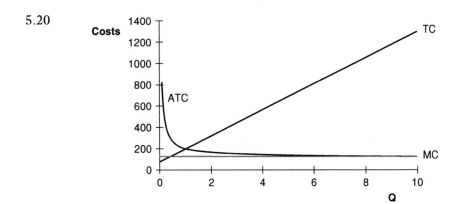

Figure 5.19 Natural monopoly cost curves

$TC = 70 + 125Q - 0.125Q^2$

$MC = 125 - 0.25Q$

Marginal cost is a straight line with a very shallow downward slope. Total cost is a curve but appears almost linear. Average total cost falls rapidly at first then gets close to marginal cost while remaining above it. The curves are shown in figure 5.19.

5.21 $E = -28 \cdot P/Q; -14, -7/3$

5.22   Figure 5.20 shows the demand curves labelled D_a and D_b. They intersect the P axis at the same point, so have the same elasticities at each price.

P		12	8	6	2	0
$E = dQ/dP \cdot P/Q$	$-\infty$	-2	-1	$-^1/_5$	0

Elasticity is -1 at $P = 6$, half the intercept of 12.

    The demand curve in problem 5.21 is shown as D_c in figure 5.20. It has a lower intercept, so is more elastic at each price.

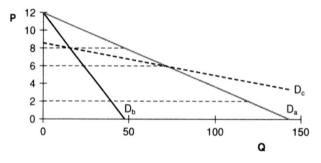

Figure 5.20

5.23   2, 4/3

5.24   (a) $5P/Q$, 50/56 (b) $14P^2/Q = 14P^2/7P^2 = 2$, regardless of the value of P.

5.25   (a) -1 (b) -3 (c) -0.3 (d) $-n$; writing the demand function in the form $Q = AP^{-n}$, elasticity is the power of P.

5.26   (a) 2 (b) 1 (c) 3 (d) 3 (e) 1.4 (f) n. The functions all comprise just one term and pass through the origin. The power of P is the elasticity.

5.27 $Y = C + I$; 5; $\Delta Y = dY/dI \cdot \Delta I = 5 \times 20 = 100$

Maximum and Minimum Values

OBJECTIVES

In this chapter you learn to
- Appreciate that economic objectives involve optimization
- Identify maximum and minimum turning points by differentiating and then finding the second derivative
- Find maximum revenue
- Show which output maximizes profit and whether it changes if taxation is imposed
- Identify minimum turning points on cost curves
- Find the level of employment at which the average product of labour is maximized
- Choose the per unit tax which maximizes tax revenue
- Identify the economic order quantity which minimizes total inventory costs

---

SECTION 6.1: Introduction

Economists usually assume that firms choose to produce the level of output that will maximize their profits. The profit functions generated by analysing firms' cost and revenue functions typically rise at low values of output, reach a maximum and then fall. With this type of profit function there is an optimal level of output at which profit is higher than it is when either a little less or a little more is produced. In this chapter we learn how the technique of differentiation can be used to help us identify points at which such optimal values occur. We shall illustrate the procedure using numerical values, but since differentiation is a general method, we shall also find that by applying it to general functions we can obtain general results. These provide criteria that can be used to identify when an optimal position is reached.

Once we have learned the technique of identifying maximum and minimum turning points we shall apply it to various different economic models. The methods are useful for analysing when various goals are achieved. In addition, being able to say where functions have turning points helps us in sketching their curves. We can mark the turning points of cost and product curves, for example, to help us in drawing their correct shapes.

Use the animated graphs in section 1 of MathEcon chapter 6 Finding Maximum and Minimum Values to see where maximum and minimum values occur. Investigate the optimization method for various economic problems using the MathEcon section Maximum and Minimum Values in Economics.

Section 6.2: Identifying Maximum and Minimum Turning Points

The maximum values we identify in this chapter are positions at which the function is higher than it is at points on either side. Point B in figure 6.1 is a maximum in this sense. It represents a turning point of the function. The function rises as it approaches the maximum value and then falls after it. Similarly, the minimum values we identify are turning points, such as point D in figure 6.1, where the function stops falling and starts to rise. Turning points can also be called critical points or stationary values. Notice that these are not the overall maximum or minimum values of the function. The function is lower than the minimum turning point at $x = 0$, and above the maximum

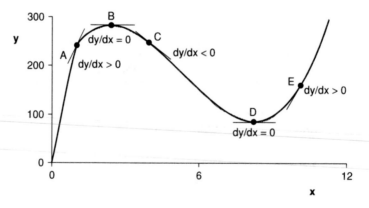

Figure 6.1

turning point at $x = 12$. The maximum and minimum values that we analyse are therefore local rather than global optima. Economic objectives such as maximum profit or minimum average cost are attained where the appropriate function reaches a value that is optimal by comparison with nearby points on either side. It is therefore maximum and minimum turning points, not global optima that correspond to points at which economic objectives are achieved. Some functions have numerous maximum and minimum turning points, although the ones that we use in the economic analysis in this chapter have at most two.

Around a turning point the slope of a curve is changing in a particular way, as we can see in figure 6.1. To the left of a maximum turning point, for example at point A, the function $y = f(x)$ has a positive slope, although it is becoming more and more shallow. At the turning point, B, the slope is horizontal, and after the turning point, at a point such as C, the slope of the curve is negative. The function shown in figure 6.1 also has a minimum turning point at D. To the left of this the slope is negative, at the turning point the curve is momentarily horizontal, and to the right of the minimum at E the slope is positive. These different changing patterns give us a means of recognizing different kinds of turning points.

We measure the slope of a curve by its derivative, dy/dx, so a useful indicator of possible turning points is to find where the derivative of the function takes the value zero. When $dy/dx = 0$ the function is momentarily neither rising nor falling, as at both points B and D in figure 6.1. To identify the maximum and minimum turning points of a function $y = f(x)$ we find the derivative, dy/dx, set it equal to zero and solve to find the corresponding values of x at which the derivative takes the value zero. We have already noted that dy/dx equals zero at both a maximum and a minimum turning point. We say, therefore, that $dy/dx = 0$ is a necessary condition for a maximum or minimum. It is not, however, a sufficient condition to guarantee that we have located a maximum or minimum and so we look for what else is required.

We can distinguish a maximum from a minimum turning point by evaluating the function at the critical value and at points that are close to it on either side. An alternative way is to look at how the derivative changes. Its precise values on either side of the zero value do not matter. As the discussion about the slope of the curve in figure 6.1 showed, we are simply concerned with whether the derivative is positive (> 0) or negative (< 0). The patterns of the signs of the derivative around the two types of turning point are as shown below:

Sign of dy/dx around a turning point

Remember...

	before	at critical value	after
Maximum	+	0	−
Minimum	−	0	+

Differentiation provides another approach for finding how the derivative changes, which is often convenient. After obtaining dy/dx, the first derivative of the function, we differentiate that and the result is called the second derivative of the original function. We write

$$\frac{d^2 y}{dx^2} = \frac{d[dy/dx]}{dx}$$

---

second derivative: is obtained by differentiating a derivative.

The screens Identifying Maximum and Minimum Values and Checking for Maximum or Minimum Turning Points in section 1 of MathEcon chapter 6 let you investigate the pattern of changes in dy/dx and d^2y/dx^2 that occur. A useful summary of the method is available on the screen titled Rules for Finding a Maximum or Minimum.

In differentiating dy/dx we are recognizing that it too is a function of x and we are looking at how it changes. Around a maximum turning point dy/dx falls as it changes from positive to negative values. This implies d^2y/dx^2 is negative. Conversely, around a minimum turning point d^2y/dx^2 is positive because dy/dx increases from negative values to positive. There is also the possibility that d^2y/dx^2 may be zero. In this case we have neither a maximum nor a minimum but the curve changes its shape, bending in the opposite direction. This is called a point of inflexion. You can see an example of a point of inflexion at a point where the curve has a positive slope in worked example 6 part (c). The requirements about dy/dx and d^2y/dx^2 are called the first and second order conditions for a maximum or minimum.

To identify possible turning points: differentiate, set dy/dx equal to zero and solve for x.

    Find d^2y/dx^2 and look at its sign to distinguish a maximum from a minimum.

    The first and second order conditions are:

	Maximum	Minimum
dy/dx	0	0
d^2y/dx^2	–ve	+ve

Remember...

The examples that follow let you see how these rules work in practice. Remember that there are both lines and curves which do not have turning points. This is the case if you find that there are no values of x for which $dy/dx = 0$ for the function you are analysing.

Find any maximum or minimum turning points for the function

$$y = 5x^3 - 30x^2 + 300$$

Find dy/dx

$$dy/dx = 15x^2 - 60x$$

For a maximum or minimum $dy/dx = 0$, so

$$15x^2 - 60x = 0$$

We need to solve this for x to find the value(s) at which turning point(s) occur. Factorizing we obtain

$$15x(x - 4) = 0$$

The value of zero occurs when either $15x = 0$ or $x - 4 = 0$, so either $x = 0$ or $x = 4$. The function has turning points at $x = 0$ and $x = 4$. To find what kind of turning points they are we find the second derivative of the function. Using

$$dy/dx = 15x^2 - 60x$$

we differentiate again with respect to x and find

$$d^2y/dx^2 = 30x - 60$$

Substitute $x = 0$, which gives

$$d^2y/dx^2 = -60$$

The negative value indicates that $x = 0$ is a maximum turning point. Substitute $x = 4$ and you find

$$d^2y/dx^2 = 60$$

Here the second derivative is positive, indicating the function has a minimum turning point at $x = 4$. The function is plotted in figure 6.2.

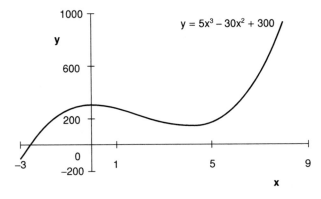

Figure 6.2

2   Find any turning points of the function $y = 15/x$, where $x > 0$.

You may find it helpful to look at a graph of this function. Figure 5.8 shows this using P and Q for y and x. The graph is close to the y axis as x gets close to zero, and close to the x axis as x becomes large.

To check for any turning points we write $y = 15x^{-1}$ and find dy/dx

$$dy/dx = -15x^{-2} = -15/x^2$$

For a turning point we require

$$-15/x^2 = 0$$

Multiplying by $-x^2$ we see that this requires that $15 = 0$, which is impossible. The function $y = 15/x$ has a negative slope $-15/x^2$ that gets shallower and shallower as x increases, but we cannot identify a value of x at which it equals zero.

Since we have a continuous function but cannot find a value where $dy/dx = 0$, the function has no turning points.

6.1   Identify any maximum or minimum turning points for the functions given

(a) $y = 3x - \dfrac{x^2}{4}$ (b) $y = 85 - 5x$

(c) $y = 12x^2 - x^3 + 40$ (d) $y = 5x + \dfrac{20}{x}$ for $x > 0$

SECTION 6.3: Maximum Total Revenue

Sales revenue maximization has been suggested as a possible alternative to profit maximization as a firm's objective. The argument is that provided a firm makes suffici- ent profit to satisfy its shareholders, its managers may prefer to maximize revenue as a way of increasing their own power and prestige. Maximization of total sales revenue is not the same thing as maximizing profit, and usually occurs at a higher level of output. We begin by showing at what level of output maximization of total revenue is achieved and in the next section we con- sider profit maximization.

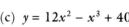

Section 5.6 defines MR as the derivative of TR.

Figure 6.3 shows a total revenue (TR) function and the corresponding marginal revenue (MR) function. Notice that MR cuts the horizontal axis at 9, the output at which TR reaches a maximum. The method used to find where TR is a maximum is:

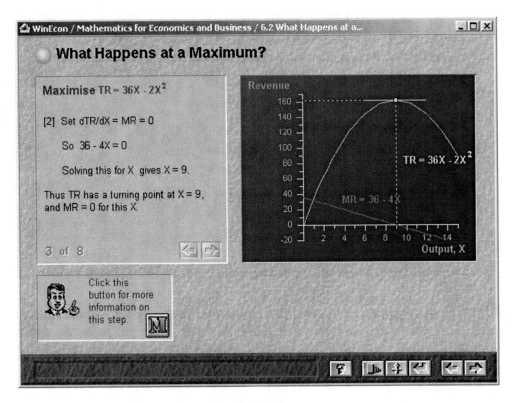

Figure 6.3

For maximum total revenue $\quad\quad\quad\quad$ **Remember...**

- differentiate the TR function with respect to output, Q
- set the derivative equal to zero and solve for Q
- find the second derivative $d^2(TR)/dQ^2$ and check that it is negative.

Show that when TR is a maximum, MR is zero.

If total revenue, TR, is a function of output, Q, we write

$$TR = f(Q)$$

$d(TR)/dQ = 0$ for maximum total revenue and so

$$MR = 0 \text{ (substituting } d(TR)/dQ = MR)$$

$$MR = 0 \text{ when total revenue is maximized.}$$

3

At what output, Q, is total revenue maximized if TR $= 147Q - 7Q^2$?

Finding d(TR)/dQ we have

$$d(TR)/dQ = 147 - 14Q$$

For a maximum, d(TR)/d$Q = 0$ so

$$147 - 14Q = 0, \text{ or}$$

$$Q = 10.5$$

To check if this turning point is a maximum, find $d^2(TR)/dQ^2$

$$d^2(TR)/dQ^2 = -14$$

Since this is negative, we have a maximum turning point at $Q = 10.5$, so total revenue is maximized at an output of 10.5.

Use the screen titled What Happens at a Maximum in section 2 of MathEcon chapter 6 to study the revenue maximizing position further.

An important relationship between marginal revenue, elasticity and maximum total revenue is shown in section 7.5. If you prefer just to use the result, you can now go through worked example 6 in chapter 7 and do practice problems 7.4 and 7.5.

6.2

Demand is given by

$$P = 80 - 6Q$$

What is the total revenue function, and at what output is it maximized? What is the value of MR at that output?

Section 6.4: Maximum Profit

In economic analysis, the objective that is most commonly assumed for firms is that they aim to maximize profit. Regardless of whether the firms are operating in competitive or monopolistic markets, their business goal is generally assumed to be profit maximization. Profit is defined in section 1.11 as total revenue, TR, minus total cost, TC

$$\pi = TR - TC$$

where both TR and TC are functions of output, Q. You may be familiar with finding the output that maximizes profit by identifying the point at which marginal cost, MC, equals marginal revenue, MR, with MC cutting MR from below. Another approach is to plot both TR and TC and find where the former exceeds the latter by the largest amount. Because it is a general method, we use differentiation to find where profit is maximized. We also apply the technique to a general statement of the profit function and thus show that using the marginal cost and revenue curves is an equivalent procedure.

The method used here is explained on the MathEcon screen titled Example One – Maximum Profit while the screens Profit Maximization 1 and 2 and Profit Maximization by a Monopolist 1 and 2 show the two graphical approaches using cost and revenue curves.

Remember…

For maximum profit, $\pi = TR - TC$

- substitute the expressions for TR and TC in the profit function so $\pi = f(Q)$
- differentiate the profit function with respect to output, Q
- set the derivative equal to zero and solve for Q
- find the second derivative $d^2(\pi)/dQ^2$ and check that it is negative.

4

A firm faces a demand function given by

$$P = 180 - 10Q$$

and has the total cost function

$$TC = 84 + 42Q - 12Q^2 + 1.5Q^3$$

Show at what output profit is maximized, finding price and the maximum value of profit.

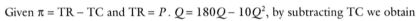

Given $\pi = TR - TC$ and $TR = P . Q = 180Q - 10Q^2$, by subtracting TC we obtain

$$\pi = -84 + 138Q + 2Q^2 - 1.5Q^3$$

To find where profit is a maximum, differentiate it with respect to Q

$$d\pi/dQ = 138 + 4Q - 4.5Q^2$$

To locate a possible maximum point, put this equal to zero and solve for Q

$$-4.5Q^2 + 4Q + 138 = 0$$

Using the formula we have

$$Q = \frac{-b \pm \sqrt{b^2 - 4ac}}{2a}$$

$$= \frac{[-4 \pm \sqrt{(16 + 2484)}]}{-9} = \frac{(-4 \pm 50)}{-9}$$

$$= -5.11 \text{ or } 6$$

Only a positive output is meaningful, but we must check to see if 6 gives a maximum turning point.

$$d^2\pi/dQ^2 = 4 - 9Q$$

This equals −50 when $Q = 6$. The negative value shows that $Q = 6$ is a maximum turning point. Now substitute in the demand function to find the price

$$P = 180 - 10(6) = 120$$

To find the value of profit substitute $Q = 6$ in the profit function.

$$\pi = -84 + 138(6) + 2(6^2) - 1.5(6^3) = 492$$

The profit maximizing firm sells an output $Q = 6$ at a price $P = 120$ and makes a profit of $\pi = 492$.

TAXATION

Indirect taxation can be regarded as an addition to cost. A lump sum tax, T, increases fixed cost but does not affect marginal cost or average variable cost. Alternatively, if a per unit tax, t, is imposed on sales, the average and marginal cost curves shift up by the amount of the tax and total cost increases by $t \cdot Q$, where Q is the quantity of output sold. We study the effects of these two kinds of tax in this worked example.

5

For the firm whose demand function and total cost function are given in worked example 4, what is the effect on the profit maximizing position if taxation is imposed as (i) a lump sum tax of 120 or (ii) a per unit sales tax of 24?

The original total cost function was $TC = 84 + 42Q - 12Q^2 + 1.5Q^3$ and the profit function was $\pi = -84 + 138Q + 2Q^2 - 1.5Q^3$

(i) If a lump sum tax of 120 is imposed the new total cost function is

$$TC' = 204 + 42Q - 12Q^2 + 1.5Q^3$$

and profit becomes

$$\pi' = -204 + 138Q + 2Q^2 - 1.5Q^3$$

Since only the constant has changed, differentiating gives the same function as before

$$d\pi'/dQ = 138 + 4Q - 4.5Q^2$$

and so again $Q = 6$ maximizes profit. Price remains unchanged at 120, but profit falls by the amount of the lump sum tax since substituting $Q = 6$ in the new profit function gives $\pi' = 372$.

(ii) If instead a unit tax of 24 is imposed, it adds $24Q$ to total cost. This changes the profit function to

$$\pi'' = -84 + 114Q + 2Q^2 - 1.5Q^3$$

and so

$$d\pi''/dQ = 114 + 4Q - 4.5Q^2 = 0 \text{ (for a maximum)}$$

$$Q = \frac{[-4 \pm \sqrt{(16 + 2052)}]}{-9} = \frac{(-4 \pm 45.475)}{-9} = -4.608 \text{ or } 5.497$$

Choosing the positive value we have $Q = 5.497$, so the quantity sold is lower when a per unit tax is imposed. Substituting we obtain

$$P = 180 - 10(5.497) = 125.03$$

Price has risen by 5.03.

$$\pi'' = -84 + 114(5.497) + 2(5.497^2) - 1.5(5.497^3) = 353.9$$

The per unit tax reduces profit, but its effect is shared between the producer and buyers of the good because price rises, whereas a lump sum tax is borne entirely by the producer.

PROFIT MAXIMIZED WHEN MR = MC

Show that when profit is maximized, marginal revenue equals marginal cost and marginal cost cuts marginal revenue from below.

$\pi = TR - TC$. When profit is maximized, $d\pi/dQ = 0$.
   Applying the sum-difference rule of differentiation to the general expression for profit gives

$$d\pi/dQ = d(TR)/dQ - d(TC)/dQ = 0$$

Identifying the derivatives of the total functions as the corresponding marginal functions we have

$$MR - MC = 0, \text{ or}$$

$$MR = MC$$

This is a possible maximum position, but we also require that $d^2\pi/dQ^2$ is negative. Since $d\pi/dQ = MR - MC$

$$d^2\pi/dQ^2 = d(MR)/dQ - d(MC)/dQ$$

This represents the slope of the MR curve minus the slope of the MC curve. The larger slope must be that of MC for the expression to be negative. If MC has a positive slope while MR has a negative one, the condition holds. Profit is maximized when an upward sloping MC curve cuts

MR from below. A maximum position is also possible if both MR and MC are downward sloping. It occurs if the slope of MC is shallower than that of MR, as in figure 6.4. Again marginal cost cuts marginal revenue from below.

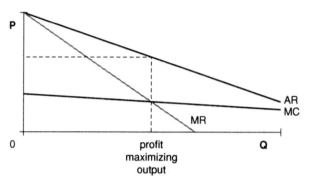

Figure 6.4   MC slopes downwards; shallower slope than MR

6.3   Find the profit function for a monopoly with the total cost function

$$TC = Q^3 - 10Q^2 + 300Q + 10,000$$

and the demand curve

$$P = 1900 - 20Q$$

At what output is maximum profit achieved? At what price is the output sold? What is the monopolist's profit?

6.4   A natural monopoly has the total cost function

$$TC = 2750 + 125Q - 0.125Q^2 \text{ for } 0 < Q < 500$$

and its demand curve is

$$AR = 400 - 1.5Q$$

Calculate the profit maximizing output and price for the firm and the profit it obtains. Is it producing where MC = MR and MC cuts MR from below?

SECTION 6.5: Minimum Average Cost

For a firm to stay in business it must in the long run at least cover its average cost and therefore it is useful to be able to find the minimum value of an average cost function. This information is also useful in sketching cost curves and in discussing relationships between them. Economic theory says marginal cost intersects the average cost curve at its minimum point, and we shall check this.

The MathEcon screen in figure 6.5 shows a quadratic average cost function and the U-shaped curve that it generates. The linear derivative is also plotted.

> Cost relationships are discussed in sections 1.10, 2.10 and 5.8.

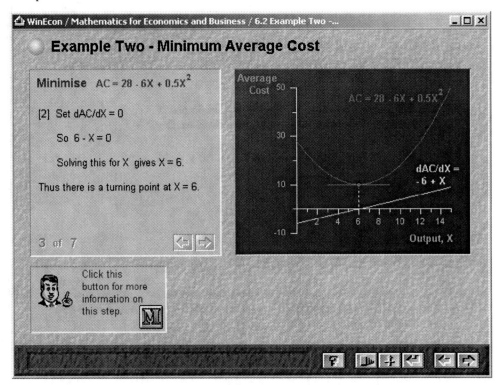

Example Two - Minimum Average Cost

Minimise $AC = 28 - 6X + 0.5X^2$

[2] Set $dAC/dX = 0$

So $6 - X = 0$

Solving this for X gives $X = 6$.

Thus there is a turning point at $X = 6$.

$AC = 28 - 6X + 0.5X^2$

$dAC/dX = -6 + X$

Output, X

3 of 7

Click this button for more information on this step.

Figure 6.5

A firm has total costs given by

$$TC = \frac{Q^3}{3} - 5Q^2 + 30Q$$

(a) Find the firm's average total cost, AC, function and show at what output it is at a minimum. What is the minimum value of AC?

(b) Find also marginal cost, MC. What value does it have when AC is a minimum? At what output is MC a minimum?

(c) Sketch the AC and MC curves, and on a different scale the TC curve. What can you say about their shapes?

6

(a) AC = TC/Q and therefore

$$AC = Q^2/3 - 5Q + 30$$

To find where AC is a minimum, differentiate it with respect to Q and set the derivative equal to zero

$$d(AC)/dQ = 2/3Q - 5 = 0$$

$$2/3Q = 5$$

So, $Q = 7.5$ is a turning point. To check whether it is a minimum we find the second derivative

$$d^2(AC)/dQ^2 = 2/3$$

This is a positive constant, so $Q = 7.5$ is a minimum.
   To find the minimum value of AC we substitute $Q = 7.5$

$$AC = \frac{7.5^2}{3} - 5(7.5) + 30 = 11.25$$

(b) MC = d(TC)/dQ

$$MC = Q^2 - 10Q + 30$$

At $Q = 7.5$ we have

$$MC = 7.5^2 - 10(7.5) + 30 = 11.25$$

This is the same value as AC, so the two curves intersect at this point.
   We now find where MC has a minimum. Differentiating it and setting the result equal to zero gives

$$d(MC)/dQ = 2Q - 10 = 0$$

So, $Q = 5$ at a turning point. To see whether this is a minimum we find the second derivative

$$d^2(MC)/dQ^2 = 2$$

This positive value tells us we do have a minimum at $Q = 5$.

(c) We have some information about MC and AC at $Q = 5$ and 7.5. Substitute a few more values for Q and you can sketch the curves shown in figure 6.6. Notice that when MC is a minimum TC changes from curving downwards to curving upwards. The second derivative of TC, the derivative of MC, is zero at this point. This is an example of a point of inflexion where the curve changes from bending one way to bending another.

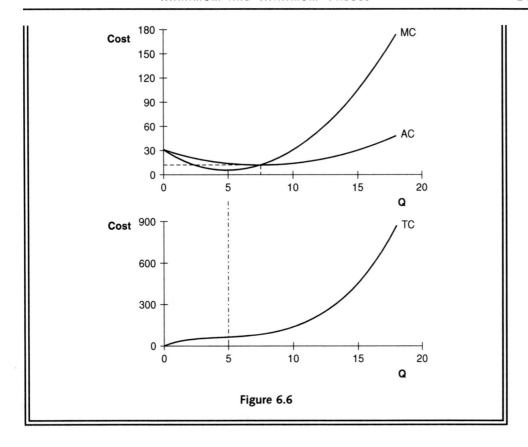

Figure 6.6

A firm in perfect competition has the total cost function

$$TC = 50 + 12X - X^2 + 0.04X^3$$

What is the minimum value of the firm's average variable cost curve? What is the firm's short-run supply curve? How much will the firm supply at a price of 12? At what output is marginal cost a minimum?

SECTION 6.6: Average and Marginal Product of Labour

The average product of labour is defined in section 1.12 as output divided by labour employed, $APL = Q/L$. The function shown there has an upside-down U shape and so has a maximum value. For a similar APL function, we shall identify the employment level at which it reaches a maximum and show it is crossed at that point by MPL, where $MPL = dQ/dL$ is the marginal product of labour, as discussed in section 5.7.

7

A firm's short-run production function is given by $Q = 140L^2 - 5L^3$. Find the marginal and average products of labour. Check that when average product is maximized, APL = MPL.

$$MPL = dQ/dL = 280L - 15L^2$$

$$APL = Q/L = 140L - 5L^2$$

To find maximum APL we differentiate

$$d(APL)/dL = 140 - 10L = 0 \text{ (for a maximum)}$$

So, $L = 14$ is a turning point. The second derivative is

$$d^2(APL)/dL^2 = -10$$

The negative sign indicates a maximum, so APL is a maximum at $L = 14$.
Substituting in APL and MPL we find

$$APL = 140(14) - 5(14^2) = 980$$

$$MPL = 280(14) - 15(14^2) = 980$$

APL and MPL intersect at the maximum value of APL. The curves are shown in figure 6.7. Notice that MPL reaches a maximum at a lower value of L. From that point there are diminishing marginal returns, since the marginal product of labour is falling.

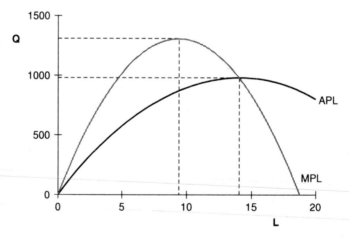

Figure 6.7 Average and marginal product of labour

6.6 For a firm with the short-run production function

$$Q = 30L + 18L^2 - 0.6L^3$$

find APL and show at what number of employees it reaches a maximum. Find also MPL and show when there are diminishing marginal returns.

SECTION 6.7: Tax Rate which Maximizes Tax Revenue

Section 2.4 shows that when a per unit tax, t, is imposed in a demand and supply model we can incorporate its effects by rewriting the supply function, replacing P by $P - t$. We now choose a value of t to maximize the tax revenue raised. For each unit of output sold the tax paid is t, so the tax revenue is $t \cdot Q$. To find a maximum we differentiate this with respect to t, the variable whose value we are choosing, but first we must substitute for Q using the condition for market equilibrium.

Choose the per unit rate of tax, t, which maximizes tax revenue in the market described by the equations

$$\text{Demand: } P = 100 - 4Q$$

$$\text{Supply: } P = 10 + 5Q$$

assuming equilibrium.

8

After tax supply: $P - t = 10 + 5Q$, or

$$P = 10 + 5Q + t$$

In equilibrium, price is the same whether determined by the demand equation or the supply equation, so we may equate the right-hand sides of the after tax supply and demand equations.

$$10 + 5Q + t = 100 - 4Q, \text{ which gives}$$

$$Q = 10 - t/9$$

We now have an expression for Q which assumes market equilibrium is achieved. Notice that to obtain this we began with the supply and demand equations written in the form $P = f(Q)$.

$$t \cdot Q = \text{tax revenue}$$

Substitute for Q

$$t \cdot Q = 10t - t^2/9$$

Differentiate with respect to t and set equal to 0 for a maximum

$$d(t \cdot Q)/dt = 10 - 2t/9 = 0$$

$$t = 45$$

To check for a maximum, find the second derivative

$$d^2(t \cdot Q)/dt^2 = -2/9$$

This is negative, so we have a maximum, therefore $t = 45$ is the per unit tax that maximizes tax revenue.

SECTION 6.8: Minimizing Total Inventory Costs

When a firm buys components from an external supplier it usually buys a batch and uses them steadily over a period of time. The components are held as inventory, or stock, until they are required. There are two types of cost associated with holding inventory. One type of cost is reduced by ordering larger batches, but the other is reduced by smaller batches. The best quantity, Q, to order in one batch is the quantity that minimizes the sum of these two types of cost.

Consider a time period of a year during which a total of D components are used. The number of orders that are placed is D/Q. The order cost, C_O, is the cost of placing an order, whatever its size, and having it delivered. The annual cost of ordering is $C_O \times D/Q$ and this is reduced by larger batches because less orders are required. Costs are also incurred through holding inventory. Money is tied up in the components that have been bought, storage space is occupied and there are costs of insurance, handling and deterioration. The cost of holding one item in stock for one year is C_H. Larger batch sizes mean more stock and so the annual cost of holding stock increases. If the Q components in a batch are used at a steady rate the average inventory level is $Q/2$ and we apply this to the unit holding cost to find the annual holding cost. We have

$$\text{Annual order cost} = C_O \times D/Q$$

$$\text{Annual holding cost} = C_H \times Q/2$$

The sum of these costs is the total inventory cost. The value of Q which minimizes it is called the economic order quantity, EOQ.

To find EOQ, choose Q to minimize   **Remember...**

total inventory cost $= (C_O \times D/Q) + (C_H \times Q/2)$

A lorry manufacturer uses axles at a steady rate of 81,000 per year. They are bought from a supplier with each order costing $400 regardless of its size. Holding axles in stock costs $80 per axle per year. What is the EOQ, and how many orders are placed per year? What is the total inventory cost?

9

Total used per year = $D = 81,000$

$$\text{Annual order cost} = C_O \times D/Q = 400 \times 81,000/Q$$

$$\text{Annual holding cost} = C_H \times Q/2 = 80 \times Q/2$$

$$\text{Total inventory cost} = (400 \times 81,000/Q) + (80 \times Q/2)$$

$$= 32,400,000Q^{-1} + 40Q$$

To minimize total inventory cost, differentiate with respect to Q and set equal to zero

$$d(\text{total inventory cost})/dQ = -32,400,000/Q^2 + 40 = 0$$

$$Q^2 = 810,000$$

Take the square root of both sides to give $Q = 900$ or -900, but only the positive value is meaningful.
  Check for a minimum by finding the second derivative

$$d^2(\text{total inventory cost})/dQ^2 = 64,800,000/Q^3$$

This is positive when Q is positive, so $Q = 900$ is a minimum.

The economic order quantity is $Q = 900$

Orders per year = $D/Q = 81,000/900 = 90$

Total inventory cost = $(400 \times 81,000/900) + (80 \times 900/2) = \$72,000$

6.7

A computer manufacturer uses 1170 video boards per year which are bought in from a specialist supplier. Placing an order for video boards costs $20 in phone calls, paperwork and carriage. The cost of holding video boards in stock is $1 per board per week. What is the EOQ and how many orders are placed each year?

Chapter 6: Answers to Practice Problems

6.1   (a) $dy/dx = 3 - x/2$; turning point at $x = 6$. $d^2y/dx^2 = -1/2$, which is negative, so the turning point is a maximum.

     (b) $dy/dx = -5$, a constant, so dy/dx cannot equal 0. A linear function has no turning points.

     (c) Turning points at $dy/dx = 24x - 3x^2 = 3x(8 - x) = 0$, i.e. when $x = 0$ or 8. $d^2y/dx^2 = 24 - 6x$, which is positive at $x = 0$ (value = 24) and negative at $x = 8$ (value = −24). Minimum at $x = 0$, maximum at $x = 8$.

     (d) $dy/dx = 5 - 20/x^2 = 0$ for a turning point. Rearranging gives $5x^2 = 20$ or $x = 2$, since the function is defined only for positive values of x.

     $d^2y/dx^2 = 40/x^3$, and since x is positive, d^2y/dx^2 is positive, so the turning point at $x = 2$ is a minimum.

6.2 $TR = P . Q = 80Q - 6Q^2$

     $d(TR)/dQ = 80 - 12Q$

     $80 - 12Q = 0$ at a maximum or minimum, so $Q = 6.67$

     $d^2(TR)/dQ^2 = -12$, i.e. negative, so a maximum

     $MR = d(TR)/dQ = 80 - 12(6.67) = 0$

6.3 $\pi = -Q^3 - 10Q^2 + 1600Q - 10,000$

     $d\pi/dQ = -3Q^2 - 20Q + 1600 = 0$ (for a maximum)

     $Q = 20$ or $-80/3$ (using the formula)

     $d^2\pi/dQ^2 = -6Q - 20$

     Q must be positive, so only $Q = 20$ is meaningful. Substituting we find $d^2\pi/dQ^2 = -140$, negative, so a maximum.

     If $Q = 20$, substitution gives $P = 1500$ and $\pi = 10,000$ as the maximum profit.

6.4 $\pi = -2750 + 275Q - 1.375Q^2$

     $d\pi/dQ = 275 - 2.75Q = 0$ (for a maximum)

     $Q = 100$

     $d^2\pi/dQ^2 = -2.75$, negative, so a maximum

     If $Q = 100$, we find $P = 250$ and profit = 11,000 for maximum profit

     $MC = d(TC)/dQ = 125 - 0.25Q$; marginal cost is downward sloping

     $MR = d(TR)/dQ = 400 - 3Q$

     The curves are plotted in figure 6.8. At $Q = 100$, $MC = MR = 100$ and MC cuts MR from below.

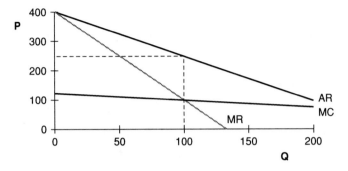

Figure 6.8 Natural monopoly cost and revenue

6.5 $AVC = 12 - X + 0.04X^2$

$d(AVC)/dX = -1 + 0.08X$; $X = 12.5$ is a turning point

$d^2(AVC)/dX^2 = 0.08$, positive, so $X = 12.5$ is a minimum

At $X = 12.5$, $AVC = 5.75$

Supply curve is MC above the minimum point of AVC

$MC = d(TC)/dX = 12 - 2X + 0.12X^2$

Supply is given by $P = 12 - 2X + 0.12X^2$ for $P \geq 5.75$

If $P = 12$, $X = 0$ or 16.67. The firm will supply at this price, so it supplies 16.67 units

$d(MC)/dX = -2 + 0.24X = 0$ for a turning point, so $X = 8.33$

$d^2(MC)/dX^2 = 0.24$, positive

$X = 8.33$ at minimum MC

6.6 $APL = Q/L = 30 + 18L - 0.6L^2$

$d(APL)/dL = 18 - 1.2L = 0$ (for a turning point)

$L = 15$

$d^2(APL)/dL^2 = -1.2$, negative

Maximum APL is at $L = 15$

$MPL = dQ/dL = 30 + 36L - 1.8L^2$

$d(MPL)/dL = 36 - 3.6L = 0$ (for a turning point)

$L = 10$

$d^2(MPL)/dL^2 = -3.6$, negative

Maximum MPL is at $L = 10$, so there are diminishing marginal returns when $L > 10$

6.7   Annual holding cost per board = $52

Total inventory cost = $(20 \times 1170/Q) + (52 \times Q/2)$

d(total inventory cost)$/dQ = -23,400/Q^2 + 26 = 0$

So, $Q = 30$ (−30 is not meaningful)

d^2(total inventory cost)$/dQ^2 = 46,800/Q^3$ (positive so a minimum)

EOQ = 30, which means 1170/30 = 39 orders per year

chapter seven

Further Rules of Differentiation

OBJECTIVES

In this chapter you learn to
- Appreciate when further rules of differentiation are needed
- Differentiate composite functions using the chain rule
- Use the product rule of differentiation
- Apply the quotient rule
- Show the relationship between marginal revenue, elasticity and maximum total revenue
- Analyse optimal production and cost relationships
- Differentiate natural logarithmic and exponential functions
- Use logarithmic and exponential relationships in economic analysis

---

SECTION 7.1: Introduction

In analysing economic relationships you often need to differentiate different functions from those we have studied so far. This chapter presents further rules of differentiation to give you more choice in economic modelling.

For these functions calculating the second derivative may be more difficult. Sometimes we shall check for a maximum or minimum by evaluating the function at the turning point and a little way on either side.

Screens in section 1 of MathEcon chapter 7 show you the Chain, Product and Quotient rules and help you to understand, remember and use them. You can click on parts of the description given to help you remember a rule and identify corresponding terms in the statement of the rule. Screens demonstrating the differentiation of Natural Logarithmic and Exponential Functions are in section 2.

SECTION 7.2: The Chain Rule

The rules you already know allow you to differentiate the function $u = 4x^3 - x^2 - 9$, where u is a function of x. They do not, however, allow you to differentiate $y = \sqrt{(4x^3 - x^2 - 9)}$. The expression we had for u now forms an inner function, and the square root of all of it is taken. Taking the square root applies a function to the expression in brackets which is itself a function of x. We describe $y = \sqrt{(4x^3 - x^2 - 9)}$ as a function of a function or a composite function. The appropriate method of differentiation is called the chain rule. Alternative names for it are the composite function, or function of a function rule. Once you recognize a function needs the chain rule to differentiate it, you substitute a variable name for the inner function. In our example we let $u = 4x^3 - x^2 - 9$ and so write $y = \sqrt{u}$. We can now use the chain rule.

The MathEcon screen titled The Chain Rule shows how the rule works.

If $y = f(u)$ where $u = g(x)$

$$dy/dx = (dy/du)(du/dx)$$

Remember...

Chain rule: multiply the derivative of the outer function by the derivative of the inner function.

1

Find dy/dx if $y = \sqrt{(4x^3 - x^2 - 9)}$

Substituting u for the inner function and writing the square root as a power we have $u = 4x^3 - x^2 - 9$ and $y = u^{1/2}$. Differentiating each of these we obtain

$$du/dx = 12x^2 - 2x, \quad dy/du = 0.5u^{-1/2}$$

The chain rule then gives the required derivative

$$dy/dx = (dy/du)(du/dx) = 0.5u^{-1/2}(12x^2 - 2x)$$

Since u is just a name we used to help us find the derivative, we should substitute back the corresponding expression in x. The result is

$$\frac{0.5(12x^2 - 2x)}{\sqrt{(4x^3 - x^2 - 9)}}$$

7.1 Differentiate with respect to x

(a) $y = (12x^2 - 25x)^3$

(b) $y = \sqrt{(10x^3 - 4)}$

(c) $y = \dfrac{50}{1 - 0.8(1 - x)}$

(d) $y = \dfrac{1}{5x^2 - 7x^4}$

SECTION 7.3: The Product Rule

If you are asked to differentiate an expression comprising two terms multiplied to-gether, you need to use the product rule if each term contains the variable with respect to which you are differentiating. For example, the function

$$y = 8x^3(1 - 7x)^4$$

comprises two terms multiplied together, namely $8x^3$ and $(1 - 7x)^4$. Each of these contains x, and so to differentiate with respect to x, the product rule is appropriate.

Sometimes an expression formed as a product can be multiplied out and you can differentiate the result. This would be possible, but tedious, with the expression above. We cannot always multiply out, however, and so the product rule is needed for economic analysis. This rule can also be used to differentiate quotients, although you may prefer to use the separate quo-tient rule shown in the next section.

As you use the MathEcon screen titled The Product Rule, click on the various items in the formula to identify the corresponding terms in the statement of the rule.

If $y = f(x)g(x)$

Remember...

$$u = f(x), \ v = g(x)$$

$$dy/dx = v \cdot du/dx + u \cdot dv/dx$$

Product rule: the derivative of the first term times the second plus the derivative of the second term times the first.

2 Differentiate with respect to x using the product rule

$$y = 8x^3(1 - 7x)^4$$

The key to using the product rule for differentiation is to identify two items that are multiplied together and call one of them u and the other v. Here $8x^3$ multiplies the expression $(1 - 7x)^4$. Let $u = 8x^3$ and $v = (1 - 7x)^4$. These separate parts have each to be differentiated with respect to x.

$$du/dx = 24x^2$$

To differentiate v, we notice that it is a composite function and choose a new variable name, w, to substitute. We have $w = 1 - 7x$ and $v = w^4$. This gives $dw/dx = -7$ and $dv/dw = 4w^3$. Using the chain rule

$$dv/dx = dv/dw \cdot dw/dx = (4w^3) \times (-7) = -28(1 - 7x)^3$$

Now substitute in the formula for the product rule, giving

$$dy/dx = v \cdot du/dx + u \cdot dv/dx$$
$$= (1 - 7x)^4(24x^2) + 8x^3(-28)(1 - 7x)^3$$
$$= 8x^2(1 - 7x)^3(3 - 21x - 28x)$$
$$= 8x^2(1 - 7x)^3(3 - 49x)$$

By now you may be feeling that differentiating a more complex function really is a more difficult procedure. Try practising using the rule, and don't worry too much about simplifying your answer after you have differentiated.

3

Using the product rule, differentiate with respect to x

$$y = \frac{5x^3}{9 - x}$$

Here we have one expression divided by another which we rewrite as a product giving the term in the denominator a negative power. We obtain

$$y = 5x^3(9 - x)^{-1}$$

Now let $u = 5x^3$ and $v = (9 - x)^{-1}$. Differentiating these with respect to x we obtain

$$du/dx = 15x^2$$

while for dv/dx we let $w = (9 - x)$ so $v = w^{-1}$

$$dv/dx = dv/dw \cdot dw/dx = -(9 - x)^{-2}(-1) = (9 - x)^{-2}$$

Using the product rule

$$dy/dx = v \cdot du/dx + u \cdot dv/dx = (9 - x)^{-1}15x^2 + 5x^3(9 - x)^{-2}$$

$$= \frac{5x^2}{(9 - x)^2} \cdot (27 - 3x + x)$$

$$= \frac{5x^2(27 - 2x)}{(9 - x)^2}$$

7.2 Use the product rule to differentiate the following functions with respect to x

(a) $y = (6x + x^2)(2x^3 - 4x + 5)$ (b) $y = 8x^{0.5}(4x^3 + 10x^2 + 3x)$

(c) $y = \dfrac{7x^3 - 2x^2 - 12}{2x^2}$ (d) $y = 12x^3\sqrt{(3x^5 - 9)}$

Section 7.4: The Quotient Rule

Although you can always use the product rule for differentiating quotients, the quotient rule which we study now may give you the answer more easily. Take care as you substitute using this rule. The rule as stated below assumes that u is the term in the numerator and v is the term in the denominator.

You can learn more about this rule on the MathEcon screen titled The Quotient Rule.

If $y = f(x)/g(x)$ **Remember...**

$$u = f(x), \ v = g(x)$$

$$\frac{dy}{dx} = \frac{v \cdot du/dx - u \cdot dv/dx}{v^2}$$

Quotient rule: the derivative of the first term times the second minus the derivative of the second term times the first, all divided by the square of the second term.

4

Find dy/dx if

$$y = \frac{7x^3}{3x^2 + 4x}$$

To use the quotient rule we let $u = 7x^3$ and $v = 3x^2 + 4x$. Differentiating each with respect to x gives

$$du/dx = 21x^2, \ dv/dx = 6x + 4$$

Using the quotient rule we have

$$\frac{dy}{dx} = \frac{v \cdot du/dx - u \cdot dv/dx}{v^2} = \frac{(3x^2 + 4x)(21x^2) - (7x^3)(6x + 4)}{(3x^2 + 4x)^2}$$

Factorizing or multiplying out the numerator and collecting terms gives

$$\frac{dy}{dx} = \frac{7x^3(3x + 8)}{(3x^2 + 4x)^2}$$

5

Differentiate

$$y = \frac{\sqrt{(4x^2 + 11x)}}{x}$$

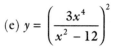

$u = \sqrt{(4x^2 + 11x)}$ and $v = x$ for the quotient rule. To find du/dx put $w = (4x^2 + 11x)$ so $u = \sqrt{w} = w^{0.5}$. Using the chain rule

$$du/dx = du/dw \cdot dw/dx = 0.5w^{-0.5}(8x + 11)$$

Substituting for w gives

$$du/dx = 0.5(4x^2 + 11x)^{-0.5}(8x + 11)$$

$$dv/dx = 1$$

Substitute in the expression for the quotient rule

$$dy/dx = \frac{v \cdot du/dx - u \cdot dv/dx}{v^2}$$

$$= \frac{0.5x(4x^2 + 11x)^{-0.5}(8x + 11) - (4x^2 + 11x)^{0.5}}{x^2}$$

$$= \frac{4x^2 + 5.5x - 4x^2 - 11x}{x^2(4x^2 + 11x)^{0.5}} = -\frac{5.5}{x(4x^2 + 11x)^{0.5}}$$

7.3   Differentiate

(a) $y = \dfrac{15x}{3x - 5x^2}$

(b) $y = \dfrac{8x + 3x^3}{4x^2 - 10x}$

(c) $y = \dfrac{7x^3 - 2x^2 - 12}{2x^2}$

(d) $y = \dfrac{(5x + 2)^2}{7x^2 - 16}$

(e) $y = \left(\dfrac{3x^4}{x^2 - 12}\right)^2$

Section 7.5: Marginal Revenue, Price Elasticity and Maximum Total Revenue

When we measure the point price elasticity of demand defined in section 5.9 as $E = (dQ/dP) \times (P/Q)$ we would also like to know how a price change will affect total revenue. A fall in price, P, increases quantity demanded, Q. As Q increases, the rate at which total revenue, TR, changes is shown by marginal revenue, MR. Since P falls as Q rises, MR can be either positive, implying that TR increases, or negative, implying that TR decreases. We now obtain a general result relating marginal revenue to elasticity and price. This shows the elasticity of demand when total revenue is maximized.

> Section 5.6 shows
> MR = d(TR)/dQ.

Show that for any demand curve, given that E is point price elasticity of demand and is negative

$$MR = P(1 + 1/E)$$

and maximum total revenue occurs when $E = -1$.

We have $MR = d(TR)/dQ = d(P \cdot Q)/dQ$, but the appropriate method of differentiation depends on what P represents. If P is just a constant, as in the special case of a firm in perfect competition, differentiation is easy. Generally, however, on a downward sloping demand curve P falls as Q increases, so P is a function of Q. To find $d(P \cdot Q)/dQ$ we need to use the product rule since we are differentiating two functions of Q multiplied together. We have

$$MR = d(P \cdot Q)/dQ$$

Let $u = P$ and $v = Q$

$$du/dQ = dP/dQ, \quad dv/dQ = 1$$

Don't worry about not knowing what dP/dQ is. Just continue, and substitute into the product rule. We obtain

$$MR = v \cdot du/dQ + u \cdot dv/dQ = Q \cdot dP/dQ + P$$

Now we need to recognize that the first term is rather like the formula for price elasticity. So that we can compare them we write down the formula for elasticity

$$E = (dQ/dP) \times (P/Q)$$

and take its reciprocal. This gives

$$1/E = (dP/dQ) \times (Q/P)$$

The first term in our marginal revenue equation is P times this and so we may write

$$MR = P/E + P = P(1 + 1/E)$$

This is the general result relating MR, P and E. It is true for any shape of demand curve. Notice that for a downward sloping demand curve, E is negative.

Marginal revenue shows how total revenue changes as the quantity sold increases when price is lowered slightly. If MR is positive, total revenue increases. Economic theory says this occurs when demand is elastic, because the quantity bought increases more than proportionately to the price change. Substituting in the formula confirms this. If demand is elastic, $1/E$ is a negative fraction and $(1 + 1/E)$ is positive, so MR is positive. Conversely, when demand is inelastic total revenue falls if price is lowered. We have $1/E < -1$ and so $(1 + 1/E)$ is negative, implying MR is negative.

Section 6.3 shows that maximum total revenue occurs when MR $= 0$, because MR $= d(TR)/dQ$. For maximum total revenue, therefore

$$MR = P(1 + 1/E) = 0$$

$$P = 0 \text{ or } (1 + 1/E) = 0$$

$P = 0$ implies TR $= 0$, so that is not a maximum value.

$$(1 + 1/E) = 0 \text{ when}$$

$$1 = -1/E$$

Therefore, $E = -1$ at a position of maximum total revenue.

The MathEcon screen titled Example One – Marginal Revenue (Product Rule) allows you to study this analysis for a particular case and also in the general form. Use both versions and compare them. The screen Price Elasticity and Total Revenue uses numerical examples and arc elasticity to show the effect on total revenue of price changes for curves of different elasticities.

6

For the demand curve $Q = 280 - 7P$ find the price elasticity, marginal revenue and total revenue at the following prices: 30, 20, 10.

To find price elasticity we begin by finding dQ/dP.

$$dQ/dP = -7$$

To find elasticity at each of the prices given we multiply by the appropriate P/Q as shown in the table below. Values of P and E are then substituted in the formula for MR and TR is calculated as $P \times Q$.

P	30	20	10
Q	70	140	210
P/Q	3/7	1/7	1/21
$E = dQ/dP \cdot P/Q$	-3	-1	-1/3
MR $= P(1 + 1/E)$	20	0	-20
TR $= P \times Q$	2100	2800	2100

We find that when $P = 30$, demand is elastic $(E = -3)$ and MR is positive (20); when $P = 20$, the demand curve has unitary elasticity and MR $= 0$; and when $P = 10$, demand is inelastic $(E = -1/3)$ and MR is negative (-20). Total revenue is maximized at $P = 20$ where $E = -1$.

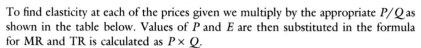

7.4

By finding price elasticity and marginal revenue at the specified prices, say what would be the impact on total revenue of a small price reduction if the demand curve is

$$Q = 100 - 10P$$

at prices of 10, 7, 5 and 3.

7.5 For each of the following functions, find an expression for price elasticity and use it to write an expression for MR in terms of price.

(a) $Q = 75/P$ (b) $Q = 100/P^2$

(c) $Q = 27/P^3$ (d) $Q = c - mP$

For these functions, can MR be negative?

7.6 For the firm facing the demand curve below, find the total revenue function and show at what output it is maximized.

$$P = (140 - 0.8Q)^{1.3}$$

Section 7.6: Optimal Production and Cost Relationships

The analysis of short-run production functions discussed in sections 5.7 and 6.6 is now developed further. General results are shown and more examples are given.

A firm's short-run production function is given by

$$Q = 15L^{0.8}(220 - 10L)^{0.5}$$

where L is the number of persons employed. What level of employment gives the maximum output?

The maximum output occurs where $dQ/dL = 0$. To differentiate we use the product rule with $u = 15L^{0.8}$ and $v = (220 - 10L)^{0.5}$. So

$$du/dL = 12L^{-0.2}$$

To find dv/dL we use the chain rule. Let $w = 220 - 10L$, so $v = w^{0.5}$.

$$dv/dL = dv/dw \cdot dw/dL = 0.5w^{-0.5}(-10) = -5(220 - 10L)^{-0.5}$$

We now apply the product rule

$$dQ/dL = v \cdot du/dL + u \cdot dv/dL$$

$$= (220 - 10L)^{0.5}(12L^{-0.2}) + (15L^{0.8})(-5)(220 - 10L)^{-0.5}$$

$$= (220 - 10L)^{-0.5}[12L^{-0.2}(220 - 10L) - 5(15L^{0.8})]$$

$$= (220 - 10L)^{-0.5}(2640L^{-0.2} - 120L^{0.8} - 75L^{0.8})$$

$$= \frac{2640 - 195L}{L^{0.2}(220 - 10L)^{0.5}}$$

For this expression to equal zero

$$2640 - 195L = 0, \text{ so}$$

$$L = 13.5$$

If a whole number of persons are to be employed we need an integer solution. It seems the maximum output occurs when 14 persons are employed.

To check, we evaluate Q for L taking the values 13, 14 and 15. The corresponding values of Q are 1107.56, 1107.997 and 1095.25, showing that the maximum value of Q occurs when $L = 14$.

MC = W/MPL AND MVP = P.MPL

We now show that there is an inverse relationship between the marginal product of labour and the firm's marginal cost. The analysis is valid for firms operating in perfectly competitive labour and product markets. They buy labour at the going wage rate and sell their product at the price determined by the market. The profit maximizing employment level for the firm is also shown.

> Section 5.8 defines
> MC = d(TC)/dQ.

A firm is operating in perfectly competitive product and labour markets where its product sells at price P and the wage rate is W. Show that (a) its short-run marginal cost curve is $MC = W/MPL$, where MPL is the marginal product of labour and (b) to maximize profits, employment is determined by $MVP = W$, where $MVP = P.MPL$ is the marginal value product of labour.

In the short run, labour is the only factor the firm can vary. To employ L workers costs $W.L$, and the firm's other costs are fixed, FC. In the short run

$$TC = W.L + FC$$

(a) Using the chain rule

$$MC = d(TC)/dQ = d(TC)/dL \times dL/dQ$$

Since $d(TC)/dL = W$ and $MPL = dQ/dL$

$$MC = W/MPL$$

(b) Profit is given by

$$\pi = TR - TC$$

$$= P.Q - W.L - FC$$

We want to choose L to maximize π. P, W and FC are all constants. Differentiate with respect to L

$$d\pi/dL = P.dQ/dL - W = 0 \text{ (for a maximum)}$$

and so

$$P.dQ/dL = W$$

and substituting MPL = dQ/dL this gives

$$P.\,\text{MPL} = W$$

MVP = W is the employment condition for profit maximization for a price-taking firm. To ensure a maximum, $d^2\pi/dL^2 = P.\,d(\text{MPL})/dL$ must be negative. This implies there must be diminishing marginal returns, with MPL falling.

A competitive firm buys labour at $W = 720$ and sells its product at $P = 5$. Its short-run production function is $Q = 24L^2 - L^3$. Find its marginal cost in terms of L and show how many workers it employs. By substituting values of L, including $L = 1, 4, 8$ and 12, find numerical values for Q, MPL, MC and also APL. Plot a graph of MPL and APL with L on the horizontal axis, and one of MC with Q on the horizontal axis.

We can write

$$\text{MPL} = dQ/dL = 48L - 3L^2$$

$$\text{MC} = W/\text{MPL} = \frac{720}{48L - 3L^2}$$

To maximize profits, the firm's employment is at the value of L where

$$P.\,\text{MPL} = W$$

Substitute and solve for L

$$5(48L - 3L^2) = 720$$

$$-15L^2 + 240L - 720 = 0$$

We find $L = 4$ or 12. MPL is falling at $L = 12$, which is therefore the optimal level of employment. The graphs are shown in figures 7.1 and 7.2. Notice that maximum MPL and minimum MC occur at $L = 8$, while $L = 12$ corresponds to maximum APL.

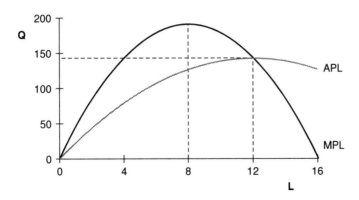

Figure 7.1 Marginal and average product of labour

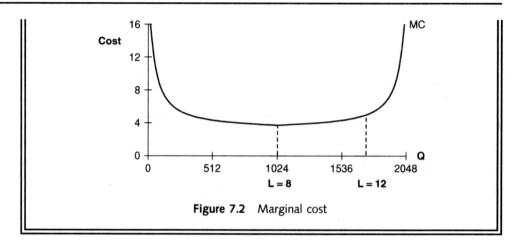

Figure 7.2   Marginal cost

MARGINAL AND AVERAGE COST

Section 6.5 shows examples identifying minimum AC. We now show a general relationship between MC and AC.

Marginal cost cuts average cost from below at the minimum point of the average cost curve.

We have seen

$$MC = d(TC)/dQ \text{ and } AC = TC/Q$$

To find the minimum point of AC, differentiate AC with respect to Q and set equal to zero for a turning point. We have

$$d(AC)/dQ = d(TC/Q)/dQ$$

For the quotient rule, put $u = TC$ and $v = Q$.

$$du/dQ = d(TC)/dQ = MC, \; dv/dQ = 1$$

Substituting in the quotient rule gives

$$d(AC)/dQ = (Q \cdot MC - TC)/Q^2$$

Dividing both the numerator and denominator by Q gives

$$d(AC)/dQ = (MC - AC)/Q$$

$$= 0 \text{ (for a minimum)}$$

$(MC - AC)/Q = 0$ at the turning point, so

$$MC = AC$$

But is this a minimum turning point? If so, as in figure 7.3, AC must be falling to the left of it and rising to the right of it. That is, $d(AC)/dQ$ is at first negative; it takes the value 0 at the turning point and becomes positive to the right of it. This implies that before the turning point $(MC - AC)/Q$ is negative or $MC < AC$. MC is below AC before a minimum turning point and at the turning point MC intersects AC from below.

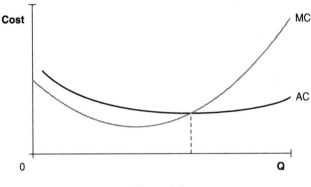

Figure 7.3

7.7 Find an expression for the marginal product of labour for a firm with the short-run production function

$$Q = \frac{30L^2 - L^3}{(1 + 2L)^2}$$

At what integer value of L is output maximized?

7.8 Find the output at which AC is a minimum for a firm with the total cost function

$$TC = 5Q^3 + 150Q + 1250$$

Find MC, and evaluate MC and AC at the output that minimizes AC to check they are equal. Is MC less than AC at a slightly lower output?

7.9 For a firm with a short-run production function of the form $Q = f(L)$, define the average product of labour, APL and the marginal product, MPL. Show that at the value of L where APL is a maximum, MPL cuts the APL curve from above.

SECTION 7.7: Exponential and Natural Logarithmic Functions

Section 2.13 discusses exponential functions and shows a graph of $y = e^x$. It is close to the x axis for negative values, rises to the value 1 when $x = 0$ and continues rising ever more steeply as x takes larger positive values. The slope of such a curve is always positive and increasing, and therefore the derivative of $y = e^x$ is always increasing.

It can be shown that for the exponential function $y = e^x$ **Remember...**

$$dy/dx = e^x$$

More generally, we can write the rule as shown below.

For the exponential function $y = ae^{mx}$ **Remember...**

$$dy/dx = mae^{mx}$$

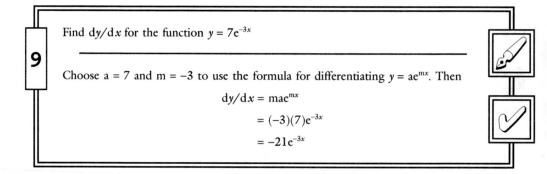

9

Find dy/dx for the function $y = 7e^{-3x}$

Choose a = 7 and m = −3 to use the formula for differentiating $y = ae^{mx}$. Then

$$dy/dx = mae^{mx}$$
$$= (-3)(7)e^{-3x}$$
$$= -21e^{-3x}$$

Logarithmic functions are explained in section 2.14. As regards their differentiation, we are solely concerned with natural logarithms, denoted $\log_e$ or ln. The shape of the curve for $y = \ln x$ is shown in figure 7.4. Notice that ln x is not defined for negative values of x. The graph of ln x starts with negative values and increases at a decreasing rate, so its slope is positive but decreasing. The slope is in fact $1/x$.

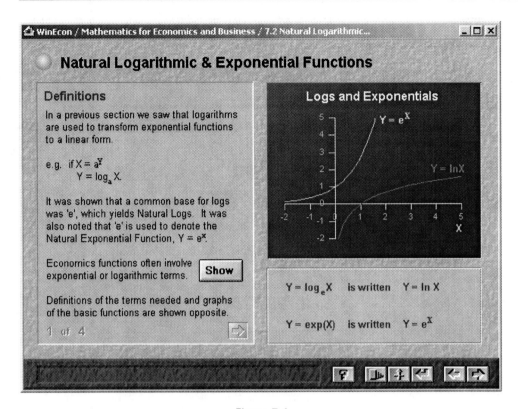

Figure 7.4

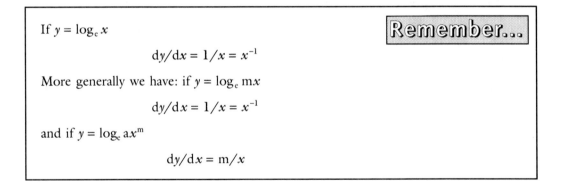

If $y = \log_e x$

$$dy/dx = 1/x = x^{-1}$$

More generally we have: if $y = \log_e mx$

$$dy/dx = 1/x = x^{-1}$$

and if $y = \log_e ax^m$

$$dy/dx = m/x$$

For explanations of these rules use the appropriate More buttons on the screen titled Rules for Differentiation of Logs/Exponentials in section 2 of MathEcon chapter 7. To see examples of differentiating exponential and log functions and of finding their second and third derivatives work through the following screen, Natural Logarithmic and Exponential Functions. There are examples for you to try on the next screen Practise Differentiating Logs/Exponentials.

Find dP/dQ for the function

$$P = -80 \ln \frac{Q}{Q+2}$$

10

For the chain rule we write $w = Q/(Q+2)$ and to find dw/dQ we use the quotient rule with $u = Q$ and $v = Q + 2$.

$$\frac{dw}{dQ} = \frac{v \cdot du/dQ - u \cdot dv/dQ}{v^2} = \frac{(Q+2) \cdot 1 - Q \cdot 1}{(Q+2)^2}$$

$$= \frac{2}{(Q+2)^2}$$

Substituting w, $P = -80 \ln w$, and so

$$\frac{dP}{dw} = -\frac{80}{w}$$

Using the chain rule and substituting for w

$$\frac{dP}{dQ} = \frac{dP}{dw} \cdot \frac{dw}{dQ} = \left[\frac{-80(Q+2)}{Q} \right]\left[\frac{2}{(Q+2)^2} \right]$$

$$= -\frac{160}{Q(Q+2)}$$

7.10   Differentiate with respect to x

(a) $y = 10e^{-4x}$ (b) $y = xe^{2x}$

(c) $y = \log_e (30x - x^2)$ (d) $y = x \log_e x$

SECTION 7.8: Applications to Economic Analysis

Exponential and logarithmic functions can be used in economic modelling. They allow us to depict relationships with particular curvilinear shapes.

11 A demand curve is defined by $P = 1000e^{-Q}$. Find an expression for price elasticity of demand.

Differentiate P with respect to Q

$$dP/dQ = -1000e^{-Q}$$

Price elasticity of demand $= (dQ/dP) . (P/Q)$

$$= -(e^{Q}/1000)(1000e^{-Q})/Q = -1/Q$$

12 A production function takes the form $Q = 4 \log_e (L + 1)$. Find an expression for the marginal product of labour.

Using the rule for logarithmic differentiation and the chain rule with $u = L + 1$

$$MPL = dQ/dL = [4/(L + 1)] . 1 = 4/(L + 1)$$

7.11 Find an expression for price elasticity of demand for the demand function

$$P = 250 - 50 \log_e (Q + 1)$$

7.12 What value of L maximizes output for the production function

$$Q = 40L^2 e^{-0.3L}$$

Chapter 7: Answers to Practice Problems

7.1 (a) $u = (12x^2 - 25x)$

$dy/du = 3u^2$, $du/dx = 24x - 25$

$dy/dx = 3(12x^2 - 25x)^2(24x - 25)$

(b) $u = (10x^3 - 4)$

$dy/du = 0.5u^{-0.5}$, $du/dx = 30x^2$

$dy/dx = 15x^2/\sqrt{(10x^3 - 4)}$

(c) $y = 50(0.2 + 0.8x)^{-1}$ (by rewriting the function)

$u = 0.2 + 0.8x$, $du/dx = 0.8$, $dy/du = -50u^{-2}$

$dy/dx = -40/(0.2 + 0.8x)^2$

(d) $y = (5x^2 - 7x^4)^{-1}$

$u = (5x^2 - 7x^4)$, $du/dx = 10x - 28x^3$, $dy/du = -u^{-2}$

$dy/dx = -(10x - 28x^3)/(5x^2 - 7x^4)^2$

7.2   (a) $u = (6x + x^2)$, $v = (2x^3 - 4x + 5)$

$du/dx = 6 + 2x$, $dv/dx = 6x^2 - 4$

$dy/dx = (2x^3 - 4x + 5)(6 + 2x) + (6x + x^2)(6x^2 - 4)$

$\qquad = 10x^4 + 48x^3 - 12x^2 - 38x + 30$

(b) $u = 8x^{0.5}$, $v = (4x^3 + 10x^2 + 3x)$

$du/dx = 4x^{-0.5}$, $dv/dx = 12x^2 + 20x + 3$

$dy/dx = (4x^3 + 10x^2 + 3x)(4x^{-0.5}) + (8x^{0.5})(12x^2 + 20x + 3)$

$\qquad = (4x^3 + 10x^2 + 3x)(4x^{-0.5}) + 2x(4x^{-0.5})(12x^2 + 20x + 3)$
$\qquad$ (since $8x^{0.5} = 2x(4x^{-0.5})$)

$\qquad = (4x^{-0.5})(4x^3 + 10x^2 + 3x + 24x^3 + 40x^2 + 6x)$

$\qquad = 4(28x^3 + 50x^2 + 9x)/x^{0.5}$

(c) $y = 0.5x^{-2}(7x^3 - 2x^2 - 12)$

$u = 0.5x^{-2}$, $v = (7x^3 - 2x^2 - 12)$

$du/dx = -x^{-3}$, $dv/dx = 21x^2 - 4x$

$dy/dx = (7x^3 - 2x^2 - 12)(-x^{-3}) + (0.5x^{-2})(21x^2 - 4x)$

$\qquad = 3.5 + 12/x^3$

(d) $u = 12x^3$, $v = \sqrt{(3x^5 - 9)}$

Chain rule to find dv/dx, letting $w = (3x^5 - 9)$

$dy/dx = 36x^2\sqrt{(3x^5 - 9)} + 12x^3(0.5)(3x^5 - 9)^{-0.5}(15x^4)$

$\qquad = 18x^2(11x^5 - 18)/\sqrt{(3x^5 - 9)}$

7.3   (a) $u = 15x$, $v = 3x - 5x^2$

$du/dx = 15$, $dv/dx = 3 - 10x$

$dy/dx = [(3x - 5x^2)(15) - 15x(3 - 10x)]/(3x - 5x^2)^2$

$\qquad = 75x^2/(3x - 5x^2)^2$

(b) $u = 8x + 3x^3$, $v = 4x^2 - 10x$

$du/dx = 8 + 9x^2$, $dv/dx = 8x - 10$

$dy/dx = [(4x^2 - 10x)(8 + 9x^2) - (8x + 3x^3)(8x - 10)]/(4x^2 - 10x)^2$

$\qquad = (12x^4 - 60x^3 - 32x^2)/(4x^2 - 10x)^2$

(c) $u = 7x^3 - 2x^2 - 12$, $v = 2x^2$

$du/dx = 21x^2 - 4x$, $dv/dx = 4x$

$dy/dx = [(2x^2)(21x^2 - 4x) - (7x^3 - 2x^2 - 12)(4x)]/(2x^2)^2$

$\qquad = (7x^3 + 24)/2x^3$

(d) $y = (5x + 2)^2/(7x^2 - 16)$

Quotient rule, $u = (5x + 2)^2$, $v = 7x^2 - 16$

and chain rule to find du/dx, $w = (5x + 2)$

$dy/dx = [(7x^2 - 16) \cdot 2(5x + 2)5 - (5x + 2)^2(14x)]/(7x^2 - 16)^2$

$\qquad = [(5x + 2)(-160 - 28x)]/(7x^2 - 16)^2$

(e) $y = [3x^4/(x^2 - 12)]^2$

Chain rule, $w = 3x^4/(x^2 - 12)$

and quotient rule to find dw/dx, $u = 3x^4$, $v = x^2 - 12$

$dy/dx = 36x^7(x^2 - 24)/(x^2 - 12)^3$

7.4

$E = dQ/dP \cdot P/Q$	$-\infty$	$-7/3$	-1	$-3/7$
$MR = P(1 + 1/E)$	10	4	0	-4
TR would:	rise	rise	remain same	fall

7.5

	(a)	(b)	(c)	(d)
$E = dQ/dP \cdot P/Q$	-1	-2	-3	$-mP/(c - mP)$
$MR = P(1 + 1/E)$	0	$P/2$	$2P/3$	$2P - c/m$
MR is	0 at all P	always positive	always positive	negative if $P < c/2m$

7.6 Method 1: $TR = P \cdot Q = Q(140 - 0.8Q)^{1.3}$
For maximum TR, $d(TR)/dQ = 0$. By using the product and chain rules
$d(TR)/dQ = (140 - 0.8Q)^{1.3} + 1.3Q(140 - 0.8Q)^{0.3}(-0.8)$
$(140 - 0.8Q)^{0.3}(140 - 1.84Q) = 0$ (for a maximum)
$0.8Q = 140$ or $1.84Q = 140$
$Q = 175$ or $Q = 76.09$
Evaluating TR we find

$$Q \qquad 75 \qquad 76.09 \qquad 77 \quad 175$$
$$\mathrm{TR} \quad 22{,}340 \quad 22{,}343.8 \quad 22{,}341 \quad 0$$

$Q = 76.09$ is therefore the output which maximizes TR.

Method 2: $dP/dQ = 1.3(140 - 0.8Q)^{0.3}(-0.8)$ (chain rule)

$$= -1.04(140 - 0.8Q)^{0.3}$$

$$E = \{1/[-1.04(140 - 0.8Q)^{0.3}]\} \times [(140 - 0.8Q)^{1.3}]/Q$$

$$= -(140 - 0.8Q)/1.04Q = -1 \text{ for maximum TR.}$$

This solves to give $Q = 76.09$

7.7 $\mathrm{MPL} = dQ/dL = L(60 - 3L - 2L^2)/(1 + 2L)^3$ (using the quotient and chain rules)

For a maximum either $L = 0$ or $60 - 3L - 2L^2 = 0$

Solving the quadratic equation gives $L = -6.3$ or 4.8

$L = 5$ (positive integer value)

To check if this is a maximum substitute $L = 4$, $L = 5$ and $L = 6$ in the production function. $Q = 5.14$, 5.17 and 5.11 respectively and so output is maximized at $L = 5$.

7.8 $\mathrm{AC} = (5Q^3 + 150Q + 1250)/Q = 5Q^2 + 150 + 1250/Q$

$d(\mathrm{AC})/dQ = 10Q - 1250/Q^2 = 0$ (for a turning point)

$10Q^3 = 1250$

$Q = 5$

$d^2(\mathrm{AC})/dQ^2 = 10 + 2500/Q^3$, positive if $Q = 5$, so this is a minimum turning point.

$\mathrm{MC} = d(\mathrm{TC})/dQ = 15Q^2 + 150$

If $Q = 5$, $\mathrm{MC} = 525$

Also $\mathrm{AC} = 525$, so $\mathrm{MC} = \mathrm{AC}$ at $Q = 5$

If $Q = 4$, $\mathrm{MC} = 390$ and $\mathrm{AC} = 542.5$, so marginal cost is less than average cost just to the left of the minimum point of the AC curve.

7.9 $\mathrm{APL} = Q/L$ where $Q = f(L)$, so differentiate using the quotient rule

$$d(\mathrm{APL})/dL = [L \cdot dQ/dL - Q]/L^2$$

$$= [dQ/dL - Q/L]/L$$

$$= [\mathrm{MPL} - \mathrm{APL}]/L \text{ (by substituting } \mathrm{MPL} = dQ/dL, \mathrm{APL} = Q/L)$$

For a maximum, $d(APL)/dL = 0$

$MPL = APL$

$d(APL)/dL$ is positive just before a maximum, so $MPL > APL$. MPL is above APL before the maximum point.

7.10   (a) $-40e^{-4x}$

    (b) $e^{2x} + 2xe^{2x}$ (using the product rule)

    (c) $(30 - 2x)/(30x - x^2)$ (using the chain rule)

    (d) $\log_e x + 1$ (using the product rule)

7.11 $dP/dQ = -50/(Q + 1)$

    $E = -[(Q + 1)/50] . [250 - 50 \log_e(Q + 1)]/Q$

      $= -[(Q + 1)/Q][5 - \log_e(Q + 1)]$

7.12 $dQ/dL = 80Le^{-0.3L} - 12L^2e^{-0.3L}$

             $= 4Le^{-0.3L}(20 - 3L)$

Turning points occur where $dQ/dL = 0$, so at $L = 0$ and $L = {}^{20}\!/_3$.

Notice that we cannot find a value of L at which $e^{-0.3L} = 0$.

Evaluating the function gives $Q = 0$ if $L = 0$ and $Q = 240.6$ if $L = {}^{20}\!/_3$.

$L = {}^{20}\!/_3$ maximizes output.

chapter eight

Partial Differentiation in Economics

SECTION 8.1: Introduction

In economic models the dependent variable is often thought to depend on a number of other variables, forming a multivariate function. An example of this is a long-run production function $Q = f(L,K)$. This function is applicable to the long run because it assumes that both labour, L, and capital, K, can take any values in the range for which the function is defined. That is, both L and K are continuous variables. In the short run the value of K is fixed at a specific value, and we have learned that the marginal product of labour, MPL, can be found by differentiating the production function with respect to L.

We would like to find the MPL for the long-run production function also, and indeed we can by using the technique of partial differentiation. This technique lets us find the rate at which a dependent variable such as Q is changing as just one of the independent variables changes. We keep fixed all independent variables other than the one whose effects we wish to investigate, and differentiate with respect to that variable. In the case of a long-run production function, without specifying a particular value for K we keep it fixed and differentiate with respect to L to find MPL. The expression for MPL obtained from a long-run production function is more general than that obtained from a short run function. It is likely to include the variable K and it gives the value of MPL for any value of K.

Furthermore, for the long-run production function $Q = f(L,K)$ not only can we find MPL but we can also find the marginal product of capital, MPK. This shows the rate at which output changes if the firm varies the amount of capital it uses by a small amount while keeping the quantity of labour it employs fixed. To find MPK we keep L fixed and differentiate the production function with respect to K. The technique of partial differentiation lets us separately investigate the rate of change of the dependent variable as any one of the independent variables changes.

> Long-run production functions are discussed and plotted in section 1.12. The marginal product of labour for a short-run production function is found in section 5.7.

Much of economic analysis is concerned with analysing the impact of changes in one variable 'other things remaining equal' and the technique of partial differentiation provides a general method for doing this. The analysis may lead us to general results, such as a relationship between the marginal products of labour and capital and the marginal rate of substitution between these inputs, as discussed in section 8.9.

> In MathEcon chapter 8, screens in section 1, Using Partial Differentiation, and section 2, Optimization of Multivariate Functions, link with this chapter. They demonstrate the methods and set out problems where you can practise your skills.

SECTION 8.2: Partial Derivatives

We begin by learning the technique of partial differentiation and practising it on various different functions. For the general multivariate function $y = f(w,x,z)$ which states that y is a function of three independent variables w, x and z we define three partial derivatives which we call $\partial y/\partial w$, $\partial y/\partial x$ and $\partial y/\partial z$. The curly ∂ symbol used in the notation indicates a partial derivative and the symbol $\partial y/\partial w$ is read as 'the partial derivative of y with respect to w'. The rules for finding partial derivatives are that we choose one variable, say w, whose effect we want to investigate and differentiate with respect to it, treating all the other independent variables as if they were constants. We then examine the separate effect of the next variable, say x. This time we treat w and z as if they were constants while we differentiate with respect to x. Similarly we can find the partial derivative of the function with respect to z. Each partial derivative is obtained by temporarily holding the other independent variables constant.

> partial derivative: measures the rate at which the dependent variable is changing as one independent variable changes, while all the other independent variables are held constant.

The rules of differentiation are those that we already know. Partial differentiation is no more difficult than differentiating with respect to one variable, except that you have to consider very carefully what is to be treated as a constant. As you find the various partial derivatives of a function, what is a variable for one partial differentiation is treated in another partial differentiation as if it were a constant. We shall see that the various partial derivatives of a function are usually different from one another and each may contain any or all of the independent variables in the original function.

As we find each partial derivative we are looking at how a small change in an independent variable will affect the dependent variable. The resulting expressions can be evaluated for any values of the independent variables to give a measure of the corresponding change. This is a much more general approach than evaluating the effect of one discrete change for particular values of the variables.

Use the MathEcon screen entitled Marginal Product of Labour and Capital to see how to find partial derivatives and what they represent. There are five questions for you to try on the screen Practise Partial Differentiation.

> **Remember...**
>
> $\partial y/\partial x$ represents the partial derivative of y with respect to x. To find it, differentiate with respect to x while holding all the other independent variables constant.
>
> Partial derivatives are found in a similar way for each of the independent variables.

1

Find the partial derivatives $\partial y/\partial x$ and $\partial y/\partial z$ for the function $y = 6x^5z^4$.

To find the partial derivative with respect to x we deal with z as if it were a constant. Write down what we are treating as constant and then multiply by the derivative of x^5 using the power-function rule. We get

$$\partial y/\partial x = 6z^4(5x^4) = 30z^4x^4$$

Next we find the partial derivative with respect to z by supposing temporarily that x is constant. We write down what is constant as regards this partial differentiation, and then multiply by the derivative of the z term

$$\partial y/\partial z = 6x^5(4z^3) = 24x^5z^3$$

2 Find the partial derivatives $\partial y/\partial w$, $\partial y/\partial x$ and $\partial y/\partial z$ for the function $y = 4x^5 + 7wz^2$.

For each partial derivative, the sum-difference rule allows us to differentiate each term separately and add the results together. To find $\partial y/\partial w$ we assume x and z are constants. If this is so, then the first term, $4x^5$, is a constant and differentiates to zero by the constant rule. For the second term we write down what is held constant and then multiply by the derivative of w with respect to w, which is 1 by the linear-function rule. We have

$$\partial y/\partial w = 0 + 7z^2(1) = 7z^2$$

For the partial derivative with respect to x we suppose w and z are constants, so the second term is constant and

$$\partial y/\partial x = 20x^4$$

For $\partial y/\partial z$ we hold w and x constant. The first term differentiates to zero and we obtain

$$\partial y/\partial z = 14wz$$

Notice that when we partially differentiate a function which is a sum of terms, any term not containing the variable that we are differentiating with respect to differentiates to zero. Hence in this example none of the partial derivatives we have calculated includes all the variables.

8.1 Partially differentiate with respect to x and z

(a) $y = 9x^3 + z^4$ (b) $y = 5x^2/z$

(c) $y = 3z^2 \ln (x)$ (d) $y = x + (x^3 - z)^2$

8.2 Find the partial derivatives $\partial y/\partial w$, $\partial y/\partial x$ and $\partial y/\partial z$ for the following functions

(a) $y = w + 10x^2/z^3$ (b) $y = (4w^2 + 6x^3 - 2z)^2$

SECTION 8.3: Small Increments Formula

A derivative tells us the rate at which a function is changing as the variable with respect to which we are differentiating alters. This rate of change strictly applies just at individual points on the function, but we can use it to obtain a useful approximation for how the value of the function changes between two points when a variable changes by a small amount. If $y = f(x,z)$, $\partial y/\partial x$ shows how y is changing as x alters, assuming z remains constant. For a small change in x, Δx, we can estimate the resulting change in y, Δy, as

$$\Delta y = \partial y/\partial x \,.\, \Delta x$$

Similarly, if we keep x constant and wish to measure the effect on y of a change in z, this may be found approximately as

$$\Delta y = \partial y/\partial z \,.\, \Delta z$$

These approximations are better the smaller are the values of Δx and Δz.

If both x and z change simultaneously we can estimate the overall change in y as the sum of the individual changes as given by the above formulae. This can be written as shown below.

The small increments formula for small changes Δx and Δz is

Remember...

$$\Delta y = \partial y/\partial x \,.\, \Delta x + \partial y/\partial z \,.\, \Delta z$$

This formula gives a useful approximation for small changes in x and z. If a partial derivative happens to be a constant the formula is valid for any size of change in the relevant variable. This occurs with linear functions.

3

If x increases by 0.1 and z decreases by 0.25, estimate the change in y given that $y = 6x^2z$. Check your result if the initial values of x and z are 4 and 10 respectively.

We first find the partial derivatives of the function

$$\partial y/\partial x = 12xz$$

$$\partial y/\partial z = 6x^2$$

Using the small increments formula and substituting we find

$$\Delta y = \partial y/\partial x \,.\, \Delta x + \partial y/\partial z \,.\, \Delta z$$

$$= 12xz(0.1) + 6x^2(-0.25) = 1.2xz - 1.5x^2$$

Notice that when we substitute for a variable which is decreasing we use a negative sign. Substituting the initial values of x and z gives

$$\Delta y = 48 - 24 = 24$$

To check the accuracy of our result we evaluate y at the initial values and new values of x and z. With $x = 4$ and $z = 10$ we obtain

$$y = 6x^2z = 960$$

while at $x = 4.1$ and $z = 9.75$ we evaluate

$$y = 6x^2z = 983.385$$

The difference between the new y value and the initial one is the true value of Δy. We have

$$\Delta y = 983.385 - 960 = 23.385$$

The value of 24 therefore provides quite a good approximation.

8.3 Find an approximate expression for the change in y that occurs when x decreases by 0.05 and z increases by 0.1 given that $y = 7z^2 + 9xz$. Evaluate the expression if the initial values of x and z are 12 and 20 respectively. Also, evaluate y at the initial and changed values and compare the true change in y.

Section 8.4: Multipliers

Using a simple macroeconomic model to describe an economy we can find the equilibrium level of income and investigate the possible effects of various changes. Sections 3.3 and 5.10 set out a method for identifying equilibrium income and showed how to use differentiation to find the investment multiplier. More generally we can define a multiplier for any exogenous change. Suppose we have an expression for equilibrium income, Y. Partial derivatives of that expression with respect to various autonomous injections or withdrawals give us multipliers.

A multiplier is: **Remember...**

- change in total income divided by the initial exogenous change which caused it
- found by obtaining an expression for equilibrium income and partially differentiating.

$$\text{Investment multiplier} = \partial Y/\partial I$$

$$\text{Government expenditure multiplier} = \partial Y/\partial G$$

$$\text{Lump sum direct taxation multiplier} = \partial Y/\partial T$$

$$\text{Tax rate multiplier} = \partial Y/\partial t$$

$$\text{Export multiplier} = \partial Y/\partial X$$

The small increments formula lets us predict the change in Y, ΔY, resulting from another specified change. For example, if G changes by ΔG, the change in Y is given by

$$\Delta Y = \partial Y / \partial G \, . \, \Delta G$$

The balanced budget multiplier (BBM) is defined as showing how equilibrium income changes with an increase in government expenditure, ΔG, and an equal increase in autonomous taxation, ΔT. Using the small increments formula we have

$$\Delta Y = \partial Y / \partial G \, . \, \Delta G + \partial Y / \partial T \, . \, \Delta T$$

Substituting for ΔT, since it equals ΔG, and taking out ΔG as a common factor we have

$$\Delta Y = (\partial Y / \partial G + \partial Y / \partial T) \Delta G$$

The balanced budget multiplier is the value by which we should multiply ΔG to find the change in income

$$\Delta Y = \text{BBM} \, . \, \Delta G$$

Balanced budget multiplier   **Remember...**

$$\text{BBM} = \partial Y / \partial G + \partial Y / \partial T$$

In our simple models we find that the government expenditure, investment, lump sum taxation and export multipliers are all constants. Each may be used to predict the change in Y that will result from either a small or a large change in the appropriate exogenous variable. Other multipliers can also be found, for example with respect to the parameters of the model although we do not show examples of these. One of the multipliers we study is not a constant. This is the tax rate multiplier, which shows how income changes if the rate of income tax changes. A multiplier that is different at different levels of income only accurately predicts the effects of very small changes from the current position.

When finding multipliers you must retain the symbols that represent injections and withdrawals as you manipulate the equations to obtain an expression for equilibrium income. Do not substitute numerical values. You need the symbols to be able to find partial derivatives.

If national income changes, there are induced changes in endogenous variables. We can predict these using the appropriate marginal propensities. For example, if the saving function is $S = f(Y,t)$, the marginal propensity to save, s, is given by the partial derivative $s = \partial S / \partial Y$. The small increments formula lets us predict the change in S, ΔS, as

$$\Delta S = s \, . \, \Delta Y$$

A simple closed economy has the consumption function $C = 280 + 0.8Y_d$ and income Y. Direct taxation, T, investment, I, and government expenditure, G, are all autonomous.

(a) Find the taxation, investment and government expenditure multipliers.
(b) If $I = 1000$, $G = 800$ and $T = 900$ find the equilibrium level of income of the economy. If G increases by 120 evaluate the new equilibrium level of income and compare the change in income with that predicted by the multiplier.
(c) What is the balanced budget multiplier? If T increases by 120 at the same time as G increases by 120, what change in equilibrium income does the balanced budget multiplier predict? Does it correspond to the actual change?

(a) Representing lump sum direct taxation as T, we have that disposable income, Y_d, is given by

$$Y_d = Y - T$$

and so the consumption function may be written

$$C = 280 + 0.8(Y - T)$$

The equilibrium condition is

$$Y = AD = C + I + G$$

where AD is aggregate demand. Substituting for C gives

$$Y = 280 + 0.8(Y - T) + I + G$$

Multiplying out the bracket and subtracting $0.8Y$ from both sides we have

$$0.2Y = 280 - 0.8T + I + G$$

Multiplying both sides by 5, the equilibrium income is given by

$$Y = 1400 - 4T + 5I + 5G$$

Partial derivatives show how equilibrium income changes if one of the exogenous variables changes. We have

$$\partial Y/\partial T = -4 = \text{the autonomous taxation multiplier}$$

$$\partial Y/\partial I = 5 = \text{the investment multiplier}$$

$$\partial Y/\partial G = 5 = \text{the government expenditure multiplier}$$

Notice that the taxation multiplier has a negative sign. An increase in direct taxation reduces equilibrium income.

(b) Equilibrium income is given by

$$Y = 1400 - 4T + 5I + 5G$$

Substituting $I = 1000$, $G = 800$ and $T = 900$ gives

$$Y = 1400 - 3600 + 5000 + 4000 = 6800$$

If G increases by 120 to 920, the new value for equilibrium income is

$$Y = 1400 - 3600 + 5000 + 4600 = 7400$$

Υ increases by $7400 - 6800 = 600$. The small increments formula predicts the change in income

$$\Delta\Upsilon = \partial\Upsilon/\partial G \,.\, \Delta G$$

$$= 5 \times 120 = 600$$

which equals the actual change.

(c) Balanced budget multiplier, BBM $= \partial\Upsilon/\partial G + \partial\Upsilon/\partial T = 5 - 4 = 1$

$$\Delta\Upsilon = \text{BBM} \times \Delta G = 1 \times 120 = 120$$

The balanced budget multiplier predicts that Υ will increase by 120. Substituting the new values of G and T gives

$$\Upsilon = 1400 - 4080 + 5000 + 4600 = 6920$$

This is 120 more than the initial value of 6800 and so accords with that predicted by the balanced budget multiplier.

   Notice that the balanced budget multiplier refers only to the change in government spending and taxation being balanced. In this economy the government budget is initially in surplus by $T - G = 900 - 800 = 100$, and the surplus remains the same when T and G both increase by the same amount.

The consumption function for a simple closed economy is given by $C = 144 + 0.72\Upsilon_d$. There is a proportional income tax at rate t. Investment and government expenditure are both autonomous.

(a) Find the investment, government expenditure and tax rate multipliers.
(b) If $I = 100$, $G = 180$ and $t = 0.2$ find the equilibrium level of income of the economy and the values of the multipliers. What change in equilibrium income is predicted if the tax rate rises by 0.01 and what is the actual change that takes place?

5

With income tax at rate t, $\Upsilon_d = \Upsilon - t \times \Upsilon = (1 - t)\Upsilon$. Substituting this in the consumption function gives

$$C = 144 + 0.72(1 - t)\Upsilon = 144 + 0.72\Upsilon - 0.72t \,.\, \Upsilon$$

The equilibrium condition is

$$\Upsilon = \text{AD} = C + I + G$$

Substituting for C we have

$$\Upsilon = 144 + 0.72\Upsilon - 0.72t \,.\, \Upsilon + I + G$$

Collecting terms in Υ on the left of the equation we obtain

$$\Upsilon(1 - 0.72 + 0.72t) = 144 + I + G$$

Dividing through by $(0.28 + 0.72t)$ we find

$$\Upsilon = \frac{144}{0.28 + 0.72t} + \frac{I}{0.28 + 0.72t} + \frac{G}{0.28 + 0.72t} = \frac{144 + I + G}{0.28 + 0.72t}$$

Notice that in a model with a proportional income tax, the tax rate, t, appears in the denominator in the expression for equilibrium income. For multipliers we find appropriate partial derivatives

$$\partial Y/\partial I = 1/(0.28 + 0.72t) = \text{the investment multiplier}$$

$$\partial Y/\partial G = 1/(0.28 + 0.72t) = \text{the government expenditure multiplier}$$

To find the tax rate multiplier we rewrite Y

$$Y = (144 + I + G) . (0.28 + 0.72t)^{-1}$$

and we then use the chain rule, letting $u = 0.28 + 0.72t$. This gives

$$\partial Y/\partial t = -(144 + I + G) . (0.28 + 0.72t)^{-2}(0.72)$$

$$= -\frac{0.72(144 + I + G)}{(0.28 + 0.72t)^2}$$

Since we have $Y = (144 + I + G)/(0.28 + 0.72t)$ we may write

$$\frac{\partial Y}{\partial t} = -\frac{0.72Y}{0.28 + 0.72t}$$

The tax rate multiplier is negative and is a function of Y. It therefore takes different values at different levels of income.

(b) Given $I = 100$, $G = 180$ and $t = 0.2$ we substitute in

$$Y = \frac{144 + I + G}{0.28 + 0.72t}$$

and find

$$Y = \frac{144 + 100 + 180}{0.28 + (0.72 \times 0.2)} = 1000$$

The equilibrium level of income is $Y = 1000$. Evaluating the multipliers

$$\partial Y/\partial I = 1/(0.28 + 0.72t) = 1/(0.424) = 2.36$$

This is the investment multiplier.

$$\partial Y/\partial G = 1/(0.28 + 0.72t) = 1/(0.424) = 2.36$$

This is the government expenditure multiplier.

$$\partial Y/\partial t = -0.72Y/(0.28 + 0.72t) = -0.72(1000)/(0.424) = -1698.1$$

This is the tax rate multiplier. Using it to predict the change in Y when $\Delta t = 0.01$ gives

$$\Delta Y = \partial Y/\partial t . \Delta t = -1698.1 \times 0.01 = -16.98$$

Equilibrium income is predicted to fall by 16.98 if the tax rate rises by 1%. Substituting the new tax rate $t = 0.21$ in the expression for equilibrium income gives

$$Y = \frac{144 + I + G}{0.28 + 0.72(0.21)} = 983.30$$

The actual fall of $1000 - 983.30 = 16.70$ is slightly different from that predicted by the multiplier because the tax rate multiplier is a point multiplier and only takes exactly the value we have calculated at the original level of income.

For the economy described by the equations below, s, t, z and w are the marginal propensities to save, be taxed, import and withdraw, all relating to total income, Y. Show that $w = s + t + z$. Find expressions for the investment, government expenditure and export multipliers and show that they are equal to $1/w$. (Hint: find the savings function and identify s.)

$$C = a + \beta Y_d \qquad \text{(consumption expenditure)}$$

$$T = tY \qquad \text{(proportional income tax)}$$

$$Z = m + zY \qquad \text{(imports)}$$

I, G and X are exogenous.

We have

$$AD = C + I + G + X - Z$$

and for equilibrium

$$Y = AD = C + I + G + X - Z$$

Disposable income is given by

$$Y_d = (1 - t)Y$$

and substituting this in the equation for C we obtain

$$C = a + \beta(1 - t)Y$$

Substituting for C and Z in the equilibrium condition gives

$$Y = a + \beta(1 - t)Y + I + G + X - m - zY$$

Collecting terms in Y on the left-hand side of the equation we find

$$Y - \beta(1 - t)Y + zY = a + I + G + X - m$$

This can be rewritten as

$$(1 - \beta + \beta t + z)Y = a + I + G + X - m$$

which gives

$$Y = \frac{a + I + G + X - m}{1 - \beta + \beta t + z}$$

To obtain multipliers we find the appropriate partial derivatives

$$\partial Y/\partial I = 1/(1 - \beta + \beta t + z) = \text{the investment multiplier}$$

$$\partial Y/\partial G = 1/(1 - \beta + \beta t + z) = \text{the government expenditure multiplier}$$

$$\partial Y/\partial X = 1/(1 - \beta + \beta t + z) = \text{the export multiplier}$$

Since all disposable income is consumed or saved we can find the savings function as

$$S = Y_d - C$$

Substituting for C we find

$$S = Y_d - (a + \beta Y_d) = -a + (1 - \beta)Y_d$$

To get saving as a function of total income we substitute for Y_d

$$S = -a + (1 - \beta)(1 - t)Y$$

The marginal propensity to save out of total income is $\partial S/\partial Y$, so

$$s = \partial S/\partial Y = (1 - \beta)(1 - t)$$

Using the expression for withdrawals $W = S + T + Z$ and substituting gives

$$W = -a + (1 - \beta)(1 - t)Y + tY + m + zY$$

The marginal propensity to withdraw, w is

$$w = \partial W/\partial Y = (1 - \beta)(1 - t) + t + z = s + t + z$$

as required. Also,

$$w = 1 - t - \beta + \beta t + t + z = 1 - \beta + \beta t + z$$

Looking at the multipliers we obtained earlier we see that each of them is indeed equal to $1/w$, as we required.

8.4 An open economy with a government is described by the equations

$$\text{Consumption: } C = 42 + 0.88 Y_d$$

$$\text{Imports: } Z = 12 + 0.13 Y$$

Taxation, T, investment, I, government expenditure, G and exports, X are all autonomous.

- Find the following multipliers: autonomous taxation, government expenditure, investment and export.
- What is the equilibrium level of national income if $T = 100$, $I = 118$, $G = 90$ and $X = 50$?
- Show that injections equal withdrawals. Find the surplus or deficit for the government budget, and also for foreign trade.
- Show the effects on the items you have calculated if exports now rise by 140.

8.5 A simple closed economy has an investment function that depends on the rate of interest, as in the IS–LM model analysed in section 3.5. Taxation takes the form of a proportional income tax and the economy is described in the equations below. R represents the rate of interest expressed as a decimal, A is autonomous investment and G is autonomous government expenditure.

$$C = 40 + 0.8 Yd$$

$$I = A - 1500R$$

$$T = 0.25 Y$$

$$MD = 0.6 Y - 2400R$$

$$MS = 1500$$

(a) Find the IS equation giving Y as a function of R and the autonomous expenditures A and G. By partially differentiating with respect to A and G find expressions for the autonomous investment and government expenditure multipliers.

(b) Find also the LM equation and calculate equilibrium income if $A = 750$ and $G = 365$.

(c) If G increases by 93 what rise in income does the multiplier predict? Calculate the actual change in income and explain any difference you find.

8.6 A closed economy with a proportional income tax at rate t has the consumption function

$$C = 96 + 0.65 Y_d$$

Investment and government spending are autonomous.

Find expressions for the government spending and tax rate multipliers and evaluate them if $I = 264$, $G = 360$ and $t = 0.2$.

SECTION 8.5: Differentials and Implicit Differentiation

Sometimes economists are interested in investigating the relationship between changes in the independent variables of a function, typically when taken together these changes leave the value of the dependent variable unchanged. This is the situation that arises, for example, with a utility function $u = f(x,y)$ as we move along an indifference curve. The quantity of one good increases and the quantity of the other is reduced in such a way that the utility of the consumer remains unchanged. To analyse this we introduce the concept of differentials. We use the symbols du, dx and dy, which are called differentials, to represent extremely small changes in the variables u, x and y respectively.

The small increments formula that we found in section 8.3

$$\Delta u = \frac{\partial u}{\partial x} \cdot \Delta x + \frac{\partial u}{\partial y} \cdot \Delta y$$

applies to small changes in the independent variables. We now replace the symbols for small changes Δu, Δx and Δy by the differentials du, dx and dy that represent extremely small changes and obtain

$$du = \frac{\partial u}{\partial x} \cdot dx + \frac{\partial u}{\partial y} \cdot dy$$

If $u = f(x,y)$ the differentials form of the small increments formula is **Remember...**

$$du = \frac{\partial u}{\partial x} \cdot dx + \frac{\partial u}{\partial y} \cdot dy$$

If we want to investigate how x and y can alter while u remains fixed, as happens when we move along an indifference curve, we set $du = 0$ and write

$$0 = \frac{\partial u}{\partial x} \cdot dx + \frac{\partial u}{\partial y} \cdot dy$$

Rearranging this we find

$$-\frac{\partial u}{\partial y} \cdot dy = \frac{\partial u}{\partial x} \cdot dx$$

Dividing both sides by $-\partial u/\partial y$ and by dx gives

$$\frac{dy}{dx} = -\frac{\partial u/\partial x}{\partial u/\partial y}$$

This formula for dy/dx is useful when we do not have an explicit function for y, but we have a function of x and y, $f(x,y)$, which equals a constant. The method is called implicit differentiation. It is valid providing $\partial u/\partial y \neq 0$, so that we are not dividing by 0 in the formula for dy/dx.

> **Remember...**
>
> Implicit differentiation of $u = f(x,y)$ where u is a constant gives
>
> $$\frac{dy}{dx} = -\frac{\partial u/\partial x}{\partial u/\partial y}$$

The method of implicit differentiation can be extended to functions of more variables. Partial derivatives are found by setting equal to zero the differentials of all variables other than those in the partial derivative we are seeking. The ratio of the differentials then represents a partial derivative.

> **Remember...**
>
> If $u = f(x,y,z)$
>
> $$du = \frac{\partial u}{\partial x} \cdot dx + \frac{\partial u}{\partial y} \cdot dy + \frac{\partial u}{\partial z} \cdot dz$$
>
> To use this formula, first set $du = 0$. We can then find the partial derivative of any one of the independent variables with respect to another by setting the differential of the third independent variable equal to 0 and rearranging the equation. For example, setting dz equal to zero the ratio dy/dx becomes
>
> $$\frac{\partial y}{\partial x} = -\frac{\partial u/\partial x}{\partial u/\partial y}$$
>
> and setting dx equal to zero the ratio dy/dz becomes
>
> $$\frac{\partial y}{\partial z} = -\frac{\partial u/\partial z}{\partial u/\partial y}$$

SECTION 8.6: Slope of an Indifference Curve

We can use the technique of implicit differentiation to show under what conditions consumers maximize their utility. For a consumer whose utility, U, depends on the amounts she has of two goods, X and Y, we write $U = f(X,Y)$. We depict the relationship by plotting indifference curves with Y on the vertical axis and X on the horizontal axis of the graph. Each indifference curve corresponds to a specific level of utility, so U is constant on a particular curve. The marginal rate of substitution, MRS, is the rate at which the consumer substitutes good Y by good X while still remaining on the same indifference curve. MRS is measured by the negative of the slope of the indifference curve, MRS $= -dY/dX$ and we can find this from the utility function using implicit differentiation.

The optimal consumption position for a consumer is at point A in figure 8.1. This occurs at a point of tangency between the budget line and an indifference curve, so that the slopes of the budget line and the indifference curve are equal. We use the result shown in section 2.7 that the slope of the budget line $= -P_x/P_y$.

Show that the consumer chooses an optimal combination of X and Y if the quantities are chosen such that

$$\text{MRS} = \frac{P_x}{P_y} = \frac{\text{MU}_x}{\text{MU}_y}$$

On a particular indifference curve we have $U = f(X,Y) = $ constant. The formula for implicit differentiation gives the slope of the indifference curve

$$\frac{dY}{dX} = -\frac{\partial U/\partial X}{\partial U/\partial Y}$$

Taking the negative of it we have

$$\text{MRS} = \frac{\partial U/\partial X}{\partial U/\partial Y}$$

Each partial derivative is obtained by differentiating the utility function with respect to one of the goods, while keeping the quantity of the other constant. The partial derivatives therefore represent the marginal utilities. We have

$$\text{MU}_x = \frac{\partial U}{\partial X}$$

and

$$\text{MU}_y = \frac{\partial U}{\partial Y}$$

Forming the ratio of these shows that

$$\text{MRS} = \frac{\text{MU}_x}{\text{MU}_y} = -\frac{dY}{dX}$$

At the point of tangency with the budget line, the slope of the indifference curve = the slope of the budget line, or

$$-\text{MRS} = -\frac{\text{MU}_x}{\text{MU}_y} = -\frac{P_x}{P_y}$$

Multiplying through by -1 gives the required result.

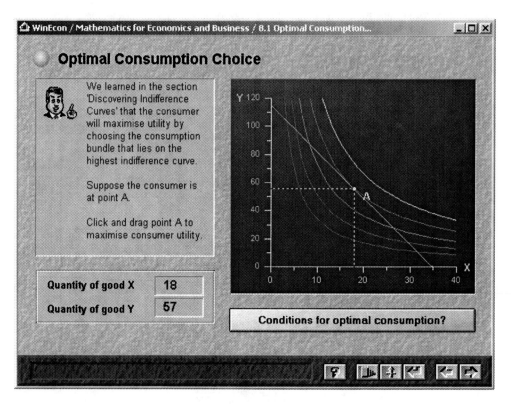

Figure 8.1

$$\text{MRS} = \frac{\text{MU}_x}{\text{MU}_y} = \frac{P_x}{P_y}$$

Remember...

The ratio of the prices of two goods equals the ratio of their marginal utilities equals the marginal rate of substitution at the optimal consumption position.

8.7   A consumer has the utility function

$$U = 10X^{1/2}Y^{2/3}$$

Find an expression for the consumer's marginal rate of substitution.
   Compare the value of the MRS at the point (45.5625, 8) with that at the point on the same indifference curve at which 9 units of X are consumed.

SECTION 8.7: Elasticities

In section 5.9 we saw that for the demand function $Q = f(P)$ the point price elasticity of demand is given by

$$\text{Point price elasticity} = \frac{dQ}{dP} \cdot \frac{P}{Q}$$

If we now have a multivariate demand function for good Y, $Q_y = f(P_y, M, P_x)$ which specifies that the quantity demanded depends not only on the price of the good itself, P_y, but also on income M and on the price P_x of another related good, X, we can use the technique of partial differentiation to find three measures of elasticity. The first of these corresponds to the demand elasticity we found in section 5.9, which we now call own-price elasticity of demand. It shows the responsiveness of the quantity of Y demanded to changes in its own price, P_y. The other elasticities we can calculate are the income elasticity of demand, which measures the impact of changes in income, M and the cross-price elasticity of demand, which shows the effect on the quantity of Y purchased of changes in the price, P_x, of the other good X. Each elasticity measures the effect on Q_y of changing just one variable while keeping the others constant. It is found by multiplying the appropriate partial derivative by the variable that is being changed and dividing by the quantity of Y. The signs of the elasticities indicate whether or not the quantity of Y changes in the same direction as the variable that is being changed. As we saw in section 5.9, own-price elasticity of demand is usually negative. The sign of the cross-price elasticity indicates the relationship between the two goods. A positive sign shows that if P_x increases, a larger quantity of Y is bought which implies Y is substituted for X. Conversely, a negative sign shows the goods are complements. Like X, less Y is bought when P_x rises. Income elasticity is positive for normal goods, since more is bought when income increases and negative for inferior goods, as less is bought when income increases.

> Use the MathEcon screen titled Cross Elasticity of Demand to check you understand the relationship.

Remember...

For good Y

$$\text{Own-price elasticity} = \frac{\partial Q_y}{\partial P_y} \cdot \frac{P_y}{Q_y}$$

(negative unless demand is upward sloping)

$$\text{Cross price elasticity} = \frac{\partial Q_y}{\partial P_x} \cdot \frac{P_x}{Q_y}$$

(positive for substitutes, negative for complements)

$$\text{Income elasticity of demand} = \frac{\partial Q_y}{\partial M} \cdot \frac{M}{Q_y}$$

(positive for normal goods, negative for inferior goods)

Demand for good Y is given by

$$Q_y = \frac{2M \cdot P_x^{0.2}}{P_y}$$

where M is income and P_x is the price of a related good. Find the own-price elasticity of demand, the cross-price elasticity of demand with X, and the income elasticity of demand. How can you describe the relationship between goods X and Y?

6

We begin by finding three partial derivatives

$$\frac{\partial Q_y}{\partial P_y} = -\frac{2M \cdot P_x^{0.2}}{P_y^2}$$

$$\frac{\partial Q_y}{\partial P_x} = \frac{0.4M \cdot P_x^{-0.8}}{P_y}$$

$$\frac{\partial Q_y}{\partial M} = \frac{2P_x^{0.2}}{P_y}$$

We now find an expression for each elasticity by substituting the appropriate partial derivative into the formula, and also substituting the original expression for Q_y. Notice that various terms then cancel.

$$\text{Own-price elasticity} = \frac{\partial Q_y}{\partial P_y} \cdot \frac{P_y}{Q_y} = \frac{-(2M \cdot P_x^{0.2}) \cdot P_y^2}{(2M \cdot P_x^{0.2}) \cdot P_y^2} = -1$$

$$\text{Cross-price elasticity} = \frac{\partial Q_y}{\partial P_x} \cdot \frac{P_x}{Q_y} = \frac{0.4M \cdot P_x^{-0.8} \cdot P_y \cdot P_x}{(2M \cdot P_x^{0.2}) \cdot P_y} = 0.2$$

$$\text{Income elasticity of demand} = \frac{\partial Q_y}{\partial M} \cdot \frac{M}{Q_y} = \frac{2P_x^{0.2} \cdot P_y \cdot M}{(2M \cdot P_x^{0.2}) \cdot P_y} = 1$$

These values are the elasticities for all price and income levels. This is a constant elasticity demand function. The cross-price elasticity is positive, so X and Y are substitutes.

Compare these elasticities with the constant price elasticity demand functions in section 5.9.

8.8 The demand function for good Y is

$$Q_y = 12 - 4P_y + 0.04M - 0.5P_x$$

Find expressions for the own-price elasticity of demand, the cross-price elasticity of demand and the income elasticity of demand. Evaluate the elasticities if $P_y = 15$, $P_x = 10$ and $M = 2000$. Are X and Y substitute goods?

> **8.9** Demand for a good is given by
>
> $$Q = M^{0.3}/P^2$$
>
> Find the own-price elasticity of demand and the income elasticity of demand.

SECTION 8.8: Logarithmic Demand Functions

Economists sometimes choose to represent demand functions with the variables measured as natural logarithms. Amongst various reasons for this is the ease with which the values of elasticities can be identified.

Show that when the demand function for good Y has the log linear form

$$\ln Q_y = -a - b \ln P_y + c \ln P_x + h \ln M$$

the values of the own-price, cross-price and income elasticities are the coefficients of the relevant variables.

We use the method of implicit differentiation shown in section 8.5. Rewriting the demand function we have

$$a = -\ln Q_y - b \ln P_y + c \ln P_x + h \ln M$$

and so

$$da = (\partial a/\partial Q_y) \cdot dQ_y + (\partial a/\partial P_y) \cdot dP_y + (\partial a/\partial P_x) \cdot dP_x + (\partial a/\partial M) \cdot dM$$

The partial derivatives of a are

$$\partial a/\partial Q_y = -1/Q_y$$
$$\partial a/\partial P_y = -b/P_y$$
$$\partial a/\partial P_x = c/P_x$$
$$\partial a/\partial M = h/M$$

Substituting these gives

$$da = -(1/Q_y) \cdot dQ_y - (b/P_y).dP_y + (c/P_x) \, .dP_x + (h/M) \cdot dM$$

Treating the parameter a as a constant, da = 0. The various partial derivatives of Q_y are found by setting combinations of two differentials in turn equal to zero. We find

dQ_y/dP_y (setting dP_x and dM equal to zero) $= \partial Q_y/\partial P_y = -bQ_y/P_y$

dQ_y/dP_x (setting dP_y and dM equal to zero) $= \partial Q_y/\partial P_x = cQ_y/P_x$

dQ_y/dM (setting dP_x and dP_y equal to zero) $= \partial Q_y/\partial M = hQ_y/M$

Now using the formulae from section 8.7 we find the various elasticities of the demand function.

$$\text{Own-price elasticity} = \frac{\partial Q_y}{\partial P_y} \cdot \frac{P_y}{Q_y} = -\frac{bQ_y}{P_y} \cdot \frac{P_y}{Q_y} = -b$$

$$\text{Cross price elasticity} = \frac{\partial Q_y}{\partial P_x} \cdot \frac{P_x}{Q_y} = \frac{cQ_y}{P_x} \cdot \frac{P_x}{Q_y} = c$$

$$\text{Income elasticity of demand} = \frac{\partial Q_y}{\partial M} \cdot \frac{M}{Q_y} = \frac{hQ_y}{M} \cdot \frac{M}{Q_y} = h$$

The elasticities therefore appear as coefficients in a log linear demand function. Own-price elasticity is the coefficient of ln (price), cross-price elasticity is the coefficient of ln (price of other good) and income elasticity is the coefficient of ln (income). Notice that a coefficient includes the sign of the term to which it belongs.

8.10   Find the own-price, cross-price and income elasticities for good Y which has the demand function

$$\ln Q_y = 1.3 - 2.1 \ln (P_y) + 0.08 \ln (P_x) + 0.6 \ln (M)$$

SECTION 8.9: Long-run Production Functions

Using a long-run production function we define output, Q, as a function of the amounts of labour, L, and capital, K, employed and write $Q = f(L,K)$.

In the long run both L and K can be varied, and the partial derivatives of the production function MPL $= \partial Q/\partial L$ and MPK $= \partial Q/\partial K$ represent the marginal products of labour and capital. The marginal rate of substitution, MRS, is the rate at which capital is substituted by labour and is the slope of the isoquant ignoring the negative sign. If the amount the firm can spend on inputs in any time period is restricted by its budget, B, we may use an isocost line to depict the various combinations of L and K that are available to the firm. We assume that the firm buys its inputs at given prices of P_l for labour and P_k for capital so that the equation of the isocost line is given by

> Section 1.12 shows how to depict such a function using an isoquant diagram. For short-run production functions the marginal product of labour is obtained as dQ/dL in section 5.7.

$$B = L \cdot P_l + K \cdot P_k$$

marginal rate of substitution: the rate at which a firm can substitute labour for capital while keeping output constant. It is the negative of the slope of the isoquant.

The optimal production position for the firm is at a point of tangency between the isocost line and an isoquant. At the point of tangency the slopes of the line and the curve are equal. The analysis using isoquants and an isocost line is analogous to that used in section 8.6 to find optimal consumption choice.

For further details see the screens titled Marginal Product of Labour and Capital, The Shape of the Isoquant: marginal rate of substitution and Producing at Minimum Cost in section 1 of MathEcon chapter 8. The terminology MPPL and MPPK is used, standing for marginal physical product of labour and of capital.

Remember...

For a long-run production function

$$\text{MPL} = \partial Q / \partial L, \ \text{MPK} = \partial Q / \partial K$$

Plotting an isoquant diagram with labour on the horizontal axis we have

$$\text{MRS} = \text{MPL}/\text{MPK}$$

Slope of the budget line $= -P_l/P_k$
At the optimal output position $\text{MPL}/\text{MPK} = P_l/P_k$

RETURNS TO SCALE

To study the returns to scale of a production function we examine how output changes when all the inputs are changed in the same proportion. For example, suppose we double the quantities of all inputs. If output also doubles we have constant returns to scale, if output more than doubles we have increasing returns to scale and if output does not rise to twice its original level we have decreasing returns to scale.

7

Increase the use of all inputs by 50% to show the returns to scale of the production function

$$Q = 12L^{0.6}K^{0.3}$$

Denote the original value of Q by Q_0 and the new value by Q_1. The original output is

$$Q_0 = 12L^{0.6}K^{0.3}$$

Increasing the use of all inputs by 50% implies that the new amounts of labour and capital used are 1.5 times their earlier values. For Q_1 we substitute these new values in the production function, taking care to raise each input to the appropriate power. This gives

$$Q_1 = 12(1.5L)^{0.6}(1.5K)^{0.3}$$

Applying the power to the individual terms in each bracket we have

$$Q_1 = 12 \times 1.5^{0.6} \times L^{0.6} \times 1.5^{0.3} \times K^{0.3}$$

Collecting terms gives

$$Q_1 = 12 \times 1.5^{(0.6+0.3)} \times L^{0.6} \times K^{0.3}$$

Noticing that $12L^{0.6}K^{0.3} = Q_0$ we write

$$Q_1 = 1.5^{0.9}Q_0$$

Thus although the inputs are all multiplied by 1.5, Q_0 is not multiplied by this but by the smaller amount $1.5^{0.9} = 1.44$. Therefore, this production function exhibits decreasing returns to scale.

Homogeneous functions

The production function above is an example of a homogeneous function of degree 0.9. When we multiply all the independent variables by a constant, λ, if we can show that the dependent variable is multiplied by λ^n, then the function is homogeneous of degree n.

8

Show the degree of homogeneity of the function $Q = 5L^{0.8}K^{0.4}$.

Starting from $Q_0 = 5L^{0.8}K^{0.4}$, multiplying L and K by λ we find

$$Q_1 = 5(\lambda L)^{0.8}(\lambda K)^{0.4}$$

$$= 5\lambda^{1.2}L^{0.8}K^{0.4}$$

$$= (\lambda^{1.2})Q_0$$

The power of the multiplier of Q_0 is the degree of homogeneity, so this function is homogeneous of degree 1.2. Notice that it has increasing returns to scale because output is multiplied by $\lambda^{1.2}$ which is larger than λ, the amount by which the inputs are multiplied. For homogeneous production functions, the degree of homogeneity determines the type of returns to scale.

A production function which is homogeneous **Remember...**

- of degree 1 has constant returns to scale
- of degree > 1 has increasing returns to scale
- of degree < 1 has decreasing returns to scale.

Euler's theorem is a general result for homogeneous functions of degree n. When we apply it to firms in competitive markets we get a useful result about factor shares, as we see in the analysis below.

Euler's theorem states **Remember...**

$$L . \partial Q / \partial L + K . \partial Q / \partial K = n . Q$$

Show that if firms with production functions that are homogeneous of degree 1 operate in competitive factor and product markets, the total factor payments exactly exhaust the value of the output.

We rewrite Euler's theorem, substituting MPL and MPK for the partial derivatives they equal, setting $n = 1$ as the degree of homogeneity and multiplying through the equation by P, the price at which the product is sold. This gives

$$L . MPL . P + K . MPK . P = P . Q$$

In competitive product markets individual firms sell all their output at P, the market price. MPL $\times P$ and MPK $\times P$ therefore represent the marginal value product for each of the factors. Firms determine the quantities of factors to buy in competitive markets by equating the marginal value products with P_l and P_k, the factor prices. Substituting these we have for firms in competitive markets

$$L . P_l + K . P_k = P . Q$$

When L employees are each paid a wage of P_l the total wage bill is $L . P_l$. Similarly the total payment to capital is $K . P_k$, while $P . Q$ is the total revenue obtained from the sale of the product. We have then that

total payment to factors of production = total sales revenue received

The total factor payments exactly exhaust the value of the output.

9

Verify that Euler's theorem holds for the function $Q = 5L^{0.8}K^{0.4}$.

The partial derivatives are

$$\partial Q / \partial L = 4L^{-0.2}K^{0.4}$$

$$\partial Q / \partial K = 2L^{0.8}K^{-0.6}$$

Substituting in the left-hand side of the theorem gives

$$L . \partial Q / \partial L + K . \partial Q / \partial K = L(4L^{-0.2}K^{0.4}) + K(2L^{0.8}K^{-0.6})$$

$$= 4L^{0.8}K^{0.4} + 2L^{0.8}K^{0.4} = 6L^{0.8}K^{0.4}$$

$$= 1.2Q$$

Euler's theorem has $n . Q$ on the right-hand side where n is the degree of homogeneity, and we showed earlier that this is 1.2. So the left-hand side equals the right-hand side, and Euler's theorem holds.

COBB DOUGLAS PRODUCTION FUNCTIONS

The production function above is an example of a Cobb Douglas production function. Such functions have the general form $Q = AL^{\alpha}K^{\beta}$. The parameters of the function α and β can be shown to have an interpretation as production elasticities.

Show that production functions of the Cobb Douglas type are homogeneous and find an expression for the degree of homogeneity. Interpret the parameters in terms of elasticities.

Starting from $Q_0 = AL^{\alpha}K^{\beta}$, multiplying L and K by λ we find

$$Q_1 = A(\lambda L)^{\alpha}(\lambda K)^{\beta}$$

$$= A\lambda^{\alpha+\beta}L^{\alpha}K^{\beta}$$

$$= (\lambda^{\alpha+\beta})Q_0$$

A Cobb Douglas production function is homogeneous of degree $\alpha + \beta$. The returns to scale depend on the sum of the parameters. Constant returns to scale occur if $(\alpha + \beta) = 1$, increasing returns if $(\alpha + \beta) > 1$ and decreasing returns if $(\alpha + \beta) < 1$.

The marginal products are

$$MPL = \partial Q / \partial L = \alpha AL^{\alpha-1}K^{\beta}$$

$$MPK = \partial Q / \partial K = \beta AL^{\alpha}K^{\beta-1}$$

Production elasticities are defined as

$$\text{Labour elasticity} = \frac{\partial Q}{\partial L} \cdot \frac{L}{Q} = \frac{\alpha A L^{\alpha-1} K^{\beta} L}{A L^{\alpha} K^{\beta}} = \alpha$$

$$\text{Capital elasticity} = \frac{\partial Q}{\partial K} \cdot \frac{K}{Q} = \frac{\beta A L^{\alpha} K^{\beta-1} K}{A L^{\alpha} K^{\beta}} = \beta$$

8.11 For a firm with the production function $Q = f(L,K)$, use the technique of implicit differentiation to show that the slope of an isoquant, $dK/dL = -MPL/MPK$. What is the MRS?

If the firm has the budget constraint $B = L \cdot P_l + K \cdot P_k$, show that the slope of the isocost line is $-P_l/P_k$.

Given that the optimal output occurs at the point of tangency between the isoquant and the isocost line, find the condition that must be satisfied for output to be optimal. (Hint: The analysis parallels the method used to find the optimal consumption choice in section 8.6.)

SECTION 8.10: Second Order Partial Derivatives

When we partially differentiate the function $y = f(x,z)$, in general the partial derivatives we obtain are each also functions of the independent variables x and z. We can therefore partially differentiate again with respect to the same variables, forming second order partial derivatives. We define second order partial derivatives as

$$\frac{\partial^2 y}{\partial x^2} = \frac{\partial(\partial y/\partial x)}{\partial x}$$

$$\frac{\partial^2 y}{\partial z^2} = \frac{\partial(\partial y/\partial z)}{\partial z}$$

These are similar to the second derivative for a function of one variable that we found in section 6.2. But now we can also define second order cross-partial derivatives

$$\frac{\partial^2 y}{\partial z . \partial x} = \frac{\partial(\partial y/\partial x)}{\partial z}$$

$$\frac{\partial^2 y}{\partial x . \partial z} = \frac{\partial(\partial y/\partial z)}{\partial x}$$

10

Find the second order partial derivatives for the function

$$y = 8x^3 - 5x^2z$$

We begin by finding the first order partial derivatives

$$\partial y/\partial x = 24x^2 - 10xz$$

$$\partial y/\partial z = -5x^2$$

To find the second order partial derivatives we differentiate $\partial y/\partial x$ with respect to x and obtain

$$\partial^2 y/\partial x^2 = 48x - 10z$$

For the second order partial derivative with respect to z we differentiate $\partial y/\partial z$ and find

$$\partial^2 y/\partial z^2 = 0$$

since $\partial y/\partial z$ is a function of x only. Cross-partial derivatives are found by differentiating $\partial y/\partial x$ with respect to z giving

$$\partial^2 y/\partial z . \partial x = -10x$$

and by differentiating $\partial y/\partial z$ with respect to x

$$\partial^2 y/\partial x . \partial z = -10x$$

Notice that the two cross-partial derivatives are equal. You will find it useful to know that this is the case for all the functions we use in economics. The result is known as Young's theorem.

8.12 Find all the second order partial derivatives for the following functions

(a) $y = 6x^4z^5$

(b) $y = 9xz^3 - 12x$

SECTION 8.11: Optimization of Multivariate Functions

Just as functions of one variable can have maximum and minimum turning points, as discussed in section 6.2, so turning points can occur with multivariate functions. For example, if the utility you obtain from consuming goods X and Y is expressed by the utility function $U = f(X,Y)$, initially as you acquire more of either good X or good Y your utility probably increases. There may be a point, however, at which you have enough of both goods, so that having more of either X or Y would actually reduce your utility. If this is the case, we can identify a maximum turning point of your utility function, U. The amounts of X and Y that you have at that point give you more utility than if you had either a little less or a little more of X, and similarly for Y. The point is a maximum with regard to both variable X and variable Y. This suggests that to identify a turning point of a multivariate function we need to examine how each of the independent variables is changing.

A necessary condition for a multivariate function to have a maximum or minimum turning point is that all the first order partial derivatives must equal zero. A maximum or minimum value of the function can only be achieved where a turning point occurs simultaneously for all dimensions of the function. Turning points that are identified using this criterion are local maxima or minima. They give the highest or lowest value of the function by comparison with other nearby values of the variables. When the variables take quite different values, it may be that the function reaches either higher or lower values than it does at the turning points.

To identify what kind of turning point we have at a point where all the first order partial derivatives are equal to zero, we can use appropriate second order conditions. These, however, are rather complex and you may prefer to evaluate the value of the function at the turning point and a small distance from it in each direction. For the function $y = f(x,w)$ the kinds of turning points that can occur are:

- a maximum, where the value of y at the turning point is greater than at nearby values of x and w,
- a minimum, where the value of y at the turning point is less than at nearby values of x and w, and

- a saddle point, where the value of y at the turning point is greater than at nearby values for one of the variables x and w, but is less than at nearby values for the other variable.

The rules below summarize the first and second order conditions for turning points of multivariate functions.

$y = f(x,w)$ has a turning point where   **Remember…**

$$\frac{\partial y}{\partial x} = 0 \text{ and } \frac{\partial y}{\partial w} = 0$$

The second order conditions for a maximum are

$$\frac{\partial^2 y}{\partial x^2} < 0, \frac{\partial^2 y}{\partial w^2} < 0 \text{ and } \frac{\partial^2 y}{\partial x^2} \cdot \frac{\partial^2 y}{\partial w^2} - \left(\frac{\partial^2 y}{\partial x . \partial w}\right)^2 > 0$$

while for a minimum they are

$$\frac{\partial^2 y}{\partial x^2} > 0, \frac{\partial^2 y}{\partial w^2} > 0 \text{ and } \frac{\partial^2 y}{\partial x^2} \cdot \frac{\partial^2 y}{\partial w^2} - \left(\frac{\partial^2 y}{\partial x . \partial w}\right)^2 > 0$$

and for a saddle point we require

$$\frac{\partial^2 y}{\partial x^2} \cdot \frac{\partial^2 y}{\partial w^2} - \left(\frac{\partial^2 y}{\partial x . \partial w}\right)^2 < 0$$

The MathEcon screen titled Optimization of Multivariate Functions shown in figure 8.2 displays the profit function for a three-product firm and lets you use a trial and error approach to finding the output combination that maximizes profit. You can also find a mathematical solution.

8.13   Identify any turning points for the function given and show what form they take

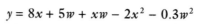

$$y = 8x + 5w + xw - 2x^2 - 0.3w^2$$

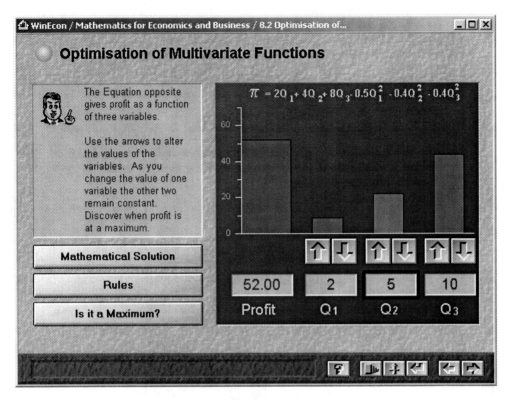

Figure 8.2

8.14 Show what quantities of X and Y maximize utility for a consumer with the utility function

$$U = 5X + 6Y + 1.2XY - 1.5X^2 - 0.6Y^2$$

SECTION 8.12: Price Discriminating Monopoly

If a monopoly supplies two separate markets with different demand curves, the firm is likely to find it profitable to sell at different prices in these markets. Examples of such situations are markets at home and overseas, or trade and retail customers. We use the technique of multivariate optimization to show how a monopolist chooses prices so as to maximize overall profit. We compare prices and profit with the best that could be achieved if the product was sold at the same price in both markets.

A monopolist supplies two markets with the demand curves $P_A = 48 - 2Q_A$ and $P_B = 60 - Q_B$. The firm's total cost function is $TC = 15 + 10(Q_A + Q_B)$.

(a) What prices in the two markets maximize total profit?
(b) If the firm could choose only a single price, what would it be, and how would profit be affected?

11

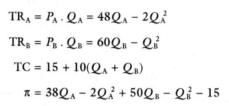

(a) We find expressions for the monopolist's total revenue in market A and in market B. Adding these and subtracting total cost gives the combined profit function which we maximize.

$$TR_A = P_A \cdot Q_A = 48Q_A - 2Q_A^2$$

$$TR_B = P_B \cdot Q_B = 60Q_B - Q_B^2$$

$$TC = 15 + 10(Q_A + Q_B)$$

$$\pi = 38Q_A - 2Q_A^2 + 50Q_B - Q_B^2 - 15$$

We choose quantities to maximize this, finding partial derivatives and setting them equal to zero.

$$\partial\pi/\partial Q_A = 38 - 4Q_A = 0$$

$$\partial\pi/\partial Q_B = 50 - 2Q_B = 0$$

Rearranging these we find that for a maximum

$$Q_A = 9.5$$

$$Q_B = 25$$

Substituting these quantities in the demand functions gives the prices at which profit is maximized

$$P_A = 48 - 2(9.5) = 29$$

$$P_B = 60 - 25 = 35$$

$$\pi = 38(9.5) - 2(9.5^2) + 50(25) - 25^2 - 15$$

$$= 790.5 = \text{maximum profit}$$

(b) If price is to be the same in both markets we find the combined market demand

$$Q_C = Q_A + Q_B$$

Rewriting the demand functions we find

$$Q_A = 24 - 0.5P_A$$

$$Q_B = 60 - P_B$$

Putting $P_A = P_B = P_C$ and adding gives

$$Q_C = 24 - 0.5P_C + 60 - P_C = 84 - 1.5P_C$$

Writing the inverse function gives

$$P_C = 56 - 0.667Q_C$$

Combined market TR and profit are

$$TR = P_C \cdot Q_C = 56Q_C - 0.667Q_C^2$$

$$\pi = 56Q_C - 0.667Q_C^2 - 15 - 10Q_C = 46Q_C - 0.667Q_C^2 - 15$$

For a maximum we differentiate and set equal to zero

$$d\pi/dQ_C = 46 - 1.333Q_C = 0$$

So, $Q_C = 34.5$ for a maximum, and therefore

$$P_C = 56 - 0.667(34.5) = 33$$

$$\pi = 46(34.5) - 0.667(34.5^2) - 15 = 778.5$$

Profit is reduced by 12 if the same price is charged in both markets.

The same analysis is shown diagrammatically in figure 8.3. The demand curves are plotted together with the corresponding marginal revenue curves and profit maximizing points are indicated where MC = MR. Reading prices from the demand curves we obtain P_A, P_B and P_C as before.

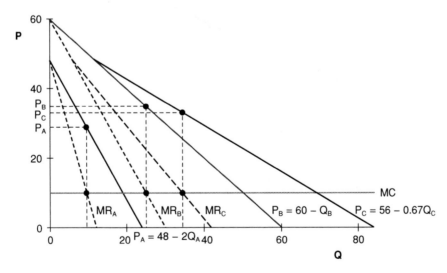

Figure 8.3 Discriminating monopolist

Chapter 8: Answers to Practice Problems

8.1   (a) $\partial y/\partial x = 27x^2$

         $\partial y/\partial z = 4z^3$

   (c) $\partial y/\partial x = 3z^2/x$

         $\partial y/\partial z = 6z\ln(x)$

   (b) $\partial y/\partial x = 10x/z$

         $\partial y/\partial z = -5x^2/z^2$

   (d) $\partial y/\partial x = 1 + 6x^2(x^3 - z)$

         $\partial y/\partial z = -2(x^3 - z)$

8.2   (a) $\partial y/\partial w = 1$

         $\partial y/\partial x = 20x/z^3$

         $\partial y/\partial z = -30x^2/z^4$

   (b) $\partial y/\partial w = 16w(4w^2 + 6x^3 - 2z)$

         $\partial y/\partial x = 36x^2(4w^2 + 6x^3 - 2z)$

         $\partial y/\partial z = -4(4w^2 + 6x^3 - 2z)$

8.3 $\partial y/\partial x = 9z$

      $\partial y/\partial z = 14z + 9x$

      $\Delta y = \partial y/\partial x . \Delta x + \partial y/\partial z . \Delta z = 0.95z + 0.9x$

      $\Delta y = 29.8$

      New y – initial y = 4989.825 – 4960 = 29.825, so Δy is a close approximation.

8.4 $Y = (30 - 0.88T + I + G + X)/0.25$

      Autonomous taxation multiplier = $\partial Y/\partial T = -3.52$

      Government expenditure multiplier = $\partial Y/\partial G = 4$

      Investment multiplier = $\partial Y/\partial I = 4$

      Export multiplier = $\partial Y/\partial X = 4$

      $Y = 800$

      $Y_d = 700$, $C = 658$, $S = 42$

      $Z = 116$

      $J = I + G + X = 118 + 90 + 50 = 258$

      $W = S + T + Z = 42 + 100 + 116 = 258 = J$

      Government surplus of 10

      Foreign trade deficit of 66

      Multiplier predicts Y will rise by 560

      With $X = 190$, $Y = 1360$, a rise of 560 as predicted

New values: $Y_d = 1260$, $C = 1150.8$, $S = 109.2$

$Z = 188.8$

$J = I + G + X = 118 + 90 + 190 = 398$

$W = S + T + Z = 109.2 + 100 + 188.8 = 398 = J$

Government surplus of 10

Foreign trade surplus of 1.2

8.5   (a) $Y_d = Y - T = 0.75Y$

$Y = C + I + G = 40 + 0.6Y + A - 1500R + G$

$Y = 100 + 2.5A - 3750R + 2.5G$ is the IS equation

$\partial Y/\partial A = 2.5 =$ the autonomous investment multiplier

$\partial Y/\partial G = 2.5 =$ the government expenditure multiplier

(b) MD = MS

$0.6Y - 2400R = 1500$

$Y = 2500 + 4000R$ is the LM equation

Equating with Y from IS and substituting A and G gives

$2500 + 4000R = 2887.5 - 3750R$

$R = 0.05$

$Y = 2700$

(c) Simple multiplier predicts Y will increase by 232.5. But R rises. New IS equation is

$Y = 3120 - 3750R$

Using this and the original LM equation gives

$R = 0.08$

$Y = 2820$

Y rises only by 120; private investment is crowded out. $I = 750 - 1500R$ falls from 675 to 630.

8.6   Substituting in the equilibrium condition and rearranging gives

$[1 - 0.65(1 - t)]Y = 96 + I + G$

so

$Y = (96 + I + G)/(0.35 + 0.65t)$

Government spending multiplier $= \partial Y/\partial G = 1/(0.35 + 0.65t) = 2.08$

Tax rate multiplier $= \partial Y/\partial t = -0.65(96 + I + G)/(0.35 + 0.65t)^2$

$$= -0.65Y/(0.35 + 0.65t) = -2031.25$$

8.7 $\partial U/\partial X = 5X^{-1/2}Y^{2/3}$

$\partial U/\partial Y = (20/3)X^{1/2}Y^{-1/3}$

$\text{MRS} = (\partial U/\partial X)/(\partial U/\partial Y) = (3/4)Y/X$

Point A in figure 8.4 has coordinates (45.5625, 8) and so MRS = 0.1317, $U = 270$

If $U = 270$ and $X = 9$, $Y^{2/3} = 9$ so $Y = 9^{3/2} = 27$, which is point B.

At point B, MRS = 2.25

Moving from B to A, MRS diminishes as X increases.

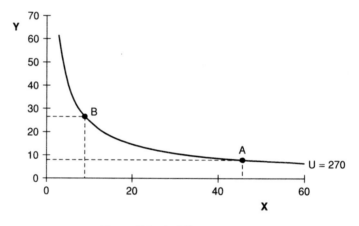

Figure 8.4   Indifference curve

8.8 $\partial Q_y/\partial P_y = -4$

$\partial Q_y/\partial P_x = -0.5$

$\partial Q_y/\partial M = 0.04$

Own-price $E = -4P_y/(12 - 4P_y + 0.04M - 0.5P_x) = -60/27$

Cross-price $E = -0.5P_x/(12 - 4P_y + 0.04M - 0.5P_x) = -5/27$

Income $E = 0.04M/(12 - 4P_y + 0.04M - 0.5P_x) = 80/27$

X and Y are complements.

8.9 $\partial Q / \partial P = -2M^{0.3}/P^3$

$\partial Q / \partial M = 0.3M^{-0.7}/P^2$

Own-price E of demand $= -2$

Income E of demand $= 0.3$

8.10 Writing $-a$ for 1.3 and rearranging we have

$a = -\ln Q_y - 2.1 \ln P_y + 0.08 \ln P_x + 0.6 \ln M$

The partial derivatives are

$\partial a / \partial Q_y = -1/Q_y$

$\partial a / \partial P_y = -2.1/P_y$

$\partial a / \partial P_x = 0.08/P_x$

$\partial a / \partial M = 0.6/M$

We can now write

$da = -1/Q_y . dQ_y - 2.1/P_y . dP_y + 0.08/P_x . dP_x + 0.6/M . dM$

Setting appropriate differentials equal to 0

$\partial Q_y / \partial P_y = -2.1 Q_y / P_y$

$\partial Q_y / \partial P_x = 0.08 Q_y / P_x$

$\partial Q_y / \partial M = 0.6 Q_y / M$

These give

Own-price $E = -2.1$

Cross-price $E = 0.08$

Income $E = 0.6$

8.11 MRS is the negative of the slope of the isoquant. On any isoquant

$Q = f(L,K) = $ constant

Implicit differentiation gives

$dK/dL = -(\partial Q / \partial L)/(\partial Q / \partial K) = -MPL/MPK = $ slope of isoquant

$MRS = (\partial Q / \partial L)/(\partial Q / \partial K) = MPL/MPK$

Rewriting the budget line

$K = B/P_k - (P_l/P_k)L$ so its slope is $-P_l/P_k$

At a point of tangency the slopes of the isoquant and the budget line are equal, so

$-MPL/MPK = -P_l/P_k$ or $MPL/MPK = P_l/P_k$

8.12   (a) $\partial^2 y/\partial x^2 = 72x^2 z^5$ (b) $\partial^2 y/\partial x^2 = 0$

         $\partial^2 y/\partial z^2 = 120x^4 z^3$ $\partial^2 y/\partial z^2 = 54xz$

         $\partial^2 y/\partial z \,.\, \partial x = 120x^3 z^4$ $\partial^2 y/\partial z \,.\, \partial x = 27z^2$

         $\partial^2 y/\partial x \,.\, \partial z = 120x^3 z^4$ $\partial^2 y/\partial x \,.\, \partial z = 27z^2$

8.13   For a turning point

$\partial y/\partial x = 8 + w - 4x = 0$

$\partial y/\partial w = 5 + x - 0.6w = 0$

So, $w = 20$, $x = 7$ at the turning point

$\partial^2 y/\partial x^2 = -4$ (negative)

$\partial^2 y/\partial w^2 = -0.6$ (negative)

$\partial^2 y/\partial x \,.\, \partial w = 1$

$(\partial^2 y/\partial x^2)(\partial^2 y/\partial w^2) - (\partial^2 y/\partial x \,.\, \partial w)^2 = (-4)(-0.6) - (1)^2 = 1.4$ (positive)

There is a maximum turning point at $w = 20$, $x = 7$.

8.14   For a turning point

$\partial U/\partial X = 5 + 1.2Y - 3X = 0$

$\partial U/\partial Y = 6 + 1.2X - 1.2Y = 0$

So, $X = 6.11$, $Y = 11.11$ at the turning point.

This gives $U = 48.611$, which is greater than its value at points such as $X = 6$, $Y = 11$, so this is a maximum turning point.

chapter nine

Constrained Maxima and Minima

OBJECTIVES

In this chapter you learn to
- Appreciate how constrained optimization problems arise in economics
- Solve constrained maximization and minimization problems using the substitution method
- Use the more general Lagrange multiplier method

SECTION 9.1: Introduction

In economic analysis we often deal with multivariate functions and have the objective of maximizing or minimizing the dependent variable. We call this the objective function. Economics, however, is also concerned with scarcity. Frequently our achievement of goals is limited by the availability of resources. The specification of this restriction is called the constraint. Up till now we have sometimes looked separately at an objective and a constraint. For example, in section 8.6 we compared the slope of an indifference curve, representing consumer utility, with the slope of the budget constraint. The optimal consumption position is a constrained maximum where the consumer achieves the maximum possible utility given the budget available. In this chapter we work simultaneously with the objective function and the constraint and see two different ways of identifying the constrained optimum position. The reason for presenting two methods is that the first one is more straightforward, although it does not always require less calculation. The second approach may be less intuitively appealing, but it is a very general method that can be extended to apply to a wide variety of situations. For the problems in this chapter you can use either solution method, but sometimes one is easier than the other.

---

constrained optimization: choosing the values of the variables that maximize or minimize the objective function from the values that are permitted by the constraint.

The methods are set out for you in step-by-step fashion. You learn them by applying them to problems in economic analysis. For example, if we have the utility function $U = f(X, Y)$ and the budget constraint $M = X . P_x + Y . P_y$, we see how to choose values of X and Y that maximize utility given the consumer's income, M. Both approaches rely on the general method for optimizing multivariate functions that is described in section 8.11. We find partial derivatives and set each of them equal to zero to locate a maximum or minimum.

Once we have identified where an optimum occurs, we should check to see whether the point is a maximum or a minimum. For an optimization problem involving a constraint the second order conditions are more complicated and they are not presented here. Generally we shall assume that the turning point we identify is either a maximum or a minimum as the economic theory requires. Another approach is to evaluate the function at and near the turning point and compare the values it takes.

The profit function on the MathEcon screen Constrained Optimization shown in figure 9.1 is the same as on the screen Optimization of Multivariate Functions in section 2 of MathEcon chapter 8, but now there is a restriction on the total output of two of the products. The firm is restricted to output combinations that do not contravene the constraint. The maximum profit the firm can achieve is therefore less than before, as you can discover by trial and error. Two further sections in MathEcon chapter 9 explain the mathematical methods for finding solution values.

Section 9.2: Substitution Method

The substitution method works by imposing the relationship between the variables that the constraint states. We rewrite the constraint to give an expression for one variable in terms of the others, and we then substitute this in the objective function. That variable is then eliminated from the objective function, and simultaneously we ensure that the constraint operates.

We go on to locate the maximum or minimum for the revised objective function by finding partial derivatives. Setting them equal to zero and solving the resulting equations gives optimal values of the variables, subject to the constraint.

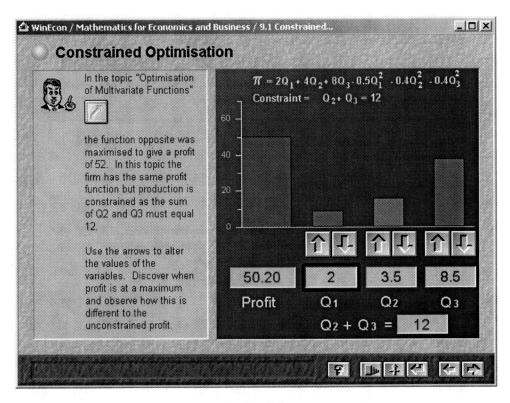

Figure 9.1

A value is still required for the variable that was eliminated. Substituting back into the constraint allows you to find its value. Substituting for the variables in the objective function gives its optimal value subject to the constraint.

You can see a demonstration of this method on the MathEcon screen titled The Substitution Method.

The substitution method   **Remember...**

1. Rewrite the constraint and substitute into the objective function, thus eliminating one variable from it.
2. Find partial derivatives.
3. Set equal to zero and solve.
4. Substitute for values of the variable eliminated earlier and the objective function.

The total cost of producing x units of model X and y of model Y is

$$TC = 5x^2 + 6y^2 - 4xy$$

If 15 items are to be produced (either of model X or Y) decide how many of each model should be produced to minimize total cost.

1

We are asked to minimize the objective function $TC = 5x^2 + 6y^2 - 4xy$ subject to the constraint that $x + y = 15$.

Step 1: We rewrite the constraint, say as

$$y = 15 - x$$

In this example you could equally well write an expression for x in terms of y, but sometimes it is easier to find an expression for one of the variables rather than the other. Substituting for y in the objective function gives

$$TC = 5x^2 + 6(15 - x)^2 - 4x(15 - x)$$

Multiplying out and simplifying we find

$$TC = 5x^2 + 1350 - 180x + 6x^2 - 60x + 4x^2$$

$$= 15x^2 - 240x + 1350$$

In this instance eliminating one variable has left us with a function of just one variable which we are to minimize.

Step 2: Differentiate with respect to x. Partial derivatives are not needed here. We obtain

$$\frac{d(TC)}{dx} = 30x - 240$$

Step 3: We set this equal to 0 for a minimum

$$30x - 240 = 0$$

$$x = 8$$

Step 4: Substituting for y, the variable we eliminated, we have

$$y = 15 - x = 15 - 8 = 7$$

We now substitute for x and y to find the value of the objective function. This gives

$$TC = 5(8)^2 + 6(7)^2 - 4(8)(7)$$

$$= 390$$

This is the minimum total cost at which 15 items can be produced, and it is achieved with $x = 8$, $y = 7$.

9.1 Choose the inputs of labour, L, and capital, K, to maximize output given

$$Q = 5K + 3L + 2LK$$

and subject to the constraint that the planned expenditure on inputs is 140. Each unit of labour costs 4 and each unit of capital costs 20.

SECTION 9.3: Lagrange Multiplier Method

The Lagrange multiplier method, named after the French mathematician who devised it, incorporates the constraint into the expression you are optimizing, forming a Lagrangian expression. Using a Lagrange multiplier, denoted λ, we add a term representing the constraint to the objective function and then apply our optimization technique. The solution values of the variables optimize the function subject to the constraint. The value of the Lagrange multiplier and the optimal value of the objective function can be found also.

Use the screen titled The Lagrange Multiplier Method in section 3 of MathEcon chapter 9 to see a worked example. Notice that the More button at step three offers you help with identifying how the partial derivatives are formed.

Lagrange multiplier: a variable that is introduced to allow the constraint to be combined with the objective function giving a Lagrangian expression.

Lagrangian expression: combines the objective function and the constraint. The maximum or minimum of the Lagrangian expression is the maximum or minimum of the objective function subject to the constraint.

The steps in the Lagrange multiplier method are: **Remember...**

1. Rewrite the constraint as an expression which equals zero and multiply by a Lagrange multiplier.
2. Add this to the objective function forming a Lagrangian expression which incorporates the constraint.
3. Differentiate partially with respect to each variable, including the Lagrange multiplier, and set all partial derivatives equal to zero.
4. Solve the resulting equations. A useful method is to move terms containing the Lagrange multiplier to the right-hand side and then divide one equation by another. We find the optimal values of the variables subject to the constraint.

A consumer budgets $100 for buying various quantities of two goods, X and Y, which sell at prices of $13 and $6 respectively. Show what quantities of the goods maximize the utility he obtains if his utility function is

$$U = 5X + 6Y + 1.2XY - 1.5X^2 - 0.6Y^2$$

At a price of $13, the consumer spends $13X$ on the first good if the quantity purchased is represented by X. Similarly he spends $6Y$ on buying Y units of the second good. The consumer's total expenditure on the two goods is $13X + 6Y$, and this must not exceed his budget of 100. The budget constraint is therefore

$$13X + 6Y = 100$$

Step 1: Rewrite the budget constraint as an expression that equals zero

$$100 - 13X - 6Y = 0$$

Multiply the left-hand side expression by the Lagrange multiplier, λ, giving

$$\lambda(100 - 13X - 6Y)$$

Step 2: Add the expression formed to the objective function. This gives the Lagrangian expression, which for convenience we call F. We have

$$F = 5X + 6Y + 1.2XY - 1.5X^2 - 0.6Y^2 + \lambda(100 - 13X - 6Y)$$

Step 3: Find all partial derivatives of F

$$\partial F/\partial X = 5 + 1.2Y - 3X - 13\lambda$$

$$\partial F/\partial Y = 6 + 1.2X - 1.2Y - 6\lambda$$

$$\partial F/\partial \lambda = 100 - 13X - 6Y$$

Setting each equal to zero gives

$$5 + 1.2Y - 3X - 13\lambda = 0 \qquad (1)$$

$$6 + 1.2X - 1.2Y - 6\lambda = 0 \qquad (2)$$

$$100 - 13X - 6Y = 0 \qquad (3)$$

Moving terms containing λ to the right-hand side helps us to eliminate λ from equations (1) and (2). We get

$$5 + 1.2Y - 3X = 13\lambda \qquad (4)$$

$$6 + 1.2X - 1.2Y = 6\lambda \qquad (5)$$

Divide the left-hand side of equation (4) by that of equation (5), and similarly divide the two right-hand sides. The resulting expressions equal one another since each side of equation (4) has been divided by something of equal value. This approach is often useful in economics problems, and the expression which results has an economic interpretation as we see below. We find

$$\frac{5 + 1.2Y - 3X}{6 + 1.2X - 1.2Y} = \frac{13}{6} \qquad (6)$$

Cross-multiplying by the divisors gives

$$6(5 + 1.2Y - 3X) = 13(6 + 1.2X - 1.2Y)$$

Multiplying out and collecting terms we obtain

$$33.6X = 22.8Y - 48 \qquad (7)$$

We have not yet used equation (3), which we now rewrite as an expression for Y

$$Y = \frac{100 - 13X}{6} \qquad (8)$$

Substituting this in equation (7) gives

$$33.6X = 3.8(100 - 13X) - 48$$

Multiplying out and collecting terms we get

$$83X = 332$$

$$X = 4$$

Substituting in equation (8) gives

$$Y = \frac{100 - 52}{6} = 8$$

The optimal consumption position for the consumer is at $X = 4$, $Y = 8$. For the level of utility achieved we substitute into the utility function

$$U = 5X + 6Y + 1.2XY - 1.5X^2 - 0.6Y^2$$

$$= 5(4) + 6(8) + 1.2(4 \times 8) - 1.5(4^2) - 0.6(8^2)$$

$$= 44$$

FURTHER RESULTS FROM THE LAGRANGE MULTIPLIER METHOD

The Lagrange multiplier method sometimes allows us to identify conditions that are specified in economic analysis as necessary for an optimum. For example, we saw in section 8.6 that the optimal consumption position for a consumer of two goods is where the ratio of the prices of the two goods equals the ratio of their marginal utilities to that consumer. This is exactly the result that equation (6) above shows. It states

$$\frac{5 + 1.2Y - 3X}{6 + 1.2X - 1.2Y} = \frac{13}{6}$$

The left-hand side is the ratio of the marginal utility of X to the marginal utility of Y, because the numerator and the denominator were formed as partial derivatives of the terms comprising the original utility function. That is, the left-hand side of the equation is

$$\frac{\partial U/\partial X}{\partial U/\partial Y} = \frac{MU_x}{MU_y}$$

The right-hand side of equation (6) is P_x/P_y because it is the ratio of the partial derivatives of the constraint part of the Lagrangian expression where the prices are the coefficients of the variables. Equation (6) of our derivation therefore states the condition for an optimum

$$\frac{MU_x}{MU_y} = \frac{P_x}{P_y}$$

The Lagrange multiplier which multiplies the constraint in the Lagrangian expression is in fact a multiplier in the economic sense. If the constraint limit changes a little, multiplying by λ gives the approximate change that ensues in the value of the objective function. We can solve for λ as we solve for the other variables. In worked example 2 we had

$$5 + 1.2Y - 3X - 13\lambda = 0 \tag{1}$$

Substituting $X = 4$, $Y = 8$ gives

$$5 + 1.2(8) - 3(4) - 13\lambda = 0$$

Solving for λ we find

$$\lambda = 0.2$$

Using the multiplier approach, the prediction is that if the consumer's budget is increased by 6 to 106, his utility will increase by $0.2(6) = 1.2$ to 45.2.

To check the accuracy of this result you have to rework the calculation above using the value of 106 in the constraint. Equations (1) and (2) are unchanged and we obtain the same relationship between X and Y as before in equation (7). Equation (3) becomes

$$106 - 13X - 6Y = 0$$

Rearranging this to form a new expression for Y and substituting it in equation (7) gives

$$33.6X = 3.8(106 - 13X) - 48$$

from which

$$X = 4.3 \text{ and } Y = 8.4$$

These values are correct to one decimal place. Substituting them in the utility function we find that $U = 45.1$, which is close to the value we predicted. Notice that the change in the budget constraint has resulted in the consumer buying more of both goods.

9.2 Use either the substitution method or the Lagrange multiplier method or both for each of the following problems.

A firm has the production function

$$Q = 12L^{1/3}K^{1/2}$$

where L and K are the units of labour and capital used in the production process. If it spends $600 on purchasing labour, L, and capital, K, at prices of $6 and $18 respectively, how much of each should it buy to maximize its output, and how much output does it then produce? Show that the ratio of the marginal products equals the ratio of the factor prices.

9.3 A student budgets $58.24 to spend on sandwiches and chocolate bars during a ten-week term. Sandwiches cost $0.64 each, chocolate bars are $0.21 each. The student's utility function is

$$U = X^{1/2}Y^{3/7}$$

where X and Y represent numbers of sandwiches and chocolate bars respectively. How many sandwiches and chocolate bars will the student buy if she wishes to maximize her utility?

Given the quantities chosen of each item, calculate the ratio of the marginal utilities of the items and show that it equals the ratio of their prices.

9.4 A firm makes three products, in quantities X, Y and Z. It wishes to maximize its profit function

$$\pi = 8X + 16Y + 4Z - 0.8X^2 - 0.8Y^2 - Z^2$$

but to satisfy customer orders it must produce a total of 24 items which are either product X or product Y. Show how many of each of its three products it should produce and find the profit it makes.

How are the firm's production decisions and profit affected if the required total of products X and Y is just 23 items?

Chapter 9: Answers to Practice Problems

9.1   Objective function: $Q = 5K + 3L + 2LK$

Constraint: $4L + 20K = 140$

Step 1: Rewrite constraint and substitute in objective function

$L = 35 - 5K$

$Q = 105 + 60K - 10K^2$

Step 2: Differentiate

$dQ/dK = 60 - 20K$

Step 3: Set equal to 0

$60 - 20K = 0$

$K = 3$

Step 4: Substitute

$L = 35 - 5K = 20$

$Q = 5K + 3L + 2LK = 195$

Maximum of $Q = 195$ at $L = 20$, $K = 3$

9.2   Objective function: $Q = 12L^{1/3}K^{1/2}$

Constraint: $6L + 18K = 600$

Step 1: Rewrite constraint and multiply by Lagrange multiplier

$\lambda(600 - 6L - 18K)$

Step 2: Add to objective function

$F = 12L^{1/3}K^{1/2} + \lambda(600 - 6L - 18K)$

Step 3: Find partial derivatives

$\partial F/\partial L = 4L^{-2/3}K^{1/2} - 6\lambda \ (= \text{MPL} - P_L\lambda)$

$\partial F/\partial K = 6L^{1/3}K^{-1/2} - 18\lambda \ (= \text{MPK} - P_K\lambda)$

$\partial F/\partial \lambda = 600 - 6L - 18K$

These $= 0$ for a maximum, so

$4L^{-2/3}K^{1/2} - 6\lambda = 0$ (1)

$6L^{1/3}K^{-1/2} - 18\lambda = 0$ (2)

$600 - 6L - 18K = 0$ (3)

Rewrite equations (1) and (2)

$4L^{-2/3}K^{1/2} = 6\lambda \ (\text{MPL} = P_L\lambda)$ (4)

$6L^{1/3}K^{-1/2} = 18\lambda \ (\text{MPK} = P_K\lambda)$ (5)

Divide corresponding sides of equations (4) and (5)

$4/6L^{-1}K = 6/18$

This shows MPL/MPK = P_L/P_K. Solving gives us

$K = L/2$

Substitute in equation (3)

$600 - 6L - 18(L/2) = 0$

$L = 40$

$K = 20$

Therefore

$Q = 12L^{\frac{1}{3}}K^{\frac{1}{2}}$

  $= 183.53$

Maximum $Q = 183.53$, with $L = 40$, $K = 20$

9.3   Objective function: $= X^{\frac{1}{2}}Y^{\frac{3}{7}}$

Constraint: $0.64X + 0.21Y = 58.24$

Step 1:

$\lambda(58.24 - 0.64X - 0.21Y)$

Step 2:

$F = X^{\frac{1}{2}}Y^{\frac{3}{7}} + \lambda(58.24 - 0.64X - 0.21Y)$

Step 3: For a maximum

$\partial F/\partial X = 1/2X^{-\frac{1}{2}}Y^{\frac{3}{7}} - 0.64\lambda = 0$ (1)

$\partial F/\partial Y = 3/7Y^{-\frac{4}{7}}X^{\frac{1}{2}} - 0.21\lambda = 0$ (2)

$\partial F/\partial \lambda = 58.24 - 0.64X - 0.21Y = 0$ (3)

Rewrite equations (1) and (2)

$1/2X^{-\frac{1}{2}}Y^{\frac{3}{7}} = 0.64\lambda$

$3/7Y^{-\frac{4}{7}}X^{\frac{1}{2}} = 0.21\lambda$

Divide

$7/6X^{-1}Y = 64/21$

$Y = 128X/49$

Substitute in equation (3)

$58.24 - 0.64X - 0.21(128X/49) = 0$, from which

$X = 49$

$Y = 128$

49 sandwiches, 128 chocolate bars.

$MU_x = 1/2X^{-1/2}Y^{3/7}$

$MU_y = 3/7Y^{-4/7}X^{1/2}$

$MU_x/MU_y = 7/6(Y/X)$

Substitute $X = 49$, $Y = 128$

$MU_x/MU_y = 64/21$

$P_x/P_y = 0.64/0.21$

$MU_x/MU_y = P_x/P_y$

9.4   Objective function: $\pi = 8X + 16Y + 4Z - 0.8X^2 - 0.8Y^2 - Z^2$

Constraint: $X + Y = 24$

Step 1:

$\lambda(24 - X - Y)$

Step 2:

$F = 8X + 16Y + 4Z - 0.8X^2 - 0.8Y^2 - Z^2 + \lambda(24 - X - Y)$

Step 3: For a maximum

$$\partial F/\partial X = 8 - 1.6X - \lambda = 0 \tag{1}$$

$$\partial F/\partial Y = 16 - 1.6Y - \lambda = 0 \tag{2}$$

$$\partial F/\partial Z = 4 - 2Z = 0 \tag{3}$$

$$\partial F/\partial \lambda = 24 - X - Y = 0 \tag{4}$$

Equation (1) gives

$\lambda = 8 - 1.6X$

Substitute in equation (2)

$16 - 1.6Y - 8 + 1.6X = 0$

$X = Y - 5$

Substitute in equation (4)

$24 - Y + 5 - Y = 0$

$Y = 14.5$

Substitute for Y

$X = 9.5$

From equation (3)

$Z = 2$

Therefore

$\pi = 8X + 16Y + 4Z - 0.8X^2 - 0.8Y^2 - Z^2$

   $= 71.6$

and

$\lambda = 8 - 1.6X = -7.2$

Reducing the product requirement by 1 will increase π by approximately 7.2. Since λ is negative these movements are in opposite directions.

   Reworking using the constraint $X + Y = 23$ gives $X = 9$, $Y = 14$, $Z = 2$ and $\pi = 78.4$.

chapter ten

Integration in Economics

OBJECTIVES

In this chapter you learn to
- Understand that integration is the inverse procedure to differentiation
- Recognize the notation and apply the rules of integration
- Find total functions from marginal functions
- Use definite integration to find the area under a curve
- Evaluate the sizes of areas on economics diagrams, giving measures of total revenue, total variable cost, consumer surplus and producer surplus

Section 10.1: Introduction

When you differentiate the function $y = f(x)$ you obtain an expression for dy/dx which in general is another function of x. If instead you started with dy/dx, could you obtain the function for y? This is the situation that we begin with when we study integration.

There are various pairs of processes in mathematics where one operation reverses the other and is called the inverse procedure. One example is multiplication and division. Multiplying and then dividing by the same number gets you back to the value you started with. Another example is taking $\log_e$ and exponentiating or raising to the power of e. The first procedure followed by the second brings you back to your original number. The inverse process to differentiation is called integration. As we shall see, however, operating the two procedures successively does not always immediately bring you back to exactly the function you started with.

Integration methods are not included in the current release of MathEcon. There is a relevant economics screen in section 1 of MathEcon chapter 10.

integration: the reverse process to differentiation.

SECTION 10.2: Rules of Integration

We begin by differentiating and then see what rule would reverse the procedure. Consider the function $y = 8x^3$. Differentiating a power function, we multiply by the power and then subtract 1 from the power. This gives $dy/dx = 24x^2$. To find the inverse procedure we reverse the rule, reversing both the operations and the order in which they take place. The resulting function is called $F(x)$. To integrate a power function we first add 1 to the power and then we divide by the new power, since division is the inverse of multiplication. Implementing these steps starting with $dy/dx = 24x^2$ we add 1 to the power of 2 so that the new power is 3 and we divide by this new power. The result is

$$F(x) = 8x^3$$

Notice that $F(x)$ is the same as the original function y in this case.

As with all new techniques, you will find the method gets easier as you practise it. Another useful tip is to always check your integration by differentiating your answer. You should get back to the expression you integrated.

To integrate a power function

Add 1 to the power and divide by the new power.

Remember...

| 10.1 | Using the rule for integrating a power function, find $F(x)$ for each of the following

(a) $5x^4$ (b) $10x^2$ (c) x^3 (d) $12x^3$ (e) $14x^6$ (f) $9x^{1/2}$ (g) $15x^{1/4}$

INTEGRATION NOTATION

If $18x^5$ is to be integrated with respect to x we show this by writing

$$\int 18x^5 \, dx$$

The elongated S, $\int$, at the front of the expression is the integral sign, while the dx at the end of the expression shows we are to integrate with respect to x. Don't worry about the notation. Just look for what is between $\int$ and dx and apply the rules to integrate it.

In general, we write the integral of $f(x)$ with respect to x **Remember...**

$$F(x) = \int f(x)\, dx$$

CONSTANT OF INTEGRATION

Consider the functions $y = 10x^4$ and $y = 10x^4 + 5$. Each of these differentiates to $dy/dx = 40x^3$, because a constant differentiates to zero. As we reverse the differentiation procedure, therefore, there is no way of immediately discovering whether there should be a constant in our answer, or what value it should have. To recognize the possibility that there may be a constant, as we integrate we add c to the expression for the integral, where c is called the constant of integration.

When integrating we use the appropriate rule and also add the constant of integration. For example, integrating $f(x) = 20x$ we have

$$F(x) = \int 20x\, dx = 10x^2 + c$$

Check that differentiating gives the original expression. For $y = 10x^2 + c$, we have $dy/dx = 20x$, which is the expression we integrated.

Although we write c for the constant of integration because we cannot immediately find its value, sometimes there is extra information in the question from which the value can be deduced. Suppose that in the above example we are also told that $F(x) = 7$ when $x = 0$. We substitute the values given. When $x = 0$ we have

$$F(x) = 10(0)^2 + c = c$$

and we know that $F(x) = 7$, so $c = 7$.

You may find it a little awkward to have to handle the concept of a constant of integration, but as you work through the economics examples in the next section you will find the constant does have an economic interpretation. In section 10.4, as you use integration to find the area under a curve, you will discover another reason why the constant of integration is less of a problem than it may at first sight appear.

POWER FUNCTION EXAMPLES

A general expression for the integral of a power function taking account of the constant of integration is shown below.

In general

$$\int ax^n \, dx = \frac{a}{n+1} \cdot x^{n+1} + c$$

Notice that we can use this rule to integrate a constant. You can regard a constant as being multiplied by x^0, since $x^0 = 1$. Substituting $n = 0$ in the above rule allows us to find, for example, $\int 9 \, dx$. We have

$$\int 9 \, dx = 9x + c$$

Check by differentiating. If $y = 9x + c$, $dy/dx = 9$, as we expect. Notice that you certainly need the dx at the end of the integral expression when you are integrating a constant. Without it you would not know what variable to put in your answer.

The rule also works for negative powers, as the next example shows. To find

$$\int 16x^{-3} \, dx$$

we substitute $a = 16$, $n = -3$ in the formula. Adding 1 to the negative power gives a new power of -2. From this we find

$$\int 16x^{-3} \, dx = -8x^{-2} + c = -\frac{8}{x^2} + c$$

Check by differentiating $y = -8x^{-2} + c$. As always, the constant of integration disappears when we differentiate and we find $dy/dx = 16x^{-3}$, the expression we integrated.

FURTHER RULES OF INTEGRATION

There is just one power of x for which the power-function rule does not work. If $n = -1$, raising it by 1 would make it zero, which causes a problem as we try to divide by it. Section 7.7 explains that if $y = \log_e x$, $dy/dx = 1/x = x^{-1}$. Applying this in reverse and remembering to add the constant of integration gives the result shown below.

To integrate x^{-1}

$$\int \frac{1}{x} \, dx = \log_e x + c$$

Notice that if we write $c = \log_e m$, where m is just another constant we have

$$\int \frac{1}{x}\,dx = \log_e x + \log_e m$$

and by the rules of logarithms

$$\log_e x + \log_e m = \log_e mx$$

We may therefore write as an alternative expression for the integral

$$\int \frac{1}{x}\,dx = \log_e mx$$

We check by differentiating. Section 7.7 shows that if $y = \log_e mx$, $dy/dx = 1/x$, which confirms our result.

Exponential functions are also considered in section 7.7 where it is shown that to differentiate

$$y = e^{mx}$$

we just multiply by the coefficient of x which gives

$$\frac{dy}{dx} = me^{mx}$$

To find the integral, then, of e^{mx} we do the opposite of the differentiation procedure and we divide by the coefficient of x. This gives the following general formula for integrating an exponential function.

To integrate an exponential function   **Remember...**

$$\int e^{mx}\,dx = \frac{1}{m}e^{mx} + c$$

To check that this is correct we differentiate the result. If $y = (1/m)e^{mx} + c$, $dy/dx = e^{mx}$ which is the function that we integrated. Integration followed by differentiation should always bring you back to exactly the expression you started with.

There is one further rule of integration that we require so that we can integrate a function which is a sum or difference of terms. This is shown below.

Integrate the terms of a sum separately and add   **Remember...**

$$\int [f(x) + g(x)]\,dx = \int f(x)\,dx + \int g(x)\,dx$$

Similarly, to integrate a difference of terms we integrate separately and then subtract.

There are a substantial number of other rules for integration, but they are beyond the scope of this book. The rules given here suffice for the economic analysis we cover.

Find

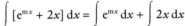

$$\int [e^{mx} + 2x]\, dx$$

1

Using the rule that allows us to write the integral of a sum as the sum of separate integrals we find

$$\int [e^{mx} + 2x]\, dx = \int e^{mx}\, dx + \int 2x\, dx$$

For the first integral we use the rule that applies to exponential functions, for the second we use the power function rule and we add a constant of integration. This gives

$$\int e^{mx}\, dx + \int 2x\, dx = \frac{1}{m} e^{mx} + x^2 + c$$

10.2 Find the integrals

(a) $\int [18x^2 + 5]\, dx$

(b) $\int [20x^4 - 8x^2 + 9x]\, dx$

(c) $\int [e^x - 4x]\, dx$

(d) $\int [14x + \frac{8}{x}]\, dx$

(e) $\int [5x^3 + \frac{10}{x^2}]\, dx$

SECTION 10.3: Finding Total Functions from Marginal Functions

The relationship between total and marginal functions in economics is explained in chapter 5. Whenever we have a total function in economics, differentiating it gives the corresponding marginal function. It follows, then, that by integrating a marginal function we can find the corresponding total function. The constant of integration represents the constant term in the total function. For example, as we integrate to find a total cost function, the constant of integration represents the fixed costs. The integral without the constant of integration therefore represents total variable costs. Finding total revenue from marginal revenue is simpler. The total revenue function takes the value zero at zero output and so it has no constant term.

These and other types of problems are illustrated by the worked examples and practice problems below. Those relating to the consumption and savings functions specify different models from the linear functions we used in chapter 3. Whereas a linear consumption function assumes the marginal propensity to consume is constant, the alternative specification in worked example 3 says people spend relatively less as income increases. In this model the marginal propensity to consume declines as income rises.

2

A firm has the marginal revenue function MR = 84 − 4Q. Find its total revenue function.

Given the marginal revenue function, we find an expression for the total revenue function by integration. Since MR = d(TR)/dQ we have

$$TR = \int (MR)\, dQ$$

$$= \int [84 - 4Q]\, dQ$$

Using the rule for a difference, that we should integrate the terms separately and then subtract, we write

$$TR = \int 84\, dQ - \int 4Q\, dQ$$

Applying the power function rule to each term we find

$$TR = 84Q - 2Q^2 + c$$

A total revenue function shows the firm's revenue associated with various levels of output, Q. If output is zero, TR is zero and this lets us evaluate the constant. Substituting for TR and Q we get

$$0 = 84(0) - 2(0)^2 + c$$

and so c = 0. This gives

$$TR = 84Q - 2Q^2$$

Checking, we find that when this expression is differentiated it gives the original MR function.

The marginal propensity to consume is given by

$$\text{MPC} = 0.5 + \frac{1}{\sqrt{Y}}$$

Find an expression for the consumption function $C = f(Y)$, using the information that when income is 25, consumption is also 25. Sketch the consumption function.

Differentiating the consumption function shows how consumption changes as income changes, and so $dC/dY = \text{MPC}$. We therefore find the consumption function by integrating MPC

$$C = \int (\text{MPC}) \, dY$$

Substituting the expression for MPC gives

$$C = \int \left(0.5 + \frac{1}{\sqrt{Y}} \right) dY$$

$$= 0.5Y + 2\sqrt{Y} + c$$

Substituting the values given for C and Y we find

$$25 = 0.5(25) + 2\sqrt{25} + c$$

and rearranging this gives $c = 2.5$. The consumption function is therefore

$$C = 0.5Y + 2\sqrt{Y} + 2.5$$

A sketch of the consumption function is shown in figure 10.1. Notice that when Y is less than 25 consumption exceeds income.

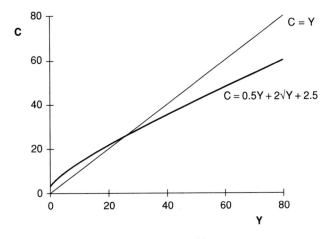

Figure 10.1 Non-linear consumption function

10.3 The marginal cost function for a firm is given by

$$MC = 3Q^2 - 28Q + 84$$

Find an expression for total cost if the fixed costs are 92.

10.4 If the marginal propensity to save is MPS = $0.3 - 0.25/\sqrt{Y}$ and saving is 20 when Y is 100, find an expression for S, the saving function.

10.5 If marginal revenue is given by MR = $120 - 8Q$, find an expression for total revenue.

SECTION 10.4: Area Under a Curve

Economic analysis based on diagrams often involves a comparison of areas. Sometimes these are rectangular areas, but the technique of integration allows us also to find the size of the area under a curve between two values of x. An example of the kind of area we can measure this way is that shaded in figure 10.2. This interpretation of an integral has useful applications in economics.

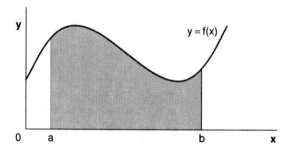

Figure 10.2 Shaded area is found by integration

The method used to find the area lying under the curve between points a and b is called definite integration. Integrating the function $f(x)$ gives $F(x) = \int f(x)\,dx$, as we saw in section 10.2. Next we substitute the higher x value, b, which gives $F(b)$ and then we similarly substitute the lower x value, a, to find $F(a)$. The difference between these values, $F(b) - F(a)$ is the value of the definite integral between the limits a and b, and is the size of the area under the curve $f(x)$ between a and b. The notation representing this definite integral is

$$\int_a^b f(x)\,dx = F(b) - F(a)$$

> definite integral from a to b: the difference between the value of $\int f(x)\,dx$ at b and its value at a.

The numbers a and b are called the limits of integration and are shown against the integral sign. In our examples, the lower limit, a, is always smaller than the upper limit, b, and also the function $f(x)$ lies above the x axis. As we integrate and find the expression for $F(x)$, we need to continue to note the limits for which we are to evaluate it. The notation for this is to enclose $F(x)$ in square brackets with the limits alongside. We write

$$[F(x)]_a^b$$

With definite integration we do not need to include a constant of integration as we find $F(x)$. If we do add a constant, it occurs in both $F(b)$ and $F(a)$ and disappears as we subtract them.

Integrate, substitute limits, subtract   **Remember...**

$$\int_a^b f(x)\,dx = [F(x)]_a^b = F(b) - F(a)$$

This gives the area under $y = f(x)$ between a and b.

4

Find $\int_4^6 3x^2\,dx$

Integrating with respect to x we have

$$\int_4^6 3x^2\,dx = [x^3]_4^6$$

Substituting $x = 6$ and $x = 4$, then subtracting

$$= (6)^3 - (4)^3 = 216 - 64 = 152$$

If the function being integrated is linear you can check your definite integration by finding the area using a geometric formula. Here is an example.

Find $\int_0^3 (9 - x)\, dx$. Mark the area your integral represents on a graph and evaluate the area geometrically also.

5

Integrating and then substituting the limits we find

$$\int_0^3 (9 - x)\, dx = [9x - 0.5x^2]_0^3 = (27 - 4.5) - (0 - 0) = 22.5$$

Notice that in this case when we substitute $x = 0$ we obtain the value zero, which simplifies the calculation.

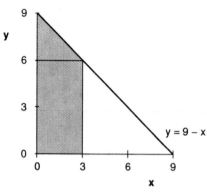

Figure 10.3

Figure 10.3 shows the graph for $y = 9 - x$ and marks the area between $x = 0$ and $x = 3$, dividing it into a rectangle and a triangle.

Area of rectangle: base × height = 3 × 6 = 18

Area of triangle: $\frac{1}{2}$ × base × height = $\frac{1}{2}$ × 3 × 3 = 4.5

Total area = 22.5

The area measured this way is the same as the value of the definite integral.

10.6 Find

(a) $\int_1^5 8x\, dx$ (b) $\int_0^3 (9x^2 + 8)\, dx$

(c) $\int_2^4 (6x^2 - 3x + 11)\, dx$

10.7 Find $\int_2^8 5\, dx$. Plot the curve representing the function you are integrating, mark the area that your integral represents and evaluate it geometrically also.

SECTION 10.5: Definite Integrals in Economics

We can now use definite integration to measure areas on economics diagrams.

TOTAL REVENUE

On a diagram showing average and marginal revenue we can now measure total revenue in two different ways. As shown in figure 10.4, for any output, *b*, we can take a vertical to the AR curve and so find the price, *c*, at which this output will be sold. Using the relationship that TR = *P.Q* we can measure total revenue as the area of the rectangle O*ceb*. The alternative approach uses the marginal revenue curve and the concept of definite integration. We find TR as

$$TR = \int_0^b (MR)\, dQ$$

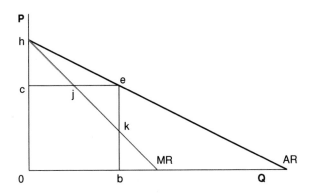

Figure 10.4   Measuring total revenue

and TR is therefore represented as the area under the marginal revenue curve from the origin to *b*. This is the area labelled O*hkb* on figure 10.4. Since the marginal revenue curve falls twice as steeply as the average revenue curve, triangles *chj* and *jek* are similar triangles with equal areas. Hence the two methods of measuring total revenue give the same result.

CONSUMER SURPLUS

Consumer surplus represents extra benefit people feel they have gained from a purchase because what they pay for it is less than the maximum they were prepared to pay. We can measure it as the area under the demand curve and

The MathEcon screen titled Market Consumer Surplus shows the geometric approach to measuring consumer surplus.

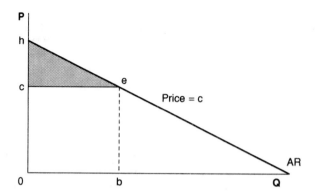

Figure 10.5 Measuring consumer surplus

above the price line, which is the triangle *che* in figure 10.5. Using the concept of direct integration we write

$$\text{Consumer surplus} = \int_{0}^{b} (\text{AR}) \, dQ - (b \times c)$$

PRODUCER SURPLUS

Producer surplus measures the amount by which the revenue received exceeds the production costs. It is the area between the marginal cost curve and the price line. For a perfectly competitive industry producing output *b* at price *c* it is measured by the area of triangle O*cf* on figure 10.6, which can be expressed as

$$\text{Producer surplus} = (b \times c) - \int_{0}^{b} (\text{MC}) \, dQ$$

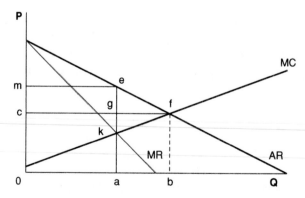

Figure 10.6 Measuring producer surplus

Comparing a monopoly with the same marginal cost curve, the monopoly would produce output a at price m. The monopolist's producer surplus includes rectangle *cmeg* (which is part of consumer surplus under perfect competition), but there is also a loss of producer surplus under monopoly measured by the triangle *kgf*. Moving from the monopolist's output a to the competitive industry's output b price falls from m to c and the change in producer surplus is

Change in producer surplus = triangle *kgf* − rectangle *cmeg*

$$= [(b - a) \times c] - \int_a^b (\text{MC}) \, dQ - [(m - c) \times a]$$

10.8 For a firm with the marginal revenue curve MR = 85 − 5Q, what is the change in total revenue if it expands its output from 2 to 6? Sketch the MR curve and mark the area representing the change.

10.9 Referring to figure 10.6, what is the change in consumer surplus if output increases from a to b? What is the change in social surplus (consumer surplus + producer surplus)?

Chapter 10: Answers to Practice Problems

10.1 (a) x^5 (b) $(10/3)x^3$ (c) $(1/4)x^4$ (d) $3x^4$ (e) $2x^7$
(f) $6x^{3/2}$ (g) $12x^{5/4}$

10.2 (a) $6x^3 + 5x + c$ (b) $4x^5 - (8/3)x^3 + (9/2)x^2 + c$
(c) $e^x - 2x^2 + c$ (d) $7x^2 + 8(\log_e x) + c$
(e) $(5/4)x^4 - 10/x + c$

10.3 $\text{TC} = \int (\text{MC}) \, dQ$
$= Q^3 - 14Q^2 + 84Q + 92$

10.4 $S = \int (\text{MPS}) \, dY$

$= 0.3Y - 0.5\sqrt{Y} + c$

and $20 = 0.3(100) - 0.5\sqrt{100} + c$ so that $c = -5$ giving

$S = 0.3Y - 0.5\sqrt{Y} - 5$

10.5 $TR = \int (MR)\, dQ = 120Q - 4Q^2 + c$

but if $Q = 0$, $TR = 0$ so $c = 0$, hence

$TR = 120Q - 4Q^2$

10.6   (a) $[4x^2]_1^5 = 100 - 4 = 96$

(b) $[3x^3 + 8x]_0^3 = (81 + 24) - (0 + 0) = 105$

(c) $[2x^3 - 3/2x^2 + 11x]_2^4 = (128 - 24 + 44) - (16 - 6 + 22) = 116$

10.7 $[5x]_2^8 = 40 - 10 = 30$

Figure 10.7 shows the area the integral represents. It is a rectangle, area = $6 \times 5 = 30$

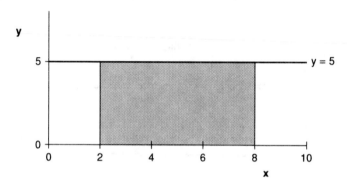

Figure 10.7

10.8 $\int_2^6 (85 - 5Q)\, dQ = [85Q - 2.5Q^2]_2^6 = 260$

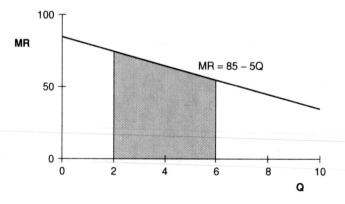

Figure 10.8

10.9 Triangle *gef* + rectangle *cmeg* = $\int_a^b (\text{AR}) \, dQ - [(b - a) \times c] + [(m - c) \times a]$ is the change in consumer surplus.

The change in social surplus = [triangle *gef* + rectangle *cmeg*] + [triangle *kgf* − rectangle *cmeg*]

= triangle *gef* + triangle *kgf*

$$= \left\{ \int_a^b (\text{AR}) \, dQ - [(b - a) \times c] \right\} + \left\{ [(b - a) \times c] - \int_a^b (\text{MC}) \, dQ \right\}$$

$$= \int_a^b (\text{AR}) \, dQ - \int_a^b (\text{MC}) \, dQ$$

= triangle *kef*

This is the deadweight loss of monopoly.

chapter eleven

Linear Programming

OBJECTIVES

In this chapter you learn to
- Appreciate the type of problems that can be solved by linear programming
- Formulate linear programming problems
- Find a graphical solution to two variable problems with a maximization example
- Appreciate how possible changes impact on the optimal solution
- Solve problems using Excel Solver
- Understand the Excel sensitivity report
- Solve minimization problems

SECTION 11.1: Introduction

Economics is concerned with making the best use of available resources, but there may be restrictions on the way the resources can be used that must be taken into account. The restrictions may be physical, for example the quantities of inputs that are needed for particular types of product. In constrained optimization problems, the objective function specifies what is to be maximized or minimized, and the restrictions are expressed as constraints. Values of the decision variables have to be chosen that maximize or minimize the function without violating any of the constraints. These values will not necessarily be integers since the decision variables are assumed to be continuous, taking any positive or zero value. Linear programming is used for constrained optimization problems where the objective function and all the constraints have a linear form. This chapter is concerned with linear models and equations and so it can be read at any time after chapter 2.

In a typical maximization problem, larger values of the decision variables increase the objective function. The decision maker then prefers to choose bigger values of the variables but the constraints put restrictions on what sizes are possible. The constraints often take the form of inequalities and state that linear functions of the variables must be less than or equal to an upper limit. It is also implied that none of the decision variables can be negative. The solution to a linear programming problem is reached when the constraints are all satisfied and a maximum or minimum, subject to these constraints, is achieved. This may occur when just some of the constraints are binding while for others the inequality holds. We discover how to set up and solve linear programming problems using examples. In the graphical approach we plot lines that represent the constraints and the objective function in the same way as we plotted budget constraints in section 2.7. We also see how to use Excel Solver to find the solution and examine its sensitivity to the specific data values given. A maximization problem is explained in detail and a minimization example follows in section 11.7.

> Constrained optimization methods for use with a non-linear objective function or constraint are discussed in chapter 9.

SECTION 11.2: Formulating Linear Programming Problems

We need to identify and write expressions for the key components of the problem as we read through its verbal specification. The worked examples below and in section 11.7 illustrate the approach.

Key components of a linear programming problem are: **Remember...**

- objective function
- decision variables
- constraints
- non-negativity conditions

1

An advertising agency has available 1200 hours of copywriter time, 440 hours of artist time and 780 hours of production staff time in the next planning period. Preparing a magazine advertising campaign requires 80 hours of copywriter time, 20 hours of artist time and 15 hours of production time. It generates a profit for the agency of $3000. Producing a television advertising campaign uses 40 hours of copywriter time, 30 hours of artist time and 60 hours of production time. It yields a profit to the agency of $6000. How many of each type of advertising campaign should the agency undertake to produce in the planning period in order to maximize its profit?

To identify the objective function we look for something that is to be maximized or minimized. Here we have to read to the end of the question to find that the agency wishes to maximize its profit. To specify the profit function we look at what generates profit for the agency. Each magazine advertising campaign and television advertising campaign generates profit, the unit profit values being $3000 and $6000 respectively. Total profit therefore depends on how many of each of these campaigns are undertaken. The numbers of each type of campaign to be undertaken are what we are asked to decide, so these are the decision variables. We choose names to identify them and write:

$$M = \text{number of magazine advertising campaigns}$$

$$T = \text{number of television advertising campaigns}$$

The profit generated by each type of campaign is the unit profit multiplied by the number of campaigns undertaken and the total profit is the sum of these amounts. This gives

$$\text{Total profit} = \pi = 3000M + 6000T$$

which is the objective function. Notice that the objective function includes both decision variables.

The constraints in this problem arise from the limits on the amounts of copy-writer, artist and production staff time that are available in the planning period. Each of the three activities imposes a separate constraint that the time used must not exceed the time available. To write down the copywriter time constraint we identify how much of this activity is needed to prepare each type of campaign. A magazine campaign requires 80 hours and a television campaign needs 40 hours. Preparing M magazine campaigns therefore uses $80M$ hours (multiplying the number of campaigns, M, by the number of hours for each) and similarly T television campaigns take up $40T$ hours. Adding these we find that for M magazine and T television campaigns

$$\text{Total copywriter time required} = 80M + 40T$$

The time used must not exceed the 1200 hours available and so we write

$$\text{Copywriter time constraint: } 80M + 40T \leq 1200$$

where the inequality sign $\leq$ means that the expression on the left is less than or equal to the expression on the right. Similarly, we write expressions for the artist time constraint and the production time constraint. In each case these set out the condition that the total time used for both types of campaign must be less than or equal to the time available. The three constraints are:

Copywriter time constraint: $80M + 40T \leq 1200$

Artist time constraint: $20M + 30T \leq 440$

Production time constraint: $15M + 60T \leq 780$

In addition, we must specify that the decision variables cannot take negative values. We write these non-negativity conditions

$$M \geq 0$$

$$T \geq 0$$

We have now formulated the problem. We require to find values of M and T that generate the largest possible value of the objective function $\pi = 3000M + 6000T$ without violating any of the restrictions. The objective function, the constraints and the non-negativity conditions have to be used together to determine the optimal values of the decision variables M and T. Notice that the resources are used in different proportions for the two different types of campaign. Magazine campaigns require twice as much copywriter time as television ones (80 hours as compared with 40 hours). As regards artist and production time, however, magazine campaigns use less time than television ones ($2/3 = 20/30$ of the artist time and $1/4 = 15/60$ of the production time). The linear programming problem arises because of these varying proportions. Television campaigns generate greater unit profit so they would be preferred to magazine campaigns, but they don't use much copywriter time. Rather than waste a lot of the available copywriter time, it may be preferable to use it in magazine campaigns even though these also require artist and production time which has to be released by reducing the number of television campaigns.

SECTION 11.3: Graphical Solution

When there are just two decision variables a linear programming problem can be solved graphically. We choose a variable to plot on each axis of the graph and mark an appropriate scale of positive values, since negative ones are not permitted by the non-negativity conditions. The boundary of each inequality constraint is plotted as a line and we check on which sides of these lines the inequalities hold. This lets us identify an area called the feasible region where all the constraints are satisfied. The points in this area comprise the set of feasible solutions. The optimal solution is the point (or points) in the feasible set that maximizes (or minimizes) the objective function. To enable us to spot the optimal combination of the decision variables we need to represent the objective function on the graph. We don't know the optimal value of the objective function but we can select possible values for it and plot the corresponding

Plotting a line by finding the points at which it intersects the axes is explained in section 2.7.

lines, giving a set of parallel lines. To identify an optimal solution we look for a point where one of these lines that represent the objective function just touches the boundary of the feasible region. For a maximum we use the highest objective function line that just touches the feasible set, while for a minimum we use the lowest.

Remember...

1. A line is plotted to represent the equality limit of each constraint.
2. The set of feasible solutions is where all the constraints are satisfied.
3. The optimal solution occurs where a line representing the objective function just touches the feasible set.

2

Plot the constraints and identify the set of feasible solutions for the advertising agency problem formulated in section 11.2.

We choose to plot M on the horizontal axis and T on the vertical one. We rewrite each constraint inequality as an equation and plot it as a line on the graph. This shows the boundary at which the constraint is just satisfied. Each line is plotted using the points at which it crosses the axes. The data are listed in the table and the resulting graph is shown in figure 11.1.

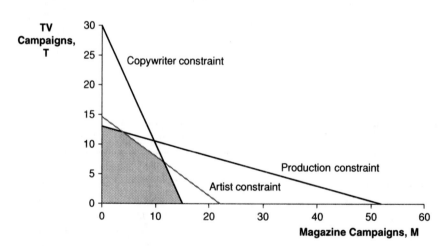

Figure 11.1

Constraint	Boundary	T axis intersection, $M = 0$, T value	M axis intersection, $T = 0$, M value
Copywriter time	$80M + 40T = 1200$	30	15
Artist time	$20M + 30T = 440$	14.67	22
Production time	$15M + 60T = 780$	13	52

The graph depicts only the positive quadrant where both M and T take positive values. This ensures that the non-negativity conditions are satisfied. Each constraint takes the form of a less-than inequality, and so it is satisfied by points below and to the left of the line that represents it, as well as by points on the line itself. Feasible solutions satisfy all the constraints. These are points that are on, or below, or to the left of all the constraint lines. The feasible region is the shaded area, including the lines that enclose it.

To find which point in the feasible region is optimal we add the objective function to the graph. We have to guess a possible value for total profit, then plot a line showing combinations of the decision variables which generate that profit. This is called an iso-profit line.

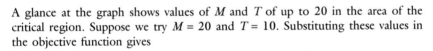

iso-profit line: a line showing combinations of the variables that generate the same profit.

Find the optimal solution for the problem discussed in worked examples 1 and 2.

3

The objective function is:

$$\pi = 3000M + 6000T$$

A glance at the graph shows values of M and T of up to 20 in the area of the critical region. Suppose we try $M = 20$ and $T = 10$. Substituting these values in the objective function gives

$$\pi = 60{,}000 + 60{,}000 = 120{,}000$$

so we choose 120,000 for our first trial value of profit. We want, therefore, to plot the iso-profit line

$$3000M + 6000T = 120{,}000$$

The line cuts the T axis at $T = 20$ and the M axis at $M = 40$. It is added to the constraint diagram in figure 11.2 and we see it lies wholly above the shaded area that represents the feasible region. A profit of 120,000 is not achievable.
  We need to try another iso-profit line, the general expression for which is

$$\pi = 3000M + 6000T$$

Rearranging this gives

$$T = \frac{\pi}{6000} - \left(\frac{3000}{6000}\right)M = \frac{\pi}{6000} - 0.5M$$

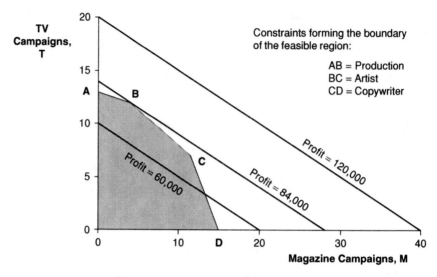

Figure 11.2

From this we can see that whatever the value of π, the slope of the iso-profit line is the negative of the ratio of the unit profit values, −3000/6000.

Figure 11.2 shows that a line with a profit of 84,000 touches the boundary of the feasible set at point B. Another line representing a profit of 60,000 is also shown. This crosses the feasible region, but higher profits are available above and to the right of it. The highest profit that is achievable given the constraints is 84,000. The values of the decision variables at point B represent the solution of the linear programming problem. The values are $M = 4$ and $T = 12$.

Solving simultaneous equations is discussed in section 2.11.

All iso-profit lines have the same slope and so they are parallel to one other. To find the highest iso-profit line that touches the feasible region we slide our line parallel to itself until we have a line that just touches the boundary formed by the constraints.

To find the solution values of the decision variables more accurately than they can be read from a diagram, we can solve the equations for the constraints lines which cross at the optimal point.

4

For the optimal solution identified in worked example 3, solve algebraically to find the values of the decision variables.

We use the artist and the production constraints which intersect at point B:

$$\text{Artist time: } 20M + 30T = 440 \tag{1}$$

$$\text{Production time: } 15M + 60T = 780 \tag{2}$$

These equations can be simplified. We divide through the artist time equation by 10, and divide through the production time equation by 15. The simplified equations are:

$$\text{Artist time: } 2M + 3T = 44 \tag{3}$$

$$\text{Production time: } M + 4T = 52 \tag{4}$$

We need M to have the same coefficient in both equations to enable us to eliminate it. Multiplying the equation (4) by 2 gives:

$$2M + 8T = 104$$

and from this we subtract equation (3)

$$2M + 3T = 44$$

to eliminate M. This gives

$$5T = 60$$

which implies $T = 12$.

We substitute $T = 12$ into any of the earlier equations, the easiest being equation (4)

$$M + 4T = 52$$

which gives

$$M + 48 = 52$$

implying $M = 4$.

$M = 4$, $T = 12$ is the optimal solution.

The advertising agency should undertake 4 magazine campaigns and 12 television campaigns. This maximizes profit, subject to the constraints, and yields a profit of

$$3000M + 6000T = 3000 \times 4 + 6000 \times 12 = 84,000$$

SECTION 11.4: The Optimal Solution and the Feasible Set

The point where the line representing the objective function touches the feasible set determines the optimal values of the decision variables. The vertex at which this occurs depends on the slope of the iso-profit line which is the negative of the ratio of the unit profit values, $-3000/6000$ in our example. If either of the unit profit values changes, the slope of the iso-profit line alters. Whether or not the optimal values of the decision variables alter as a result of this depends on how much the slope changes. A change in per unit profit obviously affects the total profit generated but it does not necessarily alter the optimal values of the decision variables. This depends on whether the new objective function line still meets the feasible set at the same vertex.

A change in the optimal solution would occur if the objective function became steeper than the artist constraint, because the highest iso-profit line would then touch the feasible set at point C in figure 11.2 and this would be the new solution. If the objective function became steeper still, so that it was steeper than the copywriter constraint, the optimal solution would be at point D and only magazine campaigns would be undertaken. Alternatively, if the slope of the iso-profit line became shallower than the slope of the production constraint the optimal solution would be at point A and only television campaigns would be undertaken. Points A and D, where one of the decision variables is zero, are called corner solutions.

It is also possible for more than one combination of the decision variables to be optimal. If the slope of the objective function happens to be the same as the slope of one of the constraints, the lines touch all along one edge of the feasible set. For example, if the slope of the iso-profit line is the same as that of the artist constraint any point between B and C in figure 11.2 is optimal. Since the decision variables are continuous there are an infinite number of solutions that all yield maximum profit.

Situations can arise when a linear programming problem does not have a solution. A maximization problem usually has at least some constraints that are less than inequalities, as occurred in the advertising agency problem. If, however, they were all greater than inequalities they would not operate to constrain the solution. The feasible set would then be unbounded and the solution values would be infinite. You should be aware of the possibility of this outcome but in realistic economic situations it is unlikely to occur.

SECTION 11.5: Using Excel Solver

The Solver tool provided in Excel is designed to solve a set of equations or inequalities and it may therefore be used for linear programming problems. You must lay out the problem in Excel in a suitable format, but then you just interact with the Solver dialogue box to obtain the solution. In addition to the optimal values of the decision variables and the objective function you can ask Solver for further reports, including a sensitivity analysis. There are many other computer programs available for solving linear programming problems, and you can use one of these if you prefer. Computer packages, including Excel, make it possible to solve more complex problems than can be handled using graphical analysis. We discover how to use Excel by applying it to the advertising agency problem set out in section 11.2.

We begin by setting out the constraint and objective function data in the spreadsheet as shown in figure 11.3. Each number requires a separate cell so that it can be used in calculations. We choose a column for each decision variable and a row for each constraint and for the objective function. The coefficients of the variables are entered in appropriate cells. The upper limits of the constraints are similarly entered in another column. As you use Solver you choose the type of inequality for each constraint, but it is useful to type the inequality signs in a column as a reminder.

	Magazine Campaigns	Television Campaigns		Inequality Sign	Upper Limit
Copywriter time	80	40		< =	1200
Artist time	20	30		< =	440
Production time	15	60		< =	780
Objective function	3000	6000			

Figure 11.3 Data for the Advertising Agency problem

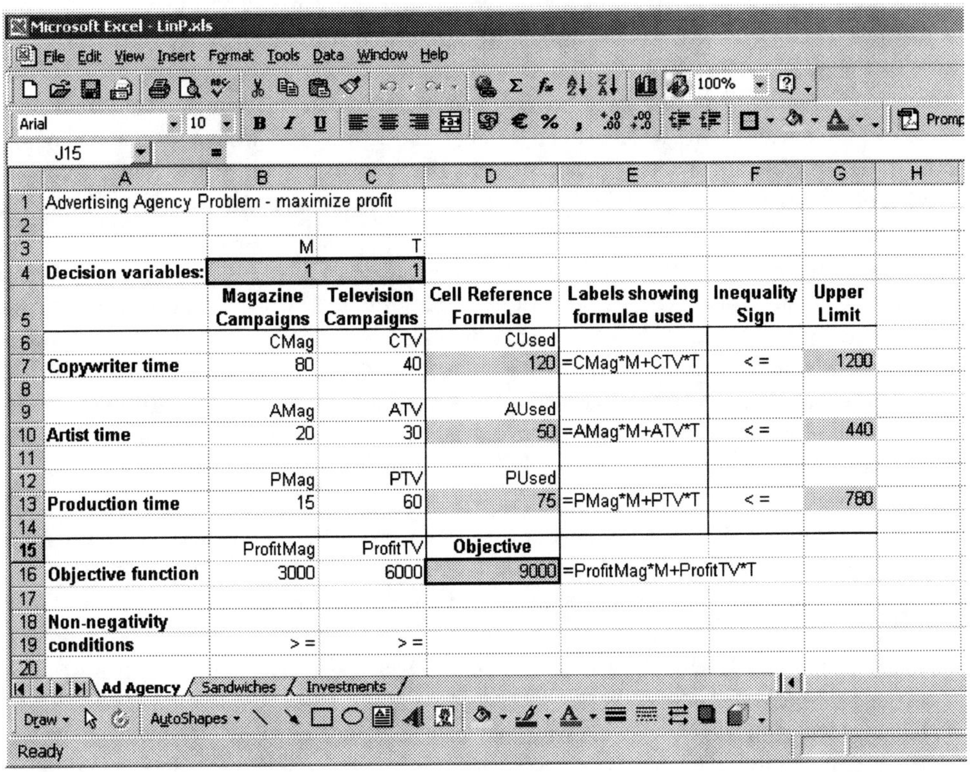

	A	B	C	D	E	F	G
1	Advertising Agency Problem - maximize profit						
2							
3		M	T				
4	Decision variables:	1	1				
5		Magazine Campaigns	Television Campaigns	Cell Reference Formulae	Labels showing formulae used	Inequality Sign	Upper Limit
6		CMag	CTV	CUsed			
7	Copywriter time	80	40	120	=CMag*M+CTV*T	< =	1200
8							
9		AMag	ATV	AUsed			
10	Artist time	20	30	50	=AMag*M+ATV*T	< =	440
11							
12		PMag	PTV	PUsed			
13	Production time	15	60	75	=PMag*M+PTV*T	< =	780
14							
15		ProfitMag	ProfitTV	Objective			
16	Objective function	3000	6000	9000	=ProfitMag*M+ProfitTV*T		
17							
18	Non-negativity						
19	conditions	> =	> =				
20							

Figure 11.4

We now add further information that Solver will need, as shown in figure 11.4. Solver asks you to nominate cells whose values it can change to find the optimal solution. These have to be the cells that contain the decision variables. We designate them above the constraint data and type 1 in each cell. These numbers are used as starting values which Solver changes as it tries to optimize them. Solver needs us to enter formulae to tell it how these cells interact with our data. Although it is not necessary to do so, naming cells that are used in formulae makes the formulae easier to read, because the cell names then appear in the formulae instead of the cell addresses. A row is inserted above cells to be named and the names are typed in. For example, in the worksheet shown B7 is named CMag, C7 is CTV and D7 is CUsed. You then select the cells containing both the names and the values to which they refer, choose 'Insert, Name, Create' from the menu and click 'OK' to 'Create Names, Top Row'. Once the various cells are named you enter formulae to calculate the values of the left-hand sides of the inequalities in the Cell Reference Formulae column and Excel immediately calculates and displays the resulting values using the current values of the decision variables, which we have set at 1. The formulae used are displayed as labels in figure 11.4, to the right of the cells in which they are entered. Notice that in Excel a formula starts with an equals sign, and a multiplication sign is represented by an asterisk. Similarly, the objective function formula calculates the current value of the objective function. We also have to tell Solver about the non-negativity conditions, so these are noted in the spreadsheet for reference. You may notice that some of the cells in figure 11.4 are shaded. These are cells that you will input in the Solver dialogue box. This worksheet is available for you to use from the Ad Agency tab in the LinP.xls file.

We are now ready to use Solver to obtain the solution. The first time you use Solver you have to make it available by choosing 'Tools, Add-Ins' on the menu, checking the Solver box and clicking 'OK'. You can now choose 'Tools, Solver' on the menu to bring up the Solver dialogue box. You set the Solver choices in turn, clicking first in a Solver box and then on the cell or cells in the spreadsheet that it is to use. Notice that it may be the cell reference rather than its name that appears in the Solver dialogue box. The various steps in the process are set out below.

- Click in the 'Set Target Cell' box and then click on the spreadsheet cell containing the objective function formula and displaying the value 9000 in figure 11.4.
- Choose 'Equal to Max' so that Solver will try to maximize the value in the target cell.
- Click in the 'By Changing Cells' box and select the cells containing the decision variables which are at present set at 1.
- Click in the 'Subject to the Constraints' box and choose 'Add'. This brings up the 'Add Constraint' dialogue box where you enter each constraint in turn, choosing 'Add' after each until you have put in all of them (including the non-negativity conditions), when you choose 'OK'. As you enter each constraint, the 'cell reference' is a shaded cell in the Cell Reference Formulae column, the type of inequality is selected from the combo box, and the 'constraint' is in the Upper Limit column. For the non-negativity conditions each 'cell reference' is one of the decision variable cells and the 'constraint' is typed as 0.
- You can safely ignore most of the 'Options' offered, but it is best to choose 'Assume Linear Model'. Clicking 'OK' returns you to the main Solver dialogue box shown in figure 11.5.
- You can now choose 'Solve' to let Solver find the solution.

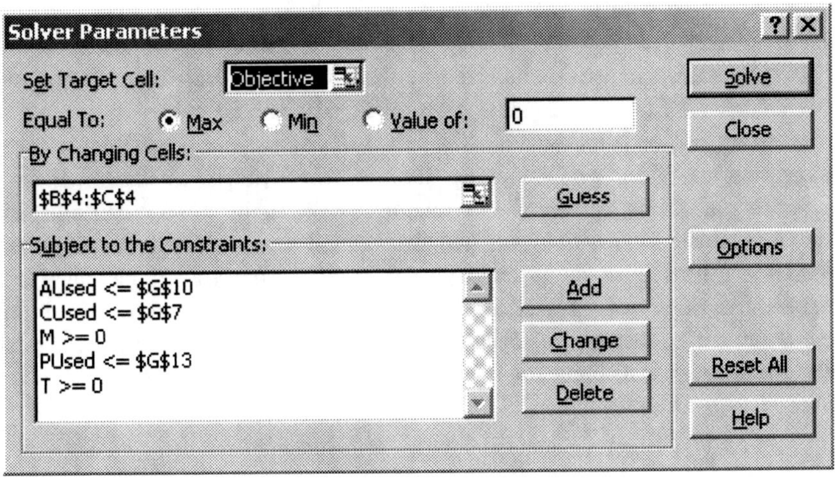

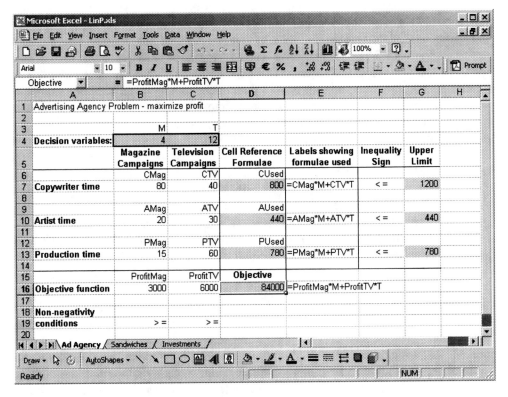

Figure 11.5 Solver dialogue box

Figure 11.6 The optimal solution

The solution is displayed in the cells outlined by boxes in figure 11.6. The decision variables take the values $M = 4$, $T = 12$ that we identified by the graphical method. Solver also calculates the profit generated by these values and displays it in the objective cell. The value of 84,000 is the maximum profit that can be achieved.

If when using Solver you don't get the solution you were expecting, but instead get a message such as 'The Set Cell values do not converge', click Cancel then choose Tools, Solver and bring up the Solver dialogue box again. Check carefully that you have included all the inequalities and that they are correctly defined. A computer works only with the information it has, and you need to ensure that it has all the correct information. As discussed in section 11.4, it is possible that a linear programming problem does not converge, but Solver's message about non-convergence is often an indicator of an error in the data it has been given.

SECTION 11.6: Sensitivity Analysis

When Solver shows the Results dialogue box it offers you the opportunity to request Reports on the solution, one of which is a sensitivity report. If you select this before you click OK to close the dialogue box, Solver provides a sensitivity report in a new worksheet which you can access by a tab at the foot of the screen. The report is shown in figure 11.7. The information headed 'Adjustable Cells' refers to the decision variables and the objective function. It shows by how much each of the coefficients in the objective function, the unit profit values in our example, can increase or decrease without the optimal solution changing. These numerical values correspond to how far the slope of the profit line can change while the decision variables stay the same, as discussed in section 11.4. Notice that the sensitivity analysis uses the comparative statics approach. Solver separately investigates the effects of changing any one of the unit profit values while everything else in the problem remains as originally specified.

In the section of the report that deals with 'Constraints', the 'Final Value' column shows how much of each type of time is used at the optimal solution. Comparing these values with the amounts available, shown in the 'Constraint R(ight) H(and) Side' column, we see that 400 hours of copywriter time was unused, whereas all the artist and production time was used up. We say that the artist and production constraints are binding, but the copywriter one is not. A resource that is fully utilized has a positive shadow price. This shows how much profit would increase if the right-hand side of the constraint increased by one unit. Shadow prices therefore indicate the maximum that it would be worth paying to obtain an extra unit of a resource. Copywriter time has a shadow price of zero because there is unused time already available. The columns headed 'Allowable Increase' and 'Decrease' show by how much the right-hand side value of the constraint could change without affecting which constraints are binding. If a constraint shifts by more than the allowable amount this alters which constraints are binding. The optimal solution is then found at the intersection of different constraints.

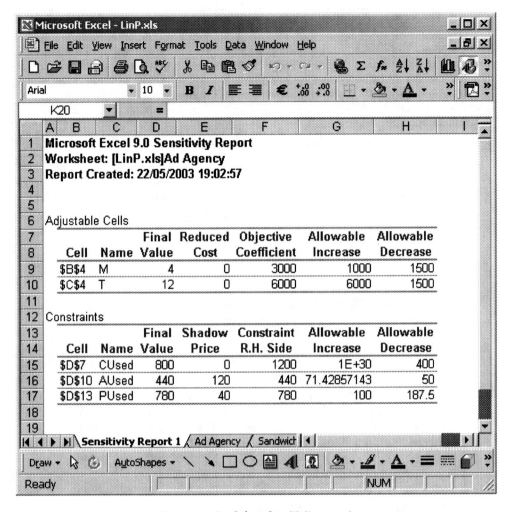

Figure 11.7 Solver Sensitivity report

SECTION 11.7: Minimization Subject to Constraints

The methods we have used to solve a maximization problem are equally applicable when the objective function is to be minimized. In this case the constraints usually take the form of greater than inequalities thus restricting how small the decision variables can be. If you use Solver to find the solution, the dialogue box allows you to set the objective to a minimum and to choose constraints with greater than inequality signs. In finding a graphical solution, the feasible set will typically be in the upper part of the positive quadrant with the constraints bounding it from below. The optimal solution will be where the line representing the objective function is as low as possible and just touches a vertex at the bottom of the feasible set. The graphical method is illustrated by a worked example.

A sandwich factory employs qualified staff at \$20 per hour and students at \$10 per hour. The former produce sandwiches at the rate of 60 per hour, while the latter produce them at the rate of 50 per hour. To provide appropriate supervision, the number of hours worked by qualified staff must be at least as great as the number worked by students. In a period when 8800 sandwiches are to be produced, for how many hours should each type of staff be employed if the factory is to minimize its total wage cost?

5

The factory's objective is to minimize its total wage cost, which depends on the number of hours for which qualified staff and students are employed. These are the values we are asked to find, so they are the decision variables. We write

Q = number of hours for which qualified staff are employed

S = number of hours for which students are employed

Hence the objective function which we wish to minimize is

$$\text{Total wage cost} = 20Q + 10S$$

since an hour of qualified staff time costs 20 and an hour of student time costs 10. The constraints relate to producing at least the required number of sandwiches and meeting the supervision requirements. We express these as:

$$\text{Production constraint: } 60Q + 50S \geq 8800 \text{ and}$$

$$\text{Supervision constraint: } Q \geq S$$

The left-hand side of the production constraint shows the total number of sandwiches that are produced using Q hours of qualified staff time and S hours of student time since the rates of production of these two groups of workers are 60 per hour and 50 per hour respectively. The non-negativity conditions are:

$$Q \geq 0 \text{ and}$$

$$S \geq 0$$

To find a graphical solution to the problem we are free to choose which variable we assign to which axis. We select the horizontal axis for S and the vertical axis for Q and plot the graph shown in figure 11.8. To find the feasible set of solutions we plot lines that represent the boundaries of the constraints and check on which side of the lines the inequalities are satisfied. As regards production, the equality limit holds when

$$60Q + 50S = 8800$$

Substituting in turn $S = 0$ and $Q = 0$ into this equation we find the line intersects the Q axis at $Q = 146.67$ and the S axis at $S = 176$. Points that satisfy the constraint $60Q + 50S \geq 8800$ are either on the line or, since they have a greater value of Q or S, above or to the right of it. The equality limit of the supervision constraint is the line $Q = S$. Choosing values for S and substituting we find at $S = 0$, $Q = 0$ and at $S = 100$, $Q = 100$. Plotting and connecting these points gives an upward sloping line through the origin that may be extended. The inequality $Q > S$ holds at points which are above the line, for example $S = 100$, $Q = 110$. The feasible set comprises points that satisfy both constraints. It is the area above both constraints that is shaded in figure 11.8.

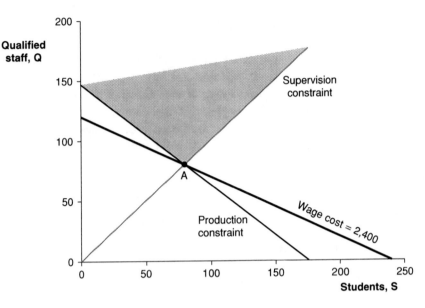

Figure 11.8

We then choose a possible value for total wage cost, plot the corresponding line and slide it, making it as low as possible yet just touching the feasible area. The line shown in figure 11.8 has a total wage cost of 2400, which is the minimum that can be achieved while satisfying the constraints. Since this line just touches the feasible set at point A where the two constraints intersect, point A is the optimal solution. To find accurate values for the decision variables we solve algebraically to find where the constraint lines cross. This occurs when

$$60Q + 50S = 8800 \text{ and}$$

$$Q = S$$

Substituting S for Q in the first equation gives

$$60S + 50S = 8800 \text{ or } 110S = 8800 \text{ from which}$$

$$S = 80$$

and, using $Q = S$

$$Q = 80$$

Minimum wage cost is achieved, subject to the constraints, by employing qualified staff for 80 hours and students for 80 hours. Total wage cost is $20 \times 80 + 10 \times 80 = 2400$.

11.1 A frozen vegetable supplier makes two brands of mixed vegetables. Brand A contains 20% beans, 25% carrots, 25% peas and 30% sweet corn and yields a profit of $500 per ton sold. Brand B contains 20% beans, 42% carrots, 28% peas and 10% sweet corn and sells giving a profit of $300 per ton. The supplier has available 3 tons of beans, 6 tons of carrots, 5 tons of peas and 2.5 tons of sweet corn. Use the graphical method to find how much of each brand of mixed vegetables he should produce to maximize profit. Which constraints are binding at the optimal solution? What is the maximum profit? Does the optimal solution alter if the profit on Brand A is only $400 per ton?

11.2 Use Excel Solver to find the solution to the sandwich factory problem that was solved graphically in section 11.7. You will need to enter a formula for the production constraint as explained in section 11.5, but the supervision constraint can be entered directly in the Solver dialogue box, using the cell references for the decision variables.

11.3 A farmers' cooperative buys winter feed from two manufacturers, X and Y at prices of $250 and $300 per ton respectively. The feed from manufacturer X contains 12% protein and 9% fibre, while that from manufacturer Y contains 8% protein and 18% fibre. Use the graphical approach to find the least cost way of buying winter feed that contains in total at least 16 tons of protein and at least 27 tons of fibre.

11.4 Use Excel Solver to solve the following problem. An investment manager is asked to invest $100,000 in either government bonds or financial or pharmaceutical company shares. The expected return on these investments is 3%, 7% and 10% respectively. The manager's objective is to maximize expected returns, but since there are different levels of risk involved certain restrictions are imposed. Neither financial nor pharmaceutical shares may form more than 40% of the portfolio. Government bonds must form at least 30% of the portfolio. The amount invested in government bonds must at least equal the amount spent buying pharmaceutical shares.

Why is it not possible to solve this problem using the graphical method that has been described?

Chapter 11: Answers to Practice Problems

11.1   Maximize $500A + 300B$ where A and B are the number of tons of each brand produced.

Subject to:

$0.2A + 0.2B \le 3$ (beans)

(weight used per ton of A) $\times A +$ (weight used per ton of B) $\times B \le$ tons available

$0.25A + 0.42B \le 6$ (carrots)

$0.25A + 0.28B \le 5$ (peas)

$0.3A + 0.1B \le 2.5$ (sweet corn)

$A \ge 0,\ B \ge 0$

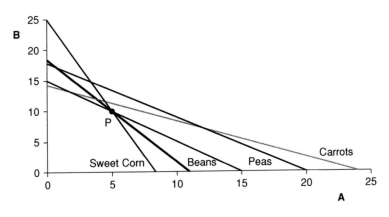

Figure 11.9

The heavy line is an iso-profit line. Profit is maximized at P where the sweet corn and beans constraints intersect. These constraints are binding.

Solving the equations

$0.3A + 0.1B = 2.5$ and

$0.2A + 0.2B = 3$ gives

$A = 5,\ B = 10$, maximum profit $= 5500$.

The profit line has slope $= -500/300 = -1.667$. If the profit on A is 400, the profit line has slope $= -400/300 = -1.333$. This line is shallower, but still steeper than the beans constraint, which has a slope of -1. $A = 5,\ B = 10$ is still the optimal solution, but the profit falls to 5000.

11.2

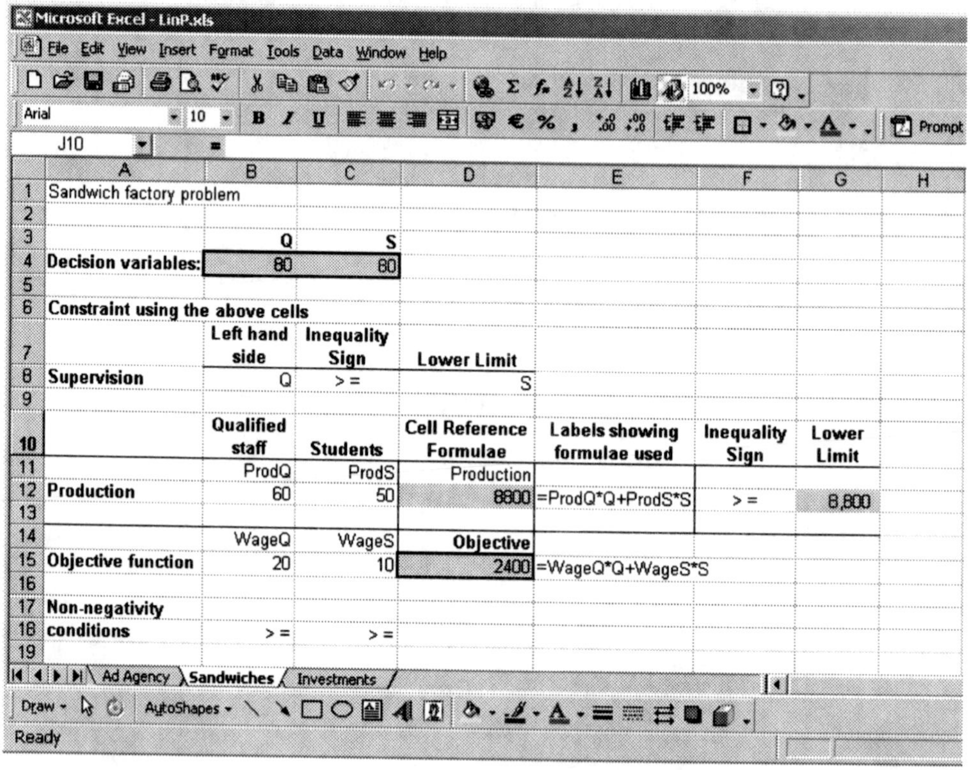

Figure 11.10

The solution can be found from the Sandwiches worksheet in LinP.xls.

11.3   Minimize cost $= 250X + 300Y$

Subject to:

$0.12X + 0.08Y \geq 16$ (protein)

$0.09X + 0.18Y \geq 27$ (fibre)

$X \geq 0, \ Y \geq 0$

Figure 11.11 shows the constraint boundaries and an iso-cost line. The feasible set is above and to the right of the lines. The solution is at point A where the constraints intersect and the iso-cost line just touches the feasible region.

Rewriting the constraint lines gives $3X + 2Y = 400$ (protein) and $X + 2Y = 300$ (fibre), and solving we find $X = 50$, $Y = 125$ at their intersection.

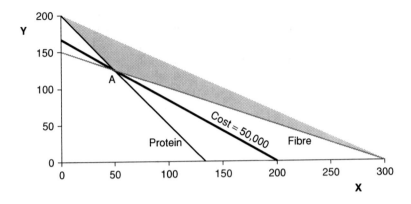

Figure 11.11

11.4

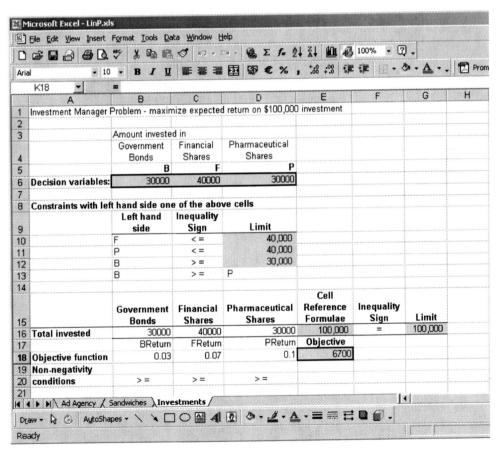

Figure 11.12

This problem has three decision variables and so cannot be solved by the graphical method of section 11.3. The solution shown uses the Investments worksheet in LinP.xls. Government bonds = 30,000, financial shares = 40,000, pharmaceuticals = 30,000. The expected return is 6700.

chapter twelve

Matrices in Economics

In this chapter you learn to
- Appreciate that using matrices you can handle an array of numbers as a single entity
- Understand the definitions of a matrix and a vector and be able to transpose them
- Carry out matrix addition and subtraction
- Multiply a matrix by a scalar or another matrix
- Use matrices to handle a system of equations
- Find the value of a determinant
- Calculate the inverse of a matrix
- Use an inverse to solve a system of equations
- Perform matrix operations in Excel and use Solver to solve a system of equations

Section 12.1: Introduction

A matrix is a rectangular array of values. The items in a matrix are called elements and their arrangement has a particular interpretation. Whether the matrix contains empirical data values or theoretical values of a variable, it is convenient to be able to manipulate the array as a whole. Matrix algebra enables us to do this. It allows us to handle a table of values as a single entity and obtain results such as the solution to a set of equations or the derivation of theoretical relationships in an economic model. The rules for manipulating and combining matrices are similar to ordinary algebraic operations.

There are, however, some restrictions. It is important that you understand how matrix operations are carried out and the various terms that are used so that you can appreciate the methods used in economic modelling.

Simple numerical examples of matrix operations are presented in this chapter so you can discover how the rules work and practise your skills. For bigger matrices the calculations become tedious, so there is an advantage in using a computer. We shall see that Microsoft Excel is a convenient computer package for handling matrices and that it offers various in-built matrix functions as well as the Solver routine that can be used to solve systems of equations. If you want additional practise at hand calculations you will find it is very easy to set up questions in Excel, try them on paper and then obtain the solutions in Excel to check that your hand calculations are correct.

This chapter also includes algebraic examples. Many economics students are primarily interested in matrix algebra to enable them to understand econometric analysis where statistical techniques are applied to empirical data sets to test theoretical models. The linear regression model is fundamental to these techniques, and practise in obtaining algebraic results relating to equation systems is a useful preliminary to its study.

SECTION 12.2: Matrices and Vectors

We denote a rectangular matrix by a capital letter formatted in bold type, or underlined if you are writing it by hand. For example,

$$A = \begin{bmatrix} 6 & 4 \\ 1 & 3 \\ 5 & 0 \end{bmatrix}$$

The rows of this matrix may represent three households and the columns may represent two goods with the values shown being the amounts that are purchased in a particular week. Each item is positioned in the matrix in the appropriate row and column for the household and the good to which it relates. You are probably accustomed to labelling a table to identify the goods and the households. While this is an excellent thing to do in presenting data, our purpose now is different. The positions of the values still have the same interpretation, but we want to work only with the values. We view them as forming a matrix.

> matrix: a rectangle of values arranged in rows and columns.
> element: the value in a particular row and column of a matrix.
> vector: a matrix with only one row, or one column.

Using this and other simple numerical examples the various terms used in matrix operations will be explained. The individual cell values in a matrix are called elements. A matrix may comprise just one row of elements, or just one column, for example

$$\mathbf{b} = \begin{bmatrix} 5 & 7 & -1 & 0 \end{bmatrix} \text{ and } \mathbf{c} = \begin{bmatrix} 42 \\ 7 \\ 31 \end{bmatrix}$$

These matrices are called vectors and we denote them again in bold type but using lower case rather than capital letters. We say that $\mathbf{b}$ is a row vector and $\mathbf{c}$ is a column vector. The use of bold letters to identify matrices and vectors distinguishes them from individual variable values and gives us a shorthand-like notation that provides a compact way of showing the matrix operations we perform and the results that follow from them.

The dimension of a matrix describes its number of rows and columns. The number of rows is given first so we write the dimension as the number of rows by the number of columns. The dimension of matrix $\mathbf{A}$ above is 3×2, since it has three rows and two columns. The dimensions of vectors $\mathbf{b}$ and $\mathbf{c}$ are 1×4 and 3×1 respectively. A square matrix has the same number of rows and columns. Matrix $\mathbf{D}$ with two rows and columns is an example. We say it is a square matrix of order 2.

$$\mathbf{D} = \begin{bmatrix} -1 & 5 \\ 4 & -2 \end{bmatrix}$$

---

square matrix: a matrix with the same number of rows as columns.
order: the number of rows and columns of a square matrix.

The elements in a matrix are arranged systematically so we have to keep them ordered. There are occasions, however, when we want to write the rows of a matrix as its columns, and vice versa. This may be for convenience, or because it forms part of a sequence of matrix operations. The transpose of a matrix is formed by writing the first row as the first column of the transpose, the second row as the second column of the transpose, and so on. The transpose of matrix $\mathbf{A}$ above, denoted $\mathbf{A}'$ (or sometimes $\mathbf{A}^T$) is

$$\mathbf{A}' = \begin{bmatrix} 6 & 1 & 5 \\ 4 & 3 & 0 \end{bmatrix}$$

The data about the households that we had in matrix $\mathbf{A}$ is now depicted in a different way. The rows of $\mathbf{A}'$ represent the two goods and the columns represent the three households. Notice that the dimensions of the matrices are different. Matrix $\mathbf{A}$ is 3×2, but matrix $\mathbf{A}'$ is 2×3. If we were to transpose matrix $\mathbf{A}'$ we would again interchange its rows and columns and so we would return to matrix $\mathbf{A}$. We have

$$(\mathbf{A}')' = \mathbf{A}$$

Matrices are equal if they have the same dimension and all the corresponding elements equal one another. As we saw with matrix $\mathbf{A}$, a matrix does not usually equal its transpose and does not have the same dimension as its transpose unless it is square. If a square matrix does actually equal its transpose it is said to be symmetric. Matrix $\mathbf{E}$ is an example of a symmetric matrix:

$$\mathbf{E} = \begin{bmatrix} 4 & 3 & 7 \\ 3 & -2 & -5 \\ 7 & -5 & 1 \end{bmatrix} \text{ and } \mathbf{E}' = \begin{bmatrix} 4 & 3 & 7 \\ 3 & -2 & -5 \\ 7 & -5 & 1 \end{bmatrix}$$

The method used to transpose a matrix in Excel is described in section 12.9 below. Examples of matrices and their transposes are included on the CD, which therefore provides additional practice problems.

so $\mathbf{E} = \mathbf{E}'$ since the corresponding elements of the two matrices are equal. In a symmetric matrix the elements above the principal diagonal that runs from top left to bottom right are the mirror image of those below the diagonal.

---

equal matrices: matrices with the same dimension and all corresponding elements equal.

principal diagonal: the elements in a square matrix that lie in the same row and column.

symmetric matrix: a square matrix where the elements above the principal diagonal are the mirror image of those below.

- The dimension of a matrix is rows × columns.
- The transpose of a matrix is found by interchanging rows and columns.

Remember...

12.1   State the dimension of each of the following matrices or vectors, and write down the transpose of each. Are any of the matrices symmetric?

$$A = \begin{bmatrix} 9 & -1 \\ 2 & 0 \end{bmatrix} \quad b = \begin{bmatrix} 5 \\ 2 \\ -3 \\ 7 \end{bmatrix} \quad C = \begin{bmatrix} -2 & 5 & 9 & 1 \\ 4 & 2 & 0 & 8 \end{bmatrix} \quad D = \begin{bmatrix} -1 & 2 & -4 \\ 2 & 7 & -9 \\ -4 & -9 & 10 \end{bmatrix}$$

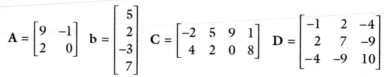

SECTION 12.3: Matrix Addition and Subtraction

Just as in ordinary arithmetic, matrix addition and subtraction lets us find sums of values and the differences between them. For example, in matrix **A** we had the amounts of two goods that were purchased by each of three households in a week. Now suppose we also have matrix **B** showing how much of the goods the households purchased in the previous week. Adding the corresponding elements in matrices **A** and **B** shows the total amount of each good purchased by each household in the two-week period. Subtracting the elements in **B** from those in **A** shows the difference between what each household purchased in the week to which **A** relates as compared with the previous week. We have:

$$\mathbf{A} = \begin{bmatrix} 6 & 4 \\ 1 & 3 \\ 5 & 0 \end{bmatrix} \quad \mathbf{B} = \begin{bmatrix} 5 & 4 \\ 0 & 5 \\ 8 & 6 \end{bmatrix}$$

Adding corresponding elements gives the sum of the matrices, **A** + **B**

$$\mathbf{A} + \mathbf{B} = \begin{bmatrix} 6+5 & 4+4 \\ 1+0 & 3+5 \\ 5+8 & 0+6 \end{bmatrix} = \begin{bmatrix} 11 & 8 \\ 1 & 8 \\ 13 & 6 \end{bmatrix}$$

To find the difference of the matrices, **A** − **B** we subtract corresponding elements

$$\mathbf{A} - \mathbf{B} = \begin{bmatrix} 6-5 & 4-4 \\ 1-0 & 3-5 \\ 5-8 & 0-6 \end{bmatrix} = \begin{bmatrix} 1 & 0 \\ 1 & -2 \\ -3 & -6 \end{bmatrix}$$

Notice that the elements of a matrix can be zero or negative. The 0s in matrices **A** and **B** occur when a household did not buy one of the goods in the relevant week. The 0 in matrix **A** − **B** indicates a household that bought the same quantity of a good in both weeks. Values in **A** − **B** are negative where households bought more of the good in the earlier week, the week to which matrix **B** relates.

The matrix operations of addition and subtraction apply to entire matrices. These must have the same dimension, otherwise for some of the elements there are no corresponding elements in the other matrix. The processes give us new matrices of the same dimension as the original ones.

If a matrix is subtracted from itself we obtain a matrix of the same dimension in which all the elements are zero. The resulting matrix is called a null matrix and denoted **0**. For example,

$$\mathbf{A} - \mathbf{A} = \begin{bmatrix} 6-6 & 4-4 \\ 1-1 & 3-3 \\ 5-5 & 0-0 \end{bmatrix} = \begin{bmatrix} 0 & 0 \\ 0 & 0 \\ 0 & 0 \end{bmatrix} = \mathbf{0}$$

> null matrix: a matrix in which all the elements are 0.

Matrices can be added and subtracted in Excel. The method is described in section 12.9 and examples are provided on the CD.

A null matrix can be formed of any dimension, so we write it as is appropriate to the dimensions of the other matrices with which we are working. The role of the null matrix in matrix algebra is similar to the way we use 0 in ordinary arithmetic.

> • Matrix addition and subtraction is applicable only if the matrices have the same dimension.
> • Add or subtract corresponding elements in the matrices.
>
> Remember...

12.2   If possible, find $A + B$, $A - B$, $A + C$, $B - C$, $C - C$, $C - 0$ where

$$A = \begin{bmatrix} 4 & 8 \\ 9 & 1 \\ 5 & 0 \end{bmatrix} \quad B = \begin{bmatrix} 3 & 7 \\ 5 & 0 \\ 5 & 2 \end{bmatrix} \quad C = \begin{bmatrix} 3 & 7 & -1 \\ 5 & 0 & 4 \\ 5 & 2 & 0 \end{bmatrix}$$

SECTION 12.4: Multiplication of Matrices

A matrix can be multiplied either by a number, known as a scalar, or by another matrix. These two types of multiplication involve different processes, so we study them in turn.

> scalar: a single value, not a matrix of values.

SCALAR MULTIPLICATION

A scalar is an ordinary value, not a matrix. When a matrix is multiplied by a scalar, every element in the array is multiplied by the scalar. For example, if matrix A is multiplied by 2, which is a scalar, every element in A is doubled. To continue our example where matrix **A** contains data on the quantities of two goods bought by three households, suppose we are asked to find a matrix **C**. This is to show the quantities purchased in a week when all the households buy double quantities of all the goods as compared with their purchases in matrix **A**. We have

$$A = \begin{bmatrix} 6 & 4 \\ 1 & 3 \\ 5 & 0 \end{bmatrix} \text{ and } C = 2A = 2\begin{bmatrix} 6 & 4 \\ 1 & 3 \\ 5 & 0 \end{bmatrix}$$

To find **C** we multiply each element in **A** by 2

$$C = \begin{bmatrix} 2\times6 & 2\times4 \\ 2\times1 & 2\times3 \\ 2\times5 & 2\times0 \end{bmatrix} = \begin{bmatrix} 12 & 8 \\ 2 & 6 \\ 10 & 0 \end{bmatrix}$$

C is the product of the matrix **A** and the scalar 2.

When we write the product of a matrix and a scalar we may write the scalar either before or after the matrix. Using k to represent a scalar, if **D** is the product of k and matrix **A** we have

$$D = kA = Ak$$

Notice that when a letter such as k is used to represent a scalar it is not written in bold, and hence it is distinguishable from a vector. With scalar multiplication the items being multiplied may be written in any order and the result is the same, as in ordinary algebra. This is called the commutative property of multiplication.

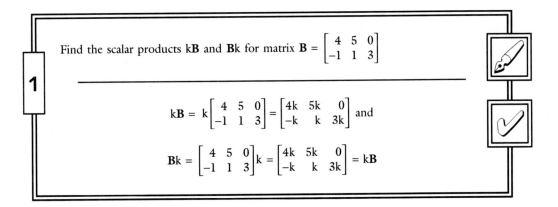

Find the scalar products kB and Bk for matrix $B = \begin{bmatrix} 4 & 5 & 0 \\ -1 & 1 & 3 \end{bmatrix}$

1

$$kB = k\begin{bmatrix} 4 & 5 & 0 \\ -1 & 1 & 3 \end{bmatrix} = \begin{bmatrix} 4k & 5k & 0 \\ -k & k & 3k \end{bmatrix} \text{ and}$$

$$Bk = \begin{bmatrix} 4 & 5 & 0 \\ -1 & 1 & 3 \end{bmatrix}k = \begin{bmatrix} 4k & 5k & 0 \\ -k & k & 3k \end{bmatrix} = kB$$

commutative property: the order in which items that are connected by an arithmetic operator are written does not affect the result.

MATRIX MULTIPLICATION

Referring again to our household data, matrix **A** gives quantities of goods purchased. If we know the prices at which the goods are sold, we may be interested in calculating the expenditures of the households. Matrix multiplication provides a way of calculating the total expenditure of each household on the goods. We write the prices of the two goods in a column vector (we shall see later why we choose a column vector) so we have

$$A = \begin{bmatrix} 6 & 4 \\ 1 & 3 \\ 5 & 0 \end{bmatrix} \text{ and } p = \begin{bmatrix} 2 \\ 7 \end{bmatrix}$$

The rule for multiplying matrix **A** by vector **p** is that we take the first row of **A**, multiply each of its elements by the corresponding element in column **p**, and add these products. This gives the first element of **Ap**. We then use the second row of **A** in a similar way to form the second row of **Ap**. Each of the elements in the second row of **A** is multiplied by the corresponding element in column **p** and the results are added. The third row of **Ap** is formed in the same way, multiplying the elements of the third row of **A** by those in column **p** and summing the products.

$$Ap = \begin{bmatrix} (6\times2) + (4\times7) \\ (1\times2) + (3\times7) \\ (5\times2) + (0\times7) \end{bmatrix} = \begin{bmatrix} 40 \\ 23 \\ 10 \end{bmatrix}$$

The resulting matrix **Ap** contains the total expenditures of the three households in buying the two goods. If we let

$$e = \begin{bmatrix} 40 \\ 23 \\ 10 \end{bmatrix}$$

the result of the matrix multiplication can be written as **Ap = e**. The condition for matrix equality implies that the corresponding elements in the two columns **Ap** and **e** must be equal, so the matrix equation is equivalent to three separate equations about the households' expenditures.

To see this we write an equation for each household's expenditure on the two goods. For each household

$$q_1 \cdot p_1 + q_2 \cdot p_2 = e$$

where q_1 and q_2 are the quantities a household buys of the two goods, p_1 and p_2 are their prices and e is the household's expenditure. Substituting for each household in turn gives the equations:

Expenditure of household 1: $(6 \times 2) + (4 \times 7) = 40$

Expenditure of household 2: $2 + (3 \times 7) = 23$

Expenditure of household 3: $(5 \times 2) = 10$

This set of equations gives the same information as the matrix equation $\mathbf{Ap} = \mathbf{e}$. The use of matrix multiplication to form the product $\mathbf{Ap}$ has given us a method of representing a system of equations. This use of matrices is developed further in section 12.5.

Not all matrices can be multiplied together. They can only be multiplied if the rows of the first matrix have the same number of elements as the columns of the second matrix so that we can pair them for multiplication. This occurs if the number of columns in the first matrix equals the number of rows in the second. In the above example matrix $\mathbf{A}$ has two columns. It can therefore only be multiplied by a matrix (or vector) with two rows. This is the reason why we wrote the prices as a column vector $\mathbf{p}$ to enable us to multiply $\mathbf{A}$ by $\mathbf{p}$.

---

conformable for multiplication: the matrices are of appropriate dimensions for their product to be formed.

Matrices which can be multiplied are said to be conformable for multiplication. To check whether this is the case it is useful to write the dimension of each matrix beneath it. In the above example we have

$$\underset{(3\times2)(2\times1)}{\mathbf{A} \quad \mathbf{p}} = \underset{(3\times1)}{\mathbf{Ap}}$$

Two matrices are conformable for multiplication if the inner numbers of their dimensions are the same, as here they are both 2. The outer numbers of the dimensions, 3 and 1 in this example, show the dimension of the resulting product, namely 3×1 in this case. Notice that although we have found the product $\mathbf{Ap}$ we cannot find $\mathbf{pA}$ since writing the dimensions below the matrices gives

$$\underset{(2\times1)(3\times2)}{\mathbf{p} \quad \mathbf{A}}$$

and the inner numbers, 1 and 3, are different. We must therefore always talk about forming a matrix product for the matrices in particular positions. Describing the example above we say that **A** was post-multiplied by **p** to give **Ap**, but that it is not possible to pre-multiply **A** by **p**. There are other occasions on which it is possible to both pre- and post-multiply one matrix by another, but the result is different. Usually, therefore, for two matrices **A** and **B**, **AB** ≠ **BA**. This is in contrast to ordinary algebra where the order in which values are multiplied together does not matter, and $ab = ba$. We say that the commutative property of multiplication does not hold for matrix multiplication.

Two properties which matrix multiplication does share with ordinary multiplication are the associative property and the distributive property. The associative property is concerned with how components are grouped before arithmetic operations are applied. When the associative property holds different groupings give the same result and so **A(BC)** = **(AB)C**. This property holds for matrix multiplication providing the dimensions of the matrices are such as to permit the different products to be formed. The distributive property allows us to multiply out brackets, distributing what is multiplying the brackets so that it multiplies the terms separately. We can state this as **A(B + C)** = **AB + AC**. These properties are illustrated by practice problem 12.4 below.

If you are going to study the properties of the linear model used in econometrics, you will need to know how the transpose of a matrix product relates to the transposes of the separate matrices. The rule is that **(AB)′** = **B′A′**. The individual transposed matrices **A′** and **B′** must be positioned in the reverse order before they are multiplied to give the same result as transposing the product **AB**. An example of this is provided in practice problem 12.7 below and another is available on the CD in Matrices.xls.

---

pre-multiply **A** by **B**: **B** is written before **A** to form the product **BA**.
post-multiply **A** by **B**: **B** is written after **A** to form the product **AB**.
associative property: the result of arithmetic operations is not affected by groupings of the components.
distributive property: one arithmetic operation can be distributed over another without changing the result.

As we work through more examples it will be useful to have a summary of the rules for matrix multiplication. The method we have used for finding the entries in a product matrix is summarized in a general statement showing which row of **A** and which column of **B** are used to form each element of the product matrix **AB** with n rows and k columns.

Write the dimension of each matrix under the proposed product. If the inner numbers of the dimensions are equal you can form the product, and the outer numbers give its dimension. Thus

$$\underset{(n\times q)\,(q\times k)}{\mathbf{A}\quad\mathbf{B}}$$

can be formed because q = q. The product is of dimension n by k.

For each entry in the product matrix **AB**, choose the appropriate row of **A** and column of **B** as shown in the table, multiply corresponding pairs of elements and sum the results

$$
\begin{array}{cccc}
A\ Row_1\times B\ Col_1 & A\ Row_1\times B\ Col_2 & \ldots\ldots & A\ Row_1\times B\ Col_k \\
A\ Row_2\times B\ Col_1 & A\ Row_2\times B\ Col_2 & \ldots\ldots & A\ Row_2\times B\ Col_k \\
\ldots\ldots & \ldots\ldots & \ldots\ldots & \ldots\ldots \\
A\ Row_n\times B\ Col_1 & A\ Row_n\times B\ Col_2 & \ldots\ldots & A\ Row_n\times B\ Col_k
\end{array}
$$

In general, **AB** ≠ **BA**, and one of these products may exist while the other does not.

(**AB**)′ = **B′A′**. The transpose of a product is the product of the separately transposed matrices in the reverse order.

We shall now see how these rules are used as we work through several examples, first numeric examples and then algebraic ones.

2

If possible form **AB** and **BA** where $\mathbf{A} = \begin{bmatrix} 6 & 0 & -2 \\ -1 & 8 & 7 \end{bmatrix}$ and $\mathbf{B} = \begin{bmatrix} 3 & 0 \\ 5 & 1 \\ 4 & 9 \end{bmatrix}$

We check first whether the matrices are conformable for post-multiplying **A** by **B**. Writing the dimensions below the matrices we have $\underset{(2\times3)\,(3\times2)}{\mathbf{A}\quad\mathbf{B}}$. Since the inner numbers of the dimensions are the same we can form **AB**. The outer numbers of the dimensions give the dimension of the product and show that **AB** will be square, of order 2.

For the top left element of **AB** we take the first row of **A** which is [6 0 −2]

and the first column of **B** which is $\begin{bmatrix} 3 \\ 5 \\ 4 \end{bmatrix}$. Multiplying corresponding pairs of values

and summing the results gives

$$(6 \times 3) + (0 \times 5) + (-2 \times 4) = 18 + 0 - 8 = 10$$

Moving along the first row, we form the second entry using the first row of **A** with the second column of **B**. Multiplying corresponding values and adding we obtain

$$(6 \times 0) + (0 \times 1) + (-2 \times 9) = 0 + 0 - 18 = -18$$

The second row of the product uses the second row of **A**. For the first entry in the row this is combined with the first column of **B**, giving

$$(-1 \times 3) + (8 \times 5) + (7 \times 4) = -3 + 40 + 28 = 65$$

The final entry is found taking the second row of **A** with the second column of **B** so that we have

$$(-1 \times 0) + (8 \times 1) + (7 \times 9) = 0 + 8 + 63 = 71$$

Now that we have calculated all the elements we write the product

$$\mathbf{AB} = \begin{bmatrix} 10 & -18 \\ 65 & 71 \end{bmatrix}$$

We now consider $\underset{(3\times2)}{\mathbf{B}}\ \underset{(2\times3)}{\mathbf{A}} = \begin{bmatrix} 3 & 0 \\ 5 & 1 \\ 4 & 9 \end{bmatrix} \begin{bmatrix} 6 & 0 & -2 \\ -1 & 8 & 7 \end{bmatrix}$. This is conformable for multiplication and gives the product matrix $\underset{(3\times3)}{\mathbf{BA}}$.

To find the element in the first row and first column of **BA** we take the first row of **B** which is $[3 \quad 0]$ and the first column of **A** which is $\begin{bmatrix} 6 \\ -1 \end{bmatrix}$. Multiplying corresponding pairs of values and summing the results gives

$$(3 \times 6) + (0 \times -1) = 18 + 0 = 18$$

For the second entry in the first row we use the first row of **B** with the second column of **A** and obtain

$$(3 \times 0) + (0 \times 8) = 0 + 0 = 0$$

The last element in the first row is formed from the first row of **B** and the third column of **A** giving

$$(3 \times -2) + (0 \times 7) = -6 + 0 = -6$$

For entries in the second row we use the second row of **B** with each column of **A** in turn. This gives

$$(5 \times 6) + (1 \times -1) = 30 - 1 = 29 \text{ for the first entry}$$

$$(5 \times 0) + (1 \times 8) = 0 + 8 = 8 \text{ for the second entry and}$$

$$(5 \times -2) + (1 \times 7) = -10 + 7 = -3 \text{ for the third entry in row two.}$$

For the third row we take the third row of **B** with each column of **A**. The elements are

$$(4 \times 6) + (9 \times -1) = 24 - 9 = 15 \text{ in the first column}$$

$$(4 \times 0) + (9 \times 8) = 0 + 72 = 72 \text{ in the second column and}$$

$(4 \times -2) + (9 \times 7) = -8 + 63 = 55$ as the final entry.

Now that we have calculated all nine elements we write the product

$$\mathbf{BA} = \begin{bmatrix} 18 & 0 & -6 \\ 29 & 8 & -3 \\ 15 & 72 & 55 \end{bmatrix}$$

Obviously the matrix products **AB** and **BA** are different from one another. Their dimensions and the values of their elements are different. This confirms that matrix multiplication is not commutative and we must be careful to write the matrices in the correct order to obtain the product we want.

In ordinary algebra we use symbols rather than numbers to allow us to study relationships. This approach is convenient also in matrix algebra. The next worked examples involve a column vector whose elements are specified as x_1, x_2 and x_3. We shall see that it is no more difficult to work with these symbols than with numbers. It just means that our results are given in terms of the x's, instead of in numerical values.

If possible, find $\mathbf{x'x}$ and $\mathbf{xx'}$ and say whether they are equal, given

$$\mathbf{x} = \begin{bmatrix} x_1 \\ x_2 \\ x_3 \end{bmatrix}$$

3

$\mathbf{x}$ is a column vector, so its transpose is a row vector, $\mathbf{x'} = [x_1 \quad x_2 \quad x_3]$. We check first to see if multiplication is possible by writing the dimensions of the vectors below the products we wish to form. This gives

$$\underset{(1\times3)(3\times1)}{\mathbf{x'x}} \quad \text{and} \quad \underset{(3\times1)(1\times3)}{\mathbf{xx'}}$$

The inner numbers match for both the proposed products so we can form them. We begin with

$$\underset{(1\times3)(3\times1)}{\mathbf{x'x}} = [x_1 \quad x_2 \quad x_3] \begin{bmatrix} x_1 \\ x_2 \\ x_3 \end{bmatrix}$$

The outer numbers of the dimensions give us (1×1) as the dimension of the product, so the result of this multiplication is in fact a single value, or scalar. We multiply the elements in the row of $\mathbf{x'}$ by the corresponding elements in the column of $\mathbf{x}$, and then add. Since the elements in the row and the column are the same, we form the sum of the squares of the x values

$$\underset{(1\times3)(3\times1)}{\mathbf{x'x}} = x_1^2 + x_2^2 + x_3^2$$

You may be accustomed to finding a sum of squares in statistics. We now have a way of representing a sum of squares using vector multiplication.

We proceed to form the product where **x** is post-multiplied by its transpose. We have

$$
\underset{(3\times1)(1\times3)}{\mathbf{xx'}} = \begin{bmatrix} x_1 \\ x_2 \\ x_3 \end{bmatrix} \begin{bmatrix} x_1 & x_2 & x_3 \end{bmatrix}
$$

The outer numbers of the dimensions show that this product will have dimension (3×3). The three rows in the vector **x** each contain just one element as do the three columns in **x'**. Taking the first row of **x**, x_1, and multiplying by the first column of **x'**, which is also x_1, we obtain x_1^2. The entry in the first row and second column is x_1x_2 (multiplying the first row of **x**, x_1, by the second column of **x'**, x_2). The third element in the first row is x_1x_3 (this time using the first row of **x** with the third column of **x'**). Notice that there is no addition when we multiply a row by a column in this case because just one pair of elements is multiplied together. The other two rows are formed in a similar way, giving

$$
\underset{(3\times1)(1\times3)}{\mathbf{xx'}} = \begin{bmatrix} x_1^2 & x_1x_2 & x_1x_3 \\ x_2x_1 & x_2^2 & x_2x_3 \\ x_3x_1 & x_3x_2 & x_3^2 \end{bmatrix}
$$

Notice that this product is quite different from **x'x**, which was the sum of the squares of x. By contrast **xx'** is a (3×3) matrix with the squares of the x's on the principal diagonal and cross products of the x's elsewhere. Since x_1, x_2 and x_3 are values, not vectors, the commutative property of multiplication does apply to their products and hence $x_1x_2 = x_2x_1$, $x_1x_3 = x_3x_1$ and $x_2x_3 = x_3x_2$. Substituting the second of these pairs by the first in each case gives

$$
\underset{(3\times1)(1\times3)}{\mathbf{xx'}} = \begin{bmatrix} x_1^2 & x_1x_2 & x_1x_3 \\ x_1x_2 & x_2^2 & x_2x_3 \\ x_1x_3 & x_2x_3 & x_3^2 \end{bmatrix}
$$

We can now see that **xx'** is a symmetric matrix. The elements below the principal diagonal are the mirror image of those above.

We have learned how to multiply matrices but have not mentioned the reverse operation, which in ordinary algebra would be division. We cannot divide one matrix by another, but there is a corresponding matrix operation as we shall see in section 12.7. The key to this is the idea that in ordinary arithmetic when something is divided by itself the answer is 1. We now define the identity matrix that plays a similar role in matrix algebra to the number 1 in arithmetic. The identity matrix, denoted **I**, is a square matrix that has 1's in the principal diagonal and 0's elsewhere. When we multiply by **I** we choose it to be of an order that is conformable to the matrix that it is to multiply. Multiplying by **I** leaves whatever was being multiplied unchanged, just as multiplying by 1 does in arithmetic. A matrix is unchanged either if it is pre-multiplied by **I** or if it is post-multiplied by **I**. We now do a worked example to illustrate this.

identity matrix: a square matrix with 1's in the principal diagonal and 0's elsewhere.

Form the products **AI** and **IA** where $\mathbf{A} = \begin{bmatrix} a & b & c \\ d & e & f \end{bmatrix}$

4

To post-multiply **A** by **I** we choose an identity matrix of order 3 and write

$$\underset{(2\times3)(3\times3)}{\mathbf{AI}} = \begin{bmatrix} a & b & c \\ d & e & f \end{bmatrix}\begin{bmatrix} 1 & 0 & 0 \\ 0 & 1 & 0 \\ 0 & 0 & 1 \end{bmatrix}$$

The matrix product is of dimension (2×3). Multiplying rows of **A** by columns of **I** and adding we obtain in the first row:

$$(a \times 1) + (b \times 0) + (c \times 0) = a \text{ (first column)}$$
$$(a \times 0) + (b \times 1) + (c \times 0) = b \text{ (second column)}$$
$$(a \times 0) + (b \times 0) + (c \times 1) = c \text{ (third column)}$$

and in the second row:

$$(d \times 1) + (e \times 0) + (f \times 0) = d \text{ (first column)}$$
$$(d \times 0) + (e \times 1) + (f \times 0) = e \text{ (second column)}$$
$$(d \times 0) + (e \times 0) + (f \times 1) = f \text{ (third column)}$$

The product matrix is therefore

$$\mathbf{AI} = \begin{bmatrix} a & b & c \\ d & e & f \end{bmatrix} = \mathbf{A}$$

and so **A** is unchanged when it is post-multiplied by an identity matrix.
To find **IA** we choose an identity matrix of order 2 and write

$$\underset{(2\times2)(2\times3)}{\mathbf{IA}} = \begin{bmatrix} 1 & 0 \\ 0 & 1 \end{bmatrix}\begin{bmatrix} a & b & c \\ d & e & f \end{bmatrix}$$

The matrix product has dimension (2×3) and again the zeros in the identity matrix ensure that there is only one non-zero term in those we sum for each entry. The elements for row 1 are:

$$(1 \times a) + (0 \times d) = a \text{ (column 1)}$$
$$(1 \times b) + (0 \times e) = b \text{ (column 2) and}$$
$$(1 \times c) + (0 \times f) = c \text{ (column 3)}$$

Similarly, in the second row we have:

$$(0 \times a) + (1 \times d) = d \text{ (first column)}$$
$$(0 \times b) + (1 \times e) = e \text{ (second column) and}$$
$$(0 \times c) + (1 \times f) = f \text{ (third column)}$$

Writing the entries in the appropriate positions in the product matrix gives

$$\mathbf{IA} = \begin{bmatrix} a & b & c \\ d & e & f \end{bmatrix} = \mathbf{A}$$

This demonstrates that **A** is also unchanged when it is pre-multiplied by an identity matrix.

Understanding when and how matrices can be multiplied is one of the cornerstones in using matrices to handle systems of equations. If, however, you simply have numerical matrices that you wish to multiply together, there is a function to do this in Excel that provides the answer instantaneously. The method of using it is described in section 12.9.

12.3 If k is a scalar, find **3a**, **kB** and **Ck** for the matrices

$$\mathbf{a} = [5 \quad 0], \mathbf{B} = \begin{bmatrix} 3 & 2 \\ 1 & 7 \end{bmatrix}, \mathbf{C} = \begin{bmatrix} 4 & 0 \\ 9 & 6 \end{bmatrix}$$

12.4 For matrices **a**, **B** and **C** in question 12.3, find

(i) **B + C**, **a(B + C)**, **aB**, **aC** and hence show **a(B + C) = aB + aC**

(ii) **BC**, **a(BC)**, **(aB)C** and hence show **a(BC) = (aB)C**

12.5 If k is a scalar, find **5A**, **kB** and **7x** for the matrices

$$\mathbf{A} = \begin{bmatrix} 1 & 3 \\ -2 & 4 \end{bmatrix}, \mathbf{B} = \begin{bmatrix} 5 & 0 & -1 \\ -6 & 7 & 8 \end{bmatrix}, \mathbf{x} = \begin{bmatrix} 9 \\ 5 \end{bmatrix}$$

12.6 For matrices **A**, **B** and **x** in question 12.5, find, where possible, **AB**, **BA**, **Bx** and **B'x**.

12.7 For matrices **A** and **x** in question 12.5, find $(\mathbf{Ax})'$ and $\mathbf{x'A'}$ and show that they are equal.

12.8 If $\mathbf{u} = \begin{bmatrix} u_1 \\ u_2 \end{bmatrix}$ find matrix expressions for $\mathbf{u'u}$ and $\mathbf{uu'}$. Find their numerical values if $\mathbf{u} = \begin{bmatrix} 3 \\ 5 \end{bmatrix}$.

12.9 For vectors **x**, **y** and **1** find matrix expressions for $\mathbf{x'1}$, $\mathbf{y'1}$, $\mathbf{x'y}$ and $\mathbf{y'x}$.

$$\mathbf{x} = \begin{bmatrix} x_1 \\ x_2 \\ x_3 \end{bmatrix}, \mathbf{y} = \begin{bmatrix} y_1 \\ y_2 \\ y_3 \end{bmatrix} \text{ and } \mathbf{1} = \begin{bmatrix} 1 \\ 1 \\ 1 \end{bmatrix}$$

Find the numerical value of the expressions if $\mathbf{x} = \begin{bmatrix} 2 \\ -1 \\ 3 \end{bmatrix}$, $\mathbf{y} = \begin{bmatrix} -2 \\ 5 \\ 4 \end{bmatrix}$

12.10 Find $\mathbf{X'y}$ for $\mathbf{X} = \begin{bmatrix} 1 & x_1 \\ 1 & x_2 \\ 1 & x_3 \end{bmatrix}$, $\mathbf{y} = \begin{bmatrix} y_1 \\ y_2 \\ y_3 \end{bmatrix}$

12.11 Show that $\mathbf{AI} = \mathbf{IA} = \mathbf{A}$ for $\mathbf{A} = \begin{bmatrix} 8 & 12 & 0 & 5 \\ -2 & 3 & 7 & 14 \end{bmatrix}$

12.12 If $\mathbf{X} = \begin{bmatrix} x_{11} & x_{12} \\ x_{21} & x_{22} \\ x_{31} & x_{32} \end{bmatrix}$ show that $\mathbf{X'X}$ is a square symmetric matrix.

SECTION 12.5: Handling Equation Systems

Economic models can involve large numbers of variables. If the relationships between the variables are linear (that is, the variables in the equations are not raised to powers such as 2 or 3) the model may be set out in a system of linear equations. We shall now see how such a system of linear equations can be written in matrix form. The advantage of doing this is that we can manipulate a matrix equation in accordance with the rules of matrix algebra. This allows us to find the solution to the set of equations (if it exists) and also to derive results in econometric modelling.

Simple systems of linear equations are solved as simultaneous equations in sections 2.11 and 2.12.

Each equation in a linear system can be written with a linear combination of the unknown variables on the left-hand side and a constant on the right. For example, the three variables x, y and z appear in the left-hand sides of the equations below

$$5x \quad -2y \quad +2z \quad = \quad 25$$
$$3x \quad +6y \quad -1z \quad = \quad 39$$
$$8x \qquad \quad +z \quad = \quad 36$$

These equations can be represented in matrix form if we write the coefficients of the variables in one matrix, $\mathbf{A}$, the variables in a column vector, $\mathbf{x}$, and the constants on the right-hand side in a column vector, $\mathbf{c}$. We have

$$\mathop{\mathbf{A}}_{(3\times3)} = \begin{bmatrix} 5 & -2 & 2 \\ 3 & 6 & -1 \\ 8 & 0 & 1 \end{bmatrix}, \; \mathop{\mathbf{x}}_{(3\times1)} = \begin{bmatrix} x \\ y \\ z \end{bmatrix} \text{ and } \mathbf{c} = \begin{bmatrix} 25 \\ 39 \\ 36 \end{bmatrix}$$

Forming the product $\mathop{\mathbf{Ax}}_{(3\times1)}$ gives a column vector that we can equate with vector $\mathbf{c}$ giving the matrix equation

$$\mathbf{Ax} = \mathbf{c}$$

On substituting into this we obtain

$$\begin{bmatrix} 5x - 2y + 2z \\ 3x + 6y - \quad z \\ 8x \qquad + \quad z \end{bmatrix} = \begin{bmatrix} 25 \\ 39 \\ 36 \end{bmatrix}$$

This is equivalent to the original set of three equations since the definition of matrix equality requires that the corresponding elements in the two vectors are equal. We have shown, therefore, that a system of equations can be written as a matrix equation.

CONDITIONS FOR A SOLUTION TO A SET OF EQUATIONS

We may wish to solve the above equations and find values for the three unknown variables, x, y and z. A system of the same number of equations as unknown variables is potentially soluble, since as we noted in section 2.11 a system of linear equations can usually be solved if the number of equations equals the number of unknowns.

The system cannot, however, be solved if one of the equations is simply a multiple of another equation, because then that equation does not add any new information. In a large set of equations, it may be that one equation is a linear combination of other equations as illustrated by the worked example below. If this is so, there is no unique solution to the equation system. For a solution to exist we must have the same number of linearly independent equations as there are unknown variables. We need, therefore, to check whether our equations are linearly independent. With the equations in matrix form this requirement can be stated as that there should be no linear relationship between the rows or between the columns of the coefficients matrix. If this is the case, the matrix is said to be non-singular, whereas a matrix that contains linearly dependent rows or columns is described as singular. In the next section we use the determinant of the coefficient matrix to discover whether or not the matrix is singular.

> linearly independent: the property that none of the equations are linear combinations of other equations.
>
> singular matrix: a matrix where one of the rows (or columns) is a linear combination of other rows (or columns).
>
> non-singular matrix: a matrix in which all the rows and columns are linearly independent.

Once we have checked that the matrix equation $\mathbf{Ax} = \mathbf{c}$ is soluble, we want to find an expression for vector $\mathbf{x}$ in terms of the other matrices. We cannot just divide through by $\mathbf{A}$ because the algebraic operation of division does not exist in matrix algebra. Instead we find what is called the inverse of $\mathbf{A}$ and use this to find the solution to the equations. We discover how to do this in section 12.7 below.

> For a solution, number of linearly independent equations = number of unknown variables. **Remember...**

5

As an example of a linear combination, find an equation that is twice the second equation minus the first for the equations

$$5x \quad -2y \quad +2z \quad = \quad 25 \quad \text{equation 1}$$
$$8x \qquad\qquad +z \quad = \quad 36 \quad \text{equation 2}$$

Multiplying equation 2 by 2 gives

$16x \qquad +2z = 72$ below which we write equation 1

$5x \quad -2y \quad +2z = 25$ and subtracting corresponding terms we get the result

$11x \quad +2y \qquad = 47$

This is a linear combination of equations 1 and 2. At the end of the next section you are asked to show that using it together with those equations will not allow us to find a unique solution for the values of x, y and z.

SUBSCRIPT IDENTIFIERS

Matrix equations are also used for econometric models. These models are estimated using statistical techniques which require there to be more equations than the number of unknowns being estimated. This kind of system of equations can also be written as a matrix equation. If there are n linear equations with right-hand side constants c_1, c_2, c_3, ..., c_n and the left-hand sides contain k unknowns x_1, x_2, x_3, ..., x_k we write the equation $\underset{(n\times k)}{\mathbf{A}} \underset{(k\times 1)}{\mathbf{x}} = \underset{(n\times 1)}{\mathbf{c}}$. Matrix **A**, which contains the coefficients, has n rows and k columns while the column vectors **x** and **c** have k and n rows respectively. Writing the elements of the matrices in the matrix equation gives

$$\begin{bmatrix} a_{11} & a_{12} & a_{13} & \cdots & a_{1k} \\ a_{21} & a_{22} & a_{23} & \cdots & a_{2k} \\ a_{31} & a_{32} & a_{33} & \cdots & a_{3k} \\ \cdots & \cdots & \cdots & \cdots & \cdots \\ a_{n1} & a_{n2} & a_{n3} & \cdots & a_{nk} \end{bmatrix} \begin{bmatrix} x_1 \\ x_2 \\ x_3 \\ \cdots \\ x_k \end{bmatrix} = \begin{bmatrix} c_1 \\ c_2 \\ c_3 \\ \cdots \\ c_n \end{bmatrix}$$

The subscripts of the constants and the unknown x's show the rows of the vectors in which these elements are placed. Since **A** is a matrix, it takes two subscripts to indicate the position of each of its elements. For example, a_{32} is the element in the third row and the second column of **A**. The elements of **A** have the general form a_{ij} where the first subscript, denoted i, indicates the row and the second subscript, j, indicates the column in which the coefficient is placed. Since **A** has n rows and k columns, i takes the values 1, 2, 3, ..., n and j takes the values 1, 2, 3, ..., k. The use of two subscripts to identify the row and column of matrix elements is a useful general notation.

---

n equations in k unknowns are written in matrix notation   **Remember...**
as

$$\mathbf{Ax} = \mathbf{c}$$

where **A** is a n × k matrix of coefficients, **x** is a k × 1 vector of unknown variables and **c** is a n × 1 vector of constants.

Once we have written a system of equations in the form $\mathbf{Ax} = \mathbf{c}$ we may manipulate it in accordance with the rules of matrices. Economists demonstrate the properties of the linear regression model used in econometrics by expressing it in matrix form.

12.13 Write the equations in matrix form

$$5x + 2y = 75$$

$$7x - y = 48$$

12.14 Data values y_1, y_2, y_3 are related to data values x_{1j}, x_{2j}, x_{3j} for each of the two x variables x_j ($j = 1, 2$) by the linear model $\mathbf{y} = \mathbf{Xb}$

where $\mathbf{y} = \begin{bmatrix} y_1 \\ y_2 \\ y_3 \end{bmatrix}$, $\mathbf{X} = \begin{bmatrix} 1 & x_{12} & x_{13} \\ 1 & x_{22} & x_{23} \\ 1 & x_{32} & x_{33} \end{bmatrix}$ and $\mathbf{b} = \begin{bmatrix} b_1 \\ b_2 \\ b_3 \end{bmatrix}$

Write the set of equations that the matrix equation $\mathbf{y} = \mathbf{Xb}$ represents.

12.15 Write the set of equations in matrix form

$$2x + 9y - 6z = -1$$

$$4y + 5z = 52$$

$$7x - 10y + 3z = 64$$

SECTION 12.6: Determinants

A determinant is a number, or scalar, associated with a square matrix. It is found by combining the elements of the array according to certain rules. The determinant of matrix $\mathbf{A}$ is denoted $|\mathbf{A}|$. It can be used to check whether the matrix is singular and to find its inverse.

Remember...

If $\mathbf{A}$ is the 2×2 matrix $\mathbf{A} = \begin{bmatrix} a & b \\ c & d \end{bmatrix}$ its determinant is

$$|\mathbf{A}| = \begin{vmatrix} a & b \\ c & d \end{vmatrix} = ad - bc$$

We shall practise finding determinants for 2×2 matrices by doing some numerical examples.

6

Evaluate $|\mathbf{A}| = \begin{vmatrix} 7 & 2 \\ 4 & 3 \end{vmatrix}$, $|\mathbf{B}| = \begin{vmatrix} 5 & -2 \\ 1 & 9 \end{vmatrix}$, $|\mathbf{C}| = \begin{vmatrix} 6 & 3 \\ -1 & 0 \end{vmatrix}$, $|\mathbf{D}| = \begin{vmatrix} 8 & 4 \\ 2 & 1 \end{vmatrix}$

Applying the rule $\begin{vmatrix} a & b \\ c & d \end{vmatrix} = ad - bc$ we multiply the pairs of values on the diagonals and subtract. This gives:

$$|\mathbf{A}| = 7 \times 3 - 2 \times 4 = 21 - 8 = 13$$
$$|\mathbf{B}| = 5 \times 9 - (-2 \times 1) = 45 - (-2) = 45 + 2 = 47$$
$$|\mathbf{C}| = 6 \times 0 - 3 \times (-1) = 0 - (-3) = 3$$
$$|\mathbf{D}| = 8 \times 1 - 4 \times 2 = 8 - 8 = 0$$

We noted in section 12.5 that if there is a linear relationship between the equations we wish to solve, the system of equations will not have a unique solution. Evidence for such a relationship is the existence of a linear relationship either between some of the rows or between some of the columns of matrix $\mathbf{A}$ in the matrix representation $\mathbf{Ax = c}$. If such a linear relationship exists, matrix $\mathbf{A}$ is said to be singular. It happens that a singular matrix has a determinant of zero. Evaluation of the determinant of a matrix therefore gives us a method of checking whether the matrix is singular. In the worked example above, matrix $\mathbf{D}$ has a determinant of 0. Looking at matrix $\mathbf{D}$ we see that the elements in the first row are four times those in the second row. There is therefore a linear relationship between the rows of matrix $\mathbf{D}$, as the zero value of the determinant indicates. Alternatively we can look for a linear relationship between the columns of $\mathbf{D}$ which reveals that the values in the first column are double those in the second.

DETERMINANT OF A 3 × 3 MATRIX

The rules for evaluating the determinant of a square matrix of order 3 are a little more complex. We first need the concept of a cofactor, which we will explain with reference to matrix $\mathbf{A}$ where the elements are identified using the double subscript notation explained above.

$$\mathbf{A} = \begin{bmatrix} a_{11} & a_{12} & a_{13} \\ a_{21} & a_{22} & a_{23} \\ a_{31} & a_{32} & a_{33} \end{bmatrix}$$

Each of the nine elements, a_{ij}, of a 3 × 3 matrix has a cofactor that we denote C_{ij}. This cofactor is the determinant of a 2 × 2 matrix, together with either a + or − sign. To find the cofactor that corresponds to a particular element we eliminate the row and column that intersect at that element from the matrix. For example, to find the cofactor for a_{21} we eliminate the second row and first column.

$$\begin{bmatrix} a_{11} & a_{12} & a_{13} \\ a_{21} & a_{22} & a_{23} \\ a_{31} & a_{32} & a_{33} \end{bmatrix}$$

This leaves 4 elements forming a 2 × 2 matrix. The cofactor we require is the determinant of this matrix, preceded by the sign that corresponds to the element's position, as shown by the matrix of signs below. Notice that the signs of the cofactors alternate in adjacent positions, beginning with a + sign in the top left of the matrix. You can also find the sign by adding the row and column numbers. If the result is an even number the sign is positive but if it is an odd number, the sign is negative.

$$\begin{bmatrix} + & - & + \\ - & + & - \\ + & - & + \end{bmatrix}$$

To find cofactor C_{21}, then, we find from its position in the matrix or by adding the row and column numbers $(2 + 1 = 3$, which is odd) that it needs a minus sign. The elements in its determinant are those that remain from matrix **A** after the second row and first column are eliminated and so

$$C_{21} = - \begin{vmatrix} a_{12} & a_{13} \\ a_{32} & a_{33} \end{vmatrix}$$

All nine cofactors can be formed in a similar way. Not all of them are needed to find the determinant, but they are all needed when in section 12.7 we find the inverse of a matrix.

For a 3 × 3 matrix, the cofactor of a_{ij} is the determinant of the 2 × 2 matrix that remains when row i and column j are deleted, together with the appropriate sign.
   The sign is + if $(i + j)$ is an even number, and − if $(i + j)$ is an odd number.

Remember...

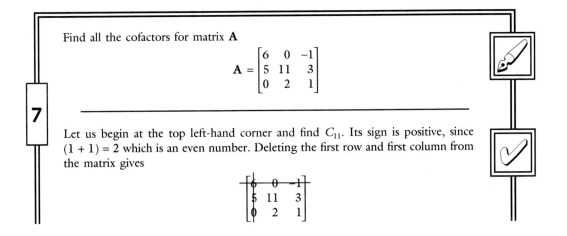

Find all the cofactors for matrix **A**

$$A = \begin{bmatrix} 6 & 0 & -1 \\ 5 & 11 & 3 \\ 0 & 2 & 1 \end{bmatrix}$$

7

Let us begin at the top left-hand corner and find C_{11}. Its sign is positive, since $(1 + 1) = 2$ which is an even number. Deleting the first row and first column from the matrix gives

$$\begin{bmatrix} 6 & 0 & -1 \\ 5 & 11 & 3 \\ 0 & 2 & 1 \end{bmatrix}$$

Taking the determinant of the remaining entries and writing the sign at the front we find

$$C_{11} = + \begin{vmatrix} 11 & 3 \\ 2 & 1 \end{vmatrix} = 11 \times 1 - 3 \times 2 = 5$$

Moving to the second element in the first row, the cofactor C_{12} has a negative sign since $(1 + 2) = 3$ which is an odd number. We delete the first row and second column from matrix **A** and form the determinant of the remaining elements, giving

$$C_{12} = - \begin{vmatrix} 5 & 3 \\ 0 & 1 \end{vmatrix} = -(5 \times 1 - 3 \times 0) = -5$$

Notice that you have to be especially careful with signs when evaluating cofactors. When a minus sign precedes the determinant, use brackets as you evaluate the determinant to ensure that you calculate the result correctly.

Working systematically through the remaining elements of the matrix we can obtain the signs of the cofactors by knowing that they alternate. Writing the appropriate determinant in each case gives the values

$$C_{13} = + \begin{vmatrix} 5 & 11 \\ 0 & 2 \end{vmatrix} = 5 \times 2 - 11 \times 0 = 10$$

$$C_{21} = - \begin{vmatrix} 0 & -1 \\ 2 & 1 \end{vmatrix} = -(0 \times 1 - (-1 \times 2)) = -2$$

$$C_{22} = + \begin{vmatrix} 6 & -1 \\ 0 & 1 \end{vmatrix} = 6 \times 1 - (-1 \times 0) = 6$$

$$C_{23} = - \begin{vmatrix} 6 & 0 \\ 0 & 2 \end{vmatrix} = -(6 \times 2 - 0 \times 0) = -12$$

$$C_{31} = + \begin{vmatrix} 0 & -1 \\ 11 & 3 \end{vmatrix} = 0 \times 3 - (-1 \times 11) = 11$$

$$C_{32} = - \begin{vmatrix} 6 & -1 \\ 5 & 3 \end{vmatrix} = -(6 \times 3 - (-1 \times 5)) = -23$$

$$C_{33} = + \begin{vmatrix} 6 & 0 \\ 5 & 11 \end{vmatrix} = 6 \times 11 - 0 \times 5 = 66$$

Now that we have calculated the cofactors of **A** we are in a position to evaluate its determinant. This will show us whether matrix **A** is singular. We use the rule:

To find the determinant of A: **Remember...**

Choose any row or column of **A**. Multiply each element in that row by its cofactor, and add these products.
    If $|\mathbf{A}| = 0$, matrix **A** is singular.

Find the determinant

$$|A| = \begin{vmatrix} 6 & 0 & -1 \\ 5 & 11 & 3 \\ 0 & 2 & 1 \end{vmatrix}$$

8

Let us evaluate $|A|$ using its first row. This process, also known as expanding the determinant, gives $|A| = a_{11}C_{11} + a_{12}C_{12} + a_{13}C_{13} = 6 \times 5 + 0 \times (-5) + (-1) \times 10 = 20$ substituting the values from the first row of A and the corresponding cofactors calculated above. If you would like to check that this calculation is correct you can evaluate $|A|$ again expanding it by a different row or column. Where possible, you may like to choose to expand a determinant using a row or column that contains a 0 since this reduces the work involved. You can see this in the expansion by the first row that we completed where a_{12} is zero. This implies that the second term in the expansion of the determinant is 0, regardless of the value of the cofactor. We therefore did not actually need to know the value of the cofactor C_{12} to be able to find the value of the determinant.

We have noted that a determinant of zero indicates a singular matrix that can prevent you from finding a solution to a set of equations. However, you should also be aware that if you use the wrong cofactors to expand the matrix, you get a zero value. For example, if you decide to expand by the first row but inadvertently use the cofactors for the second row you calculate $a_{11}C_{21} + a_{12}C_{22} + a_{13}C_{23}$ and it can be shown that this expression equals zero. In evaluating determinants care is needed both to get the correct signs for the cofactors and to use the correct set of cofactors for the expansion.

You may like to know that Excel includes a function for calculating determinants that carries out the whole process for you. This is described in section 12.9.

 Find the determinants

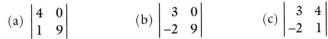

(a) $\begin{vmatrix} 4 & 0 \\ 1 & 9 \end{vmatrix}$ (b) $\begin{vmatrix} 3 & 0 \\ -2 & 9 \end{vmatrix}$ (c) $\begin{vmatrix} 3 & 4 \\ -2 & 1 \end{vmatrix}$

(d) $\begin{vmatrix} 1 & 5 \\ 1 & 9 \end{vmatrix}$ (e) $\begin{vmatrix} 2 & 5 \\ -2 & 9 \end{vmatrix}$ (f) $\begin{vmatrix} 2 & 1 \\ -2 & 1 \end{vmatrix}$

(g) $\begin{vmatrix} 1 & 5 \\ 4 & 0 \end{vmatrix}$ (h) $\begin{vmatrix} 2 & 5 \\ 3 & 0 \end{vmatrix}$ (i) $\begin{vmatrix} 2 & 1 \\ 3 & 4 \end{vmatrix}$

12.17 Find the determinants of matrices **A**, **B** and **C** (you may find you have already done some of the calculations you need in 12.16). Are any of the matrices singular?

(a) $\mathbf{A} = \begin{bmatrix} 2 & 1 & 5 \\ 3 & 4 & 0 \\ -2 & 1 & 9 \end{bmatrix}$

(b) $\mathbf{B} = \begin{bmatrix} 2 & 7 & 5 \\ 1 & 4 & 3 \\ 7 & 5 & -2 \end{bmatrix}$

(c) $\mathbf{C} = \begin{bmatrix} 1 & 9 & -1 \\ 0 & 6 & -2 \\ 3 & 0 & 7 \end{bmatrix}$

12.18 Show that it is not possible to find a solution to the equations

$$\begin{array}{rrrcr} 5x & -2y & +2z & = & 25 \\ 8x & & +z & = & 36 \\ 11x & +2y & & = & 47 \end{array}$$

SECTION 12.7: Matrix Inversion

In section 12.5 we wrote a system of equations in the matrix form $\mathbf{Ax} = \mathbf{c}$ and noted that if we could find an expression for **x** it would comprise a solution to the set of equations. We cannot divide by **A**, because the algebraic operation of division does not exist in matrix algebra. Instead, we may be able to find a matrix to pre-multiply both sides of the equation by that will help us. The matrix we require is called the inverse of **A** and denoted $\mathbf{A}^{-1}$. It has the property that when we pre-multiply **A** by it, forming $\mathbf{A}^{-1}\mathbf{A}$ we obtain the identity matrix, **I**. Pre-multiplying both sides of our matrix equation by $\mathbf{A}^{-1}$ gives $\mathbf{A}^{-1}\mathbf{Ax} = \mathbf{A}^{-1}\mathbf{c}$ and so $\mathbf{Ix} = \mathbf{A}^{-1}\mathbf{c}$ from which the expression for **x** is $\mathbf{x} = \mathbf{A}^{-1}\mathbf{c}$. Not every matrix has an inverse. Matrices that do are square and non-singular. We begin by setting out the rules for inverting a 2 × 2 matrix. We shall then check that the matrix we obtain by using them is the inverse we require. We noted above the property of an inverse that $\mathbf{A}^{-1}\mathbf{A} = \mathbf{I}$. It is also true that $\mathbf{AA}^{-1} = \mathbf{I}$, so once we have calculated an inverse we can check that it is correct by either post-multiplying or pre-multiplying it by the original matrix to see whether we obtain an identity matrix.

To have an inverse $\mathbf{A}^{-1}$, matrix $\mathbf{A}$ must be square and non-singular

The inverse has the property $\mathbf{A}^{-1}\mathbf{A} = \mathbf{A}\mathbf{A}^{-1} = \mathbf{I}$

To invert the 2×2 matrix $\mathbf{A} = \begin{bmatrix} a & b \\ c & d \end{bmatrix}$

- interchange the elements on the principal diagonal
- change the signs of the other two terms

- multiply by the scalar $\dfrac{1}{|\mathbf{A}|}$.

Notice that the third of these steps involves dividing by the determinant of the matrix. This gives us a reason why we cannot find an inverse for a singular matrix, because we cannot divide by 0. Let us apply the above rules step by step to find an expression for $\mathbf{A}^{-1}$.

Interchanging the elements on the principal diagonal gives $\begin{bmatrix} d & b \\ c & a \end{bmatrix}$ and when we change the signs of the other two terms we have $\begin{bmatrix} d & -b \\ -c & a \end{bmatrix}$. Since $|\mathbf{A}|$ is $(ad - bc)$, we multiply by the scalar $1/(ad - bc)$. Hence we find

$$\mathbf{A}^{-1} = \frac{1}{|\mathbf{A}|}\begin{bmatrix} d & -b \\ -c & a \end{bmatrix} = \frac{1}{(ad-bc)}\begin{bmatrix} d & -b \\ -c & a \end{bmatrix} = \begin{bmatrix} \dfrac{d}{(ad-bc)} & \dfrac{-b}{(ad-bc)} \\ \dfrac{-c}{(ad-bc)} & \dfrac{a}{(ad-bc)} \end{bmatrix}$$

To check that this formula is correct we post-multiply $\mathbf{A}^{-1}$ by $\mathbf{A}$ and verify that the result is an identity matrix. The working is

$$\mathbf{A}^{-1}\mathbf{A} = \begin{bmatrix} \dfrac{d}{(ad-bc)} & \dfrac{-b}{(ad-bc)} \\ \dfrac{-c}{(ad-bc)} & \dfrac{a}{(ad-bc)} \end{bmatrix}\begin{bmatrix} a & b \\ c & d \end{bmatrix} = \begin{bmatrix} \dfrac{ad-bc}{(ad-bc)} & \dfrac{bd-bd}{(ad-bc)} \\ \dfrac{-ac+ac}{(ad-bc)} & \dfrac{-bc+ad}{(ad-bc)} \end{bmatrix} = \begin{bmatrix} 1 & 0 \\ 0 & 1 \end{bmatrix} = \mathbf{I}$$

which shows that $\mathbf{A}^{-1}$ is the matrix we require.

9

Find the inverse of matrix **A** and check that $A^{-1}A = I$ given

$$A = \begin{bmatrix} 7 & 9 \\ 2 & 4 \end{bmatrix}$$

You could substitute in the formula that we found above, but it is probably easier to just work through the steps with the numerical values. This gives:

$\begin{bmatrix} 4 & 9 \\ 2 & 7 \end{bmatrix}$ when we interchange the elements on the principal diagonal and

$\begin{bmatrix} 4 & -9 \\ -2 & 7 \end{bmatrix}$ when we change the signs of the other two terms

We now need $|A| = 7 \times 4 - 9 \times 2 = 28 - 18 = 10$. Using this we form

$$A^{-1} = \frac{1}{10}\begin{bmatrix} 4 & -9 \\ -2 & 7 \end{bmatrix} = \begin{bmatrix} 0.4 & -0.9 \\ -0.2 & 0.7 \end{bmatrix}$$

If we have found A^{-1} correctly, post-multiplying it by **A** will give us an identity matrix. Forming the product we have:

$$A^{-1}A = \begin{bmatrix} 0.4 & -0.9 \\ -0.2 & 0.7 \end{bmatrix}\begin{bmatrix} 7 & 9 \\ 2 & 4 \end{bmatrix} = \begin{bmatrix} (0.4 \times 7) + (-0.9 \times 2) & (0.4 \times 9) + (-0.9 \times 4) \\ (-0.2 \times 7) + (0.7 \times 2) & (-0.2 \times 9) + (0.7 \times 4) \end{bmatrix}$$

$$= \begin{bmatrix} 1 & 0 \\ 0 & 1 \end{bmatrix} = I$$

which shows that the inverse was correctly calculated.

INVERSE OF A 3 × 3 MATRIX

To find the inverse of a 3 × 3 matrix requires us first to calculate cofactors for all its elements as we did in section 12.6. We also need to evaluate the determinant of the matrix. These components are needed to construct the inverse, as set out in the following rules:

Remember...

To invert the 3 × 3 matrix $A = \begin{bmatrix} a_{11} & a_{12} & a_{13} \\ a_{21} & a_{22} & a_{23} \\ a_{31} & a_{32} & a_{33} \end{bmatrix}$

Calculate the cofactors of the elements, place them in a matrix

$$\begin{bmatrix} C_{11} & C_{12} & C_{13} \\ C_{21} & C_{22} & C_{23} \\ C_{31} & C_{32} & C_{33} \end{bmatrix}$$

and transpose this matrix to find the adjoint of **A**. We write

$$\mathrm{Adj}(\mathbf{A}) = \begin{bmatrix} C_{11} & C_{21} & C_{31} \\ C_{12} & C_{22} & C_{32} \\ C_{13} & C_{23} & C_{33} \end{bmatrix}$$

Calculate the determinant of matrix **A**, |**A**|, and multiply Adj(**A**) by its reciprocal to form the inverse.

$$\mathbf{A}^{-1} = \frac{1}{|\mathbf{A}|} \begin{bmatrix} C_{11} & C_{21} & C_{31} \\ C_{12} & C_{22} & C_{32} \\ C_{13} & C_{23} & C_{33} \end{bmatrix}$$

We shall see how this formula works using a numerical example.

Find the inverse of matrix **A**

$$\mathbf{A} = \begin{bmatrix} 6 & 0 & -1 \\ 5 & 11 & 3 \\ 0 & 2 & 1 \end{bmatrix}$$

10

We found all the cofactors of this matrix in a worked example in section 12.6. Placing them in a matrix of cofactors we have

$$\begin{bmatrix} 5 & -5 & 10 \\ -2 & 6 & -12 \\ 11 & -23 & 66 \end{bmatrix}$$

and transposing this we find

$$\mathrm{Adj}(\mathbf{A}) = \begin{bmatrix} 5 & -2 & 11 \\ -5 & 6 & -23 \\ 10 & -12 & 66 \end{bmatrix}$$

We found in section 12.6 that |**A**| = 20 and so

$$A^{-1} = \frac{1}{20}\begin{bmatrix} 5 & -2 & 11 \\ -5 & 6 & -23 \\ 10 & -12 & 66 \end{bmatrix} = \begin{bmatrix} 0.25 & -0.1 & 0.55 \\ -0.25 & 0.3 & -1.15 \\ 0.5 & -0.6 & 3.3 \end{bmatrix}$$

By now it is probably apparent that finding the inverse of $\mathbf{A}$, $\mathbf{A}^{-1}$, can be quite laborious if the order of $\mathbf{A}$ is large. You may be pleased to learn that Excel includes an array function that only requires you to tell it the matrix of numbers for which you want the inverse and the result is immediately displayed. More information about this is provided in section 12.9.

12.19 For each of the following matrices, find its inverse, pre- or post-multiply the matrix by its inverse and check that you obtain an identity matrix

(a) $\mathbf{A} = \begin{bmatrix} 5 & 4 \\ 7 & 6 \end{bmatrix}$ (b) $\mathbf{B} = \begin{bmatrix} 8 & 11 \\ 2 & 4 \end{bmatrix}$ (c) $\mathbf{C} = \begin{bmatrix} 4 & -3 \\ 10 & 5 \end{bmatrix}$

12.20 Find the inverse of each matrix. (You may find you have already done some of the calculations you need in 12.17).

(a) $\mathbf{A} = \begin{bmatrix} 2 & 1 & 5 \\ 3 & 4 & 0 \\ -2 & 1 & 9 \end{bmatrix}$

(b) $\mathbf{B} = \begin{bmatrix} 1 & 9 & -1 \\ 0 & 6 & -2 \\ 3 & 0 & 7 \end{bmatrix}$

SECTION 12.8: Systems of Equations in Economics

Now that we can find the inverse of a matrix, we have a means of solving a set of n equations in n unknowns represented by $\underset{(n \times n)}{\mathbf{A}} \underset{(n \times 1)}{\mathbf{x}} = \underset{(n \times 1)}{\mathbf{c}}$. Given that $\mathbf{A}$ is a square matrix and providing it is not singular we can find the inverse of $\mathbf{A}$, $\mathbf{A}^{-1}$, and use it to pre-multiply both sides of the equation. This gives us $\mathbf{A}^{-1}\mathbf{A}\mathbf{x} = \mathbf{A}^{-1}\mathbf{c}$, from which, since $\mathbf{A}^{-1}\mathbf{A} = \mathbf{I}$ and $\mathbf{I}\mathbf{x} = \mathbf{x}$, we obtain the expression for the vector of unknowns $\mathbf{x} = \mathbf{A}^{-1}\mathbf{c}$.

We shall do an example to see how the method works.

11

By writing them in matrix form, solve the equations

$$7x + 6y = 53$$
$$-2x + 4y = 2$$

To write these in the general matrix form $\mathbf{Ax} = \mathbf{c}$ we define $\underset{(2\times2)}{\mathbf{A}} = \begin{bmatrix} 7 & 6 \\ -2 & 4 \end{bmatrix}$,

$\underset{(2\times1)}{\mathbf{x}} = \begin{bmatrix} x \\ y \end{bmatrix}$ and $\mathbf{c} = \begin{bmatrix} 53 \\ 2 \end{bmatrix}$. To find the inverse of $\mathbf{A}$ we first find its determinant.

$|\mathbf{A}| = 28 - (-12) = 40$ and so

$$\mathbf{A}^{-1} = \frac{1}{40}\begin{bmatrix} 4 & -6 \\ 2 & 7 \end{bmatrix} = \begin{bmatrix} 0.1 & -0.15 \\ 0.05 & 0.175 \end{bmatrix}.$$ We then pre-multiply $\mathbf{c}$ by $\mathbf{A}^{-1}$ to obtain

$$\mathbf{A}^{-1}\mathbf{c} = \begin{bmatrix} 0.1 & -0.15 \\ 0.05 & 0.175 \end{bmatrix}\begin{bmatrix} 53 \\ 2 \end{bmatrix} = \begin{bmatrix} 5 \\ 3 \end{bmatrix}$$ and setting $\mathbf{x}$ equal to this we have

$\begin{bmatrix} x \\ y \end{bmatrix} = \begin{bmatrix} 5 \\ 3 \end{bmatrix}$ which is the solution to the equations.

It is useful to understand the process of using pre-multiplication by an inverse to solve a system of equations because this will help you to study econometric models and make appropriate use of them. If your purpose, however, is to obtain a numerical solution to an equation system there are better approaches. Methods of matrix algebra have been devised to shorten the hand solution process for a set of equations. We do not study them here, because computer package programs now provide a more efficient approach. We use Excel Solver to solve a system of equations, as explained in sections 2.15 and 12.9.

12.21

By writing them in matrix form, solve the equations

$$15x + 3y = 51$$
$$7x + y = 21$$

12.22

In the ordinary least squares model used in econometrics the 'normal' equations are represented by

$$\mathbf{X}'\mathbf{Xb} = \mathbf{X}'\mathbf{y}$$

where $\underset{(n\times k)}{\mathbf{X}}$ is a matrix of observations on the independent variables, $\underset{(n\times1)}{\mathbf{y}}$ is a vector of observations on the dependent variable and $\underset{(k\times1)}{\mathbf{b}}$ is a vector of unknown parameters that are to be estimated. Find an expression for $\mathbf{b}$.

12.23 By writing them in matrix form, solve the equations

$$
\begin{aligned}
5x &\;-2y\; +2z = 25 \\
3x &\;+6y\; -1z = 39 \\
8x &\qquad\;\; + z = 36
\end{aligned}
$$

SECTION 12.9: Matrix Operations in Excel

A spreadsheet is a very appropriate medium for handling matrix calculations. You set out each matrix in Excel just as you would write it on paper, putting each matrix element in a separate Excel cell. You can then perform matrix calculations, either entering formulae for yourself or using the in-built formulae that Excel provides. This section explains how to use the Excel formulae. These are particularly useful if you have to carry out computations involving large matrices, but they are demonstrated on problems that you can also solve by hand so you can use them for additional practise if you wish.

The Excel file Matrices.xls contains worked solutions to the problems described below.

TRANSPOSING A MATRIX

You can transpose a matrix in Excel by copying it and then using the 'Paste Special' facility. Before you start the procedure you need to consider whereabouts in the spreadsheet the transposed matrix is to be placed, remembering that unless the matrix is square the transposed matrix will have a different dimension to the original matrix.

To obtain the transpose of matrix **A** in figure 12.1, select the cells that contain the matrix and choose Edit, Copy from the menu. A moving border will appear round the copied cells. Now select a position for the transposed matrix. The best way of doing this is to just click on the cell that is to become the top left-hand corner of the transposed matrix. Choose 'Edit, Paste Special' to bring up the dialogue box shown in figure 12.2. Check the 'Transpose' box at the bottom right and click 'OK'. The transposed matrix appears in the position you chose.

This problem is included in the Transpose, Add, Subtract worksheet. The values in the cells for **A'** do not contain a formula but are just numbers. This is because they have been obtained as described using the 'Paste Special' facility.

MATRIX ADDITION AND SUBTRACTION

To add or subtract two matrices, **A** and **B**, in a spreadsheet you first need to choose an area of the same dimension as each of the matrices, such as that outlined in figure 12.1,

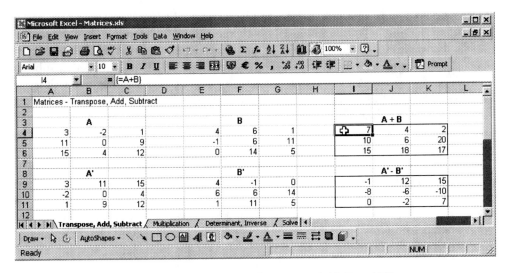

Figure 12.1 Matrices.xls shows **A** and **A′**, **B** and **B′**

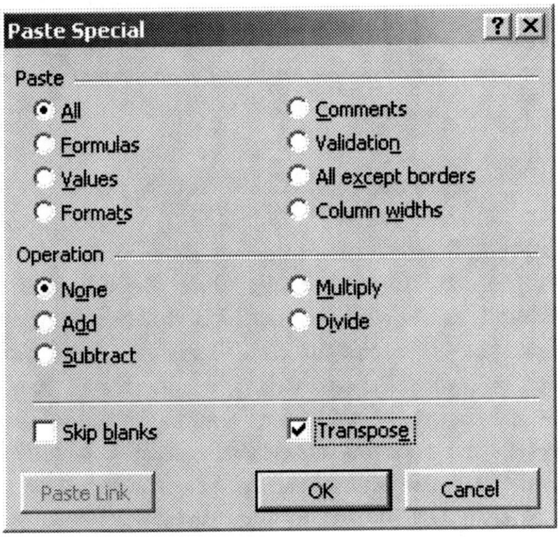

Figure 12.2 Paste Special dialogue box

where the answer is to be displayed. You could then enter a formula in the top left-hand cell to add or subtract the corresponding elements of **A** and **B**. Copying the formula down and to the right would give the sum or difference of the matrices.

There is, however, another approach which uses an Excel array formula. With this method Excel recognizes that you want to add or subtract two matrices and completes the whole answer matrix simultaneously. To use this approach you first have to name the two blocks of cells in which matrices **A** and **B** are entered. Select the nine cells containing the values of matrix **A**, choose Insert, Name, Define from the menu, type A and click OK. Similarly select the cells with the values for matrix **B** and name that matrix. Now select the block of cells of the same dimension as **A** and **B** where you want the answer to appear. Type the formula =A+B (or =A–B if you want to subtract **B** from **A**). You enter this as an array formula by holding down Control and Shift and pressing Enter. The whole answer matrix is immediately completed for you, and if you look in Excel's formula bar you will see that Excel has put braces round the formula you typed, so it is shown as {=A+B}. This indicates that it is an array formula and applies to an array of cells, not just one single cell as a normal formula does.

As you name matrices, you need to be aware that there are certain restrictions on what can be used as an Excel name. Names can include letters, numbers, periods and underscore characters, but not apostrophes. You cannot, therefore, choose A′ as the name of a matrix in Excel, but you can call it AT instead. You will also find that you cannot choose C as an Excel name. This is because C is already reserved for another purpose. Again, you should choose a different name, for example, C_matrix.

An array formula is entered in Excel using Ctrl+Shift+Enter   **Remember...**

SCALAR MULTIPLICATION

To perform a scalar multiplication that multiplies all the cells in a matrix by a scalar you need to enter an appropriate Excel formula. Once the values of the matrix and the scalar have been entered, as shown in figure 12.3 you can name them using a similar approach to that described for matrix addition. Begin by selecting the cells that contain the matrix that is to be multiplied and define a name for it. A is already in use as a matrix name in this workbook, so we choose a different name, matA, for this matrix. We also name the cell that contains the scalar, calling it k. Now we choose a position for the result of the scalar multiplication. Select a rectangle of cells of the same size as the matrix, as indicated by the outlined rectangle. Type the formula =k*matA and press Ctrl+Shift+Enter to enter it as an array formula. Values appear in all the selected cells, giving the result of the scalar multiplication. The calculation is included in the Multiplication worksheet in Matrices.xls, and you can click on the cells to see the formula used.

MATRIX MULTIPLICATION

Excel has an in-built array function that multiplies matrices for you. Figure 12.3 shows matrices **A** and **B**, together with their product **AB** in the outlined cells. You are familiar

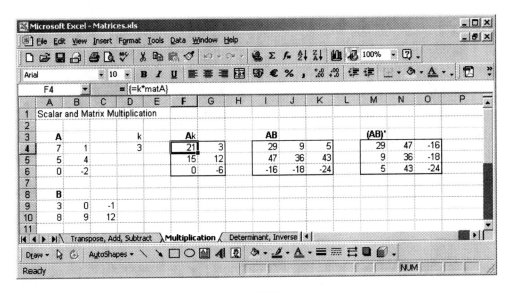

Figure 12.3 Multiplication sheet

with the idea that before you attempt to multiply two matrices you should check that they are conformable and find the dimension of the product matrix. You must still undertake these two steps for yourself when using Excel. The function warns you that the matrices must be conformable, but if you make a mistake it just gives you a #VALUE! error message. Knowing the dimension of the product matrix is essential to ensure the correct use of the Excel function because you must select a rectangle of cells to contain the product you are going to form. When you enter the array function the results are placed in the cells you selected, whether or not these have the correct dimension for the matrix product. If, for example, you select too few cells Excel will calculate the entries for the cells you have indicated and display them. It will not warn you that the answer it is giving you is actually only part of the matrix product.

To multiply **A** and **B** therefore, we check the dimensions. We see that the matrices are conformable and that $\underset{(3\times2)}{\mathbf{A}} \underset{(2\times3)}{\mathbf{B}}$ will have dimension 3×3. We select an array of cells with that dimension, such as the outlined rectangle in figure 12.3. Click the function button, choose function category Math and Trig, and function name MMULT to bring up the dialogue box shown in figure 12.4. Click on the boxes in turn and either type the name of the appropriate matrix or select its cells in the worksheet. Now press Ctrl+Shift+Enter to enter the matrix formula, and the result of the multiplication is displayed. The calculation is available for you in the Multiplication worksheet where the matrices are named matA and matB.

Now that you can let Excel do the hard work of the calculations for you, you may like to check that for the matrices in figure 12.3 $(\mathbf{AB})' = \mathbf{B}'\mathbf{A}'$. We have found **AB**, so

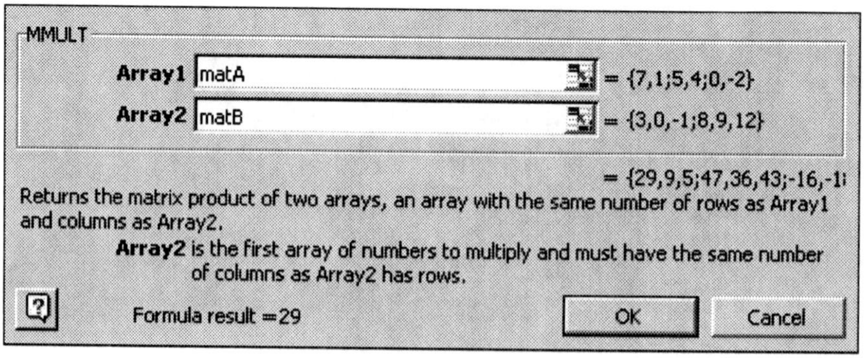

Figure 12.4   MMULT dialogue box

the next step is to transpose it. You already know that to transpose a matrix in Excel you copy it and then use the Edit, Paste Special facility. There is one additional thing to take account of when you transpose matrix **AB**, namely that the cells you are transposing contain a formula. Since Excel's formulae use references to cells in their calculations, attempting to transpose cells with the formulae in them will not give the correct result. The problem is easily solved, because when you display the Paste Special dialogue box shown in figure 12.2 you can select Paste Values in the left-hand column as well as selecting Transpose. This converts the formulae into values before transposing them and gives a transposed matrix that is comprised just of numbers. Once you have found (**AB**)′, try finding the matrices **A**′, **B**′, **A**′**B**′ and **B**′**A**′ for yourself. Check that (**AB**)′ = **B**′**A**′ and that **A**′**B**′ does not equal these matrices. All the calculations are in the Multiplication worksheet should you need them.

DETERMINANT AND INVERSE OF A MATRIX

Excel has in-built functions to find the determinant and inverse of a matrix for you. Figure 12.5 shows two square matrices **C** and **D** that are named matC and matD in the Determinant, Inverse worksheet. To find the determinant of a matrix, select the single cell where the result of the calculation is to be displayed. Click the function button, choose function category Math and Trig, and function name MDETERM to bring up the function dialogue box. Type the name of the matrix and click OK to enter the function.

The function used to find the inverse, MINVERSE, is an array function. You begin by selecting an array of cells of the same dimension as the matrix to be inverted, as outlined in figure 12.5. Click the function button, choose MINVERSE from the function name list and type the name of the matrix you want to invert. Since you are using an array function you now press Ctrl+Shift+Enter to obtain the inverse. Matrix inversion is no longer a laborious process when you have Excel to help you!

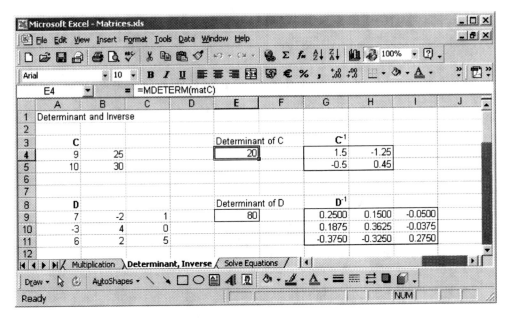

Figure 12.5

SOLVING AN EQUATION SYSTEM USING EXCEL SOLVER

Section 2.15 explains how to use Excel Solver to solve two simultaneous equations. You can solve a system of equations in the same way, using the Set Target Cell box for one of your equations and entering all the others as equality constraints. The worksheet Solve Equations in the file Matrices.xls has the equations in practice problem 12.23 set up ready for you to solve using Solver.

Chapter 12: Answers to Practice Problems

12.1 $2 \times 2, 4 \times 1, 2 \times 4, 3 \times 3$

$$\mathbf{A}' = \begin{bmatrix} 9 & 2 \\ -1 & 0 \end{bmatrix}, \mathbf{b}' = \begin{bmatrix} 5 & 2 & -3 & 7 \end{bmatrix}, \mathbf{C}' = \begin{bmatrix} -2 & 4 \\ 5 & 2 \\ 9 & 0 \\ 1 & 8 \end{bmatrix}, \mathbf{D}' = \begin{bmatrix} -1 & 2 & -4 \\ 2 & 7 & -9 \\ -4 & -9 & 10 \end{bmatrix} = \mathbf{D}$$

so $\mathbf{D}$ is symmetric.

12.2 $A + B = \begin{bmatrix} 4+3 & 8+7 \\ 9+5 & 1+0 \\ 5+5 & 0+2 \end{bmatrix} = \begin{bmatrix} 7 & 15 \\ 14 & 1 \\ 10 & 2 \end{bmatrix},\ A - B = \begin{bmatrix} 4-3 & 8-7 \\ 9-5 & 1-0 \\ 5-5 & 0-2 \end{bmatrix} = \begin{bmatrix} 1 & 1 \\ 4 & 1 \\ 0 & -2 \end{bmatrix}$

It is not possible to find **A + C** or **B − C** since **A** and **C** have different dimensions, as do **B** and **C**.

$C - C = \begin{bmatrix} 0 & 0 & 0 \\ 0 & 0 & 0 \\ 0 & 0 & 0 \end{bmatrix}$. This is a square null matrix of order 3, the same dimension

as **C**.

For **C − 0** we write a null matrix of the same dimension as **C**, giving

$C - 0 = \begin{bmatrix} 3 & 7 & -1 \\ 5 & 0 & 4 \\ 5 & 2 & 0 \end{bmatrix} - \begin{bmatrix} 0 & 0 & 0 \\ 0 & 0 & 0 \\ 0 & 0 & 0 \end{bmatrix} = \begin{bmatrix} 3 & 7 & -1 \\ 5 & 0 & 4 \\ 5 & 2 & 0 \end{bmatrix} = C$

12.3 $3a = [15 \quad 0],\ kB = \begin{bmatrix} 3k & 2k \\ k & 7k \end{bmatrix},\ Ck = \begin{bmatrix} 4k & 0 \\ 9k & 6k \end{bmatrix}$

12.4   (i) $B + C = \begin{bmatrix} 3+4 & 2+0 \\ 1+9 & 7+6 \end{bmatrix} = \begin{bmatrix} 7 & 2 \\ 10 & 13 \end{bmatrix}$

$a(B + C) = [5 \quad 0] \underset{(1\times2)}{\begin{bmatrix} 7 & 2 \\ 10 & 13 \end{bmatrix}} = [5\times7+0\times10 \quad 5\times2+0\times13] = [35 \quad 10]$

$\underset{(1\times2)}{aB} = [5\times3 + 0\times1 \quad 5\times2 + 0\times7] = [15 \quad 10]$

$\underset{(1\times2)}{aC} = [5\times4 + 0\times9 \quad 5\times0 + 0\times6] = [20 \quad 0]$

$aB + aC = [35 \quad 10] = a(B + C)$

(ii) $\underset{(2\times2)}{BC} = \begin{bmatrix} 3\times4 + 2\times9 & 3\times0 + 2\times6 \\ 1\times4 + 7\times9 & 1\times0 + 7\times6 \end{bmatrix} = \begin{bmatrix} 30 & 12 \\ 67 & 42 \end{bmatrix}$

$\underset{(1\times2)}{a(BC)} = [5\times30 + 0\times67 \quad 5\times12 + 0\times42] = [150 \quad 60]$

$\underset{(1\times2)}{(aB)C} = [15\times4 + 10\times9 \quad 15\times0 + 10\times6] = [150 \quad 60] = a(BC)$

12.5 $5A = \begin{bmatrix} 5\times1 & 5\times3 \\ -5\times2 & 5\times4 \end{bmatrix} = \begin{bmatrix} 5 & 15 \\ -10 & 20 \end{bmatrix},\ kB = \begin{bmatrix} 5k & 0 & -k \\ -6k & 7k & 8k \end{bmatrix}$

$7x = \begin{bmatrix} 7\times9 \\ 7\times5 \end{bmatrix} = \begin{bmatrix} 63 \\ 35 \end{bmatrix}$

12.6 $\underset{(2\times2)\,(2\times3)}{A\ B} = \underset{(2\times3)}{AB} = \begin{bmatrix} 1\times5 + 3\times(-6) & 1\times0 + 3\times7 & 1\times(-1) + 3\times8 \\ -2\times5 + 4\times(-6) & -2\times0 + 4\times7 & -2\times(-1) + 4\times8 \end{bmatrix}$

$$= \begin{bmatrix} -13 & 21 & 23 \\ -34 & 28 & 34 \end{bmatrix} \underset{(2\times3)(2\times2)}{\mathbf{B}\ \mathbf{A}} \text{ is not conformable, nor is } \underset{(2\times3)(2\times1)}{\mathbf{B}\ \mathbf{x}} .$$

$$\underset{(3\times2)\,(2\times1)}{\mathbf{B}'\ \mathbf{x}} = \begin{bmatrix} 5 & -6 \\ 0 & 7 \\ -1 & 8 \end{bmatrix} \begin{bmatrix} 9 \\ 5 \end{bmatrix} = \begin{bmatrix} 5\times9 + (-6)\times5 \\ 0\times9 + 7\times5 \\ -1\times9 + 8\times5 \end{bmatrix} = \begin{bmatrix} 15 \\ 35 \\ 31 \end{bmatrix}$$

12.7 $\underset{(2\times2)\,(2\times1)}{\mathbf{A}\ \mathbf{x}} = \underset{(2\times1)}{\mathbf{Ax}} = \begin{bmatrix} 1\times9 + 3\times(5) \\ -2\times9 + 4\times(5) \end{bmatrix} = \begin{bmatrix} 24 \\ 2 \end{bmatrix}$ so $\underset{(1\times2)}{(\mathbf{Ax})'} = [24\quad 2]$

$\mathbf{x}' = [9\quad 5]$ and $\mathbf{A}' = \begin{bmatrix} 1 & -2 \\ 3 & 4 \end{bmatrix}$ so $\underset{(1\times2)}{\mathbf{x}'\mathbf{A}'} = [9\times1 + 5\times3 \quad 9\times(-2) + 5\times4] = [24\quad 2]$

$= (\mathbf{Ax})'$

12.8 $\mathbf{u}'\mathbf{u} = [u_1\ u_2] \begin{bmatrix} u_1 \\ u_2 \end{bmatrix} = u_1^2 + u_2^2 = 9 + 25 = 34 \text{ if } \mathbf{u} = \begin{bmatrix} 3 \\ 5 \end{bmatrix}$

$\mathbf{uu}' = \begin{bmatrix} u_1 \\ u_2 \end{bmatrix} [u_1\ \ u_2] = \begin{bmatrix} u_1^2 & u_1 u_2 \\ u_2 u_1 & u_2^2 \end{bmatrix} = \begin{bmatrix} 9 & 15 \\ 15 & 25 \end{bmatrix} \text{ if } \mathbf{u} = \begin{bmatrix} 3 \\ 5 \end{bmatrix}$

12.9 $\underset{(1\times1)}{\mathbf{x}'\mathbf{1}} = [x_1\ \ x_2\ \ x_3] \begin{bmatrix} 1 \\ 1 \\ 1 \end{bmatrix} = x_1 + x_2 + x_3 = 4 \text{ if } \mathbf{x} = \begin{bmatrix} 2 \\ -1 \\ 3 \end{bmatrix}$

$\underset{(1\times1)}{\mathbf{y}'\mathbf{1}} = [y_1\ \ y_2\ \ y_3] \begin{bmatrix} 1 \\ 1 \\ 1 \end{bmatrix} = y_1 + y_2 + y_3 = 7 \text{ if } \mathbf{y} = \begin{bmatrix} -2 \\ 5 \\ 4 \end{bmatrix}$

$\underset{(1\times1)}{\mathbf{x}'\mathbf{y}} = [x_1\ \ x_2\ \ x_3] \begin{bmatrix} y_1 \\ y_2 \\ y_3 \end{bmatrix} = x_1 y_1 + x_2 y_2 + x_3 y_3 = (2)(-2) + (-1)(5) + (3)(4)$

$= 3$ for numerical values given.

$\underset{(1\times1)}{\mathbf{y}'\mathbf{x}} = [y_1\ \ y_2\ \ y_3] \begin{bmatrix} x_1 \\ x_2 \\ x_3 \end{bmatrix} = y_1 x_1 + y_2 x_2 + y_3 x_3 = x_1 y_1 + x_2 y_2 + x_3 y_3 = \mathbf{x}'\mathbf{y}$

$(\mathbf{x}'\mathbf{y})' = \mathbf{y}'\mathbf{x}$ but since $\mathbf{x}'\mathbf{y}$ is a scalar its transpose equals itself and so $\mathbf{x}'\mathbf{y} = \mathbf{y}'\mathbf{x}$

12.10 $\underset{2\times1}{\mathbf{X}'\mathbf{y}} = \begin{bmatrix} 1 & 1 & 1 \\ x_1 & x_2 & x_3 \end{bmatrix} \begin{bmatrix} y_1 \\ y_2 \\ y_3 \end{bmatrix} = \begin{bmatrix} y_1 + y_2 + y_3 \\ x_1 y_1 + x_2 y_2 + x_3 y_3 \end{bmatrix}$

12.11 $\underset{(2\times4)}{\mathbf{AI}} = \begin{bmatrix} 8 & 12 & 0 & 5 \\ -2 & 3 & 7 & 14 \end{bmatrix} \begin{bmatrix} 1 & 0 & 0 & 0 \\ 0 & 1 & 0 & 0 \\ 0 & 0 & 1 & 0 \\ 0 & 0 & 0 & 1 \end{bmatrix} = \begin{bmatrix} 8 & 12 & 0 & 5 \\ -2 & 3 & 7 & 14 \end{bmatrix} = \mathbf{A}$

$\underset{(2\times4)}{\mathbf{IA}} = \begin{bmatrix} 1 & 0 \\ 0 & 1 \end{bmatrix} \begin{bmatrix} 8 & 12 & 0 & 5 \\ -2 & 3 & 7 & 14 \end{bmatrix} = \begin{bmatrix} 8 & 12 & 0 & 5 \\ -2 & 3 & 7 & 14 \end{bmatrix} = \mathbf{A}$

12.12 $\underset{(2\times3)(3\times2)}{\mathbf{X}'\,\mathbf{X}} = \begin{bmatrix} x_{11} & x_{21} & x_{31} \\ x_{12} & x_{22} & x_{32} \end{bmatrix} \begin{bmatrix} x_{11} & x_{12} \\ x_{21} & x_{22} \\ x_{31} & x_{32} \end{bmatrix} =$

$\begin{bmatrix} x_{11}^2 + x_{21}^2 + x_{31}^2 & x_{11}x_{12} + x_{21}x_{22} + x_{31}x_{32} \\ x_{12}x_{11} + x_{22}x_{21} + x_{32}x_{31} & x_{12}^2 + x_{22}^2 + x_{32}^2 \end{bmatrix}$ which is square of order 2

Since the x's are values the order of multiplication may be interchanged and so

$\mathbf{X}'\mathbf{X} = \begin{bmatrix} x_{11}^2 + x_{21}^2 + x_{31}^2 & x_{11}x_{12} + x_{21}x_{22} + x_{31}x_{32} \\ x_{11}x_{12} + x_{21}x_{22} + x_{31}x_{32} & x_{12}^2 + x_{22}^2 + x_{32}^2 \end{bmatrix}$ which is symmetric.

12.13 $\begin{bmatrix} 5 & 2 \\ 7 & -1 \end{bmatrix} \begin{bmatrix} x \\ y \end{bmatrix} = \begin{bmatrix} 75 \\ 48 \end{bmatrix}$

12.14 $y_1 = b_1 + x_{12}b_2 + x_{13}b_3$

$y_2 = b_1 + x_{22}b_2 + x_{23}b_3$

$y_3 = b_1 + x_{32}b_2 + x_{33}b_3$

Since the b's and x's are scalars this may alternatively be written

$y_1 = b_1 + b_2 x_{12} + b_3 x_{13}$

$y_2 = b_1 + b_2 x_{22} + b_3 x_{23}$

$y_3 = b_1 + b_2 x_{32} + b_3 x_{33}$

12.15 $\begin{bmatrix} 2 & 9 & -6 \\ 0 & 4 & 5 \\ 7 & -10 & 3 \end{bmatrix} \begin{bmatrix} x \\ y \\ z \end{bmatrix} = \begin{bmatrix} -1 \\ 52 \\ 64 \end{bmatrix}$

12.16   (a) 36 (b) 27 (c) 11 (d) 4 (e) 28 (f) 4 (g) –20 (h) –15 (i) 5

12.17   (a) $a_{13}C_{13} + a_{23}C_{23} + a_{33}C_{33} = 5 \times 11 + 0 \times (-4) + 9 \times 5 = 100$

(b) $a_{11}C_{11} + a_{21}C_{21} + a_{31}C_{31} = 2 \times (-23) + 1 \times 39 + 7 \times 1 = 0$
Matrix **B** is singular (its middle column is the sum of the first and third columns).

(c) $a_{11}C_{11} + a_{21}C_{21} + a_{31}C_{31} = 1 \times 42 + 0 \times (-63) + 3 \times (-12) = 6$
Details of the working are available on the CD in Matrices.xls.

12.18 Expanding $|A| = \begin{vmatrix} 5 & -2 & 2 \\ 8 & 0 & 1 \\ 11 & 2 & 0 \end{vmatrix}$ by the third column gives $32 - 32 + 0 = 0$.

The matrix is singular. The third row is twice the second minus the first, as in the equation we constructed in section 12.5.

12.19 (a) $A^{-1} = \frac{1}{2}\begin{bmatrix} 6 & -4 \\ -7 & 5 \end{bmatrix} = \begin{bmatrix} 3 & -2 \\ -3.5 & 2.5 \end{bmatrix}$,

$A^{-1}A = \begin{bmatrix} (3\times5) + (-2\times7) & (3\times4) + (-2\times6) \\ (-3.5\times5) + (2.5\times7) & (-3.5\times4) + (2.5\times6) \end{bmatrix}$

(b) $B^{-1} = \frac{1}{10}\begin{bmatrix} 4 & -11 \\ -2 & 8 \end{bmatrix} = \begin{bmatrix} 0.4 & -1.1 \\ -0.2 & 0.8 \end{bmatrix}$,

$B^{-1}B = \begin{bmatrix} (0.4\times8) + (-1.1\times2) & (0.4\times11) + (-1.1\times4) \\ (-0.2\times8) + (0.8\times2) & (-0.2\times11) + (0.8\times4) \end{bmatrix}$

(c) $C^{-1} = \frac{1}{50}\begin{bmatrix} 5 & 3 \\ -10 & 4 \end{bmatrix} = \begin{bmatrix} 0.1 & 0.06 \\ -0.2 & 0.08 \end{bmatrix}$,

$C^{-1}C = \begin{bmatrix} (0.1\times4) + (0.06\times10) & (0.1\times(-3)) + (0.06\times5) \\ (-0.2\times4) + (0.08\times10) & (-0.2\times(-3)) + (0.08\times5) \end{bmatrix}$

12.20 (a) $A^{-1} = \frac{1}{100}\begin{bmatrix} 36 & -4 & -20 \\ -27 & 28 & 15 \\ 11 & -4 & 5 \end{bmatrix} = \begin{bmatrix} 0.36 & -0.04 & -0.20 \\ -0.27 & 0.28 & 0.15 \\ 0.11 & -0.04 & 0.05 \end{bmatrix}$

(b) $B^{-1} = \frac{1}{6}\begin{bmatrix} 42 & -63 & -12 \\ -6 & 10 & 2 \\ -18 & 27 & 6 \end{bmatrix} = \begin{bmatrix} 7 & -10.5 & -2 \\ -1 & 1.667 & 0.333 \\ -3 & 4.5 & 1 \end{bmatrix}$

Details of the cofactor calculations are available on the CD in Matrices.xls.

12.21 $A = \begin{bmatrix} 15 & 3 \\ 7 & 1 \end{bmatrix}$, $A^{-1} = -\frac{1}{6}\begin{bmatrix} 1 & -3 \\ -7 & 15 \end{bmatrix} = \begin{bmatrix} -\frac{1}{6} & 0.5 \\ \frac{7}{6} & -2.5 \end{bmatrix}$ and $A^{-1}c =$

$\begin{bmatrix} -\frac{1}{6} & 0.5 \\ \frac{7}{6} & -2.5 \end{bmatrix}\begin{bmatrix} 51 \\ 21 \end{bmatrix} = \begin{bmatrix} 2 \\ 7 \end{bmatrix}$

12.22   We have to pre-multiply by a matrix that will give us $\mathbf{Ib}$ on the left-hand side. First check if $\underset{(k \times n)}{\mathbf{X'}} \underset{(n \times k)}{\mathbf{X}}$ is square, which it is of order $k \times k$. We can find its inverse $(\mathbf{X'X})^{-1}$ and pre-multiply by it. This gives $(\mathbf{X'X})^{-1}\mathbf{X'Xb} = (\mathbf{X'X})^{-1}\mathbf{X'y}$ and so $\mathbf{b} = (\mathbf{X'X})^{-1}\mathbf{X'y}$.

12.23   See Matrices.xls.

Index